INDIA AND EUROPE IN THE
GLOBAL EIGHTEENTH CENTURY

India and Europe in the Global Eighteenth Century

Edited by

SIMON DAVIES, DANIEL SANJIV ROBERTS
and GABRIEL SÁNCHEZ ESPINOSA

VOLTAIRE FOUNDATION
OXFORD

www.voltaire.ox.ac.uk

© 2014 Voltaire Foundation, University of Oxford
ISBN 978 0 7294 1080 9
Oxford University Studies in the Enlightenment 2014:01
ISSN 0435-2866

Voltaire Foundation
99 Banbury Road
Oxford OX2 6JX, UK
www.voltaire.ox.ac.uk

The correct style for citing this book is
S. Davies, D. S. Roberts and G. Sánchez Espinosa (*Eds*), *India and
Europe in the global eighteenth century*, Oxford University Studies in
the Enlightenment (Oxford, Voltaire Foundation, 2014)

Cover illustration: *Les vrays Indes dits Grand Indes ou Indes Orientales par
N. de Fer* (1705). National Library of Australia MAP RM 2556

MIX
Paper from
responsible sources
FSC® C013056

FSC® (the Forest Stewardship Council) is an independent organization established to
promote responsible management of the world's forests.

This book is printed on acid-free paper

Printed in the UK by TJ International Ltd, Padstow, Cornwall

OXFORD UNIVERSITY STUDIES IN THE ENLIGHTENMENT

INDIA AND EUROPE IN THE
GLOBAL EIGHTEENTH CENTURY

The long eighteenth century was a period of major transformation for Europe and India as imperialism heralded a new global order. Eschewing the reductive perspectives of nation-state histories and postcolonial 'east vs west' oppositions, contributors to this book put forward a more nuanced analysis. Adopting multi-disciplinary approaches and using eastern as well as western sources, they examine the complexities of the historical, political and cultural interactions between Europe and India during this period.

Eighteenth-century history / colonialism and imperialism / social and cultural history

Histoire du dix-huitième siècle / colonialisme et impérialisme / histoire sociale et culturelle

Contents

Acknowledgements

This volume presents revised versions of selected papers from a symposium held at Queen's University Belfast in 2011 with additional, invited contributions. The symposium was organised by the Centre for Eighteenth-Century Studies. The organisers wish to thank Research and Regional Services at Queen's for their generous financial support. We are also grateful for invaluable assistance from the School of Modern Languages, the School of English, the University Library and the Ulster Museum.

Jonathan Mallinson, the general editor of Oxford University Studies in the Enlightenment (previously *SVEC*), encouraged the idea of this volume from its inception and we thank him for his patience and expert guidance. We very much appreciate the help and advice of our editor, Lyn Roberts. We are also grateful for the detailed comments and suggestions of an anonymous assessor.

Simon Davies
Daniel Sanjiv Roberts
Gabriel Sánchez Espinosa

List of illustrations

Introduction

DANIEL SANJIV ROBERTS

> I doubt whether there be any king in the world
> that hath more [of gold, silver and precious
> stones]
>
> François Bernier, *History*, 1671

> I have never found one among [oriental scholars]
> who could deny that a single shelf of a good
> European library was worth the whole native
> literature of India and Arabia
>
> T. B. Macaulay, 'Minute' on
> Indian education, 1835

A gulf separates the French philosophical traveller to India, François Bernier, towards the end of the seventeenth century, from the English utilitarian thinker Thomas Babington Macaulay, at the beginning of the Victorian era. Travelling to the fabled Indies, a land offering trading opportunities and adventure to Europeans, Bernier affirms the material wealth and power of the Mughal emperor as was apparent in his enormous armies and limitless stores of gold and precious stones. In 1700, the emperor Aurangzeb, whom Bernier estimated to be the wealthiest monarch in the world, ruled over a land mass that stretched in the north from modern Afghanistan to the eastern region of Assam and down, in the south, to the tip of the Indian peninsula. By the 1830s, however, much of that land mass was firmly under the control of the East India Company which had become de facto colonial ruler of India. In comparison with Bernier, Macaulay's denigration of Indian pretensions to knowledge represents an intellectual valuation of India rather than a material one, and clearly the confidence underlying such a claim was born of imperial power. Whereas Bernier, writing to his correspondents at the court of Louis XIV, based his observations on his immersion in the court culture of Mughal India, Macaulay could make his recommendation for English-language education to Governor-General William Bentinck on the basis of a general acceptance on the part of British administrators in India of the superiority of western science over Oriental forms of knowledge. Whereas Bernier learned Persian and pursued his career in India under the patronage of a Mughal nobleman,

Macaulay argued that the East India Company would transact its business most efficiently, and in the best interest of Indians, in English. The contrast between Bernier and Macaulay affirms the familiar understanding of European history as India succumbed during the course of the eighteenth century from the position of being a valued trading partner inducing European rivalry to one of overwhelming colonial subjection to European powers following the notable victories of the French over Madras (Chennai) in 1746 and of the British at the Battle of Plassey (Palashi) in Bengal in 1757.

Yet even such a broad contrast might suggest several nuances which could be added to that understanding. Despite his affirmation of the emperor's fabulous wealth and power, Bernier's observations were far from overawed in tone. Though the emperor possessed vast stores of precious stones and metals, he frequently found it difficult to collect revenues from many of the areas he nominally governed, and was in fact often stretched to pay his enormous army its wages. The army itself, which marched with the king's seraglio in tow, was powerful, but also cumbersome in the extreme. The Mughal princes were often scheming against each other and at war with the Mahratta confederacy and other contending factions of pre-colonial and early colonial India. Contemplating the ravages of internecine warfare between the Mughal princes vying for the throne, Bernier was moved to comment:

> These great and prodigious Armies, 'tis true, do sometimes great things; but when once terror seizeth, and disorder comes among them, what means of stopping the commotion? 'Tis like a great River broke through its dams; it must overrun all, without a remedy. Whence it is that as often as I consider the condition of such Armies, destitute of good order, and marching like flocks of sheep, I perswade myself, that, if in these arts one might see an Army of five and twenty thousand men of those old Troops of Flandres, under the conduct of *Monsieur le Prince*, or of *Monsieur de Turenne*, I doubt not at all but they would trample under foot all those Armies how numerous soever they were.[1]

Bernier's confidence in European troops is based on a belief in the science of warfare, a form of knowledge which European mercenaries were even then imparting to the armies of native Rajas in Mughal India with limited success. Hence, despite their significant differences, Bernier's portrait of a divided and unwieldy Mughal empire on the brink of implosion, and his faith in the greater efficacy of European troops, might have seemed a century and a half later remarkably prophetic to the likes of the evangelically-minded Macaulay, justifying

1. François Bernier, *The History of the late revolution of the empire of the Great Mogol*, vol.1 (London, Moses Pitt, Simon Miller, and John Starkey, 1671), p.126-27.

his sense of the legitimacy of a civilising mission for India along the lines of the European Enlightenment. Certainly, such aspects of discursive continuity, despite notable transformations in perspective, inform Edward Said's influential thesis regarding orientalism: 'without examining orientalism as a discourse one cannot possibly understand the enormously systematic discipline by which European culture was able to manage – and even produce – the Orient, politically, sociologically, militarily, ideologically, scientifically and imaginatively during the post-Enlightenment period.'[2] Said's insistence on a pan-European investment in the project of orientalism, and his dating of the beginnings of this phenomenon to the eighteenth century, have rendered his work of seminal importance to recent scholarly engagements in the field.

Nevertheless, despite the broadly European dimensions of his argument, few scholars have seriously sought to address the breadth of European experience in the East.[3] Doubtless this is because individual scholars are largely limited by disciplinary training as well as by the linguistic and material resources which would make such an undertaking possible. Moreover, the field is dauntingly large. Significant attempts to engage with the pan-European dimensions of 'Enlightenment orientalism' such as the recent work of literary scholars such as Ros Ballaster and Srinivas Aravamudan, have creditably sought to counter traditional accounts of eighteenth-century realist fiction through their discussions of the oriental tale and its associated genres – a phenomenon which constituted a new mode of imagining the East that spread widely through Europe, introducing a popular fabular tradition that was as much oriental as it was indeed a western invention – and yet such works despite their breadth of learning are perforce restricted by their specialist subject matter.[4] The present volume seeks however to fill this lacuna and commence such an engagement. At the same time, as several of the articles in this volume show, Said's contentions have not remained definitive, but have been contested, reaffirmed and revised in the decades that have followed his work. Perhaps the most telling criticism of Said's work however is an ontological one. Said's critique of Eurocentrism paradoxically tells the story of western imperialism from the point of view of a European gaze on the East. Correspondingly, some scholars in this volume have eschewed Said's binary approach in favour

2. Edward Said, *Orientalism* (London, 1995; first edition New York, 1978), p.3.
3. Some notable exceptions which exemplify the breadth and diversity of this field include Kate Teltscher, *India inscribed: European and British writing on India, 1600-1800* (Oxford, 1995); Paul Gifford and Tessa Hauswedell (eds), *Europe and its Others: essays on interperception and identity* (Oxford, 2010), and Holden Furber, *Rival empires of trade in the Orient, 1600-1800* (Oxford, 1976).
4. Ros Ballaster, *Fabulous Orients: fictions of the East in England, 1662-1785* (Oxford, 2005) and Srinivas Aravamudan, *Enlightenment orientalism: resisting the rise of the novel* (Chicago, IL, 2012).

of genealogical, ethnographical and history-of-ideas approaches (among others) which sidestep stark oppositions between coloniser and colonised, and examine instead the processes, entanglements and transitions, rather than the confrontations and antagonisms that mark the relationship between Europe and India in the long eighteenth century. Reverting once more to the example of Bernier, it becomes clear that his work is not merely a foreshadowing of Macaulay's imperialism, but suggests instead a far more intimate and intricate relationship between him and the India he describes. While he reports on India to the West, he also subjects himself to the authority of the Mughal ruler, living the life of a Mughal courtly intellectual, translating the works of western philosophy into Persian and perceiving the majority Hindu population of India through a distinctly Mughal-elite mode of access. His writing and career in the subcontinent might be seen as exemplifying what one scholar in this volume describes as the intersection of various global imperia in Mughal India.

Attending the widely-held recognition that the eighteenth century ushered in the key transformations in European relations with India and vice-versa that would beget colonialism, there has been much recent discussion with regard to how that transformation was achieved. Such discussions have greatly increased our understanding of the complexities and nuances of that process. The grand narrative of British colonialism which premised the Raj on the basis of oriental despotism replaced by moral and enlightened English government has long been countered by critiques of imperialism, and not merely in the wake of post-colonial theory. Some of the earliest of these criticisms emerged during the eighteenth century itself, from what may be termed the peripheries of empire, from Irish statesmen and journalists such as Edmund Burke or William Duane, or from the mythologising of French imperial figures such as Joseph Dupleix and Thomas-Arthur de Lally as purveyors of a supposedly superior French system of colonialism.[5] Alongside such critical voices from the peripheries of empire, one might add the perspectives of Scottish and Welsh participants who contributed significantly to the British Empire but not without imparting their own regional inflections to the prevailing accents of English hegemony.[6]

5. See P. J. Marshall (ed.), *India: the launching of the Hastings impeachment* (1991), vol.6, in *The Writings and speeches of Edmund Burke*, ed. Paul Langford, 9 vols (Oxford, 1981-); Nigel Little, *Transoceanic radical, William Duane: national identity and empire, 1760-1835* (London, 2007); and Kate Marsh, *India in the French imagination: peripheral voices, 1754-1815* (London, 2009) p.78-84.
6. See Andrew Mackillop, 'A union for empire? Scotland, the English East India Company and the British Union', *Scottish historical review* 87 (2008), p.116-34; and Huw Bowen (ed.), *Wales and the British overseas empire: interactions and influences, 1650-1830* (Manchester, 2012).

Thus, far from constituting a monolithic imperial presence in India even by the end of the eighteenth century, the British Empire, despite its massive success throughout much of the subcontinent, was riven by criticisms, contradictions and contestations from within and without. Over the past three decades historians of India have contested the notion of a revolution in the political order of India caused by colonialism, suggesting a more delicate evolution of systemic change which emerged from the intricate series of exchanges between competing European players and native elites and intermediaries who modified and adapted prevailing practices of society during the course of the eighteenth century.[7] Furthermore, alongside the chronicles of military history within the war-torn regions of eighteenth-century India, there has been greater appreciation in recent years of the influence of economic structures and commercial operations on the advancement of empire.[8] Inevitably, the present collection of articles is informed by these parallel and often argumentative developments in literary and historical scholarship.

The volume commences with a consideration of history writing and translation of histories of India for European consumption. Raynal's history of European trade and colonisation in the Orient and the New World, *Histoire des deux Indes*, was a best-seller throughout Europe and North America in the last decades of the eighteenth century. As Anthony Strugnell shows in his chapter 'A view from afar: India in Raynal's *Histoire des deux Indes*' (p.15-27), Raynal and the most significant contributor to his history, Diderot, neither of whom had any direct experience of the Indian subcontinent, nevertheless conveyed an authoritative account of the history, culture and contemporary situation there. They did so principally by drawing on published works, particularly British ones, while incorporating their own ideological and geopolitical perspectives. The resulting accounts, in their attempts to reconcile the principles of the French Enlightenment with French interests in the region, heavily compromised by the defeat in the Seven Years War, offer a necessarily distant, yet strongly articulated, vision of India which contrasts with the British one drawn from direct experience. Chapter 2, by Claire Gallien, 'British orientalism, Indo-Persian historiography and the politics of global knowledge' (p.29-52) is a study of the narratives on Indian history translated by eighteenth-century British orientalists from Persian into English. Following British expansion in India in the second half of the eighteenth century, the directors of the East India Company started to

---

7. See P. J. Marshall (ed.), *The Eighteenth century in Indian history: evolution or revolution* (New Delhi, 2003).
8. See Huw Bowen, *The Business of empire: the East India Company and imperial Britain 1756-1833* (Cambridge, 2005).

commission works and translations that would help them set up a colonial administration. Thus, before the 'Oriental Renaissance', as defined by Raymond Schwab, a new corpus of Persian narratives on the history and administration of India, collected and translated by British orientalists with the help of local scholars, was produced. Gallien challenges Said's presentation of orientalism as a monolithic form of knowledge and argues that one cannot understand the existence of such a corpus without taking into account its dialogical and polyphonic nature, in which the voices of orientalists and native scholars intersected, resulting in the production of hybrid narratives. Yet, she concludes, such histories did not in the end challenge the parameters of Enlightenment historiography, but rather sought to include native traditions within them, always in the service of European interests.

The significant impetus of Persian scholarship on orientalism is viewed in yet another light in Javed Majeed's chapter 'Globalising the Goths: "The siren shores of Oriental literature" in John Richardson's *A Dictionary of Persian, Arabic, and English* (1777-1780)' (ch.3, p.53-77) which examines John Richardson's oft-reprinted work 'A dissertation of the languages, literature, and manners of Eastern Nations' prefixed to his *A Dictionary of Persian, Arabic, and English*. Majeed traces the genesis, rationale and the colonial and domestic contexts of Richardson's *Dictionary*, drawing attention to his reflections on the cultural and political origins of 'Englishness'. As Majeed demonstrates, Richardson constructs a global narrative of the 'Gothic' as a political category that underpins distinctively English freedoms and institutions, and in doing so produces a transcultural account of romance as a mode of writing. Richardson's arguments are placed against the backdrop of wider debates in Britain and India in the eighteenth century, and are related to his own complex subject position as a Scotsman whose class identity was fluid. Majeed argues that Richardson aims to re-educate his readers by broadening their cultural horizons beyond the Hellenistic legacy of European civilisation.

A major English poet whose work has often been regarded as Hellenistic in orientation, though hitherto rarely related to India, was the English Romantic, John Keats. Seeking to revise the estimation of literary history with regard to Keats, Deirdre Coleman's chapter '"Voyage of conception": John Keats and India' (ch.4, p.79-100) suggests that several of Keats's aesthetic conceptions – including 'negative capability' and its closely related paradox of 'diligent indolence' – were touched by his understanding of Indian thought. Towards the end of his brief life Keats went searching for an alternative belief system. Rejecting the gloom of Christianity's 'system of Salvation', he formulated his 'vale of Soul-making', a conception which invoked as part of its definition other world religions, including the 'Hindoos' and 'their Vishnu'. Keats's circle also included two great literary champions of India, the critic William Hazlitt and the radical journalist Leigh Hunt, whose newspaper *The Examiner* carried notices and reviews of Keats's poetry alongside reports of Britain's 'Indian atrocities'. These contexts suggest a wider framework embracing public and private perceptions of India which inform Keats's aesthetic vision.

Appearing contemporaneously with Keats's poetry, *The Orientalist*, a quirky novel by an Irish author, was subsequently less successful in literary history, but offers nevertheless an interesting insight into regional inflections of orientalism in Britain. Sonja Lawrenson's chapter '"The country chosen of my heart": the comic cosmopolitanism of *The Orientalist, or Electioneering in Ireland, a tale, by myself*' (ch.5, p.101-22) delineates how this novel refracted contemporary anxieties regarding accelerated British imperial expansionism in the East through the particularised political prism of post-Union Ireland. Identifying *The Orientalist* as the work of a female novelist with a learned interest in 'Hindu' culture, Lawrenson argues that the tale offers a parodic exposition of both Romantic nationalism and Romantic Orientalism, whilst simultaneously disrupting the gender prescriptions of both. In so doing, she not only demonstrates why this long-forgotten novel merits further scholarly attention, but uncovers the subtle insights into the intricacies of regional attitudes to imperial politics that its jocular irony affords. Another chapter contrasting English and Irish attitudes to India, though focusing in this case on literary influence and appropriation, is the study on 'Orientalism and "textual attitude": Bernier's appropriation by Southey and Owenson' (ch.6, p.123-40). This investigation shows how Bernier's highly influential *History* was taken up in the context of a growing evangelical spirit in Britain to articulate widely differing attitudes to proselytisation. The study explores the ideological transformations that attend Bernier's absorption into English literary tradition, uncovering the subtle revisions that Southey and Owenson undertook so as to incorporate his work into their diametrically opposed texts.

Commercial imperatives and representations relating to India, certainly a major theme in the literature of the period, receive attention next. Felicia Gottmann's chapter (ch.7, p.141-55) on 'Intellectual history as global history: Voltaire's *Fragments sur l'Inde* and the problem of enlightened commerce' examines Voltaire's *Fragments sur l'Inde* to show that the Enlightenment could espouse a universalist vision that was truly global. *Fragments* was published in 1774 after decades of defence on Voltaire's part of commerce and luxury as the hallmarks of human civilisation. Yet without warning, the *Fragments* demolished his earlier arguments. India was the crucial factor in this. Gottmann argues that even seen in context with the contemporary debates about Euro-Indian trade, with a renewed interest in Indian culture, and a nascent anti-colonialist discourse, Voltaire's stance was radical. He perceived India as Europe's equal and finding that luxury and commerce did not, in their interaction, lead to increased material comfort, humanity and civilis-ation, as he was wont to argue, but instead to its very opposite, namely oppression, slavery and exploitation, he roundly rejected all of his previous pro-commerce discourse. Thus, the global and universalist nature of his vision of Enlightenment ultimately won out over his European pro-commercial stance. Turning from criticism to fiction, James Watt's study (ch.8, p.157-73) on 'Fictions of commercial empire, 1774-1782' focuses primarily on three novels, the anonymous *Memoirs of a gentleman, who resided several years in the East Indies* (1774), Helenus Scott's *The Adventures of a rupee* (1782), and Robert Bage's *Mount Henneth* (1782), which it reads in the context of metropolitan debates about the gulf between the civilising possibilities of transnational commerce and the actual operations of the East India Company. Watt argues that these rhetorically unstable works at once rehearse anti-Company polemic and provide counter-narratives to the familiar story of corrupt nabobs. If they invoke the metaphor of circulation as a means of apprehending 'global connections', however, they are – unsurprisingly – unable to represent an India 'civilised' by commerce, and they generally eschew the sentimental tropes that other contemporary works mobilised in an attempt to negotiate spatial distance. As a result, it is suggested, the novels in question draw attention to the fictionality of their narratives of commercial empire, while rendering India – though also the scandal of empire – still more remote for their metropolitan readers.

At yet another remove from the heart of empire, the chapters 9 and 10, by Gabriel Sánchez Espinosa and John McAleer, investigate the movement of books and objects relating to India through translation and exhibition abroad. Although Spain did not develop a colony in India, it was nevertheless clearly interested in representations of India. Sánchez Espinosa's chapter (p.175-97) considers the fate of the Spanish translation of Bernardin de Saint-Pierre's *La Chaumière indienne* (1791), first published in Salamanca in 1803 by the printer-bookseller Tójar, who specialised in exotic, Rousseauian novellas. The work quickly caught the attention of both the Spanish reading public and the Spanish Inqui-sition. This was possibly because it expressed the anxieties and inner doubts among the Spanish reform-minded minority about the feasibility of the Enlightenment programme, as well as its rejection of the ortho-doxies of traditional Spanish Catholicism. The text was soon reprinted in Valencia in 1811 amid the chaos of the Peninsular War, and was widely read both by patriot liberals and Spanish *afrancesados*. After the restoration of Ferdinand VII, it was repeatedly prohibited by secular and religious authorities. However all these prohibitions came to nothing against the tide of its continuous success with the reading public, as indicated by its multiple reprints up to the 1820s. Turning to the appropriation of material objects and their display, John McAleer's chapter (p.199-221) gives us an insight into how the East India Company, its history and the story of Britain's diverse encounters with eighteenth-century India, can be understood through the production, collecting and display of objects and artefacts. Material culture formed a crucial part of the Company's mercantile, corporate and political identities. Cultural artefacts – variously collected, commented upon and displayed by the Company and its officials – had a significant impact on British under-standings of India and Indians. And, through its collecting activities and the establishment of the India Museum, the Company also influenced the development of museum collections and played a role in shaping museum narratives. The chapter concludes by considering how changing historiographical trends have influenced the interpretation of this material culture in the recent past. In doing so, it suggests that the East India Company, its history and its material culture can act as a springboard for introducing both British encounters with India in the long eighteenth century and broader themes in the history of the British Empire.

While the English East India Company founded in 1600 was the earliest and most successful of European trading companies in India, garnering much of the attention given to eighteenth-century European trade with India, it was by no means the only such company. Dutch, Danish, French and Portuguese companies were all formed at different times in the seventeenth century and operated for at least a part of the eighteenth, except for the short-lived Portuguese company which ceased to trade in 1633. Inspired by their success, Swedish and Austrian East India companies were founded in the eighteenth century too. Mogens Nissen's study (ch.11, p.223-40) of the economic history of the Danish Asiatic Company which was established in 1616 and lasted until 1843, focuses on the period between the early 1730s and the 1790s when the Company peaked financially. Nissen draws out the economic and political interests of the Danish Company, examining the debates regarding the Company's privileges and responsibilities, including the contentious issue of whether it was to continue as a monopoly or as a liberalised free trade open to all Danish merchants.

Chapters 12 and 13 return us to Mughal and early colonial India. Examining the discursive processes of imperial formation, and including a salutary emphasis on the maritime trade, Lakshmi Subramanian's study (p.241-65) examines the ways in which piracy in the context of Indian waters was defined and regulated. Studies on buccaneer ethnography in

the eighteenth century have revealed insights into the links between
privateers and the making of empire, and on how representation of
outlaws configured British colonisation and impacted on maritime
power and the language of imperialism. While the processes of nation-
and empire-building found it critical to negotiate and articulate the
legitimacy of subjects and citizens, making reclamation of the savage
European pirate possible, and even desirable, the same could not be said
for the Indian pirate whose ethnographic examination was framed
within a paradigm of lawlessness which proved less malleable. Much of
the ethnography on pirates and privateers of Kathiawar was spearheaded
by British naval officers and administrators, whose conceptions were as
informed by considerations of power and strategy as by notions of
traditional rights, clan honour and bravery. However, the existing parameters of legitimacy and authority were understood differently by
various agents and actors. As Subramanian shows, politics and market
dynamics entered into and complicated these various understandings of
maritime violence and contravention.

Florence D'Souza's chapter (p.267-81) also discusses trading relations
between Europeans and native Indians in relation to Surat. However
D'Souza turns to an earlier period to suggest a far more open-ended view
of commercial interactions from 1670 onwards until the establishment
of English hegemony over the region. Based on the observations of the
trading centre of Surat by three significant European commentators –
the English medical doctor John Fryer (1650-1733), the Anglican clergyman John Ovington (1653-1731) and the French orientalist scholar
Anquetil Duperron (1731-1805) – this chapter highlights Surat's ethnic
and religious diversity and the improvised trading practices used by the
different trading communities (Indian and European) in Surat. Constant
adaptation to evolving circumstances by all the groups concerned seems
to have prevailed over any legalised fixities or any stable, long-term
arrangements. The European travel accounts discussed by D'Souza furnish lively details on the role of Surat in the politics and trade of both
Europeans and Indians.

The volume concludes with a challengingly revisionist view of social
change in the eighteenth century by Seema Alavi, 'The Mughal decline
and the emergence of new global connections in early modern India
(p.283-300)'. Focusing on the perceptions of individuals from the spheres
of religious, military and medical practice, Alavi shows how the social
transformations which have been characterised as 'Mughal decline' in
the eighteenth century in fact involved the forging of new global connections that shaped the political culture and the formation of state
apparatus in the nineteenth century. Contesting the Eurocentric notion
of colonialism dictating the course of history, Alavi argues for the

significance of ideas, including the notion of decline itself, as a shaping force of change. Rather than viewing India primarily as the object of European conquest, Alavi draws attention to a rich tapestry of inter-woven traditions and schools of thought including the Islamic ecumene and its Arabicist strand as well as the European-French strands which intersected with British hegemony during this period.

Traversing a wide spectrum of eighteenth-century European engage-ments with India, it is yet inevitable that some significant individual figures receive but little or passing mention in the following pages. Our emphasis has been on seeking new connections rather than re-examining older and better established ones. The impact of Sir William Jones's translation of Kalidasa's famous drama of *Sacontala, or The Fatal ring* (1789) across all of Europe was central to Schwab's conception of the 'Oriental Renaissance' and has been examined in depth by Michael Franklin in his recent biography of Jones.[9] The painter Johann Zoffany (1733-1810), who was born in Frankfurt, trained in Rome, and finally settled in England, also lived in Lucknow for several years and made a fortune from painting European society in India. His portraits, and those of the Company School of artists, include revealing details of eighteenth-century life in India, depicting Europeans, often with native elites or servants, watching *nautches* and cockfights, and smoking *hookahs*. Indian artists in turn adapted traditional Mughal and Hindu styles of painting to appeal to their new patrons and depicted Indian rulers socialising with Europeans. Such instances testify to the rich cultural syntheses that Indian and European cultures could achieve during this period, and have fed into commendable and popular works of eighteenth-century colonial history.[10] From the point of view of this volume, however, these subjects have received significant attention elsewhere. Without excluding refer-ences to such subjects, our aim has been to encourage new directions in researching the field.

The tendency of histories to be written from the viewpoint of conquering forces and victorious outcomes has meant that conceptions of Indian colonial history in relation to the rest of Europe have largely been British in scope. Other European nations have contributed sub-sidiary and competing narratives. Yet few studies have sought to examine concertedly the complex interconnections between the leading

---

9. Michael J. Franklin, *'Orientalist Jones': Sir William Jones, poet, lawyer, and linguist, 1746-1794* (Oxford and New York, 2011). See in particular ch.7, 'Europe falls in love with Śakuntalā', p.251-86.

10. See for example Percival Spear, *The Nabobs: a study of the social life of the English in eighteenth-century India* (London, 1998), William Dalrymple, *White Mughals: love and betrayal in eight-eenth-century India* (London, 2002) and Maya Jasanoff, *Edge of empire: conquest and collecting in the East, 1750-1850* (London, 2005).

European powers and their impact on social, political and cultural forms in India during the period when these processes ran their course. Such investigations often reveal interesting and hitherto overlooked perspectives. When the Irish novelist Charles Johnston went to India in the early 1780s he noted with comic dismay the mixture of 'Frenchified English, and Angli[ci]sed French' that characterised Kolkata society of the time. For Johnston, who had made his reputation as a novelist in the 1760s in the context of English and French rivalry during the Seven Years War, such a mixture was akin to compounding oil and vinegar: 'nothing but beating can make them even seem to assimilate'. Yet Johnston's staunchly British Protestant perspective in *The Calcutta gazette* was subtly undermined, as he realised, by his own Irishness, which reveals itself in the character of the 'Teague' who is his narrator. His realisation of the provisional nature of national and ethnic groupings in the context of European colonialism is so acute that he displaces the action of his narrative to the moon, figuring India as a lunar realm wherein all the common prejudices of nationality are challenged: 'as for your country! Suspend your patriotism for a few minutes, and you shall see enough to make you sick of it for ever.'[11] While European national interests were of course instrumental to the politics of empire in India, this volume seeks to challenge the belief that such categories were constitutive of the relations forged through colonialism, and to demonstrate the extent to which they were negotiated, modified and reconstituted by that historical experience.

The editors of this volume have not attempted to impose a single theoretical or disciplinary focus on the collection. The contributors have been drawn from a wide range of humanities and social science backgrounds including literary studies (English, French and Spanish), critical theory, political history, cultural history, economic history and museum curation. The chapters examine aspects of Enlightenment theory; European and Persian historical representations of India; economic history; war and piracy; material culture and display; book history and translation; travel writing, critical theory and fiction; European missions and British evangelicalism; Hellenism and orientalism and Mughal history and culture, among other topics. While the editors have sought to arrange these chapters in a form that will allow such concerns to speak to each other and to generate a narrative, we are conscious that other narratives might be constructed and that other scholars, present and future, are likely to perceive affinities and connections between the articles which escape us at the present moment. We do not offer this

11. Daniel Sanjiv Roberts, 'Newly recovered articles from *The Calcutta gazette* by Charles Johnstone', *Eighteenth-century Ireland* 26 (2011), p.140-69 (151, 158).

volume as comprehensive survey (if such a feat were possible) of the remarkable global connections between Europe and India that were forged in the eighteenth century (and continue to exert an influence on our world). Rather, we hope that it will provoke interest in the many fertile areas investigated within its pages, as well as provide a stimulus for future research, debate and re-evaluation.

A view from afar: India in Raynal's
Histoire des deux Indes

ANTHONY STRUGNELL *— needs*
orts to kate
+ me!

Anyone in Europe or North America in the last decades of the eighteenth century seeking an authoritative digest of information on the history and contemporary state of European trade and colonisation in the Orient and the New World would have turned to Guillaume-Thomas Raynal's *Histoire philosophique et politique des établissements et du commerce dans les deux Indes*. The *Histoire des deux Indes*, to give it its short title, was during its three editions of 1770, 1774 and 1780[1] by far the most popular bestselling history of its day. 'The two Indies' was the contemporary shorthand for the Orient and the New World, originating in the early sixteenth-century mistaken assumption that circumnavigation of the globe both eastward and westward would eventually lead to landfall on the Indian subcontinent. Raynal's history was translated into all the major European languages. Published extracts from it, such as *La Révolution de l'Amérique*, became best-sellers in their own right, and it was endlessly pirated by unscrupulous publishers out to make a quick profit from its popularity. In Britain it graced the libraries of the wealthy and well-connected across the land, and the records of the Bristol Lending Library show that it was borrowed as frequently as Gibbon's *Decline and fall* and Robertson's *History of America*.[2]

One of its great virtues, apart from the readable concision of the information it purveyed, gleaned by Raynal from a vast range of printed and private sources, was its ease of consultation. It was by its 1780 edition divided into nineteen books, five devoted to European trade and colonisation in the Orient, principally the Indian subcontinent, the East

1. *Histoire philosophique et politique des établissemens & du commerce des Européens dans les deux Indes* (Amsterdam, 1770); *Histoire philosophique et politique des établissemens & du commerce des Européens dans les deux Indes* (La Haye, Gosse fils, 1774); *Histoire philosophique et politique des établissemens & du commerce des Européens dans les deux Indes*, 4 vols in-4° (Genève, Jean-Léonard Pellet, 1780). A modern critical edition is currently being prepared for publication; the first volume (*HDI* Ferney, I) and the accompanying atlas were published in 2010 by the Centre international d'étude sur le XVIIIe siècle at Ferney-Voltaire.
2. See Anthony Strugnell, 'La réception de *l'Histoire des deux Indes* en Angleterre au dix-huitième siècle' in *Lectures de Raynal*, ed. Hans-Jürgen Lüsebrink and Manfred Tietz, *SVEC* 286 (1991), p.262.

Indies, the Philippines, Indochina and China, thirteen to the New World
and a final one, devoted to a survey of the advantages and disadvantages
of colonisation. Each major European trading power was dealt with in
turn in each of the geographical areas covered, an analytical index was
provided in each volume and the text was accompanied by detailed
statistical tables and a separate atlas.

The *Histoire des deux Indes* was not just a highly informative account,
fully updated in each of its three editions, of the global effects of
European trade and colonisation. It was a history which was, as it
described itself in its title, *philosophique et politique*. While the term *politique*
retained a neutral sense, referring to the description of the geopolitical
relationships of states, the term *philosophique* carried all the charged
meaning of a critical interpretation driven by the agenda of the French
Enlightenment. In many respects Raynal's history was the true heir to the
Encyclopédie and carried forward in its pages the ideological programme
of the latter. This was centred on rationalist, secular values which
sustained a progressive vision of fraternity between nations based on
free trade, mutual respect, human rights and popular sovereignty. It
comes therefore as no surprise that the *Histoire des deux Indes* carried a
powerful critique of the excesses of European colonialism, condemned
slavery and the slave trade, and opposed tyranny, despotism and domination in all its forms. It championed the American Revolution,
discredited the economic and philosophical justifications of slave-
owners, and denounced those who exploited others for their own
rapacious gain.

Yet, the highly principled aspirations of Raynal's history, on closer
enquiry, reveal themselves to be more problematic than might at first
appear to be the case. Nowhere is that more so than in the books devoted
to the history of trade and colonisation in the Indian subcontinent, not
least with regard to the record of the more recent involvement of the
European powers there. The problem arises from the fact that writing on
the recent and current situation in India could not be abstracted from
the contemporary geopolitical context; in other words, the fallout from
the Seven Years War, the world war of Anglo-French rivalry which in
both North America and the Indian subcontinent had seen France suffer
a resounding defeat at the hands of Britain. Not only did that defeat
mean that France's presence in those regions was severely diminished; it
also created a situation whereby anyone seeking knowledge of the
contemporary state of affairs there had to have recourse necessarily to
British sources of information. This, as we shall see, was overwhelmingly
the case as far as the account of India in the *Histoire des deux Indes* was
concerned. Furthermore, both the information drawn from English
sources and the way that information was reworked through the process

of redrafting and integration into a necessarily different national perspective ensured that it would take on a new and distinctive hue, one in
which national ambitions would vie with the universalising pretensions
of the French Enlightenment to which Raynal, Diderot[3] and their fellow
contributors laid claim.

The prominence of British works on India as sources used by Raynal
and his team does not mean that they were indifferent to French
publications. As Guy Deleury has demonstrated in his anthology of the
writings of French travellers to India and the Indian Ocean,[4] a number of
French accounts of the subcontinent had been published between 1750
and 1780, the year of the appearance of the third and last edition of the
Histoire des deux Indes directed by Raynal during his lifetime.[5] Among the
authors whose writings were available to the public during that period,
well-known names such as Anquetil-Duperron, Bernardin de Saint-
Pierre, Law de Lauriston and Poivre jostled for readers' attention
alongside a cohort of obscure travellers who sought to take advantage
of the contemporary enthusiasm for detailed accounts of distant lands
and the Orient in particular.[6] If one turns to the first volume of the new
critical edition of the *Histoire des deux Indes* which contains the first five
books all devoted to the activities of the Europeans in the Orient, one
will find that some fifteen titles on India and the Indian Ocean region
written by French authors have been identified as sources. However,
compared with the material drawn from British sources, the contribution from domestic ones is of less significance. By and large the
information gathered from them is of a factual nature, relating to the
history and customs of the peoples of India, as well as to the history of the
commercial and colonising projects of the Europeans in the subcontinent and the islands of the Indian Ocean. But even here, as we shall see,
when it comes to offering a record of contemporary India, British
sources are to the fore. Not only do they dominate the informational
horizon of Raynal's history; they also provide a unique perspective drawn
from the direct and immediate experience of their authors of India in

3.   In the case of Diderot, for example, the radical anti-colonialism, which he manifested in
     his attitude to European activities in the New World, was substantially compromised by
     his desire to see France re-established as a major commercial presence in India. See
     Anthony Strugnell, 'Diderot's anti-colonialism: a problematic notion' in *New essays on
     Diderot*, ed. James Fowler (Cambridge, 2011), p.74-85.
4.   Guy Deleury, *Les Indes florissantes: anthologie des voyageurs français (1750-1820)* (Paris, 1991).
5.   A fourth edition, prepared by Raynal, was published posthumously in 1820. See *HDI*
     Ferney, I, p.xlvii-xlviii.
6.   A curiosity aroused in the French reading public in the late seventeenth and early
     eighteenth centuries by Jean-Baptiste Tavernier, *Six voyages de J. B. Tavernier* (Paris, G.
     Clouzier, 1679-1682) and Jean Chardin, *Voyages en Perse et autres lieux de l'Orient*
     (Amsterdam, Delorme, 1711).

much, if not all, of its teeming diversity. They reflect the ambition of the new masters of India to explore the complexity of their dominion, the better to govern it and draw a sustained commercial benefit therefrom.

The remarkable team of writers which supported Raynal, and which included many of the progressive thinkers of the French Enlightenment, most notably Denis Diderot, the editor of the *Encyclopédie*, scanned these printed sources for up-to-date material to incorporate into the history. But two caveats have to be made at this point: the first is that none of them,[7] as far as we can tell, had direct experience of the Orient or the New World of which they wrote, yet, on the other hand, neither can it be said that the *Histoire des deux Indes* was simply a hack work of compilation. Raynal and his team, Paris-based as they were, may have been viewing the events of which they wrote from afar, but the sense of urgency with which they imbued their writing gave it an impressive immediacy. Of this the account in the *Histoire des deux Indes* of the evolution of the European presence in India offers a significant illustration.

Following the end of the Seven Years War and the Treaty of Paris in 1763, France's presence in the Indian subcontinent had been severely curtailed, being reduced to seven coastal trading counters. This state of affairs strongly coloured both the choice of sources exploited in the drafting of Books I to V in which Indian affairs feature prominently, and also the perspective adopted by Raynal and his team. Let us explore further the sources used. Here, as elsewhere in his history, Raynal resorted not only to the printed sources already mentioned, but to private written and oral sources as well. In the case of his quest for information relating to contemporary British trading and colonial activities in India he relied on both questionnaires and personal contacts. These were individuals who had direct personal experience, primarily as servants of the East India Company, whom he met during a cross-Channel fact-finding visit in 1777.[8] During his travels, he was received by Lord Shelburne, who had been First Lord of Trade[9] in the Grenville Ministry, and Edmund Burke, and gathered information from a number of retired East India Company hands and others on home leave, most of whom he would have encountered at the home of William James, who kept open house in London. Prominent among them, he established close ties with Robert Orme, the Company's historian, whose

---

7. See 'Raynal et ses collaborateurs' in *HDI* Ferney, I, p.xxx-xxxiv.
8. For a detailed account of Raynal's visit see Gianluigi Goggi, 'Autour du voyage de Diderot en Angleterre et en Hollande: la mise au point de la troisième édition de l'*Histoire des deux Indes*' in *Raynal, de la polémique à l'histoire*, ed. Gilles Bancarel and Gianluigi Goggi, *SVEC* 2000:12, p.371-98.
9. A ministerial post later to be known as President of the Board of Trade.

History of the military transactions of the British nation in Indostan was a valuable source for the *Histoire des deux Indes*.[10]

Another of his contacts who acted as an intermediary regularly sending him documentation from London was Eliza Draper. For those of us even slightly familiar with Laurence Sterne and his work the name will ring a bell. Eliza was his muse, his 'Bramine', in an intense but platonic relationship which ended with Eliza's return to India to join her husband, a servant of the East India Company, in what was by all accounts a fraught marriage. Eliza, who had been born and brought up on the Malabar Coast, and who counted herself one of the 'children of the sun', eventually fled once more her unhappy marriage and returned to Europe via Paris where she met Raynal. He was smitten by this highly intelligent and independent-minded young woman who in turn became not only a source of information on India but a profound inspiration for the elderly bachelor, though she was suffering from an illness – most likely cancer or tuberculosis – from which she was soon to die. In many ways Eliza, to whom Raynal dedicated an eloquent eulogy in Book III of the *Histoire des deux Indes*, penned on his behalf by Diderot, incarnated the muse of history which he served. Like his other British sources on India, her engagement with the subcontinent provided him and his team with a feeling for that country, with unparalleled insights into both its people and their colonisers, unobtainable elsewhere.[11]

Although Raynal's systematic use of source material is well attested,[12] rarely, in the case of either his private or his printed sources, does he directly acknowledge them. To a modern reader the absence of footnoted references to sources or even of a bibliography, little compensated for by the occasional oblique reference in the narrative to an author whose work has been exploited, may be perplexing. It is not as if a proper referencing of sources was unknown in contemporary historiography. Indeed, the authors of one of Raynal's most important British sources, the vast compendium of the *Universal history*,[13] were meticulous in indicating, with a

---

10. See C. P. Courtney, 'The abbé Raynal, Robert Orme and the *Histoire philosophique des deux Indes*', *Revue de littérature comparée* 54 (1980), p.356-59, and *HDI* Ferney, I, p.317, note 256 and p.415, note 312.
11. For a detailed account of Raynal's dealings with Eliza Draper see Anthony Strugnell, 'A la recherche d'Eliza Draper' in *Raynal, de la polémique à l'histoire*, ed. Gilles Bancarel et Gianluigi Goggi, *SVEC* 2000:12, p.173-86.
12. One of the main functions of the new critical edition, *HDI* Ferney, is to identify the sources used. Since few of Raynal's private sources have survived in identifiable form, most of the research is directed at the identification, where possible, of printed sources.
13. *The Modern part of an universal history, from the earliest account of time, compiled from original writers* (London, S. Richardson, T. Osborne [et al.], 1759-1766) and *Histoire universelle, depuis le commencement du monde, jusqu'à présent: traduite de l'Anglois d'une Société de gens de lettres* (Amsterdam et Leipzig, Arkstée & Merkus, 1742-1802). Both the original English edition

precision which leaves little to be desired, the sources exploited in their narrative. Footnotes giving full bibliographical details, along with extensive quotations, abound. One is left in no doubt about the compilatory nature of this vast survey of human history and the endeavours of its authors to use the most authoritative accounts available. But this is where the *Histoire des deux Indes*, together with other histories, such as Voltaire's *Essai sur les mœurs*, differs radically from the type of compilatory history represented by the *Universal history*. Of necessity, the former also drew most of their material from readily available sources; but that is where the similarity ends. Raynal's history, like Voltaire's, is an *histoire philosophique*. As such, it does not simply *transpose* the material, gleaned from its sources, into its narrative; rather it takes that material and *rewrites* it, in order to create a critical perspective which serves its own ideological purposes. Since we have no means of knowing how this procedure may have operated in the case of the information which Raynal amassed from private oral or written sources, very little of the latter having survived, his printed sources will serve to assess the way in which the process of rewriting generated a distinctive vision of India. There is no sense in which Raynal would have been prepared to accept the kind of intellectual subordination to a higher authority which such referencing would imply. One must conclude, therefore, that the process of rewriting, of taking pre-existing material and refashioning it to serve an intellectual purpose which transcends the purely informational, was held to render it the property of its author, thereby making redundant, with very few exceptions, referencing to a pre-existing source.

   Of the British authors drawn on by Raynal and Diderot to furnish their account of India in the *Histoire des deux Indes*, the four most important are John Zephaniah Holwell, Alexander Dow, Nathaniel Halhed and William Bolts. The last was, in fact, of Dutch origin, but had been an employee of the East India Company and his book, which drew attention to the shortcomings of the Company in its dealings with the indigenous population of Bengal, was written in English and published in London. Holwell, like the other three, was a servant of the East India Company, eventually to become for a time acting governor of Bengal. He used his extensive experience of India and of the Company to write a highly regarded account, his *Interesting historical events relative to the provinces of Bengal and the empire of Hindostan* (1766-1771).[14] Dow served as an officer in

---

and its French translation were used, the former to access material which had not yet been published in the latter.

14. Holwell first came to the attention of the public with his celebrated, if overdramatised, account of the suffering of British prisoners in the so-called Black Hole of Calcutta in 1756 at the hands of Siraj ud-Daula, the last independent Nawab of Bengal.

the Company's army, publishing a *History of Hindostan* in a number of editions (1768-1772), which was a translation of a Persian text by Firištah, an indigenous historian, to which Dow added a section on Brahman religion and philosophy, and an appendix on the last years of the history of the Mughal empire. Of the four, Halhed was by far the most scholarly, having acquired Persian while at Oxford. He used his linguistic know-ledge to good effect in the service of Warren Hastings who called on him to produce a translation of a digest of jurisprudence, *A Code of Gentoo laws* (1778) which was to provide the basis for the British administration of justice to the Hindu population. Bolts, despite having served in the East India Company, unlike the other three felt no sense of allegiance to his former employer, publishing his *Considerations on Indian affairs; particularly respecting the present state of Bengal and its dependencies*, which first appeared in 1772. In it he roundly attacked the Company's discreditable attitude towards the native population, producing a further damning volume in 1775. All four books raised awareness in Britain of the activities of the East India Company, its rapid progress in establishing a dominant commercial, administrative and political role in the sub-continent, achieved as often as not through a cynical deployment of military power, and the accompanying self-aggrandisement of its senior functionaries, the so-called 'nabobs'. Parisian publishers, deprived of informed French accounts, were quick to bring out translations of these English authors which would serve, not only to satisfy their readers, curiosity regarding a unique encounter between East and West, but, more significantly, pro-vide some insight into the means by which their erstwhile adversaries had been so successful in establishing themselves in the Indian subcontinent where they had signally failed.[15]

Both the original editions and the French translations of Holwell, Dow, Halhed and Bolts were reviewed in the *Journal encyclopédique* which, as its title suggests, was close to the *philosophes*, as well as in Fréron's *Année littéraire*. The reviews revealed a genuine curiosity about all aspects of the Indian peoples and about the history of the Mughal Empire which were presented by the English authors in unprecedented detail. However, behind this seemingly disinterested curiosity, one can detect a highly politicised reading of the British authors' works.[16] Voltaire, for example,

15. The French translations are John Zephaniah Holwell, *Evenemens historiques intéressans relatifs aux provinces de Bengale, et à l'empire de l'Indostan* (Amsterdam, Arkstée and Merkus, 1768), Alexander Dow, *Dissertation sur les mœurs, les usages, le langage, la religion et la philosophie des Hindous* (Paris, Pissot, 1769), Nathaniel Halhed, *Code des loix des Gentous ou Réglemens des Brames* (Paris, Stoupe, 1778), William Bolts, *Etat civil, politique et commerçant du Bengale, ou Histoire des conquêtes et de l'administration de la Compagnie angloise dans ce pays* (La Haye, Gosse fils, 1775).

16. See, for example, C.-F. Bergier's *Préface* to his translation of Dow, Robinet's *Avertissement* to his translation of Halhed, and Démeunier's *Préface* to his translation of Bolts.

in his *Fragments historiques sur l'Inde* turns to both Holwell and Dow as irreproachable sources in his attack on the incompetence of the French government in India and its placing the blame for France's military defeat by the British on Lally de Tollendal, the general leading the French forces in India.[17] Compared with Holwell, however, Dow did not enjoy an entirely uncritical reception in France, the reviews they received in the *Journal encyclopédique* giving some idea of the different reactions their books prompted. Whereas Holwell, who had spent thirty years in India, was seen as offering a reliably impartial view of India[18] – in other words not using his history as special pleading for Britain's increasing domination of the peoples of the subcontinent – Dow was not held to be entirely innocent of that charge. Notwithstanding his augmented translation of Firištah, Alexander Dow had been first and foremost a military man, and was therefore not above the suspicion, indeed the French reviewer's conviction, that he was promoting the view in his book that the British by their presence in India were freeing the people from Mughal oppression.[19] However, with Bolts' unfettered attack on the East India Company's cynical exploitation of its power to subject the indigenous population to its rule and milk India of her wealth, the full measure of British hypocrisy became apparent. The response of the reviewer in the *Journal encyclopédique* was indicative of the sea-change that had overcome French attitudes to Britain.[20] Gone was the anglophilia of the first half of the century, to be replaced by the realisation that the nation which had invented freedom for the modern age did not extend that privilege to the peoples it had colonised. The *philosophes* who held to the high principles of *les Lumières* could not but conclude that they could offer a more worthy vision of cooperation between nations of East and West than their foremost rivals. And nowhere could that have been better demonstrated than in India, the prospect of which had been denied them by the outcome of the recent war.

   Within that context, the last three chapters of Book IV of the *Histoire des deux Indes* provide the key to the underlying intentions of Raynal and

17. *Œuvres complètes de Voltaire* (henceforward *OCV*) ed. Cynthia Manley and John Renwick, vol.75B (Oxford, 2009), p.85. In his *Fragments historiques*, Voltaire attempted to rehabilitate the memory of Lally who, following the defeat of the French army under his command at Pondicherry, had been found guilty of treason and executed.

18. *Journal encyclopédique* (1769), II, ii, p.202-203.

19. *Journal encyclopédique* (1773), II, p.249-50. For a more detailed account of Holwell and Dow's reception in France see Anthony Strugnell, 'Mixed messages: orientalism and empire in the early British histories of India and their reception in France' in *Das Europa der Aufklärung und die außereuropäische koloniale Welt*, ed. Hans-Jürgen Lüsebrink (Göttingen, 2006), p.292-96.

20. See Strugnell, 'Mixed messages', p.298-99.

Diderot in response to the parlous situation in which France was spending 2,000,000 livres per annum on its trading counters for a paltry return of 200,000 livres. The solution to this unacceptable state of affairs, according to the *Histoire des deux Indes*, was to re-establish France's strategic position in the Indian Ocean by upgrading facilities on the Ile de Bourbon (today's Ile de la Réunion) and the Ile de France (today's Mauritius), which had been allowed to fall into disrepair, in preparation for a return in force to the subcontinent. This would be made possible once an inevitable and widespread insurrection took hold against the British who had stretched themselves too thinly across the territories they controlled, and by their oppression had provoked the Indians' undying hatred. Then, claims Diderot, in Chapter 33:

> [L]es François, regardés comme les libérateurs de l'Indostan, sortiront de l'état d'humiliation auquel leur mauvaise conduite les avoit réduits. Ils deviendront l'idole des princes et des peuples de l'Asie, si la révolution qu'ils auront procurée devient pour eux une leçon de modération. Leur commerce sera étendu et florissant, tout le tems qu'ils sauront être justes. Mais cette prospérité finiroit par des catastrophes, si une ambition démesurée les poussoit à piller, à ravager, à opprimer (*HDI* Ferney, I, p.544).

Unlike the government at Versailles, the *philosophes* gathered around the *Histoire des deux Indes* had not thrown in the towel following defeat in the Seven Years War. On the contrary, faced with a victor refusing the freedoms it had inherited to those across the globe on whom it imposed its rule, the challenge was to present to mankind a new order of relationships between nations based on the principles of the French Enlightenment. It could be said that it is less easy to identify in the French writings a desire to dominate the colonised peoples, which is arguably one of the principal features of the English writing. That, however, did not preclude a close scrutiny of British sources preferred to French ones, as they offered a direct hands-on experience of dealing with the indigenous population. Indeed, British surveys of Indian culture and mores, far from being disinterested and scholarly, sought knowledge as a means of controlling the populations under their authority. Yet, despite the principles of fraternity and cooperation between the nations which shine out from the pages of Raynal's history, when it came to practical considerations, they take on another hue. Beneath the high-sounding rhetoric a different programme can be discerned, one which derives from a perspective seemingly far removed from that which is characteristic of the British accounts of India, yet one which turns out to be equally suspect.

French enlightened thought, as represented by the *Histoire des deux Indes*, might not seem to envisage a controlling role if, at some time in the

future, France were able to return in strength to India. The British
sources' detailed insights into the Indian mindset could well be used to
more positive and humane effect. However, an examination of the way in
which one notable British source was explored and reworked in the
Histoire des deux Indes will illustrate not simply the difference between the
French and British approach. It will also underline a paradox, namely
that while the British close involvement in Indian affairs was frequently a
recipe for exploitation and oppression, the distant French perspective
did not guarantee a humane and disinterested response which
enlightened values might be expected to generate. The source in question is Nathaniel Halhed's *Code of Gentoo laws* (1776) with a French
translation (1778). Drafted at the request of the governor-general, Warren Hastings, it was conceived as a reference work which would allow the
British colonisers to understand the essentials of Brahmanic jurisprudence which influenced every aspect of the lives of the Hindu population. Far from being a disinterested enquiry into the foundations of
Hindu society, it was a tool designed for the express purpose of
reinforcing administrative control of the subject peoples through the
acquisition of a detailed knowledge of the legal and religious practices
governing their lives. Halhed was an early example, as were Holwell and
Dow, of Edward Said's deconstruction of the orientalist as a colonialist
wolf in sheep's clothing.[21]

Not that Halhed lacked respect for the subject of his enquiry, and in
that he differed sharply from Diderot whose commentary on his *Code*
makes up the lengthy chapter 7 of Book I of the *Histoire des deux Indes*.
Halhed's introduction to his work reveals him as a latitudinarian
Anglican, open to every form of faith system albeit remaining quietly
sceptical as to their validity. With regard to Hinduism, he demonstrates a
cultural relativism and an awareness of the role of historical evolution in
the fashioning of that religion and culture which are impressive. Contrast that with Diderot who draws on Halhed's *Code* in a highly selective
manner. As he summarises and comments on the Shastras or legal
stanzas which embody the cosmogony, the sacraments, rites and laws
of Hinduism, he does so from an almost exclusively French enlightened
standpoint. There is little of the sceptical tolerance and objectivity which
characterises Halhed's approach and which was essential if he were to
enter the mindset of the peoples under British sway. On the contrary,
Diderot is repulsed by the profound irrationality of the Hindu world
view as he understands it, and more particularly of the caste system to
which it has given rise and for which it provides a permanent justification. The caste system with the priestly Brahmans at its head demon-

21. Said, *Orientalism*.

strates 'la plus profonde corruption, et le plus ancien esclavage. Elle décèle une injuste et révoltante prééminence des prêtres sur les autres conditions de la société, et une stupide indifférence du premier législateur pour le bonheur général de la nation' (*HDI*, Ferney, I, p.53). He admits that the Brahmans in the distant past were noted for their wisdom, and moreover that the Brahmans of today are constrained by circumstances 'qui ne permettent souvent au législateur de donner à un peuple que les meilleures loix qu'il peut recevoir' (*HDI*, Ferney, I, p.60). However, a passing nod in the direction of a tolerant cultural relativism does not detract sufficiently from the fact that Diderot sees the India in Halhed's *Code* as not so much refracted through the latter's sceptical tolerance as coloured by his, Diderot's, hostility to the established order in France and by the supposedly universal principles of enlightenment designed to combat it. In other words, for Brahmans read the Catholic priesthood, and for the complexities of Hindu law and religion read the stranglehold imposed by the church on most aspects of French life under the *ancien régime*. Halhed and Diderot offer contrasting and representative readings of Indian society. The distance of the French *philosophes* from the realities of the sub-continent ensured that the universal principles of the French Enlightenment could be applied without being subject to modification through direct experience. On the other hand, English empiricism sat comfortably with its growing imperial role in Bengal, Gujarat and beyond, without inhibiting its increasingly negative aspects.

But what of the *philosophes*' aspiration that France should return in strength to India, this time imbued with the fraternal intentions that enlightenment would inspire? We have gained some insight through Diderot's bookish encounter with Indian culture via Halhed of the attitude one might expect. And when it comes to sketching out the framework for France's prospective return to India, the same ambivalence is discernible. In the final chapter of Book IV, entitled 'Principes que doivent suivre les François dans l'Inde, s'ils parviennent à y rétablir leur considération et leur puissance', in which the modus operandi of enlightened colonialism is set out, Diderot is once again the author. On the face of it the model recommended by the *Histoire des deux Indes* would install an entirely equitable and respectful relationship between France and the indigenous peoples:

> Un peuple sage ne se permettra aucun attentat ni sur la propriété, ni sur la liberté. Il respectera le lien conjugal; il se conformera aux usages; il attendra du tems le changement dans les mœurs. S'il ne fléchit pas le genou devant les dieux du pays, il se gardera bien d'en briser les autels. Il faut qu'ils tombent de vétusté. C'est ainsi qu'il se naturalisera (*HDI*, Ferney, I, p.451).

In other words, an enlightened nation will not seek to impose its values,

but nor will it curry favour by going native. It will allow the passage of
time to free the populations from bondage to superstition, and by its
non-intervention gain their confidence. But the relationship proposed,
it is fairly clear, is not one of equals. Despite the apparent recognition of
and respect for cultural difference, and the stern rejection of the
predatory role so often played by European colonisers, the tone of
moral and intellectual superiority cannot be mistaken. The virtuous
European has only to bide his time until the scales fall from the eyes of
the benighted peoples he has come to engage with. His attitude is one of
tolerance, but of a limited kind, a non-intrusive tolerance which has
simply to await the passage of time before they rise to his level of
understanding and enlightenment. There is no question of a meeting of
minds to be achieved, with the philosophical European seeking as much
to understand the history, values and customs of the host community as
to facilitate its passage to enlightenment. The movement is to be all one
way.

If one looks elsewhere in Book IV, that suspicion is amply borne out.
The underlying agenda is the one which has lain at the heart of France's
view of her role in the world since the eighteenth century and even
before, that of her *mission civilisatrice*. For it is not simply a question of
awaiting the passage of time for the host community to cast off its
ignorance and move towards enlightenment. That process has to be
helped forward by the incoming nation, in other words, France, through
a programme of social engineering:

> En quelque endroit que vous vous fixiez, si vous vous considérez, si vous
> agissez comme des fondateurs de cités, bientôt vous y jouirez d'une puis-
> sance inébranlable. Multipliez-y donc les conditions de toutes les espèces; je
> n'en excepte que le sacerdoce. Point de religion dominante. Que chacun
> chante à Dieu l'hymne qu'il lui croit le plus agréable. Que la morale
> s'établisse sur le globe. C'est l'ouvrage de la tolérance (*HDI*, Ferney, I, p.452).

In that short paragraph are embedded the basic characteristics of the
new social order to be fashioned by the tenets of the French Enlightenment: entrepreneurial energy and initiative wedded to a vigorously
optimistic vision of human potentialities, made possible through the
unleashing of a vast diversity of talents. And all of this enabled by a
pervasive atmosphere of tolerance which no priestly caste will be allowed
to infringe. This is the key to resolving the moral defects of an alien
culture, in this particular instance Hindu, but it can equally apply to any
non-European culture, seen from a European, but more specifically a
French perspective. What puts the stamp of the Parisian *philosophes* on
the proposed formula is the rejection of any form of priesthood or
religious orthodoxy without any consideration of the problems which

will arise in attempting to impose, albeit gradually, an essentially secular culture on a profoundly religious society.

But Diderot's audacity, not to say his missionary zeal to bring the light to those who live in the penumbra of antiquated beliefs and customs, takes him beyond mere tolerance to formulate a novel programme of intrusive social engineering. In order to guarantee that the new social order should not only survive but flourish, an injection of European blood is prescribed, presumably to mix and marry with the native population: 'Le vaisseau qui transporteroit dans vos colonies des jeunes hommes sains et vigoureux, de jeunes filles laborieuses et sages, seroit de tous vos bâtimens le plus richement chargé. Ce seroit le germe d'une paix éternelle entre vous et les indigènes' (*HDI*, Ferney, I, p. 452). Is it too much to see in this early idealised vision of future European migration to countries already long populated by ancient civilisations a prefiguration of French migration less than a century later to Algeria, New Caledonia and elsewhere? The assumption behind the thinking of Diderot and his fellow *philosophes* was that there was a bad colonialism as practised currently by the British in India and a good colonialism which would follow the principles of equity and humanity most fully realised by them. Such a naively idealistic programme could only have been conceived by thinkers living thousands of miles from the peoples with whom they hoped to establish a new relationship of parity and mutual respect. The *philosophes* were more at ease in meeting morally and intellectually the challenge of the preliterate peoples of the New World, whom they raised to the status of the noble savage, incarnating an ideal, uncomplicated humanity which they themselves had lost yet hoped to regain. The ancient literate civilisations of the Orient offered a different challenge altogether, one which could not be satisfactorily met either by the rough, self-seeking empiricism of the British merchant class or the deluded idealism of the French *philosophes*. In the latter case it was an idealism which was incapable of thinking beyond the bounds of its Francocentric value system; one which in today's terms may be described as imperialistic in its consequences as was the lack of a value system which characterised the actions, and contributed towards the success, of its foremost rivals.

British orientalism, Indo-Persian historiography and the politics of global knowledge

CLAIRE GALLIEN

[T]he person to whose judgement and care the whole had been submitted [...] was no less than an eminent historian in a nation that has now taken the lead of all Europe after having been for several centuries shockingly defective in that branch of literature.[1]

Of that country I only profess to give the native accounts from its own writers; which will, I hope, at least gratify the curiosity of those who wish to learn the former state of this part of India, and fill up a chasm in history.[2]

The first quotation, expressing confidence in the superiority of British orientalist histories, is taken from the *Sëir Mutaqharin; or, View of modern times* (1789). Written in Persian in 1781-1782 by the Indian historian Ghulam Husain Khan Tabatabai, it was translated by 'nota manus', the anonymous translator now identified as M. Raymond.[3] The translator explains that he had put a manuscript version of his work in the hands of an eminent historian and a native of Britain, a nation which led Europe in history writing. The second quotation, purporting to remedy the defects of British histories of India, is taken from another translation of an Indo-Persian historiographical text, namely *Ferishta's History of Dekkan*, published by Jonathan Scott in 1794. The translator reveals the intellectual motivations underpinning his own effort, namely to translate his Persian sources so as to fill the 'chasm in history' left by British historians of India. These paradoxical visions concerning the state of British historiography with regard to India – the former exuding confidence, the latter revealing a deficiency – expressed by translators publishing on the same topic and with an interval of only five years, establish the frame

1. 'Proposal for publishing by subscription a translation of the Sëir Mutaqharin', in *A Translation of the Sëir Mutaqharin*, trans. M. Raymond, 3 vols (Calcutta, James White, 1789), vol.1, p.iv.
2. *Ferishta's History of Dekkan*, trans. Jonathan Scott, 2 vols (Shrewsbury, J. and W. Eddowes, 1794), vol.1, p.vi.
3. The translator dedicates the book to his patron, Warren Hastings (1732-1818), governor general of India from to 1774 to 1785. Michael Franklin has identified the translator as M. Raymond, also known as Haji Mustafa, a French Creole employed by the East India Company; see Michael Franklin, ed., *Romantic representations of British India* (London and New York, 2006), p.8. See also W. H. Carey, *The Good old days of Honorable John Company*, 2 vols (Calcutta, 1882-1887), vol.2, p.238.

in which the corpus of Indo-Persian historiography translated into
English was to develop. Indeed, in the second half of the eighteenth
century, a wealth of Persian manuscripts, mostly on the history of
Mughal and pre-Mughal India, were translated into English by British
civil servants of the East India Company, the majority stationed in
Bengal. Their patrons were the directors of the Company and the
governors-general of India, and their motivations were both intellectual
and political. By translating these texts, they provided knowledge concerning the history of the territories then placed under Company rule,
information on local customs, on indigenous legal and judicial systems,
and gathered intelligence material.

Company servants, such as Jonathan Scott (1753-1829), who had
become proficient in orientalist learning,[4] perceived a gap in the knowledge of the British public concerning India's past and its contemporary
affairs, and were confident about their ability to fill it. Their confidence
stemmed from their knowledge and skills, but also from their belief in
the capacity of British historiography to digest these Indo-Persian texts
into a coherent corpus. The rules of history writing, devised by Greek
and Roman historians,[5] and, according to orientalist translators, brought
to perfection by British scholars, were considered as universally applicable. If the source texts diverged from them, these would either have to
be transformed or would be discarded. Thus, by insisting not on what it
lacked, but on its capacity to transform and integrate supplementary
material, these translators reasserted the superiority of British historiography and, by extension, of the British nation, even when (as in the
case of M. Raymond, translator of the *Sëir*) they converted to Islam,
dressing and living in Indian style thereafter.

This corpus of Persian texts on the history of India translated at the
time constitutes fascinating material for the study of orientalism. Indeed,
by exposing their methods and aims, these orientalists exhibited a
complex vision of the field in which they worked, which can neither be
reduced to the homogenous and hegemonic definition of 'Orientalism'
as presented by Edward Said,[6] nor be strictly considered as a hybrid
discourse, according to Homi Bhabha's definition of the term. For
Bhabha, hybridity is a force of disruption produced by and working

4. Jonathan Scott was employed as Captain of the East India Company and personal Persian
    secretary to Warren Hastings. He was a member of the Asiatic Society in Calcutta created
    by Sir William Jones in 1784.
5. These rules may be briefly listed as follows: first, a scepticism concerning supernatural
    elements, second, the adherence to the *audi alteram partem* (or, 'hear the other side too')
    principle and third, a preference for first-hand oral information over stories gathered at
    second-hand. These rules were delineated and followed by ancient historians, such as
    Herodotus, Thucydides and Tacitus.
6. Said, *Orientalism*. See especially the introduction.

from within colonial discourses, and is defined as the site of reclaimed authority and resistance for colonised voices.[7] This article will provide a better understanding of this branch of knowledge as it developed in India in the second half of the eighteenth century, and my argument is that this understanding may be reached by availing ourselves of both Said's and Bhabha's conceptions of orientalism.

Indeed, the history of India, within orientalist scholarship, reveals that orientalism could be based on local sources and rely on Eastern scholars while reinforcing, rather than disrupting, British authority and rule. In other words, for the corpus under consideration at least, it seems that polyphony should be prised apart from resistance and tied in with authority. Thus, the integration of Indo-Persian historiography indicates that British orientalism developed as a form of global knowledge, while serving the universalist claims of British erudition.

By using Said's presentation of the nexus formed between orientalist knowledge and colonial power and Bhabha's perception of hybridity within colonial discourses, I aim to open up a critical space that would enable us to perceive the polyphonic nature of orientalist scholarship, in which the voices of the orientalist and of native scholars intersect, while recognising the fact that the hybrid narratives resulting from this process were presented not as forces of resistance and disruption but as reinforcing the colonial enterprise.[8] Hybridisation is not a force of liberation per se. In the case of Indian history in Persian, it was recognised and integrated only when subjected to alterations and redirected to serve the political and ideological interests of British colonialism. Integration meant selection, compilation, translation and considerable rewriting. Thus, the Indo-Persian corpus was altered in order to comply with the rules of British historiography, and only once transmogrified did it enter the realm of global knowledge in English.

This chapter considers firstly, how the history of India had been written in Britain before the middle of the eighteenth century, and

7. 'If the effect of colonial power is seen to be the *production* of hybridization rather than the noisy command of colonialist authority or the silent repression of native traditions, then an important change of perspective occurs. It reveals the ambivalence at the source of traditional discourses on authority and enables a form of subversion founded on that uncertainty, that turns the discursive conditions of dominance into the grounds of intervention', in Homi Bhabha, *The Location of culture* (London, 1994), p.112.

8. For the notions of polyphony and dialogism, see Mikhail Bakhtin, *The Dialogic imagination: four essays* (Austin, TX, 1981). More specifically on the question of hybridisation in the eighteenth-century Indian context, see Muzaffar Alam and Seema Alavi, *A European experience of the Mughal Orient: the I'jāz-i arsalānī (Persian letters 1773-1779) of Antoine-Louis Henri Polier* (New Delhi, 2007); Jasanoff, *Edge of empire*; Nigel Leask, '"Travelling the other way": the travels of Mirza Abu Talib Khan (1810)', in *Romantic representations of British India*, ed. Michael J. Franklin (London, 2006), p.220-37; Daniel O'Quinn (ed.), *The Travels of Mirzah Abu Taleb Khan* (Peterborough, 2009).

then presents the corpus of Indo-Persian historiography translated by
the British orientalists stationed in India in the second half of the
eighteenth century. Particular attention will be paid to the originality
of this corpus of texts and to the colonial motivations underpinning this
intellectual enterprise. Finally, the last part proposes a reflection on the
transformations of Indian sources and the creation of a global historiographical discourse based on the universal claims of British scholarship.

The orientalist turn

By the middle of the eighteenth century, British interest in India had
taken a determinate turn, shifting its sights from trading to conquest.
Major battles, such as the battle of Plassey in 1757 or the battle of Buxar
in 1764, were fought and won by the British, and the East India Company
took control of large portions of territory, starting with the regions of
Bengal, Bihar and Orissa in 1765. These profoundly significant changes
impacted on the newly burgeoning field of Indian studies. Some of the
servants of the East India Company, working for its civil or military
branches, took an interest in oriental learning and were sometimes
granted leave from the Company for the completion of their scholarly
projects. Being funded by the Company, they had to prove useful to the
British interests in India, and the scholars who undertook such projects
were always keen to underline this aspect. Thus, this period of intense
commercial and political involvement with India also constituted a shift
in orientalist learning in the sense that the new body of scholars were
formed on the ground. They had usually received no orientalist formation before arriving in India, took on their scholarly activities as a
pastime and were interested in fields of studies related to India's past
and present, rather than to the Ottoman, Arab, or Persian worlds. Their
activities were coordinated thanks to the creation of the Asiatic Society in
Calcutta in 1784 and to the publication of the *Asiatic researches*. They were
marked by the variety of fields covered, from the collection of manuscripts
and coins, to the publication of translations, grammars, dictionaries,
surveys and essays on the history, geography, customs, languages,
religions, literatures and arts of India, and by the reliance on local
intellectual networks. The corpus of primary sources constituting the
present enquiry, namely Indian historiographical texts written in Persian
and translated into English, was part of this orientalist turn.

   At the time, it was generally believed that there was a lack of reliable
knowledge concerning the history of India. Orientalists highlighted this
deficiency in almost every publication dealing with the topic and
emphasised the originality and timeliness of their publications. Indeed,
before British orientalists embarked on this enterprise of translating

Indo-Persian historiographical texts, the only books available were the accounts by classical authors, and by medieval and early-modern travel writers. Megasthenes and Arrian's accounts of the campaigns of Alexander the Great in India as well as Herodotus's descriptions of India were well known and they provided both the factual and the fabulous material on which early-modern travellers would base their narratives. In the fragments still preserved from Megasthenes's *Indika*, the factual is interwoven with the fabulous – sections on the boundaries and size of India, on its rivers, and the manners of its population, on the seven castes and on the administration of public affairs are combined with descriptions of 'the race of men without a mouth', and with the 'the gold-digging ants'.[9] Of the remaining fragments in Megasthenes's *Indika*, only one paragraph deals with the history of ancient India[10] and in Arrian's, a short section introduces the reader to the mythological history of India at the time of Dionysus and Heracles. Arrian concluded this fragment by adding: 'Let this be said by way of a digression to discredit the accounts which some writers have given of the Indians beyond the Hyphasis, for those writers who were in Alexander's expedition are not altogether unworthy of our faith when they describe India as far as Hyphasis. Beyond that limit we have no real knowledge of the country'.[11]

Medieval travel writers, such as Marco Polo and Sir John de Mandeville, fed on the fabulous tradition set by the classics in their accounts of India. In the third book of his *Travels*, Marco Polo indicated a series of Indian kingdoms he visited and took particular notice of the idolatry of the people he met and of the commerce in these regions. Apart from these two recurring descriptive elements, the traveller supplied no historical information. Sir John de Mandeville devoted two chapters to India, 'Of Greater and Lesser India', and 'Of divers strange and remarkable wonders in the kingdom of India', in which he expounded on the qualities of diamonds to be found there, and described the 'many strange things', such as the eels 'thirty foot long', the men 'of evil colour, yellow and green' and the many wonders, such as the well of youth, he encountered there.[12] As in Marco Polo's text, the reader

9.   John W. McCrindle (ed.), *Ancient India as described by Megasthenês and Arrian* (New Delhi, 2000).

10. 'For the Indians stand almost alone among the nations in never having migrated from their own country. From the days of Father Bacchus to Alexander the Great, their kings are reckoned at 154, whose reigns extend over 6451 years and 3 months'; quoted in McCrindle, *Ancient India*, p.115-16.

11. Quoted in McCrindle, *Ancient India*, p.202. The Hyphasis is the name given to the Beas River by ancient Greek writers. It is a tributary of the Satluj River and flows in the state of Punjab in India. It is also known as the limit of Alexander the Great's conquest.

12. John Mandeville, *The Travels and voyages of Sir John Mandeville* (London, J. Osborne, n.d.), p.79.

learns about the inhabitants of the diverse Indian islands and kingdoms and about their idolatrous practices. The only historical reference is a fabulous one since it refers to Prester John as 'great Emperor of Inde'[13] but here the traveller did not provide chronological data.

India was thus imagined outside chronological frames. Its people were caught between primitivism and paganism. They went naked and worshipped oxen and snakes. As Mandeville wrote, contrary to Europeans who live under the Moon, Indians depended on Saturn. He further argued that since the Moon went through the twelve zodiac signs in a month, and Saturn in thirty years, Europeans were prone to 'much moving and stirring', while Indians had 'no good will to stir'. Early-modern British travellers had read these descriptions of India and repeated them in their own narratives, by referring to the *mirabilia* tradition and by perpetuating the vision of an ahistorical India.

Bernier's *Histoire de la dernière révolution des états du Grand Mogol* published in 1669 and translated into English in 1671,[14] was arguably the first attempt to write a full account of contemporary Indian history. Before Bernier, the few seventeenth-century travellers who were sent on diplomatic missions to the court of the Mughal emperors in Agra, such as Thomas Roe between 1615 and 1619, brought back with them observations concerning life and politics at the Mughal court, as well as information concerning the genealogical tree of Mughal emperors, concerning their political systems, and the history of their conquests and reigns. Rahul Sapra underlined in *The Limits of orientalism* that a real difference existed between the representations of Muslims and of Hindus in these travel narratives. If the Islamic rulers were described in positive terms, 'the Hindus are generally looked down on as inferior "others" by most English travel writers in the seventeenth century'.[15] A clear line was drawn between primitive Hindus and modern Mughals, who were interconnected with European nations.

Thus, it is fair to say that before British orientalists translated Persian manuscripts on the history of India in the second half of the eighteenth century, European historiography on ancient or modern India was very sparse. These orientalists frequently denounced the deficiencies of travel writers and complained about the lack of interest on the part of historians. Sir William Jones (1746-1794) warned against second-hand accounts of travellers who did not have the philological expertise

13. Mandeville, *Travels and voyages*, p.125.
14. Bernier, *The History of the late revolution of the empire of the Great Mogol*. The second edition in English was published in 1676. Bernier also published *A Continuation of the memoires of Monsieur Bernier* (London, Moses Pitt, 1672).
15. Rahul Sapra, *The Limits of orientalism: seventeenth-century representations of India* (Newark, NJ, 2011), p.89.

required to criticise their sources: 'we are forced to depend upon reports of reports, echoed from the ignorant natives to inquisitive travellers, and brought by them to Europe decorated with a thousand ornaments.'[16]

Jones not only censured the practice of gullible travellers, he also indicated – in this preface at least – a sense of general mistrust towards contemporary natives. We should remember, however, that this disparagement was written by a man who had not travelled to India yet and that it would later be mitigated in his Indian correspondence, where he talks about his links with local scholars and describes relations of trust. If, in agreement with the paradigm of the contemporary degenerate state of India repeated by Jones, European scholars should avoid second-hand information, especially when imparted orally, they would be still permitted to resort to Indian historiography when the authors had participated in the events recounted. In other words, synchronicity was a badge of reliability: 'It must be allowed, that his [Mirza Mahadi's] testimony is not wholly free from suspicion; but his narrative [of the life of Nadir Shah] must necessarily be more authentick, than that of travellers, who could not possibly be acquainted with the facts, which they relate so confidently.'[17] Thus, Indian historiography was the best tradition orientalists could rely on in order to, as Jonathan Scott put it in his translation of *Ferishta's History of Dekkan*, 'fill up a chasm in history'.[18] And since Persian was the language used by the Mughal elite, and generally the first language orientalists would learn in India, it was towards texts written in Persian that they first directed their attention.

Other British writers had documented the transactions and military conquests of the East India Company in India. Robert Orme (1728-1801), East India Company servant, historian of India and first official historiographer of the East India Company with his book on the *History of the military transactions of the British nation in Indostan* (vol.1, 1763; vol.2, 1778), was arguably the most famous amongst them. The narrations of British success in India penned by Richard Owen Cambridge (1717-1802), John Henry Grose (fl.1750-1783), William Thomson (1746-1817), and Alexander Dirom (d.1830),[19] were also well known amongst the circle of British officials and scholars involved in Indian affairs.[20] There is some evidence, from the catalogues of books that could be borrowed in

16. Sir William Jones (trans.), *The History of the life of Nader Shah, King of Persia* (London, J. Richardson, 1773), p.xxii.
17. Jones, *History of the life of Nader Shah*, p.xxv.
18. Scott, *Ferishta's History of Dekkan*, p.vi.
19. Richard Owen Cambridge, *An Account of the war in India, between the English and French* (London, T. Jefferys, 1761); John Henry Grose, *A Voyage to the East Indies*, 2 vols (London, S. Hooper, 1772); William Thomson, *Memoirs of the late war in Asia* (London, J. Murray, 1788); Alexander Dirom, *A Narrative of the campaign in India* (London, W. Bulmer, 1793).
20. Jonathan Scott refers to them and to Orme in *Ferishta's History of Dekkan*.

circulating libraries, that these narratives were also known by the British public at large.[21]

The books written by the first historians of the British Empire in India were meant to apprise the reading public at home about the recent colonial wars. They provided patriotic narratives of British exploits and glorified the new heroes of empire, such as Major-General Stringer Lawrence, Robert Clive, Sir Eyre Coote and the Marquis Charles Cornwallis. These accounts were part of a larger constitutional debate, which at the time opposed the ones who defended the case of a greater military and political involvement in India and those who, like Edmund Burke, believed that Britain's intervention and intermingling in Indian affairs could corrupt its political principles.[22] The Indo-Persian historiographical texts translated into English formed a corpus that was not directly meant to address the issue of British intervention in India. However, it was clear for the translators, for their patrons, and for their readers that, by learning more about Indian history, they would facilitate the transition from Mughal rule to Company rule.

Indo-Persian historiography and colonial interests

From Alexander Dow's *History of Hindostan* onwards,[23] a large corpus of Indian historiographical texts written in Persian was translated into English by British orientalists, who worked primarily for the civil or military branches of the East India Company. It was constituted of direct (and not relay) translations from Persian into English of the annals, chronicles and institutes of Mughal emperors by Indian historians, usually employed at the court of Mughal governors or of the emperor in person, as in the case of Abū al-Faẓl with Akbar. Indeed, the servants of the company who devoted their spare time to Eastern learning were first directed to Persian, which was the language used in Mughal administrative documents and literary productions. Thus, when searching for 'native' historiographical texts they looked first into manuscripts available in Persian. These documents being the production of mostly Muslim historians working for Mughal rulers, it was predictable that the periods covered should extend from pre-Mughal to Mughal times. Apart from

---

21. For instance, Cambridge's *Account of the war in India* is to be found in *A New catalogue of Bell's circulating library* (London, 1774), p.33. See also *A Catalogue of Dyer's circulating library* (Exeter, R. Trewman, 1783), p.9; *A New catalogue of Hookham's circulating library* (London, 1785), p.45; *Catalogue of the London and Westminster circulating library* (London, 1797), p.15; and *Earle's new catalogue* (London, J. Nichols, 1799), p.5.

22. Nicholas B. Dirks, *The Scandal of empire: India and the creation of imperial Britain* (Cambridge, MA, 2006).

23. Alexander Dow (trans.), *The History of Hindostan*, 2 vols (London, T. Becket and P. A. de Hondt, 1768).

the *Tarikh-i Firištah*, translated by Alexander Dow as the *History of Hindostan*, and containing a first part on 'The history of the Hindoos, before the first invasion of Hindostan by the Mahomedans', all other accounts translated by the British orientalists in the second half of the eighteenth century dealt with Muslim India and focused more specifically on the Mughal rulers and on contemporary events in India.

This 'Indo-Persian' phase in English, which started with Dow in 1768, was quite limited in time. It was preceded by the publications of relay translations from Persian into French or Dutch and then into English between Pétis de la Croix's 1723 translation of the *History of Timur Bec* and the 1741 *Genuine history of Nadir-Cha* and it was followed by a phase of Sanskrit translations contained in the first five volumes of the *Asiatic researches* in 1799. The first phase comprised manuscripts which only remotely dealt with India but focused instead on the history of Eastern conquerors, such as Timūr and Nāder Shāh. In the later Sanskrit phase, which to some extent superseded the Indo-Persian one, British orientalists focused their attention on Hindu chronology and its compatibility with Mosaic chronology, on the Hindu measurement of time and on ancient Indian history and rulers. These accounts were pieced together from inscriptions written on ancient monuments and from relevant passages taken from the Puranas, the *Mahābhārata*, the Upanishads and the Vedas,[24] although in the case of Vedic literature the passages were more likely to be paraphrased and explained than translated, since divinely revealed literature (or *shruti*) could not be transmitted and circulated outside certain Brahmin castes.[25]

24. At the time, very few orientalists had achieved a good command of Sanskrit. There were numerous essays related to Sanskrit literature and inscriptions published in the first five volumes of the *Asiatic researches* in 1799 but they were usually written or translated by the same persons – Sir William Jones, Charles Wilkins, Samuel Davis, Francis Wilford and the pandits who worked for them. In these essays, the reader found translations of Sanskrit inscriptions left on monuments and of excerpts from Sanskrit literature, used for chronological and historiographical purposes. See *Asiatic researches*, 20 vols (London, printed for J. Sewell; Vernor and Hood; J. Cuthell; J. Walker; R. Lea Lackington, Allen, and Co.; Otridge and Son; R. Faulder; and J. Scatcherd, 1799-1839). [In relation to the transcription and translation of inscriptions, see vol.1, p.131-44, 284-87, 379-82, vol.2, p.167-69, vol.5, p.135-42; the translation of administrative documents, see vol.1, p.123-30, 357-68, vol.3, p.39-54; and the translation of Sanskrit literature and cosmology, see vol.1, p.340-56 ('On the literature of the Hindus from the Sanscrit'), vol.2, p.111-47 ('On the chronology of the Hindus'), p.225-87 ('On the astronomical computations of the Hindus'), p.288-306 ('On the antiquity of the Indian zodiac'), p.389-403 ('A supplement to the essay on Indian chronology'), vol.3, p.209-28 ('On the Indian cycle of sixty years'), p.257-94 ('The lunar year of the Hindus'), vol.4, p.2-17 ('Indian civic history'; this essay contains no translation but is very useful since it lists all the texts in Sanskrit which the orientalists at the time were using to learn about Indian ancient history), vol.5, p.241-97 ('On the chronology of the Hindus'), p.315-44 ('Remarks on the principle aeras and dates of the ancient Hindus')].

25. Thus, in the catalogue of Sanskrit manuscripts collected and annotated by Sir William

The Indo-Persian and Sanskrit phases may have overlapped, since the texts published in the 1799 volumes of the *Asiatic researches* were actually written in the late 1780s, yet the orientalists working in these fields did not pursue the same ends. Indeed, they were just beginning to translate Sanskrit texts and inscriptions, often encountered great difficulties in accessing Sanskrit literature for reasons of exclusivity, and discovered texts of great antiquity, which could not simply be regarded as texts of history. The Puranas, for instance, are composed of five parts – the *sarga*, or creation of the universe, the *pratisarga*, or secondary creations, or re-creations after dissolution, the *vamsa*, or the genealogy of gods and sages, the *manvantara*, or the creation of the first human beings and the *vamsanucaritam*, or the histories of the patriarchs of the lunar and solar dynasties. Considering the antiquity of these texts, orientalists used them not to study ancient Indian history – the texts were considered full of fables[26] – but to compare with and confirm Mosaic chronology and to advance knowledge on Hinduism.[27] The case of Persian texts was very different. Indeed, British orientalists dealt with identifiable historio-graphical traditions (*tarikh* in Arabic, *nameh* in Persian) and with limited periods of time, namely India under Muslim rule, and more particularly under Mughal rule. Thus, the primary purpose of translating Indo-Persian historiographical texts was to garner information on the political history of Mughal rulers and their administrative records, as well as to gain a better understanding of contemporary politics.

The first of these manuscripts to be translated into English was the

Jones and Lady Jones and presented to the Royal Society by Charles Wilkins, only two entries on parts of Vedic texts are to be found – entry 30 'Vrihadaranyaca. Part of the Yajur Veda, with a gloss, by Sancara' and entry 33 'Chandasi. From the Sama Veda'. The catalogue contains two copies of the *Mahābhārata*, two copies of the *Ramayana*, eleven manuscripts of various Puranas, including the *Sri Bhagavata*, or life of Krishna. The rest of the catalogue is comprised of Sanskrit poems, tales, treatises, grammars, dictionaries, dramas and farces. See Wilkins, *A Catalogue of Sanscrita manuscripts* (London, 1798).

26. The notion that Hindus never developed an historical consciousness and thus never established proper historiographical traditions had become an orientalist topos. In 1768, Alexander Dow wrote that the *Mahābhārata* was 'at best, but an historical poem, in which a great deal of fable is blended with little truth' (see Dow, *History of Hindostan*, p.vi and viii), and, in 1794, Jonathan Scott noted: 'Their [the Hindus'] origin, like that of all nations, is involved in obscurity; to clear up which is vain', in Scott, *Ferishta's History of Dekkan*, p.x. Today, historians challenge this topos and stress the interactions between Hindus and Muslims in the production of historical records. See for instance Catherine B. Asher and Cynthia Talbot, *India before Europe* (Cambridge, 2006), p.131-51. They also warn against ethnocentrism and reflect on alternative perceptions of time in early modern Indian historiography. See Velcheru Narayana Rao, David Shulman, Sanjay Subrahmanyam (ed.), *Textures of time: writing history in South India, 1600-1800* (Delhi, 2001).

27. See Thomas R. Trautmann, *Aryans and British India* (Berkeley, CA, 1997), especially ch.2 and 3 on 'The mosaic ethnology of Asiatick Jones' and 'British Indomania'. See also P. J. Marshall, *The British discovery of Hinduism in the eighteenth century* (Cambridge, 1970).

Tarikh-i Firištah, by Mohammad-Qāsem Hendušāh Astarābādī, also known as Firištah (1572-1620). The manuscript was completed for the first recension in 1606-1607, and for the second in 1609-1610. This history of Muslim rule in India was based on a compilation of oral accounts, annals and events that Firištah witnessed during his lifetime at the service of the sultans of Ahmadnagar and of Bijapur.[28] Almost the entire work is devoted to the history of Muslim rule in India, with only a brief section on Hindu beliefs, a brief history of India prior to Muslim rule, and a section on Indian saints. Alexander Dow's 1768 translation of the text, entitled The *History of Hindostan*, was actually not a translation of the whole text but only of the first and second *maqalah* (discourses), to which Dow added 'A dissertation concerning the customs, manners, language, religion and philosophy of the Hindoos', and 'A catalogue of the gods of the Hindoos'. James Anderson (1738-1809) translated the eleventh *maqalah* dedicated to the region of Malabar in the *Asiatic miscellany* of 1786, and Jonathan Scott (1753-1829) translated the fourth *maqalah* on the Deccan region in his *Ferishta's History of Dekkan* in 1794.

Numerous translations of Indo-Persian historiographical texts were published during the 1780s, and more precisely in 1785 and 1786, at a time of great political unrest in Westminster concerning the future of British India. Indeed, the East India Company was accused of a series of scandals, which resulted in the passing of the India Act in 1784 and the creation of a Board of Control nominated by the British government and supervising the military and political operations of the Company in India. The Governor-general, Warren Hastings (1732-1818), who had used his political influence to support orientalist learning, was called back to England in order to defend himself against accusations of corruption, administrative mismanagement and military errors.[29] Thus, it appears that the concentration of translations in 1785 and 1786 was no mere coincidence and that it indicates the orientalists' concern to impart knowledge but also to take a clear political stance in favour of Hastings and of British India. The *History of the first ten years of the reign of Alemgeer* translated by Henry Vansittart (1732-1770) was published in 1785,[30]

28. For more information see C. A. Storey, 'History of India, general', in *Persian Literature: a bio-bibliographical survey* (London, 1927-1997), vol.1, section 2, fasc.3, p.442-46. Available online via the PHI–Persian Literature in Translation website: ‹http://persian.packhum. org/persian/main›. See also the article 'FEREŠTA,TĀRḴ-E' in the *Encyclopædia Iranica* online: (http://www.iranicaonline.org/articles/ferestatarik-).
29. On Hastings's return to England, impeachment and trial see P. J. Marshall, *The Impeachment of Warren Hastings* (Oxford, 1965) and Sara Suleri, *The Rhetoric of English India* (Chicago, IL, 1993), p.50-74. On the political and constitutional debates related to Company rule in India, see Dirks, *The Scandal of empire*.
30. Henry Vansittart (trans.), *The History of the first ten years of the reign of Alemgeer* (Calcutta, Daniel Stuart, 1785). Muḥammad Sākī's text is actually the abridgment of Muḥammad

along with Abū al-Faẓl's *Ayeen Akbery*.[31] The *Akbery* corresponds to the third volume of the *Akbar-nāmah*, which the author completed between 1596 and 1602. The first two volumes deal with the history of Akbar's ancestors and of the first forty-six years of his reign, while the third volume is a detailed report on Akbar's institutions. This volume attracted the attention of Francis Gladwin (1744/5-1812), who then translated and published it between 1783 and 1786.[32] Also in 1786, Jonathan Scott, personal Persian translator to Warren Hastings, published his translation of the *Tārīkh-i Irādat Hān*, entitled *Memoirs of Eradut Khan*.[33] The book, written by a member of the Mughal nobility who had placed himself during his lifetime in the service of Aurangzeb (1658-1707), relates the seven years following Aurangzeb's death, until the accession of Farrukhsiyar to the throne in 1713. As the title of the translation suggests, and as hinted in the preface, Scott's aim was not merely to 'add somewhat to the store of public information respecting the extensive empire of Hindostan, of which', the translator did not fail to adjoin, 'Great-Britain possesses so large a share', but to reflect on a period 'to us more important, as nearer to our time', compared with the periods covered in Dow's *History of Hindostan* and to find 'the causes of the very precipitate decline of the Mogul Empire in India' in the religious zeal, tyranny and half-conquests of Aurangzeb and his successors.[34] This publication was clearly intended for the instruction and edification of the British administrators who were ultimately to replace the Mughal rulers in India.

Francis Gladwin's translation of *The History of Hindostan during the reigns of Jehangir, Shahjehan and Aurangzebe* was published in 1788, which was again an important moment for those involved in East Indian affairs since the trial of Warren Hastings began the same year in Westminster. The main body of the text was based on Mir Salim's *Jahangīr-nāmah*. It relates the regulations established by the emperor Jahangir, and the

---

Kāẓim's *Ālamgīr-nāmah*, known as *Muntakhabat i Ālamgīr-nāmah*. The English translation also contains a description of Assam extracted directly from the *Ālamgīr-nāmah*. Muḥammad Kāẓim served as the *munshi* (secretary) of Mughal Emperor Alamgir I (also known as Aurangzeb, 1658-1707). He produced the *Ālamgīr-nāmah* at the emperor's request, was ordered to discontinue the work after the first ten years of the latter's reign (1657-1667) and presented the book to the emperor in 1689.

31. Abū al-Faẓl (1551-1602) arrived at the court of Akbar in 1574 and soon became his leading courtier and most trusted confidant. He was crucial in helping formulate Akbar's policy of religious toleration, but was murdered at the request of Akbar's son Salīm (later to become Mughal ruler Jahāngīr) in 1602.

32. See Francis Gladwin (trans.), *Ayeen Akbery, or, The Institutes of the emperor Akber*, ed. Michael J. Franklin (London, 2000).

33. Jonathan Scott (trans.), *A Translation of the memoirs of Eradut Khan* (London, John Stockdale, 1786).

34. Scott, *A Translation of the memoirs of Eradut Khan*, p.v-vi.

routes he took during his multiple campaigns. Gladwin also added passages reporting on Akbar's relation with sultan Salim, the lists of the *subahdar* (governors) of Bengal and Bihar during the years of Jahangir's reign, and, finally a list of words in Arabic, Persian and Urdu used in the text, which he explained for English readers.

With this new translation, Gladwin presented his readers with a further enquiry, after his *Ayeen Akbery*, into the constitutional history of Mughal India. It was dedicated to Cornwallis, the new governor general of India, and aimed to provide reliable information based on 'authentic Persian manuscripts' to English readers. Orientalists would also be content with the inclusion in the volume of the original versions of the edicts, laws and regulations. As he indicated in his preface, Gladwin considered that his mission was to confront European prejudices regarding oriental despotism with the reality of Muslim rule in India. Gladwin's notion of constitutional progress in India under the reign of the successive Mughal rulers, from Akbar to Aurangzeb, was meant to supersede prejudices held against Eastern governments, and achieved a recognition that a safe common ground could be found between Mughal and British administrations. This analysis was most timely to the pro-Hastings camp, which was accused of interacting with Indian rulers and thus debasing the British constitution and compromising the moral standards of the British administration in its pursuit of commerce and wealth. Gladwin demonstrated that a common constitutional ground could be found in India, where the law and the principles of liberty and tolerance were respected. Referring to the system established by Akbar and his vizier, Abū al-Faẓl, Gladwin wrote:

> The skill and sagacity displayed in these arrangements, for every department, with the regard shewn throughout for the security of the life and property of the meanest peasant, give us an high idea of the government; and it astonishes us to hear the minister of an absolute prince, bred up in a faith notorious for its intolerant spirit, discussing with freedom the rights of humanity; boldly reprobating persecution, and maintaining that the Almighty is the common parent of all mankind: but we contemplate with still higher admiration and reverence, the monarch, who in opposition to the prevailing maxims of despotism, could not only adopt such enlarged sentiments himself, but have the generosity to authorise their promulgation, in order to diffuse general happiness, by establishing peace and unanimity amongst his such opposite persuasions, as the followers of the Bedes, and those of the Mohammedan faith.[35]

Gladwin's enthusiastic praise for Akbar's system of governance contrasted with the concerns of British administrators involved in Indian

35. Francis Gladwin (trans.), *The History of Hindostan during the reigns of Jehangir, Shahjehan and Aurangzebe* (Calcutta, Stuart and Cooper, 1788), p.iii.

affairs, namely the question of property rights, religious tolerance and
social harmony between the different religious communities constituting
the empire. Thus, this work, which was meant for the enlightenment of
the British public and for the development of orientalist studies, was also
responding to a specific political context.

Similarly, the publication of the *Sëir Mutaqharin* in 1789-1790 was
closely related to contemporary issues of empire and more specifically to
the ongoing trial of Warren Hastings. Ghulam Husain Khan Tabatabai
(1727-1728, died after 1781), *munshi* and political intermediary by profession,[36] was the author of this popular history of India written in
Persian in 1781 and entitled the *Siyar al-Mutahahirin*, and translated as
Sëir Mutaqharin eight years later in 1789-1790, when the trial of Hastings
was in its second year. The anonymous translator, identified as M.
Raymond,[37] dedicated the volumes to Hastings, and included the copy
of a heart-rending letter, in which he expressed his thankfulness, respect
and his deepest regret at having lost such a competent administrator. He
also indicated that the volumes had been 'hurried to London merely to
afford some timely assistance to that great man by elucidating upon so
competent and so unconcerned an evidence as our historian [Ghulam
Husain Khan], several articles that went far towards clearing the
governor's character'.[38] The competence and impartiality of the Persian
writer and his positive account of Hastings would support the translator
in his unswerving and emotional backing of the governor and could be
put to immediate use by the defence.

Indeed, the translator insisted on differentiating between Hastings on
the one hand and the Company servants on the other hand. Thus, in the
copy of his letter to Hastings he noted, in a characteristic celebratory
tone, the 'love which the Natives more than once forcibly expressed' for
the governor, and, in the preface, highlighted Ghulam Husain Khan's
fierce condemnation of British administrators in India and deep resent-
ment at the discrepancy between the British rule of law in England and
its flawed version in India.[39] Furthermore, in the second volume, Ghulam
Husain Khan devoted a section to the causes (twelve) which contributed

---

36. For a complete biography of Ghulam Husain, see Arif Naushahi, 'ĠOLĀM-ḤOSAYN
    KHAN ṬABĀṬABĀʾT, in the *Encyclopædia Iranica* ‹http://www.iranicaonline.org/articles/
    golam-hosayn-khan-tabatabai›. See also M. A. Rahim, 'Historian Ghulam Husain
    Tabatabai', *Journal of the Asiatic Society of Pakistan* 8 (1963), p.117-29.
37. See n.3 above.
38. 'Proposal for publishing by subscription a translation of the Sëir Mutaqherin', in *Sëir
    Mutaqharin*, vol.1, p.iii-iv.
39. 'On my going into one of the Nawab's seats, an old woman, among other article of sale,
    offered me some broken leaves of a decayed book, in which the author talked with
    encomiums of the English Parliament in Europe, and with some asperity of the English
    Government in Bengal', in *Sëir Mutaqharin*, p.21.

to the ruin of Bengal, clearly distinguishing between English misman-agement, rapacity and distance from the population, and Warren Hastings's rejection of tyranny and respect for local customs. The words of the Persian historian are reinterpreted as ominous warnings against an impending disaster:

> The general turn of the English individuals in India, seems to be a thorough contempt for the Indians (as a national body). It is taken to be no better than a dead flock, that may be worked upon without much consideration, and at pleasure: But, beware! That national body is only motionless, but neither insensible, nor dead. There runs throughout our author's narrative a sub-terraneous vein of national resentment, which emits vapours now and then, and which his occasional encomiums of the English, can neither conceal nor even palliate.[40]

Similarly, the rearrangement of the contents of books is redolent of colonial preoccupations. The *Siyar al-Mutahahirin* comprises three vol-umes. The first volume containing the general history of ancient India to the accession of Aurangzeb, the topography of the subcontinent and its various provinces, copied from the *Ā'in-e akbari* and the biographies of the religious leaders of India,[41] was not included by Raymond in his translation. The translator focused on the contemporary history of India and thus worked on Ghulam Hussain Khan's second and third volumes. The second volume deals with the events in India from the death of Aurangzeb in 1707 to Nāder Shāh's departure from India in 1739. The third covers the years from 1740 to 1781 and is devoted mainly to events in Bengal and the British wars. It also contains an epilogue about Aurangzeb's capture of Bijapur and Golconda in 1687, with comments on his character and style of government.

This focus on contemporary history was not due to Raymond's ignor-ance of the existence of a first volume. Indeed, in his preface, he explained that he had found by chance some stray leaves from the second volume – the pages in which Ghulam Hussain Khan is said to extol the British parliament but disparage the British government in India – and that this discovery aroused his curiosity. He goes on to describe how he understood that the leaves were part of the second volume, how he found the first and the third volumes too, and then started his translation.[42] As a result of this rearrangement, events which were of primary interest to the British in India were accorded some historical depth – as in the parts dealing with the succession of Mughal

40. *Sëir Mutaqharin*, p.22-23.
41. Apparently, the first volume was added to the first two volumes, and, according to Charles Ambrose Storey, it was 'little more than a transcript of the Ḳolāṣat al-tawārikh' by Sujān Rāy Bhandāri; see Storey, *Persian literature*, vol.1, p.455 and 636.
42. *Sëir Mutaqharin*, p.21-22.

rulers and the analysis of their systems of governance, or with the origin and rise of local dynasties and their relations with the imperial centre – and were presented in a clear and detailed manner – for instance, in the case of the rivalries and conspiracies between various factions vying for the title of emperor or sultan, of the revolts in Deccan and of British transactions with local and central powers. Thanks to this work, and with the help of explanatory notes, the translator aimed to render Indian affairs transparent to European readers.[43] In the case of the *Sëir*, the boundary between history writing and intelligence gathering became very fine indeed.

Similarly, when William Francklin (1763-1839) published the *History of the reign of Shah-Aulum* in 1798, he clearly placed the focus of his enquiry on contemporary India and contemporary politics in India. As the title suggests, the book deals with the history of 'the present emperor of Hindostaun' and about 'the transactions of the court of Delhi and the neighbouring states', and the tracts contained in the appendix, such as 'A narrative of the late revolution at Rampore in Rohilcund in 1794', also deal with contemporary India. The translator's status as member of the Asiatic Society meant that his readers could trust him in terms of orientalist expertise. However, his professional occupation as captain of the East India Company in Bengal encouraged him to use his scholarly expertise for the benefit of his patrons and more generally for the British establishment in India. Indeed, the *History of the reign of Shah-Aulum* covers topics, such as the relationships between Delhi, the Marathas, the Rohillas and the *nawab* of Awadh, which are central to the Company because it was involved in transactions with these powers and was hoping to find the best strategy for setting up alliances. Thus, Francklin's professional occupations were crucial in directing his enquiries, not only in terms of the choice of topics tackled but also in relation to the logistical aspect of his enquiries. For instance, the geographical remarks interspersed by Francklin in his translation were obtained during the survey he undertook for the Bengal government. Furthermore, his access to manuscripts depended on the help of other Company servants,[44] which meant that the choice of manuscripts was, up to a certain extent, conditioned by the Company network.

---

43. *Sëir Mutaqharin*, p.7.
44. Francklin acknowledged that he received the help of 'Major Charles Reynolds, surveyor-general of the Bombay establishment, Mr Johnstone of Lucknow, Major Kirkpatrick, Colonel Palmer, and Captain Salkeld, of the Bengal establishment' in the procurement of Persian manuscripts; in William Francklin (trans.), *The History of the reign of Shah-Aulum, the present emperor of Hindostaun* (London, Cooper and Graham, 1798), p.xix.

The politics of knowledge

Clearly, late eighteenth-century British orientalists and their patrons saw the advantage of using native sources in order to supplement the European historiographical corpus on India, which they presented as lamentably defective. This incorporation led to the creation of a hybrid and polyphonic corpus with the voices of Indian scholars intersecting with those of their translators. Yet, it would be problematic to interpret hybridity and polyphony in this case as a token of epistemological weakness on the part of British orientalists or as a sign of native resistance, through the disruption of homogeneous and monolithic colonial discourses. It is true that the reading of this Indo-Persian corpus of texts requires a certain level of cultural adaptation on the part of the readers, especially in the prefatory sections, where the historians complied with indigenous generic rules, such as the praises to Allah. However, the difficulties for the general reader were more likely to be related to a complete ignorance of the matter at hand than to questions of rhetoric and style. Indeed, the corpus translated by British orientalists went through several stages, from compilation to selection, and then adaptation, so much so that these historiographical documents, being transferred from India to Europe, went through transformations that affected their very textures. In the end, it was not doubt or anxiety that were expressed concerning the capacity of the British historiographical corpus to integrate native sources, but rather a sense of pride in its inclusive quality and in its ability to produce universal knowledge and, therefore, embody that universal knowledge.

Collecting, compiling, selecting

Acquiring manuscripts in order to establish new collections and expand the universal libraries of scholars and men of letters was an activity which had occupied early orientalists of the seventeenth and eighteenth centuries. The collection of material was facilitated by the expansion of networks of European scholars in India and by the help of local intermediaries. Indeed, numerous correspondences testify to the exchanges of manuscripts, information and commentaries. For instance, Jonathan Scott indicated that 'Mr R. Johnson, who, in his residency with the Nizam of Hyderabad, collected many curious Persian manuscripts relative to Dekkan',[45] and 'Colonel POLIER, whose long residence and connections at the court of Dhely enabled him to obtain the best information of public and private transactions',[46] favoured him with the manuscripts he needed for the completion of *Ferishta's History of Dekkan*.

45. Scott, *Ferishta's History of Dekkan*, vol.2, part iv, no.2.
46. Scott, *Ferishta's History of Dekkan*, vol.2, part v, p.129.

The purpose of the translators was not to establish a definitive edition of these texts, but to fill in the gaps left in European knowledge on India. Thus, multiple manuscripts emanating from different sources would be collected, compiled and published as one single work. A good example of this process would be *Ferishta's History of Dekkan*, translated by Scott and published in two volumes in 1794. Indeed, the first volume contained the history of Dekkan by Firištah, but the second volume, albeit being presented in continuity with the first, with pages and chapters running from one volume to the next, contained other manuscripts. Part III, which opens the second volume, corresponds to 'An account of Aurungzebe's operations in Dekkan, based on the journal of an Indian army officer'.[47] Part IV on the history of Aurangzeb's successors starts with a new pagination and the translator explains that the account was taken from the 'Masser al Amra, or Biography of nobility, written by Sumsam ad Dowlah Shaw-nowauz Khan, prime minister to Sullabut Jung, brother and predecessor in power to the present Nazim of Dekkan'. Part V is a continuation of the history of Aurangzeb's successors, based on various manuscripts and part VI corresponds to 'The history of Bengal, from the accession of Aliverdee Khan Mahabut Jung', compiled from a Persian manuscript and translated in part by, Ghulam Husain Khan, 'a learned and respectable character'.[48]

Scott's use of a variety of Persian manuscripts corresponded to a desire to extend the geographical and chronological limits of Firištah's *History of Dekkan*. William Francklin's interplay of sources in the *History of the reign of Shah-Aulum* was even more complex, as they were not simply added to one another but fully integrated and interwoven. The main sources used by Francklin were the 'Shah-Aulum Nameh', and the manuscripts of 'Syud Rezzi Khan, containing the transactions of the last nine years of the reign of Shah-Aulum' and of 'Munnoo Loll, a Hindu, containing the thirteen first years of the reign of Shah-Aulum'.[49] Additionally, it appears that the 'Ousafi Asof: a genealogical account of the reigning family of Oude' was used at the end of chapter IV, where Scott provides an 'Account of the Oude family', and that a manuscript entitled 'Operations in Sindiah and Mahomet Beg Khan Hamdani, written in the Persian language' was used in chapters 8 and 9. Finally, the 'Hudeeka Al Akauleem: a geographical account of the different provinces of Hindostan, written in the Persian language' must have been Scott's main source in the section on 'the principalities of Oudipore, Joudpore, Jypore' in chapter 6.

47. Scott, *Ferishta's History of Dekkan*, vol.2, part iii, p.ii.
48. Scott, *Ferishta's History of Dekkan*, vol.2, part vi, p.311-12.
49. See Francklin, 'List of authorities quoted for the present work', in *History of the reign of Shah-Aulum*, n.p.

Thus the texts presented to the British public had strictly speaking no equivalent in Persian. Similarly, the translation process, albeit part of a project to open up European historiography to Indian perspectives, fundamentally modified the texture of the sources in order to adapt them to European standards.

Translating, transforming, integrating

The last stage in this cultural transfer of Eastern scholarship from India to Europe,[50] after the collection, compilation and selection of manuscripts, was their translation. Orientalists were aware of the fact that translating a work of Indian historiography into English for a European audience not only meant changing the language but also implied rewriting the texts in order to adapt them to the expectations of their readers in terms of genre and style. It also meant adding a paratextual apparatus that could be considered as a further intrusion of the orientalist into the Persian texts. Furthermore such translations added a new function to works that recorded historical events in India and the lives of Mughal emperors: this was the provision of instruction to a European audience, and most importantly to Company servants, whether already in service or preparing for it.

In terms of generic requirements, the rules for historical writing, drawn from Cicero and other classical writers, were clearly defined at the time, and historians were expected to follow them.[51] The types of narratives which registered as 'history' were also well-known,[52] and focused primarily on genealogical accounts and on the chronicles of

50. The term 'cultural transfer' is taken from Michel Espagne and Michael Werner's seminal study of the notion in *Transferts: les relations interculturelles dans l'espace franco-allemand* (Paris, 1988) and *Les Transferts culturels franco-allemands* (Paris, 1999). I borrow from Michel Espagne's definition of the term the idea that a cultural transfer implies both a move and a transformation of the cultural item translated from one cultural sphere to the other, and that the receptor culture is never passive but plays a crucial role in the reshaping of the object circulated.

51. On eighteenth-century historiography, see Laird Okie, *Augustan historical writing: histories of England in the English Enlightenment* (Lanham, MD, 1991); Daniel Woolf, 'From hystories to the historical: five transitions in thinking about the past, 1500-1700', in *The Uses of history in early modern England*, ed. Paulina Kewes (San Marino, CA, 2006), p.31-68; Blair Worden, 'Historians and poets', in *The Uses of history in early modern England*, p.69-90; Karen O'Brien, *Narratives of Enlightenment: cosmopolitan history from Voltaire to Gibbon* (Cambridge, 1997); John Kenyon, *The History men: the historical profession in England since the Renaissance* (London, 1983).

52. Du Pin, in *The Universal library of historians* (1709) lists several such sources for histories. These included accounts of past events based on ancient monuments and memoirs; the contemporary accounts of witnesses and the memoirs and biographies of great men; the historical records of a country including its origin, progress, manners; religious history; and the 'universal history' of the world based on biblical or mythical narratives. See Louis Ellies Du Pin, *The Universal library of historians* (London, R. Bonwicke, 1709), p.28.

dynasties. As such, they were very close to the historiographical (or *nameh*) tradition in Persian.

What distinguished a European from an Eastern historian, according to orientalists, was the style employed. Indeed historians were considered as both writers and scholars and they were expected to develop a style that would neither be too bombastic nor too dry. When orientalists found the Persian narratives they translated too distant from the stylistic requirements of European historiography, they did not hesitate to tamper with the texts, or to 'clip the wings' of Eastern writers, as Dow put it.[53] Equally, when Indian historians were praised for the quality of their prose, the criteria for evaluating that quality were established on European standards, thus implying their superiority over Eastern ones.

Alexander Dow elaborated a compromise, which consisted in disparaging the style of Eastern writers in general, calling it 'turgid', 'florid', 'false' and 'vicious' and in being generally disdainful of Eastern historians for being 'too diffuse and verbose', while praising the qualities of style of the particular historian he was translating.[54] If, in general, Eastern poets failed to meet the expectations of Europeans, there was always room for one or two exceptions, and 'amidst the redundancy of [their historians], there appears sometimes a nervousness of expression, and a manliness of sentiment, which might do honour to any historical genius in the west',[55] and, according to Dow, Firištah was one of them. If his prose was sometimes found defective, when, for instance, in order to 'comprehend in a small compass every material transaction, [he] crowded the events too much together, without interspersing them with those reflections which give spirit and elegance to works of this kind', the qualities of the historian's style had to be acknowledged:

> Upon some occasions, especially in the characters of the princes, he shews a strength of judgment, and a nervousness and conciseness of expression which would do no dishonour to the best writers in the west [...] He never passes a good action without conferring upon it its due reward of praise, nor a bad one, let the villainous actor be never so high, without stigmatizing it with infamy. In short, if he does not arrive at the character of a good writer, he certainly deserves that of a good man.[56]

Thus, if Firištah's narrative was worthy of attention and his style worthy of praise, it is always on account of its capacity to be measured up against

---

53. 'The translator, however, being sensible of the impropriety of poetical diction, in the grave narration of historical facts, has, in many places, clipped the wings of Ferishta's turgid expressions, and reduced his metaphors into common language, without however swerving in the least from the original meaning of the author', in Dow, *History of Hindostan*, p.xi.
54. Dow, *History of Hindostan*, p.ix-x.
55. Dow, *History of Hindostan*, p. ii.
56. Dow, *History of Hindostan*, p.ix.

a European yardstick. The final apology sounds ironic and certainly creates a sense of distance between the British translator and the Indian historian, while at the same time reinforcing the proximity between the former and his readers in Britain and Europe. Indeed, Dow's statement rested on the principle of a system of evaluation shared between translator and readers, which implied the possibility of a joint decision to include or exclude Firištah from the category of historians and from the field of historiography, and to demote him to the rank of 'good man'.

Just a couple of years later, Sir William Jones added some further remarks concerning the question of style in history writing in the preface to *History of Nader Shah*. After reminding his readers of the rules of the genre as set down by Cicero,[57] he commented on the difficulties of finding, amongst historians in general, and Eastern historians in particular,[58] a style which, in being 'smooth, flowing and natural, without any graces but perspicuity',[59] would match the stylistic requirements of the genre.

However, orientalists concurred that there was a way to make amends for the deficiencies of Eastern scholars by cleaning up their texts. For instance, Jones, even though asked to produce a literal translation, preferred to '[strip] the original of its affected flowers and ornaments' and to 'present the English reader with all the interesting facts in a plain and natural dress'.[60] The same attitude towards Eastern texts was adopted by Francis Gladwin, who asserted that he 'never [took] the liberty to obtrude any expression that [was] not to be found in the original', but, at the same time, that he avoided rendering his translation in a strictly literal manner so as not to 'disgust the reader'.[61] Avoiding being too literal meant here dispensing with what a European audience would have judged superfluous and inadequate,[62] even if this erasure came at the expense of the cultural specificities of the texts.

This question of style was a recurrent problem, which all orientalists addressed, not only on aesthetic grounds, but also on epistemological

---

57. Jones, *History of the life of Nader Shah*, p.xv-xvi.
58. '[V]ery few [are] written with taste and simplicity, and none, which answer in any degree to the Ciceronian idea of perfection: they contain, however, the best materials for an History of Asia from the age of Mahomed to the present century', in Jones, *History of the life of Nader Shah*, p.xxv.
59. Jones, *History of the life of Nader Shah*, p.xvi.
60. Jones, *History of the life of Nader Shah*, p.xxvii.
61. Gladwin, *Ayeen Akbery*, p.viii.
62. 'In the original, every regulation is introduced by a profusion of fulsome and laboured praises of Akber, which to an English reader would be insufferable: and therefore I have generally suppressed them. I have also entirely omitted Fizee's poem [...] as from the insignificancy of the subject, it would have made but a poor figure in English prose'; in Gladwin, *Ayeen Akbery*, p.viii.

ones. Indeed, questions of trust and truth resurfaced behind questions of
style. As Jonathan Scott clearly demonstrated in his translations of the
Memoirs of Eradut Khan: 'The authenticity of the facts he relates is
undoubted in Hindostan, and the simplicity of his style regarded as a
strong proof of his veracity'.[63] Convolutions were then regarded as a sign
of biased views and misleading reasonings, whereas plainness of style was
considered as an infallible indication of the veracity of an account.

Furthermore, the confrontation with new and foreign sources and the
practical use for which they were, at least partially, intended, imposed a
redirection of the discipline. Indeed, if in the eighteenth century,
historians were still expected to glorify great men and to improve on
the events they related in order to accomplish a commemorative and
didactic mission,[64] the orientalists of the second half of the century set
up a different agenda. The purpose of their translation was not so much
to educate by presenting historical models as to inform their readers on
the nature and functioning of Mughal power in India. By highlighting the
informative and instructive functions of history, they contributed to a
change of direction in the discipline, prior to its nineteenth-century
codification as a branch of positivist science.

Finally, the texts were adorned with a paratextual apparatus, essentially in the form of footnotes, to guide the readers, most of them being
British colonial administrators and men of letters, through the maze of
what must have seemed abstruse historiography at first. Jonathan Scott,
for instance, added his notes and commentaries for a public of non-
specialists, as he knew they constituted a majority.[65] These annotations
secured a successful cultural transfer of Indian material into Europe.
However, in transplanting the texts, and in modifying their languages
and their textures, the orientalists also performed an act of recreation,[66]
therefore presenting the British public not so much with original documents as with hybrid creations.

Indeed, if the addition of marginal annotations produced a form of
polyphony, with the two voices remaining separate, the fusion of the
voice of the orientalist scholar into the textual fabric reinforced the
dialogic nature of the narrative.[67] For instance, Sir William Jones

---

63. Scott, *Memoirs of Eradut Khan*, p.vii.
64. Gibbon states in the first volume of his *History of the decline and fall of the Roman Empire* that:
    'Wars, and the administration of public affairs, are the principal subject of history'; see
    Edward Gibbon, *The History of the decline and fall of the Roman Empire* (London, W. Strahan
    and T. Cadell, 1776), vol.1, ch.ix, p.24.
65. See Scott, *Memoirs of Eradut Khan*, p.xii; and Scott, *Ferishta's History of Dekkan*, p.vii.
66. See Walter Benjamin, 'La tâche du traducteur', in *Œuvres* I (Paris, 2000).
67. As defined by Bakhtin in *The Dialogic imagination*, dialogism is not polyphony. Polyphony
    implies speaking many languages. Applied to a novel, for instance, it means that the voices
    (idiolects and sociolects) of many characters may be heard in it. Dialogism refers to the

indicated in his 1772 translation of the *History of Nader Shah* that he 'interpose[d] [his] own judgment upon counsels, acts and events [...] and ha[d] occasionally interwoven the description of remarkable places'.[68] Twenty-two years later, Jonathan Scott gave the same indications and only trusted the perspicuity of his readers to notice 'the variation of idiom' and 'distinguish them [his remarks] from the parts translated'.[69]

Only through these <u>direct interventions on the Indo-Persian corpus</u> <u>would these texts be integrated into the British historiographical canon.</u> <u>The fact that these integrations were possible and even successful was</u> <u>then regarded as a further proof of the universal scope of British</u> <u>historiography</u>.

On the face of it, the notion that Eastern historiography could be considered as valid in a scholarly sense and used by Europeans as a trustworthy source of information on the history of India seems to contradict Edward Said's vision of a monolithic form of orientalism. Yet, this endeavour to integrate native sources emanated from scholars deeply involved in Indian affairs and whose purpose it was to serve the colonial cause. Indeed, knowing more about the history of Mughal rule in India was clearly intended to help the new British colonial administrators in their tasks. Furthermore, their publications may also be interpreted in the light of contemporary constitutional debates taking place in Westminster. Using the paradigm of the rise and fall of empires they suggested the legitimacy and even the necessity of British intervention in India, presenting themselves as coming to replace the then defunct Mughal power. By expounding rationally on Indian governance, they attempted to remove fears of succumbing, themselves, to the intoxication of oriental despotism. In other words, removing long-held prejudices against 'oriental despotism' did not mean prising apart orientalism from a colonial agenda.

Thus, the notion of orientalism turning global in the second half of the eighteenth century through the interactions with and involvement of native scholars and through the integration of sources in Persian, Sanskrit and other Indian languages, remains problematic. Indeed, by making room for 'other' voices, orientalism presented itself as an inclusive form of knowledge, which could potentially involve 'the whole world'. Its production relied on the interconnections and interactions of scholars from various countries and cultural backgrounds, on the hy-

---

notion that no voice is self-foundational but that it stems from the influences of many voices that cut through it. Its textual equivalent is the notion of intertext.

68. Jones, *History of the life of Nader Shah*, p.xxvii.
69. Scott, *Ferishta's History of Dekkan*, vol.2, part 5, p.130.

bridisation of texts and literary traditions and on a worldwide circulation from Calcutta to London.

However, the general framework in which this process took place, and
the functions it endorsed, were defined in Europe. Never were the layers
of time, language and cultural difference considered as insurmountable
impediments to the translation of texts. Never were the rules of
European historiography challenged. Rather, the compatibility of Eastern sources with these rules was always underlined. The returns of this
production, that is, the extension of knowledge, were not intended for
Indians but for Europeans.[70] In other words, the global nature of
orientalism in the eighteenth century became more evident as the
number of contacts between India and Great Britain rose, and as the
degree of mutual exposition increased; however this globalisation of
orientalism, by highlighting the inclusive capacities of European knowledge, only served to reiterate its claims to universalism.

70. 'Every accumulation of knowledge and especially such as is obtained by social communication with people over whom we exercise a dominion founded on the right of conquest
is useful to the state: it is the gain of humanity: in the specific instance which I have stated
it attracts and conciliates distant affections; it lessens the weight of the chain by which the
natives are held in subjection; and it imprints on the hearts of our own countrymen the
sense and obligation of benevolence', in Warren Hastings, 'To Nathaniel Smith, Esquire',
in *The Bhagvat-Geeta*, translated by Charles Wilkins (London, C. Nourse, 1785), p.13.

Globalising the Goths: 'The siren shores of Oriental literature' in John Richardson's *A Dictionary of Persian, Arabic, and English* (1777-1780)[1]

JAVED MAJEED

Introduction

This chapter examines John Richardson's (1740/41-1795) 'A dissertation of the languages, literature, and manners of Eastern Nations', which was prefixed to his *A Dictionary of Persian, Arabic, and English* (2 vols, 1777 and 1780). John Gilchrist, the compiler of *A Dictionary, English and Hindoostanee* (1787-1790), described the 'Dissertation' as 'the most recondite dissertation that perhaps ever accompanied any work of that kind'.[2] While Richardson's *Dictionary* was revised and updated, as well as criticised by others, his 'Dissertation' appeared to have a weight of its own. Charles Wilkins detailed the many alterations and additions he made in his revised edition of Richardson's *Dictionary* of 1806, but he nonetheless begins with Richardson's 'Dissertation', whose arguments he makes no attempts to refute. This is then followed by Wilkins's own preface.[3] Similarly, Francis Johnson's 'new edition, considerably enlarged' of Richardson's *Dictionary* also reproduces the 'Dissertation', again without challenging its content, while listing the many alterations to the *Dictionary*.[4] This wholesale reproduction of the 'Dissertation' alongside extensive revisions of the *Dictionary* is testimony to the arresting quality of Richardson's arguments in the former. These outline a transcontinental history and narrative of the categories of the 'Gothic' and 'Gothic

1. This study emerges out of some of the research I did as a British Academy Research Fellow 2006-2008.
2. John Gilchrist, *A Dictionary, English and Hindoostanee, in which the words are marked with their distinguishing initials; as Hinduwee, Arabic, and Persian: whence the Hindoostanee, or what is vulgarly but improperly, called The Moor Language, is evidently formed*, 2 vols (Calcutta, Stuart and Cooper, 1787-1790), vol.1, p.iii.
3. Charles Wilkins, *A Dictionary, Persian, Arabic, and English; with a dissertation on the languages, literature, and manners of Eastern Nations, by John Richardson, a new edition, with numerous additions and improvements, by Charles Wilkins*, 2 vols (London, 1806-1810).
4. Francis Johnson, *A Dictionary, Persian, Arabic, and English; with a dissertation on the languages, literature, and manners of Eastern Nations. By John Richardson. Revised and improved by Charles Wilkins; a new edition, considerably enlarged, by Francis Johnson* (London, 1829).

romance', in the process reflecting on the ethnohistorical and political nature of 'Englishness'.

The genesis of Richardson's *Dictionary*

Richardson's *Dictionary* was originally conceived as a new version of Franciscus Meninski's magisterial *Thesaurus linguarum orientalium* (1680-1687), that glossed Turkish, Arabic and Persian in Latin. Its coming into being as a separate text involves tracing its disentanglement from Meninski, with whose name Richardson's own was often subsequently twinned, although not always in complimentary ways. In 1770, sensing a market opportunity for Persian lexicography created by the East India Company's increasing expansion in India, a number of individuals approached the East India Company's Court of Directors with proposals for dictionaries. The East India Company's Correspondence Committee of 2 August 1770 refers to two proposals which throw light on the evolution of Richardson's *Dictionary*, one forwarded by William Crichton on behalf of some printers (not specified) 'for publishing a new Edition of Meninski's Dictionary of the Oriental Languages under the Patronage and with the assistance of Dr Gregory Sharpe, master of the Temple', and the other a proposal by the printers Archibald Hamilton and George Nicols for 'printing at Oxford a new Oriental Dictionary and Grammar principally compiled from the latest Lexicographers of the East'. At this stage the Committee opted for the latter, since the former 'according to the author's own account was compiled purposely for teaching the Turkish language', while the latter focused on Persian and would require a 'new set of Persian types, agreeable to the most modern and approved method of forming their letters wherein the Persic books hitherto printed in Europe have been as defective as to render them unintelligible to the Asiaticks'. However, the linguistic contours of this remain blurred, perhaps reflecting the multilingualism of the Indian ocean as a region[5] and the subcontinent itself at the time, as the Committee then states that Hamilton and Nicol should ensure that 'the work shall comprise the Persian, Latin, English, Portuguese and any other modern languages the undertakers shall judge most proper to render it universally useful'.[6] In November 1770 William Jones, also sensing an opportunity for lexico-graphical and grammatical work on Persian, approached the Court of Directors with a request to them to publish his *A Grammar of the Persian*

---

5. For an examination of this multilingualism, see Pier M. Larson, *Ocean of letters: language and creolization in an Indian Ocean diaspora* (Cambridge, 2009).
6. Reports and resolutions of the Committee of Correspondence 1719-1834. IOR D/26: 5th Sept 1769- April 9th 1771, p.222-23. I am indebted to Huw Bowen for pointing me to this series.

language,[7] which he linked to his interest in reprinting Meninski, saying that:

> the same reasons, which induced me to compile a grammar, persuaded me to undertake the conduct of reprinting Meninski's dictionary; that my studies might tend to make the Persian language known to my countrymen in India, which it could never be without a knowledge of the arabick. I always had the highest opinion of that work, which opinion was confirmed by the great assistance afforded me in my translation of the King of Denmark's manuscript, which I could never have finished without that assistance: and I may confidently affirm not only that it will answer every purpose of the East-India company, but that a dictionary composed upon any other plan would not enable an Englishman to interpret even the letters from the Indian princes, much less the many excellent volumes written in Persick upon the history, the production and the revenues of India.[8]

He also refers to the competing proposal to print 'a dictionary meerly Persian' at Oxford, which he criticises on various grounds, including, in an implicit reference to Meninski, the fact that a knowledge of Arabic is needed to understand Persian and that the 'the Turkish language is highly useful in every part of Asia'.[9] This appears to be the proposal that the East India Company had already agreed to patronise, referred to above. In his *A Grammar of the Persian language* (1771) Jones also argued that 'whoever professes the admirable work of Meninski will have no occasion for any other dictionary of the Persian tongue',[10] and in 1771 he himself composed a proposal to reprint Meninski.[11]

In January 1771 John Richardson addressed the Court of Directors with a proposal for 'Preparing for the press under patronage of the Universities of Oxford and Cambridge and the East India Company, an improved edition of Meninski's Dictionary of the Persian, Arabic and Turkish languages', which was to be revised and corrected by William Jones, with an English translation and index. The proposal repeats many of Jones's arguments for the usefulness of Meninski as a Dictionary of Arabic, Persian and Turkish, as opposed to 'Dictionaries of the Persian only, [that] have been considered as imperfect and comparatively use-

7. Jones had composed his famous Persian grammar some years before (*A Grammar of the Persian language* (London, W. and J. Richardson, 1771)); see *The Letters of Sir William Jones*, ed. Garland H. Cannon, 2 vols (Oxford, 1970), Jones to John Eardley-Wilmot, 27 June 1769, p.29-30.
8. East India Company General Correspondence IOR E/1/54, Letters 185-6, 19 November 1770.
9. See previous note.
10. Jones, *A Grammar*, p.xvii.
11. See William Jones, *Sous la protection des Universités d'Oxford et de Cambridge, et celle des Compagnies Angloises des Indes et de Turquie, prospectus de la réimpression par souscription d'un dictionnaire des Langues Arabe, Persanne, et Turque, compilé et originairement publié à Vienne par Meninski en quarter volumes in folio: revû et corigé par Mr Jones* (Paris, 1771).

less'.[12] In a letter of March 1771 Jones refers to the progress of his work on this edition of Meninski but he later withdrew from the project to focus, it seems, on his legal career.[13] In a letter of July 1773 he refers to having dropped the 'Persian dictionary'; this may refer to his earlier intention to compile such a dictionary.[14] Thus in 1773 the linguistic contours of the dictionary are still flexible, the description of it as 'Persian' reflecting how the Dictionary was to emerge finally without a Turkish section, but retaining an Arabic section on the grounds of its importance for understanding Persian. Jones also mentions in this letter how he agreed, though, to revise the dictionary.[15]

It appears, then, that Richardson's *Dictionary* emerged as a compromise between the two proposals submitted to the Company in 1770, one for a translation of Meninski and the other for a Persian dictionary alone. This is borne out by a letter from the printers Hamilton and Nicol to the East India Company in February 1776, where they refer to how their proposal for a Dictionary had been supported by the East India Company, and how the Court of Directors had also encouraged the proposal for an improved edition of Meninski by Jones and Richardson. Consequently, a 'coalition' between the 'proposers of these great and arduous undertakings' took place, but 'delays and difficulties occasioned by the several preparatory steps, especially cutting the types, and teaching the printers the use of them, were almost insurmountable, would have proved entirely so, had it not been for the ingenuity and perseverance of Mr Richardson'. Added to these difficulties was the fact that Jones was called to the Bar, but the efforts to execute this plan, they argued, had the effect of stimulating the study of oriental languages. They claimed an offshoot of this project was the publication of Jones's *A Grammar of the Persian language* (1771) and Richardson's *A Grammar of the Arabic language* (1776), both of 'which have justly given the world a favourable opinion of the future labours of the authors of those valuable works'.[16]

While reflecting on the beauties of Persian literature in his *Grammar*, Jones also stressed the usefulness of his work to East India Company officials in the light of the importance of Persian as the language of diplomacy in India, adding that 'it was found highly dangerous to employ the natives as interpreters, upon whose fidelity they could not depend'.[17] He also argues that 'whoever professes the admirable work of Meninski

12. IOR E/1/55 John Richardson to Sir George Colebrooke, 24 January 1771, Letters 15-16.

13. Cannon (ed.), *Letters* 1, Jones to Charles Reviczky, March 1771, p.82-87.

14. Cannon (ed.), *Letters* 1, Jones to Lady Spencer, 23 July 1773, p.129-31 and Jones to John Eardley-Wilmot, 27 June 1769, p.29-30.

15. Cannon (ed.), *Letters* 1, Jones to Lady Spencer, 23 July 1773, p.129-31.

16. IOR E/1/60 Archibald Hamilton to Court of Directors, 6 February 1776, Letter 26, folio 49-51.

17. Jones, *A Grammar*, p.xii.

will have no occasion for any other dictionary of the Persian tongue',[18] and stresses the importance of acquiring a knowledge of Arabic, 'which is blended with the Persian in so singular a manner, that one period often contains both languages wholly distinct from each other in expression and idiom, but perfectly united in sense and construction'.[19] A knowledge of both Persian and Arabic can also be a grounding for acquiring other languages in the middle East, north Africa and India, especially Turkish, so that 'there is scarce a country in Asia or Africa from the source of the Nile to the wall of China, in which a man who understands Arabick, Persian, and Turkish may not travel with satisfaction, or transact the most important affairs with advantage and security'.[20] In his *A Grammar of the Arabic language* (1776), Richardson refers to Jones's *Grammar* 'as the model I have attempted to follow'[21] and, like Jones, he argues that Arabic is 'peculiarly essential to the just understanding of that Eastern language of correspondence and state affairs, the Persian'.[22] It is for this reason that 'it is equally impossible to compile a Persian dictionary without the assistance of the Arabick'.[23]

Thus Richardson's *A Dictionary of Persian, Arabic, and English* emerged as a text in response to a British-Indian market created by the expansion of the East India Company in India, in which competing proposals were made to the Court of Directors soliciting their patronage. The planned revised edition of Meninski, and the proposal for a Persian dictionary, are combined in his *Dictionary*, which deals with Persian, Arabic and English, but not Turkish. The text was therefore re-shaped in response to the changing geopolitics of British expansion abroad. Richardson's introduction to his work is a culmination of previous arguments about the usefulness of Persian and the necessity of knowing Arabic to understand it, that circulated in letters addressed to the Court of Directors and in Jones's and his own *Grammar*, which he retrospectively linked to the former. He makes it clear that his *Dictionary* is 'chiefly intended [...] for the Persian student: and particularly for the gentlemen in the service of the Honourable East India Company', the main aim of the project being to 'make it practically useful to those who visited India'.[24] He is keen to

18. Jones, *A Grammar*, p.xvii.
19. Jones, *A Grammar*, p.xxi-xxii.
20. Jones, *A Grammar*, p.xxiii.
21. John Richardson, *A Grammar of the Arabic language. In which the rules that are illustrated by authorities from the best writers; principally adapted for the service of the honourable East India Company* (London, 1801), p.viii-ix.
22. Richardson, *A Grammar*, p.iv, ix-x.
23. Richardson, *A Grammar*, p.x.
24. John Richardson, *A Dictionary of Persian, Arabic, and English. To which is prefixed a dissertation of the languages, literature, and manners of Eastern Nations*, 2 vols (Oxford, Clarendon Press, 1777-1780), 'Plan of the work', 2, p.xiii.

point to the 'high political consequence of the Persian, in the affairs of India', and also through Persian, of Arabic, which 'has never been viewed, in Hindostan, by Europeans, in the important light it merits'.[25] In the second volume of his *Dictionary* Richardson reproduces a long letter, dated 8 March 1780, from William Davy, who was one of the Persian Secretaries in the East India Company in India, validating its practical value for East India Company officials such as himself who had to learn Persian in India without the scholarly apparatuses of grammars and dictionaries available to the European student of Latin and Greek, or of modern European languages, and apparently in his case, solely reliant on 'a Mahommedan native, totally unacquainted with English, and of no great erudition'.[26] That Indian officials were the targeted market of the work is also clear from the subscribers listed in the second volume, the majority of whom were British officials in Madras and Bengal. The East India Company took 150 sets of the *Dictionary*, and Richardson acknowledges the patronage he received from the Company, as well as the 'polite attention' of the Court of Directors, 'polite' because it seems that the Company did not finance it outright. In January 1778, though, they did agree to his request that the Company buy 150 copies of the Dictionary for ten guineas a set, rather than the originally agreed price of seven guineas. They also agreed to advance 'the further sum of two guineas a sett on his giving security to repay the same, if his proposals for publishing his Dictionary shall not be within the space of eighteen months'.[27]

Unlike Meninski, who translated from and into Latin, Richardson brought English into direct contact with Persian and Arabic within the same framework, thereby laying open these languages to each other and also in Davy's words to 'the unlearned man of parts, as well as to the scholar'.[28] Interestingly, one of the reasons the Company's Correspondence Committee gave in August 1770 for supporting the proposal for a Persian dictionary, rather than a revised edition of Meninski, was its 'not only facilitating the Persic to the English but the English to the Persian'.[29] Richardson's *Dictionary* therefore also included this strand of previous proposals that had been endorsed by the Committee. He refers to how the difficulties of translating from English into Persian and Arabic, and vice versa, meant he had to resort to 'periphrasis' with the result that 'in the choice of those Persian and Arabick words which correspond with

25. Richardson, *A Dictionary*, 2, p.vii-viii.
26. Richardson, *A Dictionary*, 2, p.xiv.
27. Richardson, *A Dictionary*, 2, p.xiii. IOR D/29, Committee of correspondence, 23 January 1778.
28. Richardson, *A Dictionary*, 2, p.xv.
29. IOR D/26 Committee of Correspondence, 2 August 1770, p.222-23.

ours, I have been copious'.[30] This lexicographical context of opening out these languages to each other, the fragility of translations and their oblique handling and the slipperiness of transferring meanings across languages, forms the background to Richardson's reflections on the cultural and political origins of 'Englishness'. Here he outlines a global narrative of the 'Gothic' as a political category that underpins distinctively English freedoms and institutions, and produces a transcultural account of romance as a mode of writing. In doing so, he also aims to re-educate his readers by broadening their cultural horizons beyond the Hellenistic legacy of European civilisation, thereby also widening and deepening their own sense of antiquity.

Greek piracy

The 'Dissertation' addresses two topics, the status and validity of Greek histories in their representations of Persia and the genre of romance narratives. Richardson connects both subjects in a variety of ways through the category of the 'Gothic' and his reflections on romance as a cross-cultural mode of writing follow on from his criticisms of Greek, and to a lesser extent, Roman histories.

Richardson's lexicography on Arabic and Persian leads him to question the effects of classical Hellenistic legacy in European civilisation, and especially its historical narratives. Firstly, he questions Greek ethnocentrism and how this structures their representations of Persia in particular and the 'East' in general: 'Too proud to consider surrounding nations [...] in any light but that of Barbarians; they [the Greeks] despised their records, they altered their language and framed too often their details, more to the prejudices of their fellow citizens, than to the standard of truth or probability.'[31] Secondly, he casts doubts on Greek histories by means of thought experiments that question the basis of the claims made in those histories. Thus Marathon, Salamis and other battles may have been 'real events' but 'Grecian writers, to dignify their country, may have turned the hyperbole into historic fact; and swelled the *Thousands* of the *Persian Satrap in the millions* of the *Persian King*' in their accounts of these events.[32] This leads him to unpick the Greek heroic self-image purveyed in these accounts, including in such legends as Jason and the Argonauts that formed such an important part of the materials for romance writing in the modern period:

> Some of these famed events, it is not impossible too, might have been the mere descents of pirates or private adventurers; either with the view to

30. Richardson, *A Dictionary*, 2, p.ii-iv.
31. Richardson, *A Dictionary*, 1, p.ix.
32. Richardson, *A Dictionary*, 1, p.xii.

plunder, or to retaliate some similar expedition of the Greeks, who appear very early to have been a race of free-booters extremely troublesome to the surrounding coasts. The Argonauts, if such heroes ever did exist, are not entitled to a more reputable appellation: and indeed the practice seems to have been too universal to carry with the Greeks the remotest imputation of dishonour. If we look into Homer, Thucydides, Diodorus, and others, we shall discover piracy to have been considered a profession: but without connecting with it the least opprobrious idea.[33]

Here Richardson echoes the mock heroic sensibilities of the Augustan age of John Dryden and Alexander Pope that preceded his own career as a lexicographer. However, while Pope and others might have been ambivalent towards the Greek models they felt obliged to imitate, for them the mock heroic epic also reflected the inadequacies of their own age and society to match the greatness of Greek epics and the society that produced them. Richardson in part develops this complex literary sensibility of the earlier part of the eighteenth century by literalising its mockery; that is, it is not the inadequacies of eighteenth-century English society that need to be satirised in relation to the heroism of the Greek epic, rather Greek heroism itself is questioned and rendered bathetic. The theme of the mock heroism of the Greeks is developed in another thought experiment that also calls into question the extent of Greek power in the ancient world:

In this honourable profession of pirates there may have been many subjects of the Persian empire. Greece, as well as other countries, may have been often the theatre of their rapine and devastation: whilst their success or discomfiture must have been events of too little moment to reach the ears or engage the attention of the Shahinshah, or King of Kings, at the remote cities of Persepolis and Balkh. Suppose, if such an illustration may be allowed, an English pirate to have landed in former times on Madagascar; suppose him to have called himself *King of England;* and suppose, after putting that island into dreadful alarm, he had been at length defeated. The Madagascar historians, if any they had, to raise the glory of their nation, might compose a pompous detail of their Marathons and Plataeas: they might repulse the English monarch at the head of any myriads the victors should vauntingly give out, or tradition magnify: and this might undoubtedly gain credit in Madagascar and in the adjacent isles; whilst the splendid event, unfelt, and even unknown to the British nation, found not a single line in their historic page.[34]

This leads to the third point in Richardson's argument. In order to assess their validity Greek narratives on the 'East' and Persia have to be compared to narratives in Persian and oriental languages themselves.

33. Richardson, *A Dictionary*, 1, p.xii.
34. Richardson, *A Dictionary*, 1, p.xii.

Richardson avers that from about 610 BC until the Greek conquest we have a history of Persians as given by Greeks, and as given by Persians themselves. He adds:

> Between those classes of writers, we might naturally expect some difference of facts; but we should as naturally look for a few great lines, which might mark some similarity of story: yet, from every research which I have had an opportunity to make, there seems to be nearly as much resemblance between the annals of England and Japan, as between the European and Asiatic relations of the same empire.[35]

Developing this further, he argues:

> In a few circumstances they [Persian historians] coincide with the writers of Greece and Rome; this strengthens history: there are many upon which they are silent; this naturally leads to doubt and enquiry: there are numbers in which the opposition is pointed: whom are we to believe? The natives, or the native enemies of a country? Those who might have had access to genuine records, or those who probably never could?[36]

The fourth plank in Richardson's argument is to disabuse his readers of what we today would call their 'Eurocentric' assumptions. He argues that because of the cultural prestige of the Greeks in the European imagination, his readers are predisposed to accept their narratives uncritically, even when these are highly improbable: 'The Grecians are already in full possession of our imaginations; we imbibe a reverence for them in our early years, which it is impossible ever to eradicate; and we are dragged with difficulty to give a candid review to accounts, which, though fully within the line of probability, contradict ideas which we have so long fostered with care.'[37] These Eurocentric assumptions include compilers of ancient history viewing 'the languages and literatures of the East under one general unsupported assertion, that they are wild, uninteresting, and obscure',[38] whereas, Richardson argues, the annals of Persians and other 'Asiatics' are on an equal footing with those of Western nations, they are 'remarkably attentive to the annals of their country', 'their materials for ancient history are upon a footing of respect not inferior to those of more Western nations' and 'their traditions are upon a ground as substantial as those of the Greeks, the Egyptians, and other people of high antiquity'.[39] In addition, Richardson gives specific reasons as to why 'Eastern' historians are preoccupied with

35. Richardson, *A Dictionary*, 1, p.xi.
36. Richardson, *A Dictionary*, 1, p.ix.
37. Richardson, *A Dictionary*, 1, p.xiii. He also points to how 'an attachment to the chronology of Greece' leads to other chronologies being 'forced into an analogy with their imaginary eras' (p.xix).
38. Richardson, *A Dictionary*, 1, p.xvii.
39. Richardson, *A Dictionary*, 1, p.xvi.

genealogy, and how this produces critical historical knowledge.[40] What is
of key importance, he argues, is that 'Truth ought to be searched for
wherever it can be found; and a well authenticated fact, if told by a
Persian, an Arab, or a Chinese, should remove an improbability, though
adorned with all the eloquence of Greece or Rome'.[41] His conclusion,
then, comes as no surprise to the reader: 'the *Greeks* and *Romans*, in their
ancient histories, especially of distant countries, are often wrong; and, in
general, liable to suspicion: that their accounts of the East, as well with
regard to manners, as historic facts, are inconsistent with the Asiatic
authors; irreconcilable with Scripture; contradictory in themselves; and
often impossible in nature.'[42]

The British intervention in the Indian subcontinent had profound
intellectual consequences for the production of knowledge about and in
India and its adjoining regions, not least in the area of historiography
and questions about the very possibility of a historical narration of
'Asian' antiquity. These questions were also central to and continue to
animate post-colonial societies and nationalisms, and are integral to
their own fraught sense of political and historical identities.[43]
Richardson, by focusing on the question of sources in Asian languages
in the writing of history especially as it relates to Persian antiquity, was
writing in the wake of the work of such scholars as Anquetil-Duperron's
Zend-Avesta, ouvrage de Zoroastre (1771), which approached an Asian text
totally independent of the classical and biblical traditions, and therefore
introduced European scholarship to an antiquity that was independent
of these traditions.[44] He was also looking forward to Sir William Jones's
'Third Anniversary Discourse' of 1786 which focuses on the source
materials for the writing of ancient Indian history. In effect, his 'Dissertation' was partly arguing for a new global and cosmopolitan cultural and
linguistic imagination, for which an expanded notion of antiquity
grounded in enhanced linguistic expertise was crucial:

> Should the Arabic and Persian languages ever become therefore, like the
> Greek and Latin, objects of general education; and learned men, freed from
> the fetters of prejudice, be once brought to suppose, that Grecian and
> Roman information may *sometimes* be assisted or corrected by a judicious
> study of Eastern authors, many discoveries must evidently be expected;

40. Richardson, *A Dictionary*, 1, p.xv-xvi.
41. Richardson, *A Dictionary*, 1, p.xvii.
42. Richardson, *A Dictionary*, 1, p.xxi.
43. The secondary literature on this area is too vast to cite here, but for a recent intervention
    see Rama Mantena, *The Origins of modern historiography in India. Antiquarianism and philology
    1780-1880* (New York, 2012).
44. Raymond Schwab, *The Oriental Renaissance: Europe's rediscovery of India and the East, 1680-
    1880* (1950); transl. Gene Patterson-Black and Victor Reinking (New York, 1984), p.17.

which may furnish a variety of useful clues to the dark labyrinths of Ancient Mythology, History, and Manners.[45]

However, also underpinning Richardson's argument for a different cultural imagination embedded in an expanding lexicography is a distinctive form of identity politics which is also globalised. This comes to the fore in his ruminations on romance narratives.

The amusing wildness of romantic fables and Gothicism

Richardson's critical attitude to Greek histories also stems from a sobering sense of how difficult it is to ascertain and represent 'truth' in historiography, difficulties which he outlines in some detail.[46] He gives some telling examples of how events have been represented in widely differing ways by a variety of historians, depending on their ideological position, and argues that historical facts are always provisional ('few facts, either of ancient or modern times, are so fully authenticated as to render further enquiry improper').[47] This question of the uncertainty of historical truth leads him to examine romance narratives and fables and whether these can be interpreted in ways that can recover historical facts.

Richardson argues that one source of historical information from ancient and medieval eras is 'tradition'. Under this category he groups epic poems, 'romantic tales', 'legendary tales', songs, 'older compositions', 'romantic fables' and 'Heroic Ballads'. It is in these forms of 'oral record' and compositions that 'public events' are registered when the 'written memorials of a people are few, and where fewer still can read them'.[48] He argues that 'If any dependence then is placed on those Western tales, in the absence of more convincing evidence, candour ought to allow a proportionate degree of weight to those of the East.'[49] As 'many events may have been in this manner preserved in [Persian and Arabic] poems and legendary tales, like the Runic fragments of the North, the Romanzes of Spain, or the Heroic Ballads of our own country, seems to be highly probable', so too 'such materials may have originally suggested to Firdousi many of the adventures of his *Shah namé*; which, like Homer, when stript of the machinery of supernatural beings, is supposed to contain much true history, and a most undoubted picture of the superstition and manners of the times'.[50] The 'ground-work of truth' can

45. Richardson, *A Dictionary*, 1, p.xxii.
46. Richardson, *A Dictionary*, 1, p.ix-x.
47. Richardson, *A Dictionary*, 1, p.x; the events he mentions are the Bartholomew Massacre in France and the suppression of the Monmouth Rebellion in England.
48. Richardson, *A Dictionary*, 1, p.xiv-xv.
49. Richardson, *A Dictionary*, 1, p.xiv.
50. Richardson, *A Dictionary*, 1, p.xv.

be recovered from the 'embroidery of the imagination' in these Oriental tales, as in 'the Gieurusalemme of Tasso, or the Lusiade of Camoens'.[51] The result is that 'much rational information will therefore be discovered, not only in their [Persians' and Arabs'] more ferocious traditions, but also amidst the amusing wildness of their romantic fables'. In fact, the Arabian Nights and other tales show a 'truer picture of Eastern manners and beliefs, than in all the Grecian writers; or in hundreds of other books, more generally resorted to as authorities'.[52]

The question of the status of historical 'truth' in the wildness of 'romantic fables', and in other literary and cultural productions such as epics, was to be raised later in an Indian context by Sir William Jones in his essays 'On the Gods of Greece, Italy and India' (1788) and 'Asiatick History, Civil and Natural' (1794). However, Richardson's 'Dissertation' also resonates with debates in Britain during the eighteenth century about the status of romance narratives as histories. David Fairer has discussed how eighteenth-century critics and writers reflected on the nature and possibilities of romance through their engagement with Spenser's *Faerie queene* (1590-1596). The perceived clash between the imaginative visions of the 'fancy' opening up new areas of experience and perception, and the critical ratiocinative faculties of 'reason' was central to the problematic status of the poem and its evaluation. Similarly, while novelists such as Defoe, Richardson and Fielding preferred the descriptive label 'History' for their own works, they nonetheless also reworked conventions of romance within these works so labelled.[53] Richardson's own translations of the term 'romance' in his *Dictionary* reflects this fluidity of romance as a genre, and its slipperiness in the eighteenth century, as well as the way it cut across the boundaries of 'fiction' and 'history'. Thus, he translates 'A romance' into Persian as 'qissa', 'dastan', 'hikayet' and 'afsana', and in the same entry refers the reader to 'fable, lie, fiction'. 'Qissa' is glossed as 'a history, tale, romance, fable, apologue', while 'afsana' is translated into English as 'a narration, history, commentary' as well as 'a fiction, tale, fable, romance, parable'. This ambiguity is continued in the gloss for 'hikayet' as 'history, heroic romance, fable, tradition, a relation, narrative'. 'Hikayet-e kitabi' is glossed as 'a book of history or romance, and 'dastan' as 'history, fable, romance, a narrative, tale, news'.[54] Thus, Richardson's transcontinental

51. Richardson, *A Dictionary*, 1, p.xiv.
52. Richardson, *A Dictionary*, 1, p.xiv.
53. David Fairer, 'The *Fairie queene* and eighteenth-century Spenserianism' (p.216-32) and Clive Probyn, 'Paradise and cotton-mill: rereading eighteenth-century romance' (p.251-68, 257-58) in *A Companion to romance from classical to contemporary*, ed. Corinne Saunders (Oxford, 2004).
54. Richardson, *A Dictionary*, 2, p.1672, 1389, 183, 743, 823.

history of romance was in part secured by the multilingual, cross-cultural instability of the term, exemplified by the entries in his *Dictionary*.

Richardson's reflections, then, on the question of historical 'truth' in romance and allied narratives needs to be seen in terms of a series of debates about the subject in a variety of locations across the globe, from a British domestic literary space to Calcutta as one of the centres of British authority in India. However, a globalising framework is also integral to, and not just the context for, Richardson's own argument in the 'Dissertation' in relation to the question of the 'Eastern origin' of 'Romantic Fiction'. This argument is framed by a broader narrative 'on the extensive subjects of Eastern manners' and an attempt to trace 'their probable influence on those of modern Europe'.[55] Here the 'Dissertation' resonates with the intellectual history of the category of the 'Gothic' as a political and aesthetic idea in seventeenth- and eighteenth-century England.[56] It draws upon and engages with the different facets of 'Gothicism' as a key concept in English intellectual life during this period. Its examination of 'Romantic Fiction' and its 'Eastern origins', flowing from its lexicographical interaction with Arabic and Persian in the context of a burgeoning colonialism in India, becomes in part a reflection on the origins of the English as a people and their distinctive institutions, in the very period when Britain itself was entering its second phase of global expansion after American independence.

This question of the origins of the English was a key part of 'Gothicism'. As Robert Young has pointed out, Dr Johnson's *Dictionary* of 1755 included a chart showing the derivation of English from 'Gothick or Teutonick'.[57] Kliger has shown how the term 'Gothic' originally referred to one of the three Germanic tribes that invaded England, but by the seventeenth century the term had been expanded to refer to the Germanic origins of the English people in general.[58] Richardson takes this Gothic ancestry of the English for granted, referring in passing to 'our Gothic ancestors'.[59] Another important component of Gothicism in the seventeenth and eighteenth centuries was the idea that the English constitution and distinctive English freedoms also had their origins in Gothic institutions.[60] This idea was given an extra urgency in the seventeenth century, when the term 'Gothic' was used by Parliamentary leaders to defend the prerogatives of Parliament against the pretensions

55. Richardson, *A Dictionary*, 1, p.xxviii-xxix.
56. The classic work here is Samuel Kliger, *The Goths in England. A study in seventeenth and eighteenth century thought* (Cambridge, MA, 1952).
57. Robert Young, *The Idea of English ethnicity* (Oxford, 2008), p.24.
58. Kliger, *The Goths*, p.11-19.
59. Richardson, *A Dictionary*, 1, p.xxix.
60. Kliger, *The Goths*, ch.1-2.

of the king's absolute right to govern England. However, the notion of
the Gothic origins of the English constitution continued to be expressed
as late as 1828, when in *History of the Anglo-Saxons* Sharon Turner declared
that 'our language, our government, and our laws, display our Gothic
ancestors in every part'.[61] Again, Richardson echoes these staples of
Gothicism when he discusses the features of 'Gothic government', including a 'constitutional Parliament', juries, the feudal system and a love
of liberty.[62] He echoed the tendency in Gothicism to connect 'Gothic'
history with a national apotheosis of democracy in England, so that
English freedoms were described as 'Gothic' liberties.[63]

Moreover, Richardson examines in detail the 'hypothesis of *Oden's flight
from the Euxine to Scandinavia*' that has been adopted to account for 'the
early prevalence amongst our Gothic ancestors' of 'Romantic fiction'.[64]
He also refers to the theories of Jordanes, regarding the *officiana gentium*
from which 'barbarians' poured into the civilised parts of the world. As
he says, Jordanez looked to Scandinavia and the northern parts of
Germany for 'those bodies of fierce warriors' who in the early ages of
Christianity 'overturned the government, and changed the manners of
Europe'.[65] Kliger has pointed out that the history of the Goths, their
conquests and their gradual spread over Europe was a magnificent
record of Gothic greatness in Jordanes' *De origine actibusque Getarum*
(551 CE). The primary importance of Jordanes for the modern revival
of interest in Gothic antiquity rested on the credence he gave to the
theory that all German tribesmen were generically 'Goths', stemming
from the group which, migrating from Scandza in the north, peopled
Europe.[66] Kliger also outlines the different uses to which the Odin myth
was put in outlining the origins and movements of Goths from the
north.[67] In examining this myth, Richardson concludes that 'there is no
probability in the tale of Oden', and in this case, history cannot be
recovered from 'the province of Romance'.[68] However, the Odin myth
also located the Goths in an 'Asiatic' home,[69] and this aspect of the myth
is utilised in Richardson's own argument about the Asian origins of
Gothic institutions, customs and romance literature. Richardson also
refers in passing to how theories of the 'Eastern origin' of 'Romantic
Fiction' sometimes referred to the Crusades as a channel of transmission

61. Kliger, *The Goths*, p.9.
62. Richardson, *A Dictionary*, 1, p.xxxiv-xxxv.
63. Kliger, *The Goths*, p.19.
64. Richardson, *A Dictionary*, 1, p.xxix.
65. Richardson, *A Dictionary*, 1, p.xxx.
66. Kliger, *The Goths*, p.11-12.
67. Kliger, *The Goths*, p.7, 95-103, 212-17, 234.
68. Richardson, *A Dictionary*, 1, p.xxix-xxx.
69. Kliger, *The Goths*, p.95, 97, 212-17.

for this genre of literature,[70] again echoing previously circulated theories.

In his 'Dissertation', then, Richardson engages with different strains in Gothicism while reproducing some of its basic tenets. In doing so, he makes two interventions. The first is to develop the idea of the 'Oriental' origins of Gothic institutions and customs, and the second is to argue for the Persian, rather than Arabian, origins of 'Romantic Fiction'. Regarding the first, Richardson refers to Jordanez's argument that Scandinavia and northern Germany were the originating places for 'those bodies of fierce warriors' who in early ages of Christianity 'overturned the government, and changed the manners of Europe'. He counters this by arguing it is from Tartary that 'myriads of barbarians' have come into the 'cultivated regions of the earth', adding that 'These people [Tartars] possess, as we may observe, the whole interior almost of the Asiatic and European continent' and 'they have burst repeatedly upon every adjacent country'. When they settled, the previous inhabitants would adopt some of the manners and beliefs of the 'Eastern strangers', and these in turn fell in with 'habits and ideas peculiar to the aboriginal people'. In time 'nations' formed known by names such as Goths, Vandals, Lombards and Franks, 'whose roaming, rapacious, Tartar genius, became afterwards conspicuous, in the destruction of the Roman empire'.[71] Richardson concludes this stage of his argument:

> Every observation, indeed, on the habits of those roving, daring people, strikingly displays their love of liberty, and their similitude of character with the *old Gothic nations*. Their aversion to the culture of the ground; their pastoral life; their idleness; their eagerness for plunder, and martial excursion; with many customs and beliefs, clearly Eastern: form all together a chain of internal proofs, stronger perhaps than direct historical assertion [...] nothing can surely approach nearer in resemblance than the original northern invaders of the Roman states, and those inundations, *immediately from Tartary*, who, under the names of *Alans* and *Huns*, led by the famous *Attila* and other bold chiefs, overwhelmed the empire, towards the close of the fourth century, and gave a final blow to the chains of Roman servitude.[72]

However, Richardson also makes some specific points in relation to the apparently Asian origins of the feudal system in Europe, which he argues was 'an exotic plant' in Europe. Whereas lawyers, historians and antiquarians have seen the feudal system that laid 'great foundation of the jurisprudence of modern Europe' as 'introduced and diffused over Europe by the conquerors of the Roman power', Richardson goes further

---

70. Richardson, *A Dictionary*, 1, p.xxix. For these theories, see Kliger, *The Goths*, p.223-24, 227-28.
71. Richardson, *A Dictionary*, 1, p.xxx-xxxi.
72. Richardson, *A Dictionary*, 1, p.xxxii.

by arguing that the feudal system actually originated in Persia, Tartary, India and other 'Eastern' nations. He focuses in particular on how the power of the sovereign in these societies was always limited by a degree of dependence on 'secondary kings', drawing on the examples of the Caliphate, Tartary, the Mughal empire and parts of the Ottoman empire.[73] He also refers to examples of governance and assemblies among the Tartars that resemble the meeting of estates and the Diets of 'Gothic nations'.[74] He also notes that even when Genghis Khan nominated his second son as his successor, this had to be acknowledged by 'the meeting of the Great Assembly two years afterwards'.[75] In making these arguments, Richardson is clearly echoing the notion of the Gothic constitution and the idea of a 'Gothic balance' of powers, such as in the constitution of England, as being a form of constitutional or limited, and not absolute, monarchy.[76] Moreover, in notions of Gothic liberty the idea of the king not as a hereditary *princeps* but an elective *dux bellorum* elevated in a war crisis from a military captaincy to a kingship, was an important one.[77] Richardson alludes to this in his argument that Tartar chiefs issued orders for the attendance of vassals before embarking on military expeditions.[78] Richardson concludes, then, that in these Asian polities we can see 'several strong traces of Gothic government' such as 'the ruder draughts of States General, of Parliaments, of Juries; and, in the circumstances of the Electors and Elected, some striking features of that system, which still unites the great Germanic Body', which were then developed and modified in Scandinavia and Germany.[79]

Shifting from the 'Eastern' origins of Gothic manners, customs and polities, in the second part of his 'Dissertation' Richardson considers the 'Eastern' origins of romance writing and what he calls the '*Mythology of romance*'.[80] Discussing the fabulous geography, plots and structures of these 'Eastern' romances in detail,[81] he argues that Persia, and not Arabia, is the 'great classic ground of Eastern fiction; and the centre whence it seems to have spread to almost every surrounding and distant country'. Referring to the many 'singular' resemblances between the 'wild imagery of this stile of fabling, with that which prevailed in after-times in *Europe* [...] we must either suppose, in the writers, a wonderful coincidence of luxuriant imagination, or conclude, that the West must

73. Richardson, *A Dictionary*, 1, p.xxxii-xxxiv.
74. Richardson, *A Dictionary*, 1, p.xxxiv.
75. Richardson, *A Dictionary*, 1, p.xxxiv.
76. For the history of these ideas, see Kliger, *The Goths*, p.164-67, 203-207.
77. Kliger, *The Goths*, p.117, 200.
78. Richardson, *A Dictionary*, 1, p.xxxiv.
79. Richardson, *A Dictionary*, 1, p.xxxv.
80. Richardson, *A Dictionary*, 1, p.xxxvii.
81. Richardson, *A Dictionary*, 1, p.xxxv-xxxvii.

have borrowed from the East'. Opting for the latter, he suggests that in the romances of Europe, and in 'the nobler works of *Ariosto, Tasso*, and *Spencer*, we can discover the counter part of all their fanciful machinery in the fictions of *Persia*'.[82] Discussing the 'peculiar and distinct species of machinery' underlying Romance, he focuses on Persian narratives and their fabulous transmuting creatures, their non-realistic plots, the 'Peri system' of fairies and other supernatural beings, the 'machinery of Angels',[83] talismans and amulets[84] and 'chivalry or Knight-errantry', here arguing that 'the institution of Chivalry in Europe [appears] to have been long familiar in the East'.[85] In this context he also argues that duelling and 'private War' and revenge were better regulated in early Islamic society than in medieval Europe.[86] However, Richardson makes special mention of 'that respectful attention to women which formed no part of the national character of the Greeks or Romans', and argues that 'The attention of the Arabians and Tartars to the Fair Sex seems indeed to have been conducted upon such principles of delicate sensibility, as would hardly be expected from that fierceness of temper, for which they have been characterized.'[87] Here again Richardson's argument resonates with the discussions of the war-like ethos of the Germanic tribes and their idealisation of women in Gothicism,[88] except that he traces this ethos and the idealisation of women to the romances and customs of the Arabs and Persians. His 'Dissertation' therefore also represents an early intervention in what was to become a central issue in the production of knowledge during the colonial period, namely the assessment of the civilisational qualities of different societies in relation to the position of women. Richardson's remarks on the respect paid towards women in his argument about Gothic romances and their origins also reflects a broader concern with gender and romance narratives in eighteenth-century England, especially in relation to the possible ill-effects of this literature on women readers. Contemporary critics have addressed these anxieties in terms of the transgressive possibilities afforded to women within the complex gender order of eighteenth-century England. As one critic puts it, in Radcliffe's romances the female Gothic becomes a

---

82. Richardson, *A Dictionary*, 1, p.xxxvii.
83. Richardson, *A Dictionary*, 1, p.xxxviii-xl.
84. Richardson, *A Dictionary*, 1, p.xxxviii.
85. Richardson, *A Dictionary*, 1, p.xliv.
86. Richardson, *A Dictionary*, 1, p.xlv-xlvi, and note.
87. Richardson, *A Dictionary*, 1, p.xlii; the discussion of the idealisation of women by Arabs and Tartars is on p.xlii-xliii.
88. Kliger, *The Goths*, p.72-78, 210 on how the Goths were supposed to be the first people in history to venerate women, institute monogamous marriage, and undertake adventure on behalf of womankind, and p.220-223 on the alleged Gothic idealisation of women as a component in eighteenth-century theories of romance.

symbolic site where conflicts over the rights and construction of women are played out at the 'romantic' distance of the sixteenth to seventeenth centuries.[89]

However, Richardson's argument that respect to women was not part of the 'national character of the Greeks or Romans' reminds us again of his critical stance on the classical legacy in European culture, resonating as it does with Gothicism and the anti-classical animus that was sometimes associated with it. As we have seen, in drawing on Meninski, Richardson not only excluded the Turkish part of Meninski's lexicon, he replaced Latin as a medium of translation with English. As Kliger has shown, the meaning of Gothicism remained fixed in the seventeenth and eighteenth centuries to describe primitive Germanic culture and the medieval, as a historical narrative separate from the classic Roman narrative. 'Gothic' freedoms were seen as countering 'Roman tyranny' and 'depravity'.[90] The scope of 'Roman tyranny' was extended to include the Church of Rome as well, so that humanity was twice ransomed from Roman tyranny and depravity – in antiquity by the Goths, and in modern times by their descendants, the German reformers.[91] Furthermore, the ensemble of ideas and arguments in Gothicism also included ridding the term 'Gothic' of its connotations of barbarism in the context of elevating it against Rome.[92] This sometimes included criticising the Greeks and their animadversions of their non-Greek neighbours as barbarians, in order to validate the Goths and, ultimately, English literary taste.[93] In addition, romances such as Samuel Richardson's *Clarissa* (1747-1748) questioned higher-status genres, especially classical learning, and after Samuel Richardson, commentators on romance frequently expressed reservations about classical education, suggesting that untempered by Christianity it promoted 'licentiousness' to as great a degree as romance might be accused of doing so.[94] However, through his lexicographical project, Richardson extended the potential in Gothicism of an alternative cultural politics to bring Arabs and Persians into the 'civilised' fold. Through 'a chain of internal proofs' he connected 'Englishness' via the category of the Gothic to different parts of the 'East', thereby trying to locate 'Englishness' in a global historical context of overlapping, interconnected cultures and institutions that defied the parameters of

---

89. Probyn, 'Paradise and cotton-mill,' p.262-63, and Jerrold E. Hogle, '"Gothic romance": its origins and cultural functions', p.216-32, 226-27, in Saunders (ed.), *Romance*.
90. Kliger, *The Goths*, p.20, 31-33, 78, 84-89, 210.
91. Kliger, *The Goths*, p.33-34, 47-66.
92. Kliger, *The Goths*, p.65, 91-92, 217.
93. Kliger, *The Goths*, p.89-90.
94. Fiona Price, '"Inconsistent rhapsodies": Samuel Richardson and the politics of romance', in Saunders (ed.), *Romance*, p.269-86, 277-78.

'national' histories even as Britain was entering its second phase of overseas expansion as a world power.

It is also useful to consider Richardson's argument about the remote 'Eastern' origins of English romance narratives in relation to eighteenth-century debates about 'Englishness' and/or 'Britishness' and romance narratives. Critics have pointed out how Samuel Richardson adapted key features of French romance in order to create 'an explicitly British model of romance that rejected "foreign" narratives of authority'. Clare Reeves in *The Progress of romance* (1785) attempted to distance romance from French influence by evoking nostalgia for a hardier Gothic past which she makes implicitly British.[95] In addition, Judith Weiss has argued that the heroes of Anglo-Norman romance from the thirteenth century onwards refer repeatedly to their Englishness with a growing pride in their 'nationality', while Arthurian romance also came to be associated with the triumph of a 'native' dynasty, playing out the 'wish-fulfilment fantasy of national unity' in Geoffrey of Monmouth's *Historia Regum Britanniae*.[96] The latter, along with the myth of Alfred, came to be one of the two myths of racial origin developed for the English.[97] But by connecting English romances via Gothic romances to Persian narratives in particular, and 'Eastern' romances in general, Richardson made a distinctive intervention in the field of literary criticism and ethnohistorical reflections on the British. He countered the attempts to link Britishness and/or Englishness with a particular set of romance narratives and their reworking, in which, as it were, these categories emerged as ultimately self-contained and distinctively set apart from a wider geopolitical and global literary context.

It is also possible that Richardson as a Scot was particularly sensitive to these constructions of Englishness and Britishness. Others in British colonial society in Calcutta tended to see him as a troublesome Scotsman. William Hickey (1749-1827) in his memoirs both lampooned his broad Scottish accent, and referred to him as the 'poor Scotchman' who, because of his indifferent skills as a lawyer, was the object of the governor-general's pity. He also suggested that the reason for the Court of Directors acceding to his application to go to India was 'merely to get rid of his troublesome importunities'.[98] Given the complicated and

95. Price, '"Inconsistent rhapsodies"', p.273-74, 282.
96. Judith Weiss, 'Insular beginnings: Anglo-Norman romance', p.26-44, 40-41, and W. J. Barron, 'Arthurian romance', p.65-84, 66-68, in Saunders (ed.), *Romance*.
97. Young *The Idea of English ethnicity*, p.15 and following.
98. William Hickey, *Memoirs of William Hickey*, ed. Alfred Spencer, 4 vols (London, 1925), 4, p.82-83, 126. For references to Richardson's applications to go to India in East India Company correspondence, see BL, IOR D/31 East India Company Committee of Correspondence 3, April 1783, and IOR E/1/72 East India Company General Correspondence,

sometimes violent narrative of Scotland's integration into the Union after 1707, and the role that British expansion overseas was to play in this integration,[99] it is possible that Richardson was especially sensitive to such constructions and their histories and fluidity. To a certain extent, the form and content of his *Dictionary* plays out an ambivalent relationship to 'Englishness'. On the one hand, as we have seen, Richardson anglicised Meninski's lexicon. This is especially evident in contrast to the reprinting of Meninski in Vienna in 1780 which retained Latin as the medium of translation, as well as the Turkish sections of the lexicon,[100] and to Jones's 1771 proposal for a pan-European reprinting of Meninski, where Arabic, Persian and Turkish were to be glossed into Latin, French, English, Portuguese and Italian. Moreover, as we have seen, while drawing on Meninski Richardson shaped his *Dictionary* in relation to British expansion in India, thereby reflecting in its own constitution the globalising framework of his argument in the 'Dissertation'. But the content of that argument, precisely because of its globalising transcultural framework, hollowed out the Gothic distinctiveness of 'Englishness' which was its subject matter. The genesis and constitution of the work, and the content of its argument, mimic the dialectical interaction between the globalisation of 'Englishness' and its undoing as a distinctive ethnohistorical, political and cultural category. It was precisely this interaction that was to cause Seeley so much anxiety almost exactly a century later in *The Expansion of England* (1883).

Richardson's sensitivity to these issues may have been further deepened by the fluidity of his class identity. He was apprenticed to an Edinburgh printer at the age of twelve in 1753, but after moving to London in 1767 he studied law and Arabic and Persian, while forging connections with Oxford in the course of his lexicographical work.[101] This sense of his being seen as a *parvenu* comes across in the back-handed compliment Boswell paid to him upon reading his 'Dissertation', which he thought had the 'the appearance of research and ingenuity', adding 'and, as I had known Richardson as a printer in Edinburgh, I wondered at the great benefit he had received by studying at Oxford'.[102] While in

folio 318, letters 147-48, 31 March 1783. Hickey moved to India in 1777 where he stayed until 1808, practising as an attorney at the Supreme Court. His 742-page *Memoirs* is an important historical source that brings to life the British community in Calcutta.

99. For which see Linda Colley, *Britons: forging the nation, 1707-1837* (New Haven, CT, 1992).

100. Francisci a Mesignien, *Meninski Lexicon Arabico-Persico-Turcicum, adjecta ad singulas voces et phrases significatione Latina, ad usitatiores, etiam Italica* (Vienna, 1780).

101. P. J. Marshall, 'John Richardson', *Dictionary of national biography* (Oxford, 2004), vol.46, p.818-19.

102. James Boswell, *Boswell in extremes 1776-1778*, ed. Charles McC. Weis and Frederick A. Pottle (London, 1971), p.211.

Calcutta, Richardson styled himself Sir John Richardson, asserting his claim to succeed to a baronetcy revived by his elder brothers, since the second one had died in December 1791, leaving as his heir a child born out of wedlock but legitimised by subsequent marriage.[103] Or as Hickey put it, 'His right to the title of *Sir* was of a somewhat doubtful nature; he assumed it some time after his arrival in India, upon hearing of the death of his elder brother, who undoubtedly had succeeded to a baronetage, but who, it was equally certain, had left two legitimate sons.'[104] Schumpeter's classic study *Imperialism and social classes* (1951) characterised imperialism as a militaristic and aristocratic throwback to Europe's past, and here Richardson's self-advancement through lexicography within an imperial Indian context, culminating in a distinctive kind of self-styling, seems to be an individual illustration of this. At the same time, though, this self-styling suggests a playful exemplification of one of the conventional themes of Gothic romance itself, that of the displaced aristocrat severed from his true origins.[105] Critics have argued that issues of class and class placement are crucial to Gothic romance, and that Gothic romance is indicative not just of deep cultural contradictions, but also the contradictions and tensions between the claims of landed property and the emergent mercantile and preindustrial capitalism celebrated in Adam Smith's *Wealth of nations* (1776).[106] Richardson's own life trajectory and self-presentation, then, was imbricated with narratives of class and ethnicity within Britain and how they were played out and complicated in India in the context of imperial expansion. The 'Dissertation' resonates with his complex subject positions in multiple narratives of class, ethnicity, politics and literary history, which are brought together at the beginning of the second phase of British imperial expansion overseas within a globalised narratological space created by lexicography. The complexity of these intersecting narratives and the need to negotiate the complex subject positions it created accounts for Richardson's lexicographical style, described by himself as 'periphrasis'.[107] Boswell wrote of Richardson's style that 'though frequently incorrect and sometimes absurd from his ambition for pomp and metaphor, [it] surprised me with its abundance and choice of words'.[108] It was only through this style that Richardson was able to articulate the complexity of these intersecting and conflicting narratives,

103. Marshall, 'John Richardson'.
104. Hickey, *Memoirs*, p.126.
105. Hogle, '"Gothic" romance: its origins and cultural functions' in Saunders, p.219.
106. Hogle, '"Gothic" romance' in Saunders, p.221-22.
107. Richardson, *A Dictionary*, 2, p.ii-iv. Wilkins also described Richardson's use of 'periphrase' (Wilkins, *Dictionary*, 2, p.xxi).
108. Weis and Pottle, *Boswell*, p.211.

and his negotiation of them in a globalised lexicographical space, while simultaneously dramatising and hollowing out 'Englishness'.

Richardson's ethnopolitical and historical reflections on the origins of 'Englishness', and the originality or otherwise of European Gothic romances and their themes, are also indicative of a problem distinctive to his career as a lexicographer, namely that of originality. From the start, as we have seen, Richardson's *Dictionary* was intertwined with Meninski's, or as Charles Wilkins put it, it was 'notorious that the learned Author took the justly celebrated dictionary of *Meninski* for the ground work of his own'.[109] Some were more uncharitable. Hickey, for example, wrote that 'He [Richardson] was the reputed compiler of the Persian Dictionary published under his name, though those who were conversant with the language asserted that there was nothing original on the part of Richardson, the whole having been stolen from Meninski',[110] while Francis Johnson described the *Dictionary* as 'being little else than a limited translation from the great Thesaurus of Meninski'.[111] However, both Wilkins and Johnson, rather than producing a dictionary ab initio for which Richardson would have been one source they consulted among many, preferred to produce revised editions of Richardson's *Dictionary* instead. While Wilkins referred to the notoriety of Richardson's reliance on Meninski as his 'ground work', and drew attention to its 'considerable mistakes' and the 'many alterations and numerous additions' he had to make,[112] he also admitted errors he might himself have committed. But in the second volume, referring to the 'faults' both volumes might contain, he argued these 'cannot be fairly attributed to me, whose undertaking was to improve an old, not make a new Dictionary'.[113] While it is not clear what being 'original' as a lexicographer would entail, in a sense Wilkins's and Johnson's simultaneous reliance and denigration of Richardson as their own 'ground work' parallels the other discourse about originality in Richardson's 'Dissertation', namely that English Gothic romances are not 'original' as such; their ground work is Persian and 'Eastern' romances, to which they are connected in a transcontinental, cross-cultural literary history.

In his essay on Gothic Romance of the eighteenth century, Jerrold E. Hogle defines two features of Gothic romance; first it looked backwards and forwards in history, and second, it was a vivid indicator of cultural tensions and anxieties in general about modern identity.[114] Richardson's

109. Wilkins, *Dictionary*, 1, p.xci.
110. Hickey, *Memoirs* 4, p.126.
111. Johnson, *A Dictionary*, p.7.
112. Wilkins, *Dictionary*, 1, p.xci.
113. Wilkins, *Dictionary*, 2, p.xxiii.
114. Hogle, '"Gothic" Romance' in Saunders, p.216-32.

discussion of Gothicism and romance in a colonial lexicographical framework adds another dimension to these features. By its very nature, lexicography is concerned with the relationship between language and cultural identity, and with questions of the origins, and past and present meanings of words. As we have seen, while engaging with Persian and Arabic, Richardson looks backwards to antiquity and the origins of the English, while, it could be argued, formulating a new kind of cultural and linguistic politics better suited to the interconnected world of modernity from the 1780s onwards.[115] More immediately, the relativising of Greek and Roman antiquity in European cultural identity in relation to the 'Orient' was a defining feature of what Schwab called the 'Oriental Renaissance'.[116] This relativising was already under way before the arrival of Sanskrit texts in Europe from the late eighteenth century onwards. Moreover, as we have seen, there was a kind of built-in anticlassicism to the English Gothicism of the seventeenth and eighteenth centuries, which Richardson articulated in his own distinctive way by globalising the term 'Gothic' to expand its potential for an alternative cultural politics, bringing into the civilised fold Arabs and Persians. The British connection with India via Persian was crucial in many other ways too, as it was partly through Persian translations of Sanskrit texts that the British made their first literary contacts with Sanskrit. Charles Wilkins's translation of the *Bhagavad Gita* of 1785 was the first direct translation into English of a Sanskrit text.[117] Richardson's work on language and origins looks forward to the more systematic argument of Sir William Jones in his 'Third anniversary discourse' of 1786 where the question of origins and the Indo-European family of languages is key, and intercultural and interlingual comparisons are more rigorously grounded in the idea of similarities and differences expressed by the branches of a family network of relationships.[118] However, in a letter of February 1779, while referring to the project of reprinting Meninski and how it had been dropped, Jones reflected upon the prevalence of European words in the Persian language. This in turn led him to consider the possibility of 'a very old and almost primaeval language [...] from which not only the Celtic dialects, but even the Greek and Latin, are derived'. In this context, he gives a number of examples of similarities

115. For which see C. A Bayly, *The Birth of the modern world 1780-1914: global connections and comparisons* (Oxford, 2003).
116. Schwab, *The Oriental Renaissance*.
117. *The Bhagvat-Geeta, or Dialogues of Kreeshna and Arjoon; in eighteen lectures; with notes. Translated from the original, in the sanskreet, or ancient language of the Brahmans*, trans. Charles Wilkins (London, C. Nourse, 1785).
118. See Sir William Jones, 'On the Hindu[']s', *Asiatick researches* 1 (1788), p.414-32.

between Greek and Persian words, speculating that these might have 'sprang from the same root'.[119]

Edmund Burke also played a role both in debates of romance and questions of constitutionalism in Britain as affected by expansion in India. Burke's statement in *Reflections on the Revolution in France* (1790) that with the execution of Marie Antoinette the 'age of chivalry is gone' was seized upon by both defenders and critics of romance as part of a political and aesthetic debate in the years following the French Revolution.[120] As I have argued elsewhere, Burke depicted and defended Indian cultures and polities in the same terms in the 1780s as he was later to defend the *ancien régime* in his *Reflections*. In particular, Burke played an important role from the early 1780s onwards in the Select Committee of the House of Commons whose purpose was to investigate the administration of justice in Bengal.[121] The same confluence of constitutionalism, cultural identity and romance is to be found in Richardson's work, and here again the colonialism of East India Company rule is the background against which these issues become sharper.

Scholars have argued that in its preoccupation with the formation of identity through dangerous journeys, colonial fiction in the nineteenth century can be explicated in terms of the motifs of the 'romance quest'. The reworking of these motifs has been interpreted as revealing the characteristic concerns of colonial ideologies in Asia and Africa in the nineteenth century as writers sought to redefine European identity in unfamiliar surroundings. Thus, in his study of nineteenth- and early twentieth-century British literature and imperialism, Brantlinger considers how empire offered charismatic realms of adventure for British men, usually free from the complexities of relationships with British women. Discussing the relationship between 'domestic realism' and the adventure narrative of the romance quest, he points to how India was a 'realm of imaginative licence [...] a place where the fantastic becomes possible in ways that are carefully circumscribed at home'.[122] Robert Fraser considers the significance of the imperial quest romance in the period 1880-1920, and the importance of legends such as Jason and the Argonauts with its themes of quest and travel through dangerous regions in this mode of writing. Such legendary and mythological material was

119. Cannon (ed.), *Letters*, 1, Jones to Adam Czartoryski, 17 February 1779, p.284-86.
120. Fiona Robertson, 'Romance and the Romantic novel: Sir Walter Scott', in *A Companion to romance from classical to contemporary*, ed. Corinne Saunders (Oxford, 2004), p.287-304 (290-91).
121. Javed Majeed, *Ungoverned imaginings: James Mill's 'The history of British India' and orientalism* (Oxford, 1992), p.8-9.
122. Patrick Brantlinger, *Rule of darkness: British literature and imperialism, 1830-1914* (Ithaca, NY, and London, 1988), p.12-13.

examined in Andrew Lang's *Myth, ritual and religion* (1887). As Fraser notes, the key features of the travel romance are present in the traditional legends Lang discussed; news of distant danger, male companions pursuing a quest, a journey across uncharted regions, the reaching of the goal, and a withdrawal.[123] For these critics and others, adventure narratives and the romance quest formed the 'energising myth' of empire, although, as Brantlinger has noted, these narratives were rooted in imperial anxieties of various kinds, especially from the late nineteenth century onwards.[124] By bringing together eighteenth-century political debates about the origins of English cultural identity and the English constitution, aesthetic debates about romance literature and intellectual debates about historiography, with Persian and Arabic lexicography in English, Richardson anticipated the complex concatenation of these issues in the cultural politics of India as articulated by colonial texts in general – and the complexities of colonial romance writing of the nineteenth century in particular – in which the rediscovery of identity in unfamiliar surroundings was a central motif. In many ways, then, the imperial romance quest in relation to India was first articulated in the works of lexicographers like Richardson. In this he was to be followed by Gilchrist, the compiler of *A Dictionary, English and Hindoostanee* (1787-1790), who expressed his lexicographical subjectivity through the romance quest without reflecting upon it as such.[125] Although Richardson and Gilchrist differed in their handling of the romance quest, both fused together the negotiation and defining of interlingual meanings with the motifs of the romance quest while addressing questions of cultural and personal self-definition in a colonial and globalised context. In this sense, the romance quest in its colonial incarnation was first articulated by lexicographers in the late eighteenth and early nineteenth centuries in their work on oriental languages in India.

123. Robert Fraser, *Victorian quest romance: Stevenson, Haggard, Kipling and Conan Doyle* (Plymouth, 1998), p.5-6.
124. Brantlinger, *Rule of darkness*, ch.8; see also Martin Green, *Dreams of adventure, deeds of empire* (London, 1980), p.3, 14.
125. I am writing a study entitled 'Gilchrist, lexicographical subjectivity and the romance quest'.

'Voyage of conception': John Keats and India

DEIRDRE COLEMAN

The impact of orientalism on British Romantic literary forms and the artistic imagination is now commonly acknowledged, with excellent studies by Peter Kitson, Nigel Leask, Saree Makdisi and others.[1] But the 'Easts' which tend to attract the most attention are China, Egypt, Turkey and Arabia, with Tartary and Abyssinia featuring in studies of the period's most 'oriental' poem, Coleridge's *Kubla Khan*. More work needs to be done on the numerous connections between Indian literature, writings about India and Romantic literature of the late eighteenth and early nineteenth century. John Drew, in his *India and the Romantic imagination* (1987), made a bold and erudite start, with illuminating chapters on Coleridge and Shelley.[2] Marilyn Butler followed in 1994 with a thought-provoking chapter on orientalism,[3] while Michael J. Franklin has done most of the heavy lifting in the last fifteen years or so, having edited a collection of essays, *Romantic representations of British India* (2006), and done ground-breaking biographical work on the eighteenth-century orientalist, Sir William Jones, a key figure for establishing connections between Indian and European cultural forms.[4] Franklin has also collected the *European discovery of India* (2001) and *Representing India* (2000), multi-volume editions which enable scholars to make their own independent assessments about the place of India in Romantic writing.[5]

1. See Peter J. Kitson, *Romantic literature, race, and colonial literature* (London, 2007); Nigel Leask, *British Romantic writers and the East: anxieties of empire* (Cambridge, 1992); Leask, '*Kubla Khan* and orientalism: the road to Xanadu revisited', *Romanticism* 4.1 (1998), p.1-22; Leask, 'Easts' in *Romanticism: an Oxford guide*, ed. Nicholas Roe (Oxford, 2005), p.137-48; Saree Makdisi, *Romantic imperialism: universal empire and the culture of modernity* (New York and Cambridge, 1998), and Saree Makdisi, 'Literature, national identity, and empire' in *The Cambridge companion to English literature, 1740-1830*, ed. Thomas Keymer and Jon Mee (Cambridge, 2004), p.61-79.
2. John Drew, *India and the Romantic imagination* (Delhi, 1987).
3. Marilyn Butler, 'Orientalism', *The Penguin history of literature 4: the Romantic period*, ed. David B. Pirie (New York, 1994), p.395-447.
4. Franklin (ed.), *Romantic representations of British India*; see also Franklin's new biography '*Orientalist Jones*'.
5. Michael J. Franklin (ed.), *The European discovery of India: key Indological sources of Romanticism*, 6 vols (London, 2001); and *Representing India: Indian culture and imperial control in eighteenth-century British orientalist discourse*, 9 vols (London and New York, 2000). Franklin is also the author of various important articles, including 'Accessing India: orientalism, anti-

That there is now growing acceptance of the importance of orientalists such as Jones to British Romanticism can be seen in Jerome McGann's inclusion of three of his Hymns in the *New Oxford book of Romantic period verse* (1993), and the recent reappearance of Jones's work in the *Norton anthology of English literature*, published 2005. The latest Broadview anthology for *The Age of Romanticism* (2010) even includes an entire section entitled 'Contexts: India and the Orient'.[6]

As long ago as 1941, H. G. Rawlinson made some general but contradictory claims about the influence of Eastern literature on English literature. Whilst pointing out that the highly influential Arabian Nights 'contain a vast number of tales derived from Hindu, Greek, and Persian sources', he nevertheless concluded that English writers seem to have known nothing about the Hindu philosophy which was to stir Germany so powerfully. Yet, Rawlinson adds, 'Shelley, Wordsworth, and Carlyle are full of unconscious traces of the *Vedanta*, which reached them indirectly through German or Platonic sources'. In illustration of this he remarks that Wordsworth's 'Ode: intimations of immortality' expresses a belief in the soul's pre-existence while the following passage from 'Lines written a few miles above Tintern Abbey' embodies the doctrine of the 'World soul':

> Something far more deeply interfused
> Whose dwelling is the light of setting suns,
> And the round Ocean and the living air,
> And the blue sky and in the mind of man:
> A motion and a spirit, that impels
> All thinking things, all objects of all thought,
> And rolls through all things.[7]

Of these pantheistic lines Rawlinson adds that they are reminiscent of the Jain belief 'that not only men and animals, but also plants, minerals capable of growth, air, wind and fire possess souls (jiva) endowed with varying degrees of consciousness'.[8] Importantly for this chapter, which aims to connect John Keats with India, this is the same Wordsworth poem that inspired the young poet to formulate his 'simile of human life', namely the 'Chamber of Maiden Thought', an intoxicating place of light and pleasure at first, but whose passages gradually darken as we

"Indianism" and the rhetoric of Jones and Burke' in *Romanticism and colonialism: writing and empire, 1780-1830*, ed. Tim Fulford and Peter Kitson (Cambridge, 1998), p.48-66.

6. See Joseph Black (ed.), *The Broadview anthology of British literature, vol.4: the age of Romanticism*, 2nd edn (Peterborough, Ontario, 2010).
7. William Wordsworth, 'Lines written a few miles above Tintern Abbey', *Lyrical ballads, with a few other poems* (London, J. Arch, 1798), l.97-103.
8. H. G. Rawlinson, 'Indian influence on the West' in *Modern India and the West: a study of the interaction of their civilizations*, ed. L. S. S. O'Malley (London, 1941), p.536, 549.

mature. In Keats's view it was Wordsworth's particular genius to explore these 'dark passages'. Furthermore, his ability to 'think into the human heart' put him ahead of Milton, a sign (for Keats) of mankind's continuing intellectual progress over time.[9]

Although much research has been performed since Rawlinson's essay, the perception remains that in Britain there were relatively few scholarly sources of information about India and Indian thought systems available in the late eighteenth and early part of the nineteenth century. This is certainly true of Buddhism, the tenets of which had, according to one reviewer in 1807, 'never been satisfactorily explained' and whose relationship with Hinduism was something of a mystery.[10] As this comment suggests, however, quite a lot more was known about Hindu religion, literature and culture. Indeed, certain members of the Bengal Asiatic Society in Calcutta had, over the previous few decades, been revealing a rich array of Hindu legal, philosophical and literary texts. In 1785 Charles Wilkins's translation of *The Bhagvat-Geeta, or Dialogues of Kreeshna and Arjoon* appeared, from the ancient Hindu poem the *Mahabaratha* – the first published translation into a European language of part of a major Sanskrit work. Three years later, in 1788, many more translations, as well as essays, began to appear in the series *Asiatick researches*, all of which were extensively summarised and reviewed in the British periodicals. Indeed, the first number of the *Edinburgh review* (October 1802) carried a positive review by the Sanskritist Alexander Hamilton of the sixth volume of *Asiatick researches*. Earlier volumes of the *Researches* had also been summarised and critiqued by him in the *Monthly review* and elsewhere.[11] Some of the scholarly work under scrutiny at this time may have been somewhat fanciful – that the Hindu religion had its origin in the British isles, for instance – and some of it, as I shall show, was deeply unsettling to orthodox Christians, but most of the research was solid and credible, and well disseminated by the end of the first decade of the nineteenth century.

From the 1780s onwards, the orientalists began to make large claims for the Sanskrit language and for all aspects of Eastern thought and

9. Letter to John Hamilton Reynolds (3 May 1818), *The Letters of John Keats 1814-1821*, ed. Hyder Edward Rollins, 2 vols (Cambridge, 1958), vol.1, p.280-81.
10. '[W]e are still ignorant whether the doctrines of Buddha, universally admitted to be a native of India, bear any, and what, affinity, with the religion of Brahma. By some they are considered totally different, and of higher antiquity; whilst the Brahmans themselves class Buddha amongst their Avatara, of whom they consider him as their last'; H. T. Colebrooke, 'On the Sanskrit and Pracrit languages', *Edinburgh review* 9 (January 1807), p.287.
11. For an overview of his earlier writings, see Rosane Rocher, 'New data for the biography of the Orientalist Alexander Hamilton', *Journal of the American Oriental Society* 90.3 (1970), p.426-48.

culture. For instance, Jones was in no doubt as to the superiority of
Sanskrit to Greek and Latin, writing that it was 'more perfect than the
Greek, more copious than the *Latin*, and more exquisitely refined than
either'.[12] Such was the 'wonderful structure' and beauty of this ancient
language that he and others believed that the influence of their translations would penetrate as deeply as did the revival of Greek literature in
the fifteenth century, heralding a revivification of English poetry
through a wholly 'new set of images and similitudes', symbols and
mystical allegories.[13] The classical world's jaded Pantheon would be
refreshed by a splendid new array of mythological stories – a strange
and colourful new Indian Pantheon of gods and goddesses such as
Brahma, Vishnu, Lakshmi and hundreds more.

Jones also believed that a study of the Eastern languages would bring 'a
more extensive insight into the history of the human mind'.[14] In his
'Hymn to Surya', composed a year after the publication of Wilkins's
translation, the association of the 'celestial tongue' of Sanskrit with
labyrinthine caves and with mystery and obscurity, is captured in the
lines where the Vedic Sun-god describes him liberating Sanskrit from the
abysm of the past: 'He came; and, lisping our celestial tongue, / Though
not from *Brahma* sprung, / Draws orient knowledge from its fountains
pure, / Through caves obstructed long, and paths too long obscure'.[15]
That the association of Sanskrit with mystery and psychological complexity was a continuing theme in British commentary can be seen in a
reference in the *Quarterly review* of 1809 to 'the dark caverns of Sanscrit
literature'.[16] Ideas of darkness and difficulty were inevitable given the
much-vaunted 'high antiquity' of the Sanskrit language, with experts
claiming that Sanskrit was derived 'from a primeval tongue, which was
gradually refined in various climates, and became Sanskrit in India,
Pahlavi in Persia, and Greek on the shores of the Mediterranean'.[17] The
revolutionary implications of such 'high antiquity' for the Christian faith
gave birth to religious syncretism and comparative mythology – Jones's
'similitudes'. In his ground-breaking essay 'On the gods of Greece, Italy,

---

12. 'The third anniversary discourse, on the Hindus, delivered to the Asiatic Society, 2
    February, 1786', *Sir William Jones: selected poetical and prose works*, ed. Michael Franklin
    (Cardiff, 1995), p.355-67 (361).

13. 'An essay on the poetry of the eastern nations' (1772), Franklin (ed.), *Sir William Jones*,
    p.319-36 (336).

14. 'The poetry of the eastern nations', Franklin (ed.), *Sir William Jones*, p.336.

15. Franklin (ed.), *Sir William Jones*, p.143-52 (l.184-87).

16. Sharon Turner, with John Shore, Lord Teignmouth, 'Grammars of the Sanscrita
    language', *Quarterly review* 1 (February 1809), p.54. For the attribution, see Jonathan
    Cutmore (ed.), *Quarterly Review* Archive (http://www.rc.umd.edu/reference/qr/index/
    01.html).

17. Colebrooke, 'On the Sanskrit and Pracrit languages', p.290.

and India' (1785), Jones stopped short of a 'systematical spirit' which would insist that 'such a God of *India* was *the* Jupiter of *Greece*; such, *the* Apollo; such, *the* Mercury',[18] but enthusiastic followers of his imaginative syncretism frequently drew direct parallels between the different gods, such as the jealous Radha 'who perfectly represents the Grecian Juno in her caprices, her jealousy, and her fury'.[19] By 1810, the year in which Dean Mahomed opened the Hindoostanee Coffee-House in London, and Edward Moor published his large and lavishly-illustrated book, *The Hindu pantheon*, it was confidently asserted that the 'mythological legends of the Hindus' were the source of 'the fables and deities of *Greece* and *Italy*, and other heathen people of the West'.[20] From here it was a short and easy step to Keats's assertion in 1819: 'It is pretty generally suspected that the Christian scheme has been copied from the ancient Persian and Greek Philosophers.'[21]

Over time, the novelty of oriental scholarship and the Sanskrit translations faded, and a conservative backlash was evident in some quarters, as can be seen in Robert Southey's anti-Hindu epic, *The Curse of Kehama* (1810), followed by James Mill's 'monument of Indophobia', his *History of British India* (1817).[22] This stunting of the British public's engagement with India went hand in hand with the need to justify the expanding empire by dismissing overly optimistic accounts of Indian civilisation, emphasising instead the country's backwardness. Furthermore, in anticipation of the evangelisation of India after 1813, an attack was mounted on the heterodox implications of the Hindu chronology. The first-ever number of the conservative *Quarterly review* led the charge. Looking back from the perspective of 1809, the reviewers Sharon Turner and John Shore, Lord Teignmouth, not only downgraded the claims made for Indian literature, geography, astronomy and religion, they also complained about the 'sudden assault' made upon everybody's 'chronological repose' by 'the phantoms of Hindostan'. The 'monstrous reveries' of far-distant times dreamed up by the 'oriental literati' had threatened 'the simple and probable chronology of the Hebrews', based as it was on 'all the authentic remains of ancient history'. It was time, the reviewers

18. Franklin (ed.), *Sir William Jones*, p.349 (349-54).
19. Colebrooke, 'On the Sanskrit and Pracrit languages', p.287 and 297.
20. Edward Moor, *The Hindu pantheon* (London, J. Johnson, 1810), p.xi. In 1808, in a review of J. D. Paterson's 'Of the origins of the Hindu religion' (*Asiatic researches* 8, 1808, p.50-51), Alexander Hamilton referred to the 'often and justly remarked [...] great analogy between the ancient languages of India and of Greece', the evidence for which was most plainly seen in the 'Puranas of the votaries of Vishnu'; 'Asiatic researches', *Edinburgh review* 15 (April 1808), p.39.
21. Letter to the George Keatses (14 Feb-3 May 1819), *Letters*, vol.2, p.103.
22. P. J. Marshall, 'British-Indian connections *c*.1780 to *c*.1830: the empire of the officials', *Romantic representations of British India*, p.45-64 (56).

urged, to 'break the spell of credulity' and 'hail the dawn of reason' by rejecting the many 'abundantly extravagant' descriptions of absurd rituals and obscene legends.[23]

John Keats, Bacchus and the East

In terms of 'obscene legends' and William Jones's 'similitudes', the wine-god Bacchus was a pivotal figure, spanning the worlds of Greek and Indian mythology. According to myth, Bacchus spent many years travelling in the East, and from ancient times onwards was often depicted in the moment of his triumphal return from India, laden with the spoils of conquest. Keats probably read about Bacchus as the first conqueror of India at school, under the letter 'I' in Lemprière's *Classical dictionary*. As we know from his school mentor, Charles Cowden Clarke, this dictionary was one of his three favourite books:

> India, the most celebrated and opulent of all the countries of Asia, bounded on one side by the Indus, from which it derives its name [...] It has always been reckoned famous for the riches it contains; and so persuaded were the ancients of its wealth, that they supposed its very sands were gold. It contained 9000 different nations, and 5000 remarkable cities, according to geographers. Bacchus was the first who conquered it.[24]

There was also, according to learned opinion, a 'similitude' between Bacchus and the Hindu divinity Iswara (or Baghesa). Alexander Hamilton, in his review of J. D. Paterson's 'On the origins of the Hindu religion' (1808), argued that the two gods shared the same phallic cult: 'the same obscenities, the same bloody rites, and the same emblem of the generative power'.[25] Iswara's chief emblem was 'the phallus', and his rites consisted in its worship: with the phallus 'wrapped in a tiger's skin, and mounted on a sacred bull . . . [Iswara] is followed by a mixed crowd of males and female votaries, whose wild dances and frantic revels accompany his steps, or announce his presence'.[26] Ian Jack has rightly argued for the importance to Keats of the sacrificial or religious procession, both of which come together in the Indian maid's description of Bacchus's triumphant return from the East in her roundelay in Book IV of *Endymion: a poetic romance* (1818):

> And as I sat, over the light blue hills
> There came a noise of revellers: the rills

23. Turner *et al.*, 'Grammars of the Sanscrita language', p.65-66.
24. John Lemprière, *Bibliotheca classica; or, A Classical dictionary* (London, T. Cadell, 1792), n.p.; for Clarke's recollections, see Charles and Mary Cowden Clarke, *Recollections of writers* (London, 1878), p.123-24.
25. See Paterson, 'On the origins of the Hindu religion'.
26. Alexander Hamilton, review of J. D. Paterson, *Edinburgh review* 15 (April 1808), p.38.

Into the wide stream came of purple hue –
'Twas Bacchus and his crew!
The earnest trumpet spake, and silver thrills
From kissing cymbals made a merry din –
'Twas Bacchus and his kin!
Like to a moving vintage down they came
Crown'd with green leaves, and faces all on flame:
All madly dancing through the pleasant valley,
To scare thee, Melancholy![27]

We know from Joseph Severn that Keats was much struck by Titian's *Bacchus and Ariadne* (1520-1523) when he saw it in London in 1817 (Fig.1, p.86), just as he was beginning to compose *Endymion*. That Keats was aware of the learned discourse around Indian and Greek 'similitudes' can be seen in a passage where one of Bacchus's followers describes the homage paid to the young wine-god by all other gods, including a somewhat begrudging, father-like Brahma: 'Great Brahma from his mystic heaven groans, / And all his priesthood moans; / Before young Bacchus' eye-wink turning pale.'[28]

From the 'mad' and 'wild minstrelsy' of *Endymion* would arise the Bacchic frenzy and abandon of 'Ode on a Grecian urn': 'What men or gods are these? What maidens loth? / What mad pursuit? What struggle to escape? / What pipes and timbrels? What wild ecstasy?'[29] Bacchus's mythic journey through the East is revisited yet again in 'Ode to a nightingale': 'Away! away! for I will fly to thee, / Not charioted by Bacchus and his pards, / But on the viewless wings of Poesy.'[30] The importance of Bacchus at this time for Keats and his circle can be seen in William Hazlitt's *Lectures on the English poets* (1818), where the somewhat paltry Bacchus of John Dryden's 'Ode in honour of St Cecilia's Day' is roundly berated. Hazlitt's own vision of Bacchus was, like Keats's, a majestic one, of the wine-god 'returning from the conquest of India, with satyrs and wild beasts, that he had tamed, following in his train; crowned with vine leaves, and riding in a chariot drawn by leopards – such as we have seen him painted by Titian or Rubens'.[31]

The enthusiasm of Keats's circle for ancient, especially Greek, myth-ology went hand in hand with a renewed interest in the writings of an earlier generation of 'infidel anthropologists' such as Sir William Hamilton, Richard Payne Knight and Erasmus Darwin. As Marilyn Butler

27. *The Poems of John Keats*, ed. Jack Stillinger (Cambridge, MA, 1978), p.198. See Joseph Severn, *Letters and memoirs*, ed. Grant F. Scott (Aldershot, 2005), p.662-63, 62. For Keats and Bacchus, see Ian Jack's excellent *Keats and the mirror of art* (Oxford, 1967).
28. Stillinger, *Poems of John Keats*, p.200.
29. Stillinger, *Poems of John Keats*, p.372.
30. Keats, 'Ode to a nightingale', Stillinger, *Poems of John Keats*, p.369-72 (l.31-33).
31. William Hazlitt, *Complete works*, ed. P. P. Howe, 21 vols (London, 1930-1934), vol.5, p.81.

Figure 1: Titian, *Bacchus and Ariadne* © The National Gallery, London.

has shown, these Enlightenment thinkers provided a counter-politics for the second-generation Romantics amidst the conservative gloom of the long years of war, drawing them towards a 'free and humanistic paganism', a cheerful creed which included republicanism, guilt-free sexuality, a jovial interest in priapus and phallus worship and the pursuit of ideal love, or nympholepsy.[32] There are many ideal nymphs in Keats, including the Indian maid of *Endymion* who, in a neat piece of East-West syncretism, turns out to be one and the same as the moon-goddess Cynthia. In terms of the Indian maid's avatars, there were several striking examples for Keats to follow, such as Robert Southey's heroine, Kailyal, from *The Curse of Kehama* (1810), a poem Keats certainly knew for he alludes to it in *Isabella, or The Pot of basil* (1818) where Isabella's vision of the dead Lorenzo is described as 'like a lance, / Waking an Indian from his cloudy hall/With cruel pierce, and bringing him again / Sense of the gnawing fire at heart and brain'.[33] There was also the Indian priestess Luxima from Sydney Owenson's novel, *The Missionary* (1811), a work steeped in Jones's orientalism and syncretism. As is well known, P. B. Shelley was obsessed with this 'divine' Indian tale, urging all his friends to read it and modelling his own 'veiled maid' in *Alastor* (1816) on Owenson's priestess. 1816 is also the year in which Keats first met Shelley so it is very likely that he read *The Missionary* and that this fed into the poetical, mystical, and sensual shape of his conceptual voyaging in *Endymion*.[34]

The centrality and prominence of classical allusions in Keats's work – his reputation for 'the power of putting a spirit of life and novelty into the Heathen Mythology'[35] – are undeniable, and yet it is notable that he sometimes signalled a readiness for other, new sensations, for a new and different cosmology beyond a pagan 'creed outworn'. His preface to *Endymion* signals the prospect of change: 'I hope I have not in too late a day touched the beautiful mythology of Greece, and dulled its brightness: for I wish to try once more, before I bid it farewell.'[36] Further evidence will be outlined below to support my argument that he was fascinated by Hinduism's challenge to the originality and antiquity of Europe's Greco-Roman inheritance. That contemporaries saw his work as coloured by the East can be seen in the distinctly orientalist discourse which greeted

32. Marilyn Butler, *Peacock displayed: a satirist in his context* (London, 1979), p.109.
33. Stillinger, *Poems of John Keats*, p.255. Kehama's curse on Ladurad contains the lines: 'Thou shalt live in thy pain, / While Kehama shall reign / With a fire in thy heart / And a fire in thy brain,' Robert Southey, *The Curse of Kehama* (London, Longman, Hurst, Rees, Orme and Brown, 1810), p.19.
34. For Shelley's championing of *The Missionary* and Jones's influence on Owenson, see Michael J. Franklin, 'Passion's empire: Sydney Owenson's Indian venture: Phoenicianism, orientalism, and binarism', *Studies in Romanticism* 45.2 (2006), p.181-97.
35. Unsigned, '*The Quarterly review* – Mr Keats', *The Examiner* (11 October 1818), p.649.
36. John Keats, 'Preface', *Endymion: a poetic romance* in Stillinger, *Poems of John Keats*, p.103.

his poetry, frequently described as excessive, unmanly, luxurious and degenerate.[37] In 1826, for instance, *Blackwood's Edinburgh magazine* accused his work of outhunting Leigh Hunt 'in a species of emasculated pruriency, that [...] looks as if it were the product of some imaginative Eunuch's muse within the melancholy inspiration of the Haram'.[38]

Formative influences

Compared to Shelley and Byron, Keats struck Marilyn Butler as 'not normally much of an orientalist',[39] and the poet barely figures in Drew's *India and the Romantic imagination*. Successive editors of his letters have also ignored possible allusions to Indian religion and literature, arguing incorrectly that nothing was known about such matters in the early nineteenth century.[40] Indeed, of all the Romantic poets, it is argued that Keats's orientalism is 'primarily a question of style, an imperial heraldry uncomplicated by the anxiety of empire'.[41] Thus the generally received view of Keats's literary and intellectual development is that the only writers who mattered to him were English ones, principally Shakespeare, Spenser, Chatterton and Milton, an impression reinforced by the brief list of books left behind after his death,[42] in which there are no titles associated with Indian or other Eastern literature.

For those keen to refute Keats's reputation as an apolitical or even anti-political dreamer – more comfortable in faery land than in Regency England – it is important to go on delving into the material and historical contexts for his life and work.[43] The task of tracing the resonances and affinities of Indian philosophy in his writings is, however, an elusive one. Stuart Sperry faced similar difficulties when he set out to chart Keats's intellectual affinities with Voltaire, for the young poet seems to have held 'no fixed philosophical position'.[44] But while there may not have been any single major philosophical influence, there were plenty of ideas in

---

37. See Makdisi, 'Literature, national identity, and empire', p.76.
38. *Blackwood's Edinburgh magazine* 19 (January-June 1826), p.xxvi.
39. Butler, 'Orientalism', p.438. In a recent study of eastern religion in Romantic writing, Keats only appears in very general terms; see Mark S. Lussier's *Romantic dharma: the emergence of Buddhism into nineteenth-century Europe* (New York, 2011).
40. See note 67 below.
41. Leask, *British Romantic writers and the East*, p.125; see also Tim Fulford, 'Romanticism and colonialism: races, places, peoples, 1800-1830' in Fulford and Kitson (ed.), *Romanticism and colonialism*, p.35-47 (45).
42. 'List of Keats's books', in Hyder Edward Rollins (ed.), *The Keats circle: letters and papers* and *More letters and poems of the Keats circle*, 2 vols (Cambridge, MA, 1965), vol.1, p.253-60.
43. Twenty-five years after its special issue in 1986 on 'Keats and politics', the journal *Studies in Romanticism* has re-visited this issue; see its special issue 'Reading Keats, thinking politics' ed. Emily Rohrbach and Emily Sun, *Studies in Romanticism* 50.2 (2011).
44. Stuart M. Sperry, 'Keats's skepticism and Voltaire', *Keats-Shelley journal* 12 (1963), p.75-93.

the air, and a poetical temperament open to speculations and impressions from a number of sources. Furthermore, Keats's ideas about the progress of mankind – what he termed 'the general and gregarious advance of intellect' – incorporated wide views of world history and global linkages.[45] As the biographer of eminent orientalist H. T. Colebrooke put it: 'The acknowledged antiquity of the civilisation of the Hindus, their ancient literature, and the mystery attached to writings locked up in a dead language, excited the imagination of all who took an interest in the history of human progress.'[46] Developed amongst and reinforcing Keats's many assertions of the advance of human intellect lie his key aesthetic concepts – the 'vale of Soul-making', 'negative capability' and its closely related paradox of 'diligent indolence' – all of which were, I shall argue, touched by his understanding of Indian thought, an understanding which developed from his schooldays onwards.

Lemprière, for instance, ranged much more widely than just the Western tradition, including (as we have seen) an entry on India, together with entries on the Ganges and the 'Indian philosophers' known as Brachmanes. This last entry is quite long, describing the derivation of the name 'Brachmanes' from Brahma, 'one of the three beings whom God, according to their theology, created, and with whose assistance he formed the world'. Lemprière continues: 'According to modern authors, Brahma is the parent of all mankind, and he produced as many worlds as there are parts in the body, which they reckoned fourteen. They believed that there were seven seas, of water, milk, curds, butter, salt, sugar, and wine, each blessed with its particular paradise.'[47] Keats was also given as a school prize C. H. Kauffman's *Dictionary of merchandize* (1803), a book brimful of descriptions of exotic commodities, many with medicinal properties.[48] Of the various spices and food-stuffs associated with India and Ceylon, there were entries on cardamon, cloves, coconut, Colombo root, frankincense, gamboge, ginger and turmeric, all of which described in rich detail the tastes, smells and uses of these products. In Kauffman the young Keats would also have read about the manufacture of seductive narcotics such as opium, and the dangers of deep-sea pearl-fishing off the coast of Ceylon.

Of his other reading, Clarke tells us that Keats 'exhausted the school

---

45. Letter to the George Keatses (14 Feb-3 May 1819), *Letters*, vol.2, p.102. Letter to J. H. Reynolds (3 May 1818), *Letters*, vol.1, p.281.
46. T. E. Colebrooke, quoted in Marshall, 'British-Indian connections *c*.1780 to *c*.1830: the empire of the officials', p.47.
47. Lemprière, *Bibliotheca classica*, n.p.
48. [C. H. Kauffman], *The Dictionary of merchandize, and nomenclature in all languages: for the use of counting-houses: containing, the history, places of growth, culture, use, and marks of excellency, of such natural productions, as form articles of commerce, by a merchant* (London, 1803). I thank Nicholas Roe for bringing this book to my attention.

library, which consisted principally of abridgments of all the voyages and travels of any note; Mavor's collection, also his "Universal History".[49] William Fordyce Mavor was a compiler of educational books, principally marketed for schools, 'written with an eye to youthful innocence and female delicacy'.[50] In these pocket-size multi-volume sets, Keats would have discovered in volumes 11 and 12 of the *Universal history* histories of Hindostan; of the Mogul Empire; parts of Tartary; and of China, as well as an up-to-date history of India. In this last section there was a digest of most of what was popularly known about Calcutta and the Asiatic Society, the latter described as 'a noble monument of science in a distant country' instituted by 'the late admirable Sir William Jones'.[51] Mavor also provided an abstract of the 'genuine principles of the Hindoo religion' which inculcates 'the most sublime notions – though its rites are debased with idolatry and superstition':

> These principles teach, that the universe is governed by one supreme and intelligent Ruler, whose divine essence pervades the whole circle of nature, gives motion to the luminaries of the sky, and vivifies the animal creation; that the soul, after death, re-ascends to the immortal spirit of God, and that the body returns to dust; that he who distinguishes himself in this world by pious and charitable actions, shall attain immortality; but that he who destroys the purity of his own soul, shall dwell, for a certain time, with evil spirits in the regions which utter darkness involves, and that, after he has received the punishment due to his crimes, his spirit shall be sent back to this world, to inhabit the bodies of beasts [...]. In the Vedas, one God only is acknowledged, who is called Brahma, or the Great One. He is declared to be a being without shape, whose essence is incomprehensible, and who must therefore be worshipped through symbolical representations of his divine attributes. The triple divinity of Vishnu, Brahma, and Shiva, which are expressed by the mystical word OM, are said to be emblems of the creative, preservative, and destructive powers of the Almighty.[52]

Furthermore, in Mavor's extensive 25-volume set of the *Most celebrated voyages*, there was John Holwell's account of the infamous 'Black-Hole of Calcutta' (vol.20), and George Forster's 'Travels in the northern part of India, Kashmire, Afghanistan, and Persia, and into Russia by the Caspian Sea, performed in the years 1782, 83, and 84' (vol.24). Finally, as John Whale reminds us in his essay on William Hazlitt's 'The Indian jugglers',

49. Clarke, *Recollections of writers*, p.123.
50. William Mavor, 'Prefatory remarks', *Historical account of the most celebrated voyages, travels, and discoveries, from the time of Columbus to the present period*, 25 vols (London, Richard Phillips, 1796-1797; 1801), vol.1, n.p.
51. William Mavor, *Universal history, ancient and modern; comprehending a general view of the transactions of every nation, kingdom, and empire in the world, from the earliest records of time*, 25 vols (London, 1802-1805), vol.11, p.280.
52. Mavor, *Universal history*, vol.11, p.289-90.

the London in which Keats grew up in the early nineteenth century enjoyed frequent visits by troupes of Indian fakirs, snake-charmers, sword-swallowers and jugglers.[53]

The vale of Soul-making

That Keats saw life as a mystic drama can be seen in his famous journal letter of February-May, 1819. Here, in pursuit of a religion which would not affront his 'reason and humanity', Keats repudiates the gloomy and 'straightened' Christian teaching of life as a 'vale of tears'. The creed he groped towards in his letters during this time was the 'vale of Soul-making', a conception which invoked as part of its definition other world religions, including the 'Hindoos' and 'their Vishnu':

> Seriously I think it probable that this System of Soul-making – may have been the Parent of all the more palpable and personal Schemes of Redemption, among the Zoroastrians the Christians and the Hindoos. For as one part of the human species must have their carved Jupiter; so another part must have the palpable and named Mediator and saviour, their Christ their Oromanes and their Vishnu.[54]

The 'carved Jupiter' takes us straight to Keats's earliest lesson in syncretism and comparative religion, provided by one of his favourite school books, Andrew Tooke's *The Pantheon* (1798).[55] In the book's opening entry on Jupiter, '*the father and king of Gods and men*', we read that 'there is not one *Jupiter*, but many, who are sprung from different families [...] *Varro* reckoned up three hundred *Jupiters*; and others reckon almost an innumerable company of them; for, there was hardly any nation which did not worship a *Jupiter* of their own, and suppose him to be born among themselves'.[56] The other instructor in comparative religion was of course the sceptic Voltaire. On the list of Keats's books drawn up after his death we find Voltaire's *Dictionnaire philosophique* (Paris, 1816), *Siècle de Louis XIV*, and *Essai sur les mœurs* (Paris, 1804-1805). It is likely that Keats first read Voltaire at school under the guidance of Clarke, who was a Voltaire enthusiast. As is well known, Voltaire was an admirer of India as an ancient civilisation to which the Greeks had travelled for instruction, quipping that his contemporaries in Europe only travelled there to enrich themselves and to kill each other

---

53. See John Whale, 'Indian jugglers: Hazlitt, Romantic orientalism and the difference of view', *Romanticism and colonialism*, p.206-20 (208).
54. Letter to the George Keatses (14 Feb-3 May 1819), *Letters*, vol.2, p.101-103.
55. Clarke, *Recollections of writers*, p.123-24.
56. Andrew Tooke, *The Pantheon, representing the fabulous histories of the heathen gods, and most illustrious heroes; in a short, plain, and familiar method, by way of dialogue*, 13th edn (London, B. Law *et al.*, 1798), p.10, 12.

in the process. Hinduism, along with other world religions, was central to Voltaire's comparative mythology and anti-Christian polemic. Unlike Coleridge whose Christian apologetics led to a rejection of the Hindu chronology and Voltaire's 'levities', Keats was a self-professed deist who, 'straining at particles of light in the midst of a great darkness', was searching for an alternative, more cheerful belief system.[57] In rejecting certain Christian doctrines as inhuman and repellent, Keats resembled his friends William Hazlitt and the radical journalist Leigh Hunt. Like William Jones he might have argued: 'I am no Hindu, but I hold the doctrine of the Hindus concerning a future state to be incomparably more rational, pious, and more likely to deter men from vice, than the horrid opinions inculcated by Christians on punishments *without end*.'[58]

Leigh Hunt's *Examiner* and the British Empire in India

On the liberal side of politics, attuned to matters of empire, and keen to do some good in the world, Keats sometimes felt trapped between his muse and a more active engagement in political life.[59] For instance, at the same time that he was developing his creed of the 'vale of Soul-making', he was seriously considering a career as an Indiaman's surgeon, voyaging 'to and from India for a few years'.[60] The idea was hardly a top priority, described instead as one of 'two Poisons', the other being 'a fevrous life alone with Poetry'.[61] But why did India present itself as the setting for a more active role and, more particularly, as an alternative to the poetical life? There are several possible answers to these questions, one of which might be Leigh Hunt's editorial interweaving of notices of Keats's poetry with his ongoing coverage of Britain's crimes in India.

The subject of British rule in India had begun to take a higher profile in the public press with the passing of an amendment to the India Act in 1813, giving Christian missionaries the green light to pursue their proselytising agenda. Leigh Hunt's *The Examiner*, assiduously read by Keats, began to cover the East quite intensively from 1815, the year in which Ceylon was ceded to Britain, but Hunt had long been a diligent

---

57. Letter to the George Keatses (14 February-3 May 1819), *Letters*, vol.2, p.80.
58. Quoted in Franklin, '*Orientalist Jones*', p.253.
59. Keats's determination to take an active role in political life can be seen intermittently throughout his letters; see *Letters*, vol.1, p.267, 293, 386-87. For his awareness of empire, see his comments on Richard Carlisle's trial, *Letters*, vol.2, p.194.
60. See Keats's letter to Sarah Jeffrey (31 May 1819), *Letters*, vol.2, p.113. See also a month later to Dilke: 'my mind [h]as been at work all over the world to find out what to do [...] South America or Surgeon to an I[n]diaman – which last I think will be my fate', *Letters*, vol.2, p.114. These letters inspired William Logan to write his prize-winning poem, 'Keats in India' (1991), a blank-verse monologue which imagines a posthumous life for Keats in India in 1848; see Logan, *Vain empires* (New York, 1998).
61. *Letters*, vol.2, p.113.

observer and critic of British crimes in India, in particular the East India Company's systematic warfare in Bengal. In 1808 Hunt declared that he would look on the 'loss of India without a sigh'. The tyranny exerted by Britain over the Indians – 'grinding Nabobs into gold-dust', burning their cities and oppressing their wives and children – had ensured the natives' hatred, and all to 'enrich a few lazy individuals, who return to this country, with yellow death in their countenances [...]. The sun of India sucks up our seas to return us nothing but a few turbid and unprofitable showers'.[62]

As an opponent of dogmatism of all kinds, Hunt ran a regular feature in *The Examiner* on 'Superstition – its civil and political consequences'. Keen to promote his own cheery view of a benevolent God, and horrified (like Jones and Keats) by the Christian notion of eternal punishment, he was vehemently opposed to the evangelisation which had been unleashed on India. Happily, few converts had been found, a situation which would remain (he joked) as long as the British missionary kept on threatening the Hindoos that, if they 'do not come over to his humaner opinions, they will be tortured to all eternity!'.[63] That God 'is pleased with a diversity of religions' is an opinion for which Hindus had much better grounds than 'believing in such a thing as eternal punishment'. Hunt's positive feelings towards the Hindus only magnified Britain's offences against them. In *The Examiner* he wrote that they 'are by nature one of the gentlest and kindest people on the face of the earth, and literally would not hurt a worm; for they believe in the metempsychosis. They think it barbarous even to eat meat.'[64]

Fearless in putting forward his own radical views, Hunt was particularly concerned at the secrecy which surrounded Britain's mission in India. In the lead article of *The Examiner* for 20 September, 1818 he declared that the Anglo-Indian press was 'in the lowest state of slavery', muzzled under the direct control of government. The upshot of this was that

> the people in England seldom even think of India. [...] India only presents itself occasionally to their minds, as a great distant place with strange beasts and trees in it, where Brahmins meditate and Musselmen keep seraglios, – where white people in regimentals are always fighting for some cause or other with the dark natives in vests and turbans, – and from which sallow elderly gentlemen are every now and then coming away to enjoy the large fortunes which they have acquired, – which they cannot do for the bile.

62. 'Necessity of peace to our Indian possessions' (27 March 1808), *The Selected writings of Leigh Hunt*, ed. Greg Kucich and Jeffrey N. Cox, 6 vols (London, 2003), vol.1, p.46-48.
63. Leigh Hunt, *The Examiner* (18 October 1818), p.657.
64. Leigh Hunt, 'Superstition – its civil and political consequences', *The Examiner* (18 October 1818), p.657.

It was part of Hunt's soul-searching on British imperialism to raise the topic of India (and Ceylon) in his newspaper. He also took a wide, European perspective on Britain's imperial activities. For instance, in his leader of 20 September 1818, Hunt argued that complaints about Bonaparte's behaviour were completely hypocritical when 'we have been encroaching, and conquering, and usurping in India', and 'with less excuse' than Bonaparte in Europe. To such hypocrisy, illogicality must be added: 'Either our encroaching and conquering system in India, under the plea of bettering the natives, is a bad and unjustifiable one [...] or the same proceedings on the part of Bonaparte with regard to Spain and some other countries, where the Inquisition and slavery were to be rooted out, is good and justifiable.'[65] This leader is then followed directly by what would become a series of letters entitled 'Indian atrocities' addressed to the Editor by ex-Lieutenant George Strachan who, as a young cadet aged eighteen in 1800, was involved in the Cotiote war which ended with the 'entire extirpation of both the prince and the people known as Nairs, on the coast of Malabar'.[66] The warlike Nairs perished in the cause of their oppressed sovereign, and Strachan spares no details in describing the massacres of Nairs carried out by the British forces.

A week later, in the issue of 27 September, 1818, Hunt published on his front page a second instalment of 'Indian atrocities.' Strachan's second letter led off with a quotation from Shakespeare – 'I, from the Orient to the drooping West, making the winds my post horse, thus do ride. I speak of sudden deaths, of treasons, murders, plots, conspiracies'.[67] The regular mixing of politics and poetry was standard fare for *The Examiner*. Keats himself had been introduced under the heading 'Young poets' a few years earlier, and since that time notices and reviews of his work had appeared intermittently. What is remarkable about this particular issue, with its front-page feature, 'Indian atrocities', is that Hunt appends to his left-hand column the following sarcastic note: 'We congratulate, most *sincerely*, our young friend JOHN KEATS on the involuntary homage that, we understand, has been paid to his undoubted genius, in an article full of grovelling abuse' (Fig.2, p.96).[68] Hunt is referring, of course, to the notorious attack on his friend in the 'half-witted, half-hearted' *Quarterly review*.[69] The juxtaposition, bottom left, of the note about Keats, with the

65. Leigh Hunt, 'India', *The Examiner* (20 September 1818), p.593-94 (594).

66. For Strachan's later appeal against his court-martial, see 'Case of ex-Lieutenant G. Strachan', *The Asiatic journal and monthly register for British India and its dependencies* 21 (Jan-June, 1826), p.126-29.

67. G. Strachan, 'Indian atrocities', *The Examiner* (27 September 1818), p.609.

68. Leigh Hunt, 'Article and no article', *The Examiner* (27 September 1818), p.609.

69. For Hunt's attack on the *Quarterly* and defence of Keats's poetry, see Leigh Hunt, 'Literary notices', *The Examiner* (11 October 1818), p.648-49.

Shakespearean epigraph to 'Indian atrocities', top right, forms a striking visual emblem of the tug-of-war in Keats's letters between poetry and an active life.

Diligent indolence, or the 'drooping' East

In an essay entitled 'On the poetry of the eastern nations', which accompanied his first published collection of poems in 1772, William Jones drew a connection between indolence, Eastern warmth and Apollonian levels of poetic creativity:

> Now it is certain that the genius of every nation is not a little affected by their climate; for, whether it be that the immoderate heat disposes the *Eastern* people to a life of indolence, which gives them full leisure to cultivate their talents, or whether the sun has a real influence on the imagination, (as one would suppose that the ancients believed, by their making *Apollo* the god of poetry;) whatever be the cause, it has always been remarked, that the *Asiaticks* excel the inhabitants of our colder regions in the liveliness of their fancy, and the richness of their invention.[70]

It is possible that Jones is deliberately countering here the negative interpretation given to Eastern indolence by Luke Scrafton in his *Reflections on the government of Indostan*, first published in 1763 and reprinted in 1770. Scrafton denigrates the Hindus as a people devoid of natural passion on account of the 'enervating heat of the climate'. He also charges that

> they are strangers to that vigour of mind, and all the virtues grafted on those passions which animate our more active spirits. They prefer a lazy apathy, and frequently quote this saying from some favourite book: 'It is better to sit than to walk, to lie down than to sit, to sleep than to wake, and death is best of all.'[71]

Something of this negative flavour lingers in Coleridge's famous letter to John Thelwall of 1797, in which he draws a contrast between two different kinds of intellectual discipline, one in which he raises and spiritualises his intellect to a great height, the other involving a lowering exercise which he calls 'the Brahman Creed':

> It is better to sit than to stand, it is better to lie than to sit, it is better to sleep than to wake – but Death is the best of all! – I should much wish, like the Indian Vishna, to float about along an infinite ocean cradled in the flower of

70. Sir William Jones, *Poems consisting chiefly of translations from the Asiatick languages: to which are added two essays: I. On the poetry of the eastern nations. II. On the arts, commonly called imitative* (Oxford, Clarendon Press, 1772), p.180-81.

71. Luke Scrafton, *Reflections on the government of Indostan, 1763* (London, W. Richardson and S. Clark, 1770), p.16.

THE EXAMINER.

No. 561. SUNDAY, SEPT. 27, 1818.

THE POLITICAL EXAMINER.

Party is the madness of many for the gain of a few. POPE.

No. 546.

ARTICLE AND NO ARTICLE.

Our readers will do us the justice to acknowledge, that we very rarely indeed fail in giving them the usual article at the head of our paper ; and perhaps when it is considered that it is one and the same individual that has been in the habit of furnishing the original matter in this paper for nearly ten years, through all the various feelings of health and sickness, and the love of other studies besides politics, it may be granted by those who understand human nature (kindly and wisely, that he has not failed in his regularity as often as might be excused him. We think our courteous readers exclaim, in one of the few good things that may be imitated from Parliament,—" Hear ! Hear !"

Dr. Johnson, it is true, says that an author may always write, provided he sits down to it doggedly. And write he certainly may ; but how write is another question. Not that industry in general is not sufficient ; but even setting aside the inclination, industry itself will not always do, as is most for instance where the subject does not readily present itself, or rather where out of many subjects it is difficult to choose. A man's very industry and anxiety may then hamper him ; for he may go through so many subjects, and consider them so fastidiously as he goes, that he shall reject them one after the other from mere over-weighing and comparison. The dogged argument is very good, we must confess, to apply to journals. There would be no excuse, for instance, for the frequent short articles in such papers as the Courier, if it were not, in the nature of things, to be found in their very brevity. The Morning Post (if it is what it used to be) is bound to be in it's place at all times, like one of it's namesakes in a street ; the Sun has no reason for not shining in all weathers, as much as it does in any ; and the Editor of the Quarterly Review would have no excuse for being behind-hand with his publication, as there is always to be found a sufficient number of better-tempered spirits, agreeable women, or promising young poets, to throw him into the requisite passion.* But in proportion as Journalists differ with other Journalists, who will deny that they become excusable?

Chance Reader. Yet after all, Mr. Examiner, what is the good of an excuse?

Exam. To shew the good-nature of those who accept it.

* We congratulate, most sincerely, our young friend JOHN KEATS on the involuntary homage that, we understand, has been paid to his undoubted genius, in an article full of grovelling abuse.

INDIAN ATROCITIES.

TO THE EDITOR OF THE EXAMINER.

" I, from the Orient to the drooping West, making the winds my post horse, thus do ride.—I speak of sudden deaths, of treasons, murders, plots, conspiracies," &c.—SHAKSPEARE.

The cause and origin of that obstinate contest between the East India Company and the Niars on the coast of Malabar, which terminated in the entire extirpation of both prince and people of that country, after a struggle of ten years, attended with a series of atrocities, the subject of my last article, may be thus collected from the concurrent testimony of the natives, as well as Europeans, who were engaged on that service.

A Gentleman of the name of Peel, lately deceased, who held the office of Collector in that district, a civilian in the Company's service (with whom I was personally unacquainted), is reported to have provoked, by his conduct towards the Rajah of the Cotiote, that oppressive system of proscription which led to the annihilation of the whole race of Niars, with the loss of an equal number of British troops, who were employed with a view to root out and destroy, as the only means of subjugating that nation to the yoke of the East India Company.

The quarrel between Mr. Peel and the Rajah of the Cotiote is alledged to have arisen from the attempting to impose upon the Rajah an additional rate of tribute to that which he had voluntarily submitted to pay to the Company. The Rajah having remonstrated at this encroachment, Mr. Peel forgot to treat him with that respect which, as an independent prince and faithful ally of the Company, he had a right to expect from their representative, or rather their servant. The refusing to pull off his shoes, according to oriental custom, on entering the Palace, was construed into such premeditated personal contempt, that the Rajah, it is said, grasped his sword, and compelled this diplomatic agent of the Company, in terms of indignation, as he valued his life, that instant to consult his safety.

The next step after this (corresponding with the measures adopted towards our late faithful friend and ally, the Peishwa*), was to obtain possession of the Rajah's person or capital. The brave prince resolved to preserve his liberty, even at the expense of becoming a desperate fugitive, in arms against his pursuers ; and the consequence was, that he and his faithful adherents, or, in other words, the whole of his subjects, were proscribed and hunted down, without quarter being given, as rebels to the power and authority of the British Government.

* A series of systematic warfare, spreading over almost the whole extent of the vast peninsula of Hindostan, has been incessantly carried on in that country before and since the year 1790; namely, the war in Mysore; in the province of Trichinopoly; the Mahratta war, which is now revived; war in the Guzerat; the Napaul war; war in Cuttack; and the present war with the Peishwas Holkar and Scindia; besides various contests with the natives of India not enumerated; since it would be difficult to say at what period of their history the East India Company were not engaged in some war or other, for the purpose o subjugating, or of extirpating, the Indian nations.

the Lotos, and wake once in a million years for a few minutes – just to know I was going to sleep a million years more.[72]

That the Brahman creed invoked here was something of a cliché by 1797 can be seen in Phebe Gibbes's popular novel *Hartly House, Calcutta* (1789) where the young heroine comments on the Hindus' avoidance of 'vigorous exertions'. It is a maxim with them, she writes, 'That it is better to sit than to walk, to lie down than to sit, to sleep than to wake, and that death is best of all'.[73] While Gibbes's novel is pro-Indian and pro-Hindu (the English heroine is infatuated by her Brahmin tutor), Coleridge is already signalling his distance from the pro-Hindu scholarship of Jones and others.[74] A measure of the hardening of cultural stereotypes about Indians can be seen in Wordsworth's *Essay, supplementary to the preface* (1815), where he argues for the importance of an active reader, inspired by the text he is encountering: 'Is it to be supposed that the reader can make progress [...] like an Indian prince or general – stretched on his palanquin, and borne by his slaves? No; he is invigorated and inspirited by his leader, in order that he may exert himself; for he cannot proceed in quiescence, he cannot be carried like a dead weight.'[75]

Keats's own idea of 'diligent indolence', developed in a letter to J. H. Reynolds in early 1818, deliberately overturns all such negative stereotypes. In doing so it incorporates Keats's own version of the Hindu credo:

> Now it is more noble to sit like Jove tha[n] to fly like Mercury – let us not therefore go hurrying about and collecting honey-bee like, buzzing here and there impatiently from knowledge of what is to be arrived at: but let us open our leaves like a flower and be passive and receptive – budding patiently under the eye of Apollo and taking hints from every noble insect that favours us with a visit – sap will be given us for Meat and dew for drink.[76]

The coinage 'diligent indolence', which has its poetic counterpart in the 'ardent listlessness' of *Endymion*, occurs amidst several quotations from 'noble Books', all of which take Keats on a 'voyage of conception'. This voyage includes a couple of quotations from Shakespeare and a curious reference to 'all "the two-and thirty Pallaces"'.[77] The thirty-two palaces

---

72. Samuel Taylor Coleridge, *Collected letters*, ed. E. L. Griggs, 6 vols (Oxford, 1956-1971), vol.1, p.349.
73. Phebe Gibbes, *Hartly House, Calcutta*, ed. Michael J. Franklin (Oxford, 2007), p.81.
74. For Coleridge and the Indian orientalists, see my essay 'The "dark tide of time": Coleridge and William Hodges' India', in *Coleridge, Romanticism, and the Orient: cultural negotiations* ed. D. Vallins, K. Oishi and S. Perry (London, 2013), p. 39-54.
75. William Wordsworth, 'Essay, supplementary to the preface', *The Prose works*, ed. W. J. B. Owen and Jane Worthington Smyser, 3 vols (Oxford, 1974), vol.3, p.62-84 (82).
76. Letter to J. H. Reynolds (19 Feb 1818), *Letters*, vol.1, p.232.
77. Rollins, and later editors of the letters, have been baffled; see *Letters*, vol.1, p.231, and *John Keats: selected letters*, ed. Robert Gittings, revised by Jon Mee (Oxford, 2002), p.390.

may be a slip for one of the most famous story-books of medieval India, *Vikrama's Adventures, or The Thirty-two tales of the throne*, a narrative about a magic throne supported by thirty-two statuettes, each of which tells a tale full of miracles and fantastical adventures about King Vikrama's great valour and generosity. This may seem an obscure title for Keats to include in his list of 'noble books' but a French translation (from the Persian) had appeared in New York in 1817, bringing the story to the West for the first time.[78] Kauffman's *Dictionary of merchandize* might also be listed amongst the 'noble books', with its long entry on opium, the finest of which is 'traded at Patna, on the river Ganges'. Described by Kauffman as the most valuable of all the simple medicines – 'the most sovereign remedy for easing pain and procuring sleep' – it is both a narcotic and a stimulant: 'it stupefies, excites agreeable ideas, or occasions madness'.[79] That this 'madness' is the divine furor can be seen in the last of the three ghostly figures glimpsed by Keats in the 'drowsy hour' of his 'Ode on indolence':

> The first was a fair maid, and Love her name;
> The second was Ambition, pale of cheek,
> And ever watchful with fatigued eye;
> The last, whom I love more, the more of blame
> Is heap'd upon her, maiden most unmeek,
> I knew to be my demon Poesy.[80]

Critics usually read Keats's formulation of 'diligent indolence' as a counter to William Hazlitt's disparagement of indolence in his lecture on Thomson and Cowper, delivered the week before Keats's letter.[81] Hazlitt opens his lecture with the claim that Thomson is 'the most indolent of mortals and of poets', castigating his 'Castle of indolence' for pouring out 'the whole soul of indolence, diffuse, relaxed, supine, dissolved into a voluptuous dream'. But it soon becomes clear that, for Hazlitt, Thomson's 'indolence' is a catch-all word for his 'slovenliness', together with his deficient indignation 'against unjust and arbitrary power'.[82] Hazlitt had given a much more positive spin to the concept of indolence the previous year in his collaboration with Leigh Hunt on *The Round table* (1817). Here, in his essay 'On manner', Hazlitt praises the Hindoos as 'a different race of people from ourselves' who make it their business

78. Daniel Lescallier, *Le Trône enchanté: conte indien traduit du Persan* (New York, 1817). For a modern edition, see *Thirty-two tales of the throne of Vikramaditya*, trans. A. N. D. Haksar (New Delhi, 2006).

79. [Kauffman], *The Dictionary of merchandize*, p.241-42.

80. Stillinger, *Poems of John Keats*, p.376.

81. See Keats, *Selected letters*, p.390.

82. Hazlitt, *Complete works*, vol.4, p.85, 91, 88.

to sit and think and do nothing. They indulge in endless reverie [...]. They wander about in a luxurious dream. They are like part of a glittering procession, – like revellers in some gay carnival. Their life is a dance, a measure; they hardly seem to tread the earth, but are borne along in some more genial element, and bask in the radiance of brighter suns.[83]

That for Hazlitt India is a sign of the imagination can be seen in his mockery of James Mill's utilitarian *History of British India* (1817), reviewed in *The Examiner* in January 1818.[84] Mill's boast that 'he could describe a country better at second-hand than from original observation' struck Hazlitt as absurd, especially when that country was as poetical as India. It was his own view that 'seeing half a dozen wandering Lascars in the streets of London gives one a better idea of the soul of India, the cradle of the world and (as it were) garden of the sun, than all the charts, records and statistical reports that can be sent over, even under the classical administration of Mr Canning'.[85] Hazlitt's high valuation of Indian religion and culture at this time might well have been the prompt for Keats to think of sailing east on an Indiaman.

Richard Woodhouse, in his interleaved and annotated copy of Keats's *Poems* (1817), commented: 'There must be many allusions to particular circumstances, in his poems: which would add to their beauty and interest, if properly understood.'[86] The cult of India and Hinduism which I have identified in Keats and his circle is the missing chapter from Marilyn Butler's thesis concerning the second-generation Romantics and their 'cult of the South'. If, as she argues, the revival of Greek mythology and paganism formed the lingua franca of the international Enlightenment – a liberal, extrovert, and sunny creed which was mobilised polemically against a conservative, gloomy, and introverted Christianity – then the same might be said of Jones's religious syncretism and his championing of the ancient Sanskrit texts. On a more personal level, too, it is clear that Keats's wider thinking about world religions such as Hinduism helped him to navigate the darker passages of the 'chamber of maiden thought'. Finally, thanks to the assiduous and vigilant reporting of Leigh Hunt's *Examiner*, Keats's already strong political views on the wider world were sharpened by a sense of Britain's religious intolerance and the colonial crimes involved in consolidating

83. Hazlitt, *Complete works*, vol.4, p.45-46.

84. James Mill, *The History of British India*, 3 vols (London, 1818); reviewed in 'Literary notices', *The Examiner* (8 March 1818), p.156-58.

85. Hazlitt, 'On reason and imagination', *Complete works*, vol.12, p.51. For the dating of this essay to 'probably before April 1823' see William Hazlitt, *The Plain speaker: the key essays*, ed. Duncan Wu with an introduction by Tom Paulin (Oxford, 1998), p.39.

86. Quoted in Andrew Motion, *Keats* (London, 1997), p.578.

its hold on the Indian subcontinent.[87] Indeed, his most conspicuous
stretch of overt politicising – the so-called 'capitalist stanzas' about the
brothers' exploitative commerce in *Isabella; or, The Pot of basil* – is centred
on Ceylon's pearl-fishing industry:

> For them the Ceylon diver held his breath,
> And went all naked to the hungry shark;
> For them his ears gush'd blood; for them in death
> The seal on the cold ice with piteous bark
> Lay full of darts; for them alone did seethe
> A thousand men in troubles wide and dark:
> Half-ignorant, they turn'd an easy wheel,
> That set sharp racks at work, to pinch and peel.[88]

Recent events, such as the cession of Ceylon to the British in 1815, and
the subjugation of its inland kingdom of Kandy, may have been the most
immediate prompts for these lines, but engagement with the history of
the subcontinent had longer roots as well. The dangers of diving amongst
'monstrous fishes' on the pearl banks of the Gulf of Mannar, far-famed
from antiquity, was a lesson learnt by the school-boy Keats from his prize
copy of Kauffman's *Dictionary of merchandize*.[89]

87. An example of his strong views can be seen in his claim that the worst thing Napoleon had
    done was to teach 'the divine right Gentlemen [...] how to organize their monstrous
    armies', *Letters*, vol.1, p.397.
88. Keats, *Isabella; or, The Pot of basil*; Stillinger, *Poems of John Keats*, p.245-63 (l.113-20).
89. [Kauffman], *The Dictionary of merchandize*, p.248-51.

'The country chosen of my heart': the comic cosmopolitanism of *The Orientalist, or, electioneering in Ireland, a tale, by myself*

SONJA LAWRENSON

Alongside Charles Maturin's *Melmoth the wanderer* and Walter Scott's *The Abbot*, the year 1820 saw the publication of a markedly less renowned literary endeavour bearing the peculiar title of *The Orientalist, or, Electioneering in Ireland, a tale, by myself*. Not only written 'by myself', but also addressed and dedicated 'to myself',[1] this comic tale delineates the adventures of the 'Orientalist', Stuart Jesswunt, as he strives to win both the hand of Lady Eleanor, daughter of Irish absentee landlord Lord Clanroy, and the parliamentary seat incorporating the Clanroys' Irish estate at Glenarm Castle, North Antrim. The grandson of legendary Sikh Maharaja Runjeet Singh[2] and long-lost son of an East Indian officer, Captain Dalkieth, Duke of Dunluce, the protagonist of this novel by its denouement not only uncovers the true identity of his mother, a native Indian convert to Catholicism, but also discovers his abandoned sister, Nourhan Vatchel, married to a close friend and relative, Lord Llancharne,[3] also of County Antrim. Initially discomfited by Jesswunt's paltry 'pretensions to rank'[4] and deriding him as 'the Nabob',[5] the Clanroys warmly welcome him to their family estate on the discovery of his true identity. Angered by the revelation that Lady Eleanor had previously rejected his son's proposal of marriage on the grounds of his seemingly ignominious parentage, Lord Dunluce spurns the Clanroys' efforts to re-establish the union. On this jarring note, the novel hastily

1. Anonymous [Mrs Purcell], *The Orientalist, or electioneering in Ireland; a tale, by myself* (London, 1820), vol.1, p.v.
2. Maharaja Runjeet Singh (d.1805) ruled the princely Indian state of Bharatpur between the years 1776 and 1805. Exiled from Bharatpur during the Seven Years War as a result of a French and Mughal political alliance, Singh eventually regained his territory. Subsequent to this, Singh made strenuous efforts to strengthen diplomatic relations with the British East India Company.
3. The name Llancharne may be a transliteration of the Gaelic Eilean a' Chuirn, one of the southernmost islands of the inner Hebrides of Scotland. Less than 40 kilometres from North Antrim by sea, this island shares deep-rooted cultural and linguistic ties with the north of Ireland.
4. *The Orientalist*, vol.1, p.18.
5. *The Orientalist*, vol.1, p.3.

concludes. The newly ennobled Viscount Stuart Jesswunt Dalkieth returns unmarried to his family's Antrim estate.

With its convoluted storyline and non sequitur conclusion, not to mention its absurd title and farcical introductory dedication, it is no wonder that British reviewers responded with puzzlement and reserve. *The Monthly review* proclaimed that 'this tale does not convey a characteristic description of Irish electioneering, nor indeed anything else',[6] whilst the *Ladies' monthly museum* objected to its sympathetic portrayal of the Irish rebel, Skeffington-Murray Taswell.[7] On the other hand, *The Orientalist* garnered a much better reception within Ireland. The Dublin-based *Freeman's journal* 'earnestly recommend[ed] its perusal to any person having a moment to spare'.[8] Furthermore, whilst the text was not available in any major circulating library in Britain, libraries in both Dublin and Belfast issued the text to their varied readerships until the late 1830s at least.[9]

Abounding in intertextual allusions, generic subversions and multi-layered irony, *The Orientalist* engages inventively with the dazzling array of political and cultural discourses that circulated within Irish writing of the Romantic period. It thereby poses a challenge to established trajectories of Irish Romantic fiction by confuting what Claire Connolly describes as the widespread 're-imagin[ing of] the field of Irish and Scottish fiction in terms of a system of generic evolution'.[10] Querying Katie Trumpener's supposition that Irish Romantic fiction can be plotted chronologically from 'the emergence of the national tale out of the novels of the 1790s and the subsequent emergence of the historical novel out of the national tale',[11] Connolly 'makes a more cohesive case for the Irish novel as a single cultural phenomenon with, however, far greater evidence of generic and sub-generic diversity at work than can be conveyed by the designation "national tale"'.[12] However, whereas Connolly cautions that though 'it is possible to discern an Irish readership in this period [...] a separate Irish readership for the Irish novel remains difficult to establish',[13] *The Orientalist* clearly appealed to

6. Review of *The Orientalist*, by Mrs Purcell, *The Monthly review* 92 (1820), p.321.
7. Review of *The Orientalist*, by Mrs Purcell, *The Lady's monthly museum* (July 1820), p.35.
8. Review of *The Orientalist*, by Mrs Purcell, *The Freeman's journal* (22 September 1820), p.3.
9. In *British fiction, 1800-1829: a database of production, circulation and reception* (Cardiff, 2004), Peter Garside, Jacqueline Belanger and Sharon Ragaz record that both the 1834 catalogue of Gerrard Tyrrell's Circulating Library of Lower Sackville Street, Dublin and the 1838 catalogue of John Hodgson's Circulating Library in Belfast list *The Orientalist*.
10. Claire Connolly, *A Cultural history of the Irish novel, 1790-1829* (Cambridge, 2011), p.3-4.
11. Katie Trumpener, *Bardic nationalism: the Romantic novel and the British Empire* (Princeton, NJ, 1997), p.131.
12. Connolly, *Cultural history*, p.4.
13. Connolly, *Cultural history*, p.6.

its Irish readership in ways imperceptible to a wider British audience. What, then, attracted Irish readers to this gently parodic text?

In response to this question, this chapter explores how *The Orientalist* refracts contemporary anxieties regarding British imperial expansionism in the East through the particularised political prism of post-Union Ireland. Via its intermeshing discussions of Irish electoral politics and Indian colonial history, *The Orientalist* reveals the myriad global connections between India and Ireland in this period, and the various international and domestic conduits through which such cultural cross-currents are navigated. Identifying *The Orientalist* as the work of a female novelist with a learned interest in 'Hindu' culture, this essay argues that the tale offers a parodic exposition of both Romantic nationalism and Romantic orientalism, whilst disrupting the gender prescriptions of both. Highlighting *The Orientalist*'s vibrant textual dynamics, it demonstrates the text's potential to illuminate the unique relevance of Indian culture, history and politics to post-Union Ireland – not only with regard to Irish attempts to reconfigure Ireland's role within an expanding British Empire but also in the (by no means contradictory) struggle to construct an Irish national identity distinct from either British colonial or archipelagic identifications. In so doing, it not only elucidates why this long-forgotten novel merits further scholarly attention, but also uncovers the subtle insights into regional attitudes to imperial politics that its jocular irony affords. Ultimately, it urges an appreciation of both the Irish inflections and the gendered nuances of *The Orientalist*'s cosmopolitan perspective.

Correspondingly, this essay posits that *The Orientalist* testifies to the heightened cultural currency of the discourse of 'Irish orientalism' within this period. Informed by Joep Leerssen's argument that 'Irish cultural nationalism, grown as it has out of a culturally and politically divided country, is to a large extent an interiorised form of exoticism',[14] Joseph Lennon's *Irish orientalism* delineates how Irish writers cultivated a rich repository of orientalist tropes over the centuries by drawing on European representations of the East as remote, mysterious and antique. This is amply evidenced in the scholarship of eighteenth-century Irish antiquarians such as Sylvester O' Halloran and Charles Vallancey, where oriental texts were used to substantiate impassioned claims regarding Ireland's antiquity.[15] Under the rubric of 'Irish Romantic orientalism'

14. Joep Theodoor Leerssen, *Remembrance and imagination: patterns in the historical and literary representation of Ireland in the nineteenth century* (Cork, 1996), p.66.
15. Charles Vallancey's (1721-1812) *Vindication of the ancient history of Ireland* (Dublin, White, 1786) and his *Ancient history of Ireland, proved from the Sanscrit books of the Brahmins of India* (Dublin, Graisberry & Campbell, 1797) used comparative philology to argue that the Irish descended from ancient Phoenicia. Sylvester O'Halloran (1728-1807) published three

Lennon examines the development of such identifications in the popular writings of Sydney Owenson and Thomas Moore. According to Lennon, both Owenson and Moore 'celebrated the Celtic and oriental [...] and created a dialogue between them in their allegorical and allusive works'.[16] A semiotic symbiosis of the Oriental and the Celt offered an alternative to Britain's pejorative stereotyping of Ireland and provided an opportunity to develop a national image that highlighted the artistic, spiritual nature of the Irish. In its jarring comic fusions of Ireland and the Orient (both titular and textual), *The Orientalist* satirises but is nonetheless indebted to this self-exoticising myth. That it gained a substantial readership within Ireland testifies to a wider cultural awareness of the specific generic origins of its satiric premise.

This aspect is first evidenced in the novel's self-satirising dedication to 'my dearest self'.[17] Published under the pseudonym Mrs Purcell, the real scribe takes an almost tangible delight in ridiculing this woman's 'pretensions' to authorship. As 'Mrs Purcell' writes of herself:

> I have modestly chosen YOU as the person for whom in this world I have the highest regard [...] albeit conscious that your pretensions to rank and talent are but slender; that, your learning, to my grief during my late labours I found shallow [...] Yet, my dear Self [...] there lives not that person of whom a thorough knowledge would be to me of more inestimable value.[18]

Odd as this dedication appears, the hyperbole and slick sanctimony of this novelist's self-appraisal corresponds with the main narrative's satirical exposition of the popular genre of the Irish 'national' tale. Despite comprising a relatively limited corpus of works, this genre's popularity endured throughout the long Romantic period. However, even by 1820 the generic conventions and political tropes of the most well-known national tales must have come across as slightly shop-worn. It is thus tempting to read this preface as a light-hearted riposte to the self-fashioned inaugurator of the national tale, Sydney Owenson. Writing in the wake of the failed 1798 United Irishmen rebellion and during a period of increased agitation for Catholic emancipation, Owenson's championing of Irish political causes led to controversy regarding the suitability of such subjects for a female pen. Prone to lengthy and self-aggrandising prefaces, many of Owenson's contemporaries deemed such pre-ambulatory pronouncements a rewarding object of satire. For

---

studies in support of Ireland's eastern heritage, namely, *An Introduction to the study of the antiquities of Ireland* (London, Murray, 1770), *Ierne defended* (Dublin, Ewing, 1774) and *A General history of Ireland* (London, Hamilton, 1775).

16. Joseph Lennon, *Irish orientalism: a literary and intellectual history* (Syracuse, NY, 2004), p.141.
17. *The Orientalist*, vol.1, p.v.
18. *The Orientalist*, vol.1, p.vi-vii.

example, *The Quarterly review* acerbically concluded from the introduction to Owenson's *Ida of Athens* (1809) that 'this young lady [...] has
evidently written more than she has read, and read more than she has
thought'.[19]

Clearly, the self-dedication of *The Orientalist*'s professed authoress
should be considered in the light of Owenson's public persona. However,
it would be erroneous to surmise that *The Orientalist* shares these reviewers' anxieties over the sexual propriety of Owenson's novelistic
incursions into national and gender politics. For a text designating Irish
electioneering as its titular subject to accuse Owenson of violating
strictures of female authorship would be extraordinarily brazen given
that its author was likewise a woman writer.[20] Admittedly, *The Orientalist*'s
female protagonists correspond more dutifully to stereotypes of English
domestic femininity than Glorvina, the erudite and enigmatic heroine of
Owenson's most famous novel, *The Wild Irish girl* (1806). However,
whereas the latter text deploys Glorvina as an allegory of the Irish
nation, *The Orientalist* subverts this political strategy by overturning
what Robert Tracey terms the 'Glorvina solution', that is, the proclivity
in Irish Romantic fiction to deploy a marriage plot that terminates in the
'intermarriage/assimilation of Irish and Anglo-Irish, of modern efficiency
and ancient tradition, of legal right and traditional loyalty'.[21] Moreover,
as glimpsed in the *Lady's monthly museum*'s disapproving response to
the novel's charismatic Irish rebel, Skeffington-Murray Taswell, *The
Orientalist* arguably promotes a more radical nationalist agenda than
Owenson's fiction. Conceding this, it is worth reflecting once again upon
The Orientalist's relationship to earlier Irish Romantic fiction. For,
although much of the humour of *The Orientalist* derives from the pre-
sumptuous claims that an author such as Sydney Owenson might set
forth with regard to Ireland's oriental heritage, this novel in many ways
reproduces the sense of an underlying affinity between Irish and Indian
sensibilities.

Perhaps the most striking illustration of such mutual 'sensibility' lies in
the text's treatment of the fashionable genre of 'national melodies', as
popularised by Thomas Moore's *Irish melodies* of 1808-1834. Fleeing the
stifling atmosphere of a tumultuous ball, Jesswunt and his amiable
companion, Lord Llancharne, escape to the 'calm delight' of the
Clanroy's drawing room, where Eleanor and Nourhan are singing 'one

19. Review of *Woman; or, Ida of Athens*, by Sydney Owenson, *The Quarterly review* 1 (1809), p.50-
    52 (52).
20. In its recommendation of the novel, *The Freeman's journal* (22 September 1820) claimed
    that it had 'discovered [*The Orientalist*] to be the work of one of the fair sex', p.3.
21. Robert Tracy, *The Unappeasable host: studies in Irish literature* (Dublin, 1998), p.31.

of Sir John Stevenson's most admired duets' (1: 141).[22] A contemporary readership (particularly an Irish one) would immediately recognise this reference to the composer John Stevenson, who collaborated with Thomas Moore on his self-avowed Celticist project 'to interpret in verse the touching language of [his] country's music'.[23] Similarly, when called upon to sing, Jesswunt first adapts a sonnet from the Anglo-Irish poet Lord Strangford's much celebrated (if incredibly loose) translations of Luís de Camoens's exoticist Portuguese poetry 'to a tune he had learned in India'.[24] Then 'intreated to indulge them with a native strand of his native land' Jesswunt sings in 'Hindostanee':[25]

> Fooleah buttorteetee
> Sawra bang ko jaaur tee tee [...]
> Rung bay rung ka fool hy
> Dooleena ko sayla chy
>   Peearee Loll

The incorporation of this four-verse transliterated poem into the main body of a narrative episode set in an Irish drawing-room is undoubtedly eye-catching. Even more remarkable, however, is the way in which an advertisement for a forthcoming collection of *Oriental melodies* is intrusively interpolated into the scene. Having complied with Lady Eleanor's request that he translate this Indian song into English, Jesswunt offers to 'note it down for her'.[26] The reader is then directed to a note at the end of the volume stating that William Power (the erstwhile Dublin publisher of Moore's *Irish melodies*) 'proposes to publish [...] a collection of original Oriental melodies'.[27] Cast in the mould of Moore's *Melodies*, the symphonies and accompaniments to *A Selection of oriental melodies* were also arranged by Sir John Stevenson, although it was not Moore but the otherwise undistinguished poet Thomas Power who provided English lyrics. Power also wrote the introductory 'Advertisement', in which he declares that these *Oriental melodies* were collected 'in various parts of India, by a gentleman of acknowledged taste'.[28] Whether personally connected to this unidentified gentleman, Sir John Stevenson or either of the Powers, the author of *The Orientalist* evidently had privileged access

---

22. *The Orientalist*, vol.1, p.141.
23. Thomas Moore, *The Poetical works* (London, 1841) vol.4, p.v.
24. Purcell, *The Orientalist*, vol.2, p.143. Percy Clinton Sydney Smythe (1780-1855), 6th Viscount Strangford was a diplomat, writer and friend of Thomas Moore. However, in *British bards and Scotch reviewers* (London, Cawthorne, 1809), Lord Byron mocked Strangford for imitating Moore in his translation of Camoens.
25. *The Orientalist*, vol.2, p.143.
26. *The Orientalist*, vol.2, p.143.
27. *The Orientalist*, vol.2, p.420.
28. Thomas E. Power and John Stevenson, *A Selection of oriental melodies* (Dublin, c.1821), n.p.

to the material that appeared in *Oriental melodies* shortly after its own publication. Crucially, however, a comparison of the ways in which this material is deployed in *Oriental melodies* in contrast to *The Orientalist* indicates a subtle divergence in each work's position in relation to the orientalist scholarship from which they both draw.

Even at a cursory glance, it is clear that *The Orientalist* and *Oriental melodies* share the same undisclosed source material. One of the *Oriental melodies*, entitled 'The Gazzel [Ghazel]' is addressed to a female figure called Nourhan, a name which a subsequent footnote informs us translates as 'the morning star'. It is hardly coincidental that, in *The Orientalist*, Lord Llancharne dubs Jesswunt's long-lost sister, Nourhan Vatchel, his 'morning star'.[29] Similarly, although Power included only English lyrics in his *Oriental melodies*, his 'Bridal eve' is patently derived from the transliterated Hindi song 'Peearee Loll' that Jesswunt translates as 'Lovely darling' in *The Orientalist*. What is more, not only do both texts provide botanical annotations to indigenous Hindustani flora, but they supplement the song's nuptial theme with suspiciously similar anthropological commentaries on the dancing 'Nautch' girls that, according to Power, accompany 'an Indian bridal'.[30] In this way, both texts contribute to Edward Said's classic formulation of 'Orientalism as a Western style for dominating, restructuring, and having authority over the Orient'.[31] However, while both could be said to corroborate Said's view that, 'what inevitably goes with such work [...] is a kind of free-floating mythology of the Orient',[32] neither work fully corroborates this position. Instead, both texts offer sympathetic and appreciative interpretations of Indian culture and society. In this way, they echo the earlier conservative orientalism of major Indologists such as Sir William Jones, who sought to encourage 'the quest for knowledge about Indian customs and practices [...] allowing regional customs to flourish so long as locals submitted to an overarching imperial sovereignty'.[33] Most notably, via their representations of the Indian Sepoy and Jesswunt respectively, both *Oriental melodies* and *The Orientalist* present Indian masculinity as noble and heroic, thereby problematising Said's claim that Western writers tended

29. *The Orientalist*, vol.2, p.246. It is interesting to note that whilst Jesswunt possesses a Hindu name, his sister Nourhan possesses a Muslim one. This could indicate the author's anti-sectarian politics.
30. Power & Stevenson, *Oriental melodies*, n.p. Of course, the Indian nautch or classical dance was a sophisticated form of entertainment that had much deeper and broader significances within Indian society. See Hermione De Almeida and George H. Gilpin, *Indian renaissance: British Romantic art and the prospect of India* (Aldershot, 2005), p.74.
31. Said, *Orientalism*, p.3.
32. Said, *Orientalism*, p.53.
33. Douglas T. McGetchin, *Indology, Indomania, and orientalism: India's rebirth in modern Germany* (Cranbury, NJ, 2009), p.31.

to imagine the East as 'passive, seminal, feminine, even silent and supine'.[34] Nevertheless, though *Oriental melodies* endorses an assertively martial ideal of the Indian sepoy's masculinity, it does 'keep intact the separateness of the Orient, its eccentricity, its backwardness' if not 'its feminine penetrability'.[35] Asserting his scholarly authority, Thomas Power informs his readers that 'the partiality of the Easterns for music is such, that when under its influence they have been frequently known to commit acts almost too extravagant for belief'.[36] As this study demonstrates, *The Orientalist* brings similar orientalist assumptions into play in its referencing of India. And yet, it is worth observing how the narrative simultaneously decentres and deflects the 'flexible positional authority'[37] of this orientalism. Thus, though both texts are adroitly attuned to the colonial sensitivities of a broad Irish readership, *The Orientalist* is undoubtedly more subversive in its creative adaptations of Orientalist scholarship.

For, although Power's *Oriental melodies* professes to be 'a close imitation of the original',[38] this is belied by his admission that 'their wildness and irregularity gave [him] much trouble in adapting English words to them'.[39] Again, despite adopting a sympathetic mode of conservative orientalism, Power's exoticist view of Indian culture remains rooted (as was much other conservative scholarship) in the idiom of academic authoritarianism. *The Orientalist*, on the other hand, situates Jesswunt's Hindustani melody within a discussion of 'Scotch, Irish, German and even Hebrew melodies'.[40] Furthermore, the text's transliteration of this song is idiosyncratic; it does not render Hindu culture more accessible to its wider anglophone readerships but instead defamiliarises it. What such transliteration does achieve, then, is the privileging of the unfamiliar phonetics of the transliterated verses of 'Peearee Loll' over the English translation that succeeds it. Whereas Power assumes the authority to adapt and refine the Hindu lyrics of the unknown source melody to suit the supposedly more cultivated cadences of English, *The Orientalist* makes no effort to assimilate the song's foreignness. Moreover, it is Jesswunt, the indigenous Indian

---

34. Said, *Orientalism*, p.138.

35. Said, *Orientalism*, p.206.

36. Power & Stevenson, *Oriental melodies*, n.p. Probably a reference to the purported Hindu practice of throwing oneself under the chariot wheels of juggernaut cars. British evangelicals such as William Wilberforce sought to end these supposedly 'fearful religious customs' by adding clauses to the British East India Company's 1813 charter requiring it to commit to the 'religious improvement' of Indians. John Pollock, *William Wilberforce* (London, 1977), p.236.

37. Said, *Orientalism*, p.7.

38. Power & Stevenson, *Oriental melodies*, n.p.

39. Power & Stevenson, *Oriental melodies*, n.p.

40. *The Orientalist*, vol.1, p.142.

character, who assumes the cultural authority to translate the verses into English. Overall, the intertextual relationship between this novel and Power's musical manuscript testifies to the complexity of the former's engagement in the intellectual and literary exchanges of Irish orientalism. The novel's popularity within Ireland testifies to an Irish readership that recognised its narrative's generic lineage.

This is not to refute the fact that the autochthonic Indian voice regis-tered in *The Orientalist* is a fictional one. Though resisting the epistemo-logical complacency and hegemonising tendencies of academic orientalism, *The Orientalist* is no less obligated to its scholarly strictures than *Oriental melodies*. In truth, *The Orientalist* not only avails of the interpretative frameworks produced by the scholarly Orientalist project, but often indulges in the kinds of romanticised visions of the Orient prevalent within both British and Irish Romanticism. Despite his culti-vated manners and tastes, Jesswunt remains an exotic figure. Indeed, his intense passion for Lady Eleanor is relayed to the reader via extracts from Lord Byron's exuberantly exoticised poem of 1813, *The Bride of Abydos*.[41] However, though explicitly citing Byron, *The Orientalist* adheres more closely to the Irish orientalist strategies practiced by Owenson and Moore. Notwithstanding their unique styles and distinct political perspectives, works such as Owenson's *The Wild Irish girl* and Moore's *Lalla Rookh* imbued Irish political realities with the mystique of oriental romance.[42] By transposing its exotic oriental prince to an Irish Romantic landscape, *The Orientalist* achieves an ostensibly similar effect. Forced to seek Jesswunt's aid after a road accident, Lord Llancharne later embellishes his account of this adventure with a host of orientalist imagery familiar from *The Arabian nights* saga. 'Impelled forward by the power of magic' to 'the estate of a sorcerer', Llancharne imaginatively narrates his 'petrifac-tion' at seeing 'two black castles [spring] out of the bog at [their] approach' to this 'haunted demesne'.[43] In this way, *The Orientalist* almost paradigmatically conforms to Said's hypothesis that European narratives conceptualise the Orient as 'a place of romance, exotic beings, haunting memories and landscapes, remarkable experiences'.[44]

Of course, the narrative's setting of the North Antrim coastline somewhat undermines the discursive authority of its orientalism. Ultimately, Llancharne's romanticised retelling of this adventure is laced

41. *The Orientalist*, vol.1, p.107.
42. Obviously, as a close confidante and protégé of Thomas Moore, Byron was arguably highly attuned to the political inflections of Irish Romantic orientalism. Conceding this, it is also worth noting the ways in which the thwarted romance of *The Orientalist* might evoke the doomed love affair of Byron's poem.
43. *The Orientalist*, vol.1, p.151.
44. Said, *Orientalism*, p.1.

with irony as it is he who triggers the whole incident by driving recklessly after Lady Eleanor mistakes Jesswunt for a 'rebel or robber'.[45] His comic exaggeration thus reiterates the parodic and self-reflexive nature of *The Orientalist*'s engagement with Romantic-orientalist tropes. What is more, rather than simply burlesque the imaginative excesses of Romantic orientalism, the text alerts its readers to the ways in which such a discourse may be employed to mislead and manipulate. Recognising that his candidature for the parliamentary seat of County Antrim is threatened by Jesswunt's rival election campaign, the young Lord Glenarm relies 'on the misrepresentations of his own partisans'. Accurately accrediting Jesswunt's 'incredible popularity' with local voters to his 'goodness and munificence', Glenarm's partisans aim to sabotage the former's reputation by characterising him as a stereotypical eastern despot. Later in the novel, Lord Llancharne mischievously misinforms his supercilious aunt, Lady Clanroy, that Jesswunt is the son of the powerful ruler of Mysore and implacable enemy of Britain, Tippoo Saib (Tipu Sultan). Lady Clanroy receives Jesswunt 'with unusual condescension',[46] suspecting that he may have valuable East Indian connections. By such diverse means, *The Orientalist* both reveals the Orient to be a rhetorical construct and exposes the economic and political agendas that its recurrent tropes often served to promulgate. Furthermore, given Tipu Sultan's alliance with revolutionary France and America against Britain, the linking of Jesswunt and Tipu also carries political connotations with particular significance in Ireland at this period.

According to Joseph Lennon 'this awareness of the constructed nature of the Orient pervades Irish literary Orientalism, and occasionally exposes the Irish Celt'.[47] *The Orientalist* may capitalise on the comedic potential of Irish caricatures via its derisive portrayals of the Irish lower orders as heavily-'brogued' and wily, but it often invokes such stereotypes only to subvert them. Having 'imported [...] much prejudice' from England,[48] Lady Clanroy feels 'an insurmountable horror at the idea of visiting a country which had so lately been the scene of much bloodshed, from internal commotion; apprehending that in every peasant she might encounter a rebel'.[49] In its parodic exposition of English attitudes towards both Ireland and India, *The Orientalist* aligns itself with Irish Romantic writers such as Owenson and Moore, both of whom employed an Irish-oriental cross-colonial lens as a means of countering British imperial stereotypes. This novel both humorously draws upon, and

---

45. *The Orientalist*, vol.1, p.122.
46. *The Orientalist*, vol.2, p.242.
47. Lennon, *Irish orientalism*, p.142.
48. *The Orientalist*, vol.1, p.120.
49. *The Orientalist*, vol.1, p.16.

sympathetically responds to, the creative dynamism that lies at the heart of many Irish Romantic responses to an evolving European imperialism.

Unwilling to endorse seriously the idealised realms of Celtic-oriental romance prevalent within much Irish Romantic fiction, *The Orientalist* remains sympathetic to the political imperatives underpinning such discursive formations. Overall, *The Orientalist* is more scathing in its ridicule of English attitudes towards Irish barbarism than in its mockery of Romantic Celticism. Whilst the Anglo-Irish absentee, Lord Glenarm, regards an ancient site as 'most probably designed for some barbarous monument of sacrifice, or rude mausoleum of the aboriginal Irish',[50] the 'East Indian' Jesswunt displays an antiquarian knowledge of Ireland. When exploring the ruins of an ancient Irish castle, purportedly the family seat of Ulster's deposed Gaelic dynasty, the O'Neills, Jesswunt relates how the castle 'was dismantled by Cromwell, and finally burned and reduced to its present state in the wars of King James'.[51] In his brief allusion to the Cromwellian and Jacobite wars of the seventeenth century, Jesswunt invokes two pivotal episodes in the history of the English conquest of Ireland. More specifically, he provides a compelling example of the destructive impact of English confiscations of the property of Irish Catholic gentry as a result of these military campaigns, reflecting that 'it is much to be regretted, that a very ancient inscription cut in the Irish character upon a slab of marble, has been either removed from thence, or wilfully destroyed'.[52] The most conspicuous aspect of Jesswunt's historical account is that it conflates two authentic historic sites of County Antrim (Dunluce Castle and Shane's Castle) and relocates this historical amalgamation within the direct vicinity of Muckamore Abbey, which, in fact, is about 40 miles from the novel's primary setting of Glenarm Castle. Arguably, an underlying political motive prompts the creative realignment of these sites. As the text explicitly refers to its ancient castle as 'for centuries the subject of contention and theatre of many a bloody spectacle',[53] it is worth recalling that both Shane's Castle and Muckamore Abbey had witnessed more recent bloodshed during the 1798 United Irishmen rebellion. During the Battle of Antrim of 7 June 1798, United Irishmen had congregated at Muckamore Abbey. Government forces then proceeded to burn the contemporary residence down, killing several civilians in the process.[54] In these few passages of antiquarian interest we perhaps discern Jesswunt's latent affinities.

50. *The Orientalist*, vol.1, p.41.
51. *The Orientalist*, vol.2, p.112.
52. *The Orientalist*, vol.2, p.112.
53. *The Orientalist*, vol.2, p.112.
54. For a detailed account of this event see William Hamilton Maxwell, *History of the Irish rebellion* (London, 1845). See also Jim Smyth, *The Men of no property* (Houndmills, 1992), p.92-94.

For, although the narrative does not reveal Jesswunt's Irish paternity until its final chapter, the revelation of his family history forces a reassessment of his status as a stranger. Before the infant Jesswunt was seized from his 'afflicted' mother by her father, the Maharaja Runjeet Singh, this Indian convert to Catholicism ensured that her young son 'was hastily admitted by the name of Stuart, a member of that faith which [she] had embraced'.[55] Given the historical resonances of the aforementioned scene, Jesswunt's Christian name arguably invokes the house of Stuart – the royal lineage from which King James descended, and whose disputed hereditary claims were widely supported by Irish Catholics of the seventeenth and eighteenth centuries. As the son of an Anglo-Irish landlord and Indian Catholic mother, Jesswunt embodies the intricate web of intra-imperial connections between India and Ireland that emanate from the text. In this way, *The Orientalist* reflects the syncretistic and equivocal nature of Irish orientalism.

It also corroborates Lennon's view that, from this period onwards, 'Irish Orientalism contributed to an increased use of allegory and linguistic play through which the Irish decolonising and nationalist voices might exist'.[56] From Jesswunt's elegiac reflections on past conflicts at Muckamore Abbey to the imaginary sightings of 'rebels' by Ascendancy women such as Lady Eleanor and Lady Clanroy, a hidden leitmotif of this novel is Ireland's recent legacy of failed rebellion. Most demonstrably, its principal subplot tells the story of the fugitive Skeffington-Murray Taswell who becomes leader of a group of Irish rebels. This subsidiary plot-line introduces a radical nationalism that disrupts the more moderate political perspective provided by the main narrative. Never explicitly labelled a revolutionary, Murray is nevertheless identifiable as a kindred spirit to the hero-martyrs of the United Irishmen's rebellion of 1798 and Robert Emmet's subsequent rebellion of 1803.[57] In the bitter aftermath of these failed rebellions, sympathisers often chose to depict these revolutionaries as misguided but chivalrous figures. Fintan Cullen argues that early nineteenth-century visual representations of the dashing United Irish leader, Lord Edward Fitzgerald,

55. *The Orientalist*, vol.2, p.223.
56. Lennon, *Irish orientalism*, p.xxi.
57. Intriguingly, Taswell's full name also evokes Clotworthy Skeffington, second earl of Massereene (1742-1805). Of old Protestant lineage, the Skeffingtons possessed major landholdings in Antrim, including Antrim Castle. However, although an esteemed political family, the real-life Skeffingtons were generally unsympathetic towards Irish patriotism. Nevertheless Murray's misfortunes in *The Orientalist* do recall the unfortunate fate of Clotworthy Skeffington. Imprisoned for debts in France in 1770, Clotworthy Skeffington was only liberated nineteen years later by Parisian crowds on the eve of the fall of the Bastille.

transformed him 'from an impressive political and military strategist to a tragic yet romantic innocent'.[58]

The favourite son of the liberal patriot Taswell, Murray's envious brother brutally coerces his childhood sweetheart into marriage. Echoing contemporary biographical and fictional reports of the demise of Fitzgerald, Murray is shown to be possessed of 'an ardent adventurous disposition'.[59] And, just as Thomas Moore's later biography of Fitzgerald would claim that 'a heart overflowing with affection and disappointment conducted [this] young lover' to become a naïve disciple of Rousseau's writings, Murray 'does not anticipate the powerful effect' that his enthusiastic reading of German 'sturm und drang' dramatists such as Friedrich Schiller 'might produce in his mind'. Conspicuously, nor does he 'reflect that he was not the first youthful enthusiast whose head had been turned by a perusal of such works'. Consequently, although Murray never explicitly expresses a specific political ideology, he is figuratively associated with the tragic icons of the 1798 and 1803 Irish rebellions. Furthermore, the text's compassionate attitude towards Murray contrasts directly with its unsympathetic characterisation of 'Ensign Fortescue', the English soldier who arrests Murray when this 'gentlemanly' outlaw bursts into the funeral service of his beloved father. To a certain extent, the moral and political sensibilities of the main characters of the story are measurable by their attitude towards the 'ill-fated Murray'.[63] In contrast to the absentee Ascendancy ladies Lady Eleanor and Lady Clanroy, who live in almost perpetual fear of rebels or robbers, the Irish-Indian Stuart Jesswunt consoles 'the unfortunate Murray',[64] whilst his (as yet undeclared) sister Nourhan Vatchel assists in Murray's escape.

Once again, *The Orientalist*'s evocation of a sympathetic bond between India and Ireland aligns it with the Romantic orientalist writings of Owenson and Moore. In many ways, its attitude towards Irish revolutionary nationalism also echoes the political sentiments of these authors' works, where, in texts such as Owenson's *The Wild Irish girl*, 'revolutionary movements such as the United Irishmen are acknowledged, but ascribed to a misguided patriotism'.[65] Nevertheless, it would be remiss to view *The Orientalist*'s satirical exposition of the

58. Fintan Cullen, 'Lord Edward Fitzgerald: the creation of an icon', *History Ireland* 6.4 (1998), p.17-20 (19).
59. *The Orientalist*, vol.1, p.336.
60. Thomas Moore, *The Life and death of Lord Edward Fitzgerald* (London, 1831), p.101.
61. *The Orientalist*, vol.2, p.281.
62. *The Orientalist*, vol.2, p.281.
63. *The Orientalist*, vol.1, p.130.
64. *The Orientalist*, vol.2, p.339.
65. Thomas Tracy, *Irishness and womanhood in nineteenth-century British writing* (Burlington, VT, 2009), p.15.

orientalising tendencies of Irish Romanticism as a superficially divergent
yet complementary mode of the forms of Irish cultural nationalism
propounded in better-known Irish Romantic writing. It is not simply
that *The Orientalist* debunks national stereotypes, but that the text fundamentally rejects the models of cultural nationalism propagated in
many Irish Romantic works.

According to Julia Wright, two traditions 'inform much radical,
rationalist, national politics in Romantic-era Ireland',[66] specifically,
'antiquarian nationalism, which seeks a return to the cultural and
political past' and 'inaugural nationalism' which is based on the 'self-
consciously modern and revolutionary inauguration of a new state' and
which rests on an idea of popular sovereignty.[67] She regards *The Wild
Irish girl* as exemplary of a burgeoning antiquarian nationalism, in which
'society is not governed by globally legitimate, ahistorical paradigms but
by an antique national culture that is properly handed down from
generation to generation'.[68] However, in discussing both the writings
of the United Irishmen and Owenson's later work, Wright reveals how
'the combination of inaugural nationalism with the non-sectarian features of the antiquarian kind produced a brand of nationalism that [...]
embraced [...] universal rights, but still invoked the emotional force of an
Irish nation with specific cultural features'.[69] *The Orientalist* likewise acts
as a proxy arena for the interplay of various conceptions of nationhood
at struggle in post-Union Ireland. Through the narrative conceit of an
Irish electioneering campaign, it erects a stage upon which these different political ideologies can be surveyed as they intersect, merge and
diverge. In contradistinction to national tales such as *The Wild Irish girl*,
The Orientalist militates against any surface resolution of this political
clamour via the marriage of an Anglo-Irish hero and Gaelic Irish heroine
and instead repudiates the symbolic conflation (or, indeed, reduction) of
national politics to domestic plots. Alternatively, its parallel plotting of
intercultural marriage and Irish national politics underlines the
constructed nature of cultural identity and, by extension, the nationalist
ideology upon which it is founded.

From the opening pages, the narrative establishes an ideological
opposition between the key ideas, interests and political actors
contending for power in the upcoming parliamentary elections. Using

66. Julia M. Wright, *Ireland, India and nationalism in nineteenth-century literature* (Cambridge,
    2007), p.30.
67. Julia M. Wright, 'National erotics and political theory in Morgan's *The O'Briens and the
    O'Flahertys*', *European Romantic review* 15.2 (2004), p.229-241(229).
68. *Ireland, India and nationalism*, p.33.
69. Julia M. Wright, '"The nation begins to form": competing nationalisms in Morgan's *The
    O'Briens and The O'Flahertys*', *English literary history* 66.4 (1999), p.939-63 (942).

a heavy-handed symbolism, the different political orientations of each of the four parliamentary candidates for Antrim are signposted for readers. Whereas those supporting the representatives of Protestant Ascendancy, Lord Glenarm and Sir Edmond Harleigh, rally under the banner of a harp and crown in gold and aristocratic blue ribbands, Taswell's followers sport bunches of shamrock indicating the populist and revolutionary bent of his Irish nationalism. The supporters of the Indian candidate, Jesswunt, wear laurels, thereby associating him with a classical (and masculine) republicanism. Most suggestively, at the final rally before the election 'bunches of laurel entwined with shamrock [...] were triumphantly carried in honour of the most popular candidates'.[70] At the same rally, Taswell and Jesswunt give speeches that underline the commonalities between Taswell's revolutionary nationalism and Jesswunt's classical cosmopolitanism. Having heard Taswell exhort his followers 'to assert and vindicate [their] rights as free electors, not merely now invaded but long borne down and oppressed',[71] Jesswunt delivers a speech that draws on this longstanding Irish nationalist rhetoric of slavery and oppression yet tempers it with a globally nuanced perspective. As yet uncertain of his Irish ancestry, Jesswunt is nonetheless eager to profess his profound sense of affinity with Ireland and its inhabitants:

> What though I have not the happiness to boast, that Ireland is my native soil, is she the less dear to my soul? When, after traversing Europe and the greater part of the Eastern hemisphere, I return to her hospitable shores in search of happiness and home, as the country chosen of my heart, and as dear to me as my native clime. Proud to claim such a mother! May I not hope to be received in her bosom, acknowledged as her adopted son and to cherish with fraternal affection, and be cherished by my adopted brethren, whilst I study to render myself worthy of their esteem, by endeavouring to deserve it![72]

Through the alliance of Taswell and Jesswunt, the *Orientalist* offers a fusion of a cosmopolitan ideal of fraternal universalism and a revolutionary Irish nationalism. In this way, the text labours to recuperate United Irishmen ideals within the post-Union political context. However, whilst the text appears to marry revolutionary nationalist and cosmopolitan ideals, the insular logic of cultural nationalism is repeatedly undercut by the fact that the electoral candidates with the greatest claim to an ancient Irish lineage are in fact absentee landlords, who choose to reside not at their Irish ancestral estates but amongst fashionable London elites. Significantly, one of the central structural ironies of the narrative lies in this concern with ancestry and authenticity. In the

70. *The Orientalist*, vol.2, p.30.
71. *The Orientalist*, vol.2, p.9.
72. *The Orientalist*, vol.2, p.24.

countdown to the election, Lady Eleanor avers that 'the East Indian, although possessed of, in the eyes of the world, the most substantial recommendation – incalculable wealth; yet, not being a native, had no claim to the representation of a county in Ireland'.[73] In contrast, her brother's election campaign hinges upon his being 'heir not only to [the Glenarm] title and estates but to the Dukedom of Dunluce'.[74] The most obvious irony underpinning Eleanor's observations is that Jesswunt – unbeknownst to either the Clanroys or the reader – is in fact the long-lost son of the Duke of Dunluce and therefore the legitimate heir to this title. Yet, throughout the course of the novel, the more persistent irony of Eleanor's statement is refracted in the hypocrisy with which the Clanroys abuse their hereditary claims. Despite his acknowledged Irish aristocratic ancestry, having never visited the country before, the young Glenarm inadvertently admits that he and his family are 'strangers in Ireland'.[75] From the commencement of Glenarm's political campaign, his family's ancestry is repeatedly invoked only to be refuted by their fraudulence, self-interestedness and absenteeism.

In a desperate attempt to curry favour with the poorest of their voting public, the local forty-shilling freeholders, the Clanroys try 'by every possible exertion, to regain the popularity [they] had forfeited, by having allowed so many years to elapse since visit[ing their] estates in Ireland'.[76] A significant measure in this endeavour 'to stifle the remembrance of [their] national desertion' is the publication of electioneering squibs. In one of these pamphlets, Glenarm's devious land agent, Bromley, dis-guises himself as 'a local weaver' and castigates Taswell as a gentleman who 'blow[s] into my ears a deal about liberty and property [...] yet set[s his] land at the highest rackrent'.[77] In reality, it is Taswell who 'repro-bate[s] the system of suffering the rents to run in arrear' while Bromley has 'left the poor, too frequently miscalled *independent* forty shilling freeholders on the townland, unemployed'.[78] As this remark suggests, the independent forty-shilling freeholders were the most numerous but least powerful body within the Irish electorate of the period. Enfranchised in 1793,[79] the largely Catholic voting base of the indepen-dent forty-shilling freeholders were often under immense pressure to vote for local landlords. Notably, *The Orientalist* provides a fictional space for dissenting voices amongst the forty-shilling freeholders. This includes

73. *The Orientalist*, vol.1, p.266.
74. *The Orientalist*, vol.1, p.18.
75. *The Orientalist*, vol.1, p.37.
76. *The Orientalist*, vol.1, p.112.
77. *The Orientalist*, vol.1, p.166.
78. *The Orientalist*, vol.1, p.168.
79. This right was eventually withdrawn as part of the Catholic emancipation act of 1829.

the elderly Mahoolan who is eager to voice his political opinions to the young gentleman lodging at his inn:

> If I was a parliament man, I'd make a law, that all lords and great gentlemen [...] ought to better their lands and tenants by laying out some of the profits of one year towards the next; however [they] keep never heeding us, except when there's elections; then [...] they'd wheedle a body to b'lieve if it wasn't for sickness they'd never quit Ireland at all![80]

On discovering that he is speaking to Lord Glenarm, however, Mahoolan's fear concerning the potential repercussions of his outburst exposes his dependency upon the goodwill of this landlord. Affirming that 'anyone who voted against [the landlord] interest could expect immediate eviction', Robert Kee nonetheless argues that 'during the second decade of the nineteenth century evidence began to appear that Catholic forty-shilling freeholders could, if given support and encouragement by their priests, be brought to defy their landlords at the polls'.[81] Strikingly devoid of Catholic clergy, *The Orientalist* yet upholds Kee's assertion that 'the numerous forty-shilling freeholders were thus potentially a considerable democratic force'.[82] Published three years before Daniel O'Connell's Catholic Association mobilised the Catholic masses of Ireland into a cogent populist political movement, *The Orientalist* fictively attests to Thomas Bartlett's argument that 'in the years between 1790 and 1820 large segments of the Irish peasantry were brought to an awareness of their political weight and were made accustomed to acting together'.[83] In many ways, the text is complicit in this politicisation of the masses, as it not only provides space for the voices of these independent freeholders but gives a generous platform to the political perspective of their champion, Skeffington Taswell.

Possessing O'Connell's popularity amongst the lower orders, Taswell is also implicated in a revolutionary strand of Irish nationalism. To begin with, he is quite literally a progenitor of Irish rebellion as the doting father of the unfortunate rebel Murray. And, no less than his maverick son, the narrative (rather approvingly) associates Taswell with Irish revolutionarism. In response to Bromley's bogus squib, a supporter of Taswell writes a letter 'to the really free and independent Electors of the County of A–',[84] commending them to 'convince the haughty junction of

---

80. *The Orientalist*, vol.1, p.45.

81. Robert Kee, *The Green flag: a history of Irish nationalism* (Harmondsworth, 2000), p.182.

82. Kee, *Green flag*, p.182.

83. Thomas Bartlett, *The Fall and rise of the Irish nation: the Catholic question 1690-1830* (Dublin, 1992), p.311-12.

84. The title and rhetoric of this fictional letter are clearly inspired by the United Irishman Arthur O'Connor's radical publication, *To the free electors of the County of Antrim* (Belfast, Miles's Boy, 1797).

aristocratic power, that [they] are independent, that they know their own consequence, and will not bend to the lordly will of any conclave'.[85] Waiving his own name, the author of this pamphlet adopts 'that of a virtuous nobleman, whose blood was spilled in your cause [...] and who, if now alive, would stand forward to protect the rights and privileges of the really free and independent Electors'.[86] The signatory line of the pamphlet reveals that this pseudonym refers to 'Russell', in all likelihood the seventeenth-century British patriot Lord William Russell. As well as being hailed by eighteenth-century patriots as a glorious defender of British civic liberties, Lord Russell was especially admired by Irish revolutionaries for his championing of religious liberties. But given that the United Irishmen repeatedly signed pamphlets under the name of William Russell, the allusion might also invoke Thomas Russell, the United Irish leader who fought in Antrim during the 1798 rebellion and was hanged in 1803 for his role in Emmet's rebellion.

As Bartlett notes, the political mobilisation of the Irish peasantry in the later 1820s was 'helped immeasurably [...] by the folklore that grew up around the rebellion of 1798'.[87] *The Orientalist* corroborates Bartlett's estimation that 'the rebellion cast a long shadow before it, forming and firming attitudes for a generation or more'.[88] Even so, given that *The Orientalist*'s plot hinges on the pivotal backstory of Jesswunt's early separation from his parents during the East India Company's failed siege of his grandfather Runjeet Singh's fort at Bharatpur, it is interesting to note that, prior to his enlistment in the United Irishmen, Russell had served in India with the British army from 1783 until 1786, distinguishing himself in action in the Second Anglo-Mysore War.[89] The seeming inconsistency of Russell's twofold military career is difficult to resolve. In his 1796 'Letter to the people of Ireland', Russell denounced Irish imperial involvement in Britain's distant colonies. Yet, the only gesture he ever made towards furthering Indo-Irish colonial networks is to lobby against restrictions on Irish merchants engaging in the East India trade.[90] Hence, even the most far-sighted and cosmopolitan[91] of

85. *The Orientalist*, vol.1, p.177.
86. *The Orientalist*, vol.1, p.177.
87. Bartlett, *The Fall and rise*, p.318.
88. Bartlett, *The Fall and rise*, p.318-19.
89. The Second Anglo-Mysore War of 1779-1784 was fought in Mughal India between the British East India Company and the conjoined forces of Mysore ruler Hyder Ali and his aforementioned son, Tipu Sultan. Russell was enlisted with Crown troops sent from Britain to bolster the Company's numbers.
90. C. J. Woods (ed.), *Journals and memoirs of Thomas Russell, 1791-1795* (Dublin, 1991), p.35.
91. Having visited India, Africa, Scotland, England, Germany, Holland and France, Russell attributes his fervent nationalism to his multi-continental experiences: 'I have travelled much and seen various parts of the world, and I think the Irish the most virtuous nation

the United Irish leaders did not automatically recognise the potential for radical political affinities between colonial Ireland and India. In its ventriloquising of Russell's revolutionary rhetoric, *The Orientalist* also appears to retain some of this cross-colonial ambivalence.

For example, Jesswunt's account of his early life in India offers a comparatively conservative perspective on Indian colonial politics. Explaining that, as 'a baby, [he] was torn from his tender mother, by command of [his] grandfather Runjeet Singh, and removed to the fortress of Bhurtpore', Jesswunt relates that 'about that period the English made war against my grandfather, and many of their brave troops were slaughtered by his, before the walls of the fortress'.[92] The incident Jesswunt is referring to here is the 1805 Battle of Bharatpur, which took place in Rajasthan during the Second Anglo-Maratha War.[93] A humiliating defeat for East India Company forces, the British instigated the battle because Singh reneged on an earlier agreement by allying with their longstanding enemy, the Maratha confederacy. On 17 April 1805, Singh unexpectedly committed to a treaty with the British, causing the Marathas to suffer defeat in a war they had very nearly won. He remained an ally of the British until his death eight months later.

The broad facts of this history are recounted in Jesswunt's fictional relation of the battle's impact upon his personal fortunes, but the narrative exerts considerable creative licence in its retelling of these events. Not only is the chronology disordered but the narrative borrows from popular accounts of other landmark events in the annals of colonial India. To begin with, the Princess Jehânara was not in fact the daughter of the Jat king of Bharatpur, but the daughter of the early seventeenth-century Mogul emperor, Shah Jehan. In all likelihood, the author of *The Orientalist* appropriated this name from the first volume of James Mill's *History of British India* (1817). It is also probable that Jesswunt's characterisation of the Reverend Macdonald, 'the beloved guide and companion of his youth', was informed by Mill's resurrection of what has been referred to as 'a vast and compelling symbol of momentous change in British power and residency in India'[94] – the British hostage-taking of Tipu Sultan's young sons after his surrender of the Third Anglo-Mysore war of 1789-1792. Although the aftermath of this war reflected unfavourably upon the East India Company, British discomfort at the

on the face of the earth', *Speeches from the dock*, Timothy Sullivan and Denis Sullivan (eds), (Dublin, 1867), p.56.
92. *The Orientalist*, vol.2, p.221.
93. The Second Anglo-Maratha War of 1803-1805 was fought between the East India Company and the Maratha Confederacy, an empire which covered much of South Asia at its peak.
94. De Almeida and Gilpin, *Indian renaissance*, p.147.

recollection of their humiliating defeat in the Second Anglo-Mysore war necessitated the rendering of their discomforting settlement of the Third into a jubilant victory. By presenting the seizure of the young princes as a munificent act and casting the Indian Governor-general, Lord Cornwallis, in the role of a paternalistic benefactor, Mill's *History* revivified the longstanding chauvinistic interpretation of this hostage-taking. Similarly, by accrediting Jesswunt's Christian principles to the ameliorative influence of his British tutor, *The Orientalist* accedes to this pre-established colonial discourse.

Overall, the choice of Bharatpur as a setting for Jesswunt's early history is a politically charged one as Runjeet Singh's real-life reconciliation with the British had served to promote a self-confirming image of British rule in India as an act of benevolent paternalism. In the final volume of his *History*, for example, Mill describes how the governor-general, Lord Cornwallis, 'exercised an uncommon degree of lenity and forbearance' when apprised of Runjeet Singh's traitorous designs.[95] According to Mill, Cornwallis determined that 'the characteristic lenity and mercy of the British government, required that a due indulgence should be manifested towards the imbecility, ignorance, and indolence of the native chiefs'.[96] Philosophically committed to liberal utilitarianism, Mill presents the degeneracy of native Indian sovereigns as evidence for the necessity of a utilitarian system of reform. Interestingly, *The Orientalist*'s reimagining of this history re-enforces the conservative orientalist perspective that Mill's *History* was dedicated to eradicating. Once deeming the East India Company as one of his 'bitterest enemies',[97] on witnessing Jesswunt's grief at the death of the Reverend Macdonald, Runjeet Singh pardons Jesswunt's Anglo-Irish father and anticipates their reunion. By creatively adapting the historical record in this manner, *The Orientalist* proffers a fictional rebuff of Mill's utilitarian assessment of colonial Indian politics. Bestowing the Maharajah with the rational cognition to realise his error as well as the authority to pardon an East India Company officer, *The Orientalist* recasts the familial dynamics of British imperial relations by assigning the Hindu sovereign a limited patriarchal authority under the broader sovereignty of British imperial rule. The siege of Bharatpur thus provides the author of *The Orientalist* with an opportunity to probe the symbolic import of the patriarchal family within British imperial politics. Its vision of familial reconciliation, in turn, functions as a metonym for reconciliation at an imperial level.

In *The Orientalist*, as in many Irish novels of the period, India can at times function as a figurative terrain upon which Ireland's future role

95. Mill, *History of British India*, vol.3, p.685.
96. Mill, *History of British India*, vol.3, p.685.
97. *The Orientalist*, vol.2, p.223.

within the British Empire can be mapped. The death of Taswell and the imprisonment of Murray in the final volume appear to herald the dawn of a more conciliatory attitude towards both the Union and Irish participation in British imperialism. And yet, the denouement of the novel suggests that its conciliatory conservative orientalism is not wholly at odds with the latent radical nationalism present within the greater part of the novel. As *The Orientalist* hurtles towards its conclusion, the threads of its various plots entwine to imbue the novel's conservative appreciation of Indian cultural traditions with an anti-colonial edge. With the final resolution of Jesswunt and Eleanor's romance hinging upon the outcome of events in India, *The Orientalist* ultimately undermines any attempt to deploy the Orient as an Irish political allegory. Following the Clanroys to England in the hope of having his second marriage proposal accepted by Lady Eleanor, Jesswunt learns that his father, Lord Dalkieth, Duke of Dunluce, has just arrived in England from India on a mission to trace his son and daughter. This discovery delivers a final blow to Jesswunt and Eleanor's budding relationship. Once son and father are reunited, 'Eleanor's image [no longer] intrude[s] on [Jesswunt] Dalkieth as his every thought [is] devoted to his father'.[98] Describing *The Wild Irish girl* as the novel 'that sets the template for the integration of love and marriage within a national plot', Claire Connolly argues that its conclusion 'suggests the promise of sympathy to redress historical wrong and correct asymmetries of power, as well as the narrative instabilities attendant on such an outcome'.[99] However, as Connolly also notes, from the 1820s onwards, Irish novels 'become increasingly equivocal regarding the management of affect within plots of cross-cultural marriage'.[100] In its refusal to conform to the Anglo-Irish marriage trope, *The Orientalist* rebukes such political harmonising. Angered by the revelation that his niece previously refused his son's proposal, the Duke of Dunluce 'disdains to accept an *honour* which the Marquis of Dalkieth [Jesswunt] ought not now to crave'.[101] By brusquely thwarting the projected union between the Anglo-Irish Eleanor and the Indo-Irish Jesswunt, *The Orientalist* overturns the conventions established by Owenson's most famous Irish national tale.

In the place of an intra-imperial union of hearts and minds, *The Orientalist* founds its vision of cross-colonial solidarity on a globally oriented cosmopolitanism. If the Romantic ideal of a Celtic Ireland generates much of this text's comic momentum, the theme of a cross-colonial fraternal bond is considered in a much more serious light.

98. *The Orientalist*, vol.2, p.392.
99. Connolly, *Cultural history*, p.96.
100. Connolly, *Cultural history*, p.122.
101. *The Orientalist*, vol.2, p.418.

Though the text gently mocks the metropolitan pretensions of the Anglo-Irish gentility, this is not at the expense of a sincere cosmopolitan consciousness. By centring the plot's resolution on a fictionalised account of the East India Company's 1805 Siege of Bharatpur, the author of *The Orientalist* reveals herself to be a globally connected individual who seeks to engage seriously with socio-political realities not only in Ireland but in the modern East. Refuting the gendered premises of an allegorical union between England and Ireland (or indeed India), the novel insists that any vision of Ireland's future must rest on a more substantial political basis than allegorical romance. Furthermore, in the final chapter, the narrative severely critiques the fictional subordination of female identity to national politics via its exposition of Lady Eleanor's melancholy fate. Unable to articulate her feelings for Jesswunt, 'in his anxiety for his father' he does not observe her 'death-like paleness' at his departure.[102] Unfortunately, because Jesswunt decides to prioritise his patrilineal connection to the Duke over the possibility of a marital union with Eleanor, the narrative reinforces the allegorical subordination of its female characters that its conclusion ostensibly seeks to challenge. Nevertheless, the text's parodical and self-reflexive engagement with Celticism and Orientalism provides an exceptional insight into the mutability of Irish Romantic conceptions of India and its multivalent role in Irish literary efforts to imagine a political future for Ireland, whether based upon intra-imperial affinities, cross-colonial resistance or a global (and potentially revolutionary) cosmopolitanism.

102. *The Orientalist*, vol.2, p.391.

Orientalism and 'textual attitude': Bernier's appropriation by Southey and Owenson

DANIEL SANJIV ROBERTS

Reviewing Robert Southey's epic poem set in India, *The Curse of Kehama*, Sir Walter Scott commented in 1811 on the lengthy notes which accompanied the poetic text: 'The notes contain a profusion of eastern learning, and the massive blocks which Mr Southey has selected as specimens of Brahminical poetry and mythology, give us [...] an idea of the immense quarries, in which the author must have laboured'.[1] Like many antiquarian and orientalist writers of the period, Southey attached a vast amount of source material to his primary text, keying images of peoples, places and things, as well as geographical and historical details, taken from an impressive range of Indological works, to individual lines, incidents and characters in his poem, evidently buttressing his poetic narrative with orientalist scholarship. Turning to the modern critical edition of Southey's work which identifies his numerous sources,[2] it is striking how heterogeneous these materials are, drawn from several European and classical oriental languages, as well as representing a huge span of geographical and historical information. This feature of orientalist (and similarly antiquarian) literature appears to support what Edward Said described as a 'textual attitude' to the East among Europeans, the reliance and interdependence of European authors on a vast body of writing which supported their imaginative portrayals of the East, even as they themselves contributed to that growing corpus by producing their own works of literature.

This textual accumulation, as Said asserts, exerts over time a powerful discursive force which cannot be countered, at least until the subject nations of the East are able to 'write back' to the Empire. The evidence of a shared European compendium of Eastern knowledge suggested by the extensive footnotes to many a major work of orientalist literature would at first glance appear to support Said's thesis admirably. Despite the considerable enmities and rivalries between European powers at this time, not least in relation to their commercial and territorial ambitions in the East, it would appear that European writers were by and large

1. 'The Curse of Kehama: by Robert Southey', *Quarterly review* 5 (1811), p.40-61 (61).
2. Robert Southey, *The Curse of Kehama*, ed. Daniel Sanjiv Roberts (London, 2003).

prepared to partake in a collective conception of the Orient, hypothesised in opposition to western forms.[3] The widespread dissemination of major translations and adaptations of European orientalists and travellers to the East thus seems to attest to a subterranean discursive field underpinning European knowledge of the Orient. Hence Southey's collation and compression of these diverse sources into the mythological purview of his poem appears to fulfil Said's much discussed notion of orientalism, that it represents a discursive formation which enabled the 'enormously systematic discipline by which European culture was able to manage – and even produce – the Orient politically, sociologically, militarily, ideologically, scientifically, and imaginatively during the post-Enlightenment period'.[4]

Said's thesis regarding orientalism and his conclusions about what he considered to be its inevitable geopolitical fallout have attracted considerable criticism in recent decades, from historians, literary and art critics and critical theoreticians.[5] In relation to such attempts, this chapter seeks to examine the relatively neglected *textual* dimensions of Said's argument with regard to the long eighteenth century by paying close attention to the way in which orientalist texts were circulated, disseminated and incorporated into other works through the British Isles and the continent during this period. By placing this analysis in the wide context of European orientalism – the sphere of enquiry which Said's work explicitly addressed – a clearer picture will emerge of the textual exchanges underpinning Said's argument. While Walter Scott's tribute quoted above to Robert Southey's Indian poem suggests (in keeping with Said) a shared materiality with regard to eighteenth-century orientalism – its building blocks taken from the 'vast quarries' of Indological scholarship – the aim of this essay is to re-examine the edifice of orientalism as a textual artefact, and to query the discursive conclusions of Said's argument. The question is whether the common

3.   Despite his often Francophobic view of French authors, Southey's notes to his 'Arabian romance' *Thalaba the Destroyer* (1800) comment favourably on Antoine Galland's 'translation' of the *Arabian nights* even while rubbishing their supposed originals: 'The Arabian tales certainly abound with genius; they have lost their metaphorical rubbish in passing through the filter of a French translation.' See Robert Southey, *Thalaba the destroyer*, ed. Tim Fulford (London, 2003), p.194.

4.   Said, *Orientalism*, p.3.

5.   A broad spectrum of critical approaches to orientalism in relation to art, architecture, design, music and theatre, may be gleaned from John Mackenzie's study, *Orientalism: history, theory and the arts* (Manchester, 1995). Other significant critiques of Said's work have focused on gender, race and religion. See Meyda Yegenoglu, *Colonial fantasies: towards a feminist reading of orientalism* (Cambridge, 1998); Tony Ballantyne, *Orientalism and race: Aryanism in the British Empire* (Basingstoke, 2006); and Richard King, *Orientalism and religion: post-colonial theory, India and the mystic East* (London, 1999), among other notable responses to Said's work.

eighteenth-century practice of quoting orientalist texts implies a shared discursive understanding of the East during the period as Said argued, or whether this practice conceals discontinuities and disparities between the texts and authors involved that might disturb the ideological façade represented by orientalism. This essay focuses on the figure of François Bernier, a French traveller to the Mughal Empire during the reign of Aurangzeb in the latter part of the seventeenth century, who is quoted as the first of Southey's sources in the 'Notes' to *Kehama* in 1810. In comparison with Southey's use of Bernier we shall turn to the Irish writer Sydney Owenson's novel, *The Missionary*, published in 1811, just a year after *The Curse of Kehama*, which also crucially references Bernier's text, providing a useful test case to examine the constancy (or lack of it) of Bernier's significance for both writers. Considering Bernier's textual significance across the long eighteenth century in this way allows us to determine: firstly, whether Bernier's oft-quoted work retains any ideological consistency across more than a century of European contact between the heyday of the Mughal Empire towards the end of the seventeenth century, and the emergence of the British Empire on the ruins of its demolition by the early nineteenth; and secondly, what is involved, aesthetically and politically, in the absorption of Bernier within the English literary texts of Southey and Owenson. Finally, we shall return to the vexed issue of the western 'will to power' allegedly involved in all such textual transactions: do the intertextual links between these works serve as material evidence of what Said described as the discursive nature of orientalism?

Bernier's *Travels*, as they are commonly known in English, were first published in Paris as *Histoire de la dernière Révolution des Etats du Grand Mogol* (1670) and *Suite des Mémoires [...] sur l'empire du Grand Mogol* (1671) and was followed within the year by an English translation from London by Henry Oldenburg. A pirated edition of his work came out promptly at The Hague in 1671, and Dutch, German and Italian translations, apart from the English, appeared between the 1671 and 1675.[6] Bernier's work became the staple of several historical accounts of Mughal India during the eighteenth and nineteenth centuries, feeding into a wide range of

6. For a full bibliography of the early editions in Paris, London, Amsterdam, The Hague, Frankfurt and Milan, see *Travels in the Mogul Empire* (New Delhi, 1999), p.xxv-xxx. The imprint page of the Indian edition of 1999, itself a reprint of the 1914 London edition cited below, indicates that it is the fourth impression since 1989, attesting to its continued significance as a key source of Mughal history in modern India, though historians have drawn attention to the shortcomings of Bernier's perspective. For the purpose of this essay I shall quote from the 1671-1672 translation by Henry Oldenburg which was available to English writers of the long eighteenth century, *The History of the late revolution of the empire of the Great Mogol* (London, Moses Pitt, Simon Miller, and John Starkey, 1671) and *A Continuation of the memoires of Monsieur Bernier*, 2 vols (London, Moses Pitt, 1672).

orientalist scholarship throughout Europe, and later English translations appeared in 1826 and 1914.[7] Most notably, in the long perspective, his depiction of the Mughal imperial system has been associated with the notion of 'Oriental despotism', a staple of orientalist representations from the eighteenth century onwards; this aspect of his work has received significant attention in relation to texts as diverse as Dryden's tragedy of *Aureng-Zebe* (1675), Montesquieu's *L'Esprit des lois* (1748) and Marx's view of the so-called Asiatic mode of production which is part of his theory of historical materialism.[8] However, it should also be noted in this regard that Bernier's analysis of Mughal society based on a supposed absence of private property ownership has required considerable corrective intervention from political historians; in this respect Bernier's work is now recognised to be misleading though certainly influential. The object of this analysis however is not to evaluate the accuracy of Bernier's work, but to consider its textual significance and deployment in relation to British perspectives in the context of literary works by Southey and Owenson published in 1810 and 1811.

Turning to Bernier's work as it appeared in the 1670s, it is important to register that he was writing before the emergence of full-scale European imperialism in India, although, as he notes, European soldiers were already engaged in the internecine struggles of the warring states in Mughal India. In relation to what has been referred to as the myth of Mughal decline[9] in the eighteenth century, we may remind ourselves that by 1700, Aurangzeb's empire stretched across north India from Kabul to Assam and had extended in the south almost to Kanyakumari, the tip of the peninsular. On the other hand, European trading companies were strongly in competition with each other in India; the English (1600), Dutch (1602) and Danish (1616) East India Companies were already in operation from the early seventeenth century, and it is noteworthy that the powerful French finance minister Jean-Baptiste Colbert (who was instrumental in forming the Compagnie des Indes Orientales in 1664) received advice from Bernier. Among the most closely studied sections of Bernier's *Travels* – which included several public letters to fellow intellectuals in France interested in oriental matters – was his letter to Colbert on 'the extent of India, the circulation of gold and silver [...] the riches, forces, justice, and the principle cause of the decay of the states of Asia'. Despite the critical note struck by Bernier's *Travels* in

---

7. *Bernier's travels: comprehending a description of the Mogol Empire including the kingdom of Kashmir*, trans. John Steuart (Calcutta, 1826), *Travels in the Mogul Empire*, trans. Irving Brock (London, 1826), and *Travels in the Mogul Empire*, ed. and trans. by Archibald Constable and revised by Vincent A. Smith (London, 1914).
8. Nicholas Dew, *Orientalism in Louis XIV's France* (Oxford, 2009), p.133.
9. See the essay by Seema Alavi in this volume (p.283-300).

relation to Mughal pretensions to power – it might seem paradoxical
that he describes Aurangzeb's empire as decaying even while it was
expanding its territories – it is notable too that his philosophical and
political thinking held an obvious critical edge in relation to French
politics as well. As Nicholas Dew comments, in 'recent historiography,
the most common way of commenting on the "Letter to Colbert" is to
read Bernier's description of the politics of India as a form of allegory on
what is usually thought of as the nascent "absolutism" of Louis XIV'.[10] In
another key chapter of the *Travels*, Bernier's letter to Jean Chapelain, an
associate of Colbert, Bernier described the 'superstitions, strange
fashions, and doctrine of the native Indies, or Gentiles of Indostan', a
chapter purporting to show 'that there are no opinions so ridiculous,
and so extravagant, which the spirit of man is not capable of'.[11] However,
Bernier's criticisms of Hindu idolatry and superstition are subject to the
criticism that he was living in India under Muslim patronage during a
period of increasing Muslim orthodoxy led by Aurangzeb. We observe
that at times Bernier sides with his 'aga' (or patron) Danishmand Khan in
ridiculing the stories of Hindu pandits, including the very pandit
employed by Danishmand Khan as an informant. Yet these drawbacks,
which are important to note, were not immediately apparent to his
contemporaries.

   To a large extent Bernier's account of the Mughal Empire may have
gained credence and authority amongst his contemporaries on account
of the sceptical and philosophical approach which he brought to his
observations in India. Bernier's willingness to submit various claims he
encountered to scientific and empirical scrutiny led him to be a fierce
critic of the many fakirs and holy men he encountered in India; on
occasion he dissembled as a believer in miracles only to record in his
Travels the credulousness of common people and the artifices practised
by those he sees as religious charlatans. Philosophically speaking, Bernier
was first and foremost a disciple of Pierre Gassendi, the free-thinking
and controversial early Enlightenment figure whose work spanned the
disciplines of philosophy and theology, mathematics and astronomy,
among other areas of enquiry. Although his *Travels* have proved to be the
more enduring work, by far the greater part of Bernier's *œuvre* consists of
abridgements and defences of Gassendi's philosophy which he sought to
reconcile with Cartesian philosophy. Indeed, he translated Gassendi and
Descartes into Persian for his master Daneshmand Khan, suggesting a
strong element of cultural and intellectual interchange in Mughal India

10. Dew, *Orientalism in Louis XIV's France*, p.134.
11. Bernier, *A Continuation*, p.103 (t.3: this work is divided into four 'tomes' which are issued
    within the volume, though numbered separately).

which clearly does not apply to British administration of India in the early 1800s when Southey and Owenson produced their works. That there is today evidently no surviving text of Bernier's Persian translation – surely a significant work of intellectual exchange in its own right – might be attributed to the increasing vernacularisation of Persian studies in India over the eighteenth century,[12] and the implementation of an English-medium educational policy after the English Education Act of India in 1835. The survival of manuscripts is obviously linked to such factors even if it is difficult to ascertain the exact moment of disappearance. This examination of Bernier's work is placed therefore in a changing landscape of intellectual history with regard to India's global outlook during the *longue durée* of colonial history.

Since a comprehensive discussion of Bernier's multi-faceted representation of Mughal India is not possible within the scope of this essay, we shall turn our attention to two portions of Bernier's work which are crucially used by Southey and Owenson respectively: firstly, Bernier's critique of Hindu (or, in his terminology, 'Gentile') superstition in India, and particularly of the role of the Brahmin priests and religious authorities who in his opinion furthered such beliefs for their own ends; and, secondly, his famous and vivid account of travelling with the Emperor Aurangzeb's massive army which included 100,000 horsemen and a camp of 300,000-400,000 persons on one of the emperor's campaigns from Delhi to Kashmir, the fabled 'paradise of the East' which Bernier was the first to describe for European readers.[13] Hence, Bernier's questioning attitude to popular beliefs and customs of the Hindus, his observations on the extent of power wielded by the Mughal emperor and his vivid descriptions of travel through the harsh desert areas of Northern India prior to his arrival in the oriental paradise of Kashmir, are all integral to the later narratives devised by Southey and Owenson.

At the same time, it should be noted that both Southey and Owenson wrote in the context of considerable metropolitan interest in India, which included a hotly contested pamphlet war regarding the issue of the East India Company's role in Indian governance. Whereas the earlier commercially-driven policy of the East India Company had been not to interfere in local customs and beliefs, from the early 1800s however there were increasing calls for the Company to engage in the evangelisation and western-style education of India. The appointment of the influential Clapham Sect Evangelical, Charles Grant, as the Chairman of the Board of Directors of the East India Company in 1805 led to a marked increase in such efforts, and metropolitan debates surrounding their appropri-

12. See Seema Alavi's essay in this volume (p.283-300).
13. These portions are contained within *A Continuation of the memoires of Monsieur Bernier*.

ateness for India. Following an incident of rebellion amongst the native soldiers of East India Company against the European officers of the 69th Foot regiment in Vellore in 1806 there was a manifest polarisation of opinion regarding missionary activity in India. The incident was reputedly provoked by the insistence of the commanding officer, Sir John Craddock, that native soldiers would not be permitted to wear turbans or beards or to carry caste marks. Rumours of forced conversions by Baptist missionaries in the south of India fuelled the discontent which broke out into a 'mutiny' by the Indian soldiers in which they fired on European barracks. While the mutiny was suppressed by the execution of around 100 native soldiers, the debate regarding cultural intervention continued to rage in the decade following the Vellore mutiny/massacre.[14] While both Southey's and Owenson's works are produced in this context, our task is to examine how Bernier's text is absorbed into the framework of their narratives.

Turning to Southey's opening note from Bernier, a description of the Hindu widow-burning ceremony of *sati*, we may begin to analyse more closely his use of Bernier's text. Bernier's significance as a reliable and early witness to this controversial practice is of obvious importance here. In the context of heated public debates and controversy regarding the role of the East India Company in the governance of India during the early nineteenth century, *sati* was a particularly volatile topic, appealing strongly to public sympathy and evidently justifying a more interventionist approach on the part of the Company. Southey's poem opens with the death and funeral of the despotic Rajah Kehama's son, Arvalan, who is killed by the father of a young peasant woman, Kailyal, whom Arvalan attempts to rape. Arvalan's death is the cause for a public funeral attended by the entire city; the funeral ends with a scene of *sati* in which Arvalan's wives perish, one of them, Azla, accepting her fate with calmness and dignity, while the other, the younger queen, Nealliny, is cruelly pushed to her death by the Brahmins. Southey's notes to the poem include several descriptions of *sati* taken from Bernier (he uses the Oldenburg translation verbatim). The first of these focuses on the resolution and even cheerfulness of the woman:

> She, says Bernier, whom I saw burn herself, when I parted from *Surat* to travel into *Persia*, in the presence of Monsieur *Chardin* of *Paris*, and of many *English* and *Dutch*, was of a middle age, and not unhandsome. To represent unto you the undaunted chearfulness that appeared in her countenance, the resolution with which she marched, washed herself, spoke to the people; the confidence with which she looked upon us, viewed her little cabin, made up of very dry millet-straw and small wood, went into this cabin, and sat down

14. For an account of this pamphlet war see David Kopf, *British orientalism and the Bengal renaissance: the dynamics of Indian modernisation* (Berkeley, CA, 1969), p.136-44.

upon the pile, and took her husband's head into her lap, and a torch into her
own hand, and kindled the cabin, whilst I know not how many *Brahmans* were
busy in kindling the fire round about: To represent to you, I say, all this as it
ought, is not possible for me; I can at present scarce believe it myself, though
it be but a few days since I saw it.[15]

This note taken from Bernier supports Southey's depiction of the elder
Queen Azla's death:

> Calmly she took her seat,
> Calmly the whole terrific pomp survey'd;
> As on her lap the while
> The lifeless head of Arvalan was laid.[16]

In this regard, Southey draws on Bernier's description to emphasise the
fortitude and strength of the woman. On the other hand, while Southey
clearly bases his portrayal of the woman's calmness on Bernier, quoting
his work accurately, his poetic text erases Bernier's insistence that she
plays a central and active participant in the proceedings, kindling the
cabin in which she places herself even as the Brahmins play a secondary
and supporting role in kindling the fire around the cabin, presumably to
seal her exit. Instead, Azla is reduced to a passive role, accepting her fate
heroically.

Not so Southey's younger queen, Nealliny. She is described in pathetic
terms, struggling against her inevitable fate:

> See in her swelling throat the desperate strength
> That with vain effort struggles yet for life;
> Her arms contracted now in fruitless strife,
> Now wildly at full length
> Towards the crowd in vain for pity spread, ...
> They force her on, they bind her to the dead.
> Then all around retire;
> Circling the pile; the ministring Bramins stand,
> Each lifting in his hand a torch on fire.
> Alone the Father of the dead advanced
> And lit the funeral pyre.[17]

Line 172, 'They force her on, they bind her to the dead', is keyed to a long
note citing several sources providing evidence for forced immolations of
women, the first of which is again taken from Bernier:

'Tis true, says Bernier, that I have seen some of them, which, at the sight of
the pile and the fire, appeared to have some apprehension, and that,
perhaps, would have gone back. Those demons, the Bramins, that are there

15. Southey, *The Curse of Kehama*, p.193.
16. Southey, *The Curse of Kehama*, p.14.
17. Southey, *The Curse of Kehama*, p.14-15.

with their great sticks, astonish them, and hearten them up, or even thrust them in; as I have seen it done to a young woman that retreated five or six paces from the pile, and to another, that was much disturbed when she saw the fire take hold of her clothes, these executioners thrusting her in with their long poles.

At Lahor, I saw a very handsome and a very young woman burnt; I believe she was not above twelve years of age. This poor unhappy creature appeared rather dead than alive when she came near the pile; she shook and wept bitterly. Meanwhile, three or four of these executioners, the Bramins, together with an old hag that held her under the arm, thrust her on, and made her sit down upon the wood; and, lest she should run away, they tied her legs and hands; and so they burnt her alive. I had enough to do to contain myself for indignation.[18]

Once more, it is instructive to consider Southey's departures from his source. While Bernier is clearly prepared to accord a degree of heroism and dignity to the women who are both agents in their own destruction and the victims of social abuse, he reserves his ire for the Brahmins who in his view disseminate and inculcate such practices. While the women are either deluded or coerced into the rite, it is the Brahmins, the priestly agents of *sati*, who are the real object of Bernier's criticisms. They are described as 'executioners' and quite literally demonised by Bernier. Yet Bernier himself we may note was powerless to intervene in this instance, despite his anger at the Brahmins. In Southey's portrayal however, the final act of destruction symbolised by the lighting of the pyre is committed by the Rajah Kehama himself, the Brahmins are merely ministers of his will. What is described by Bernier (and other sources) as a cultural practice presided over by the high-caste Brahmins but also evidently accepted by lower-caste participants, is attributed in Southey's depiction, to the will of a ruling elite headed by the king himself. By focusing attention on the Rajah Kehama as the ultimate perpetrator of the act Southey redirects Bernier's intellectual critique (against the ecclesiastical caste of Brahmins) to one that is directed to governance (the Rajah). Apart from Bernier, Southey cites an impressive range of travel sources, Pietro Della Valle, John Splinter Stavorinus, Bernard Picart and Charles Dellon to illustrate his point regarding the supposedly deluded and forced nature of many *satis*. Such sources are ranged against the views of Captain Mark Wilks, a supporter of the non-interventionist policy of the East India Company:

Yet if we are to believe the anti-missionaries, none but fools, fanatics, and pretenders to humanity, would wish to deprive the Hindoo women of the right of burning themselves! 'It may be useful (says Colonel Mark Wilks), to examine the reasonableness of interfering with the most exceptionable of all

18. Southey, *The Curse of Kehama*, p.194.

their institutions. It has been thought an abomination not to be tolerated, that a widow should immolate herself on the funeral pile of her deceased husband. But what judgement should we form of the Hindoo, who (if any of our institutions admitted the parallel) should *forcibly* pretend to stand between a Christian and the hope of eternal salvation? And shall we not hold him to be a driveller in politics and morals, a fanatic in religion, and a pretender in humanity, who would forcibly wrest this hope from the Hindoo widow'.[19]

Apart from his *sati* representations, Southey drew heavily on Bernier's depiction of the Jagannath procession and his imputations of sexual improprieties on the part of the priests at Jagannath in crucial later sections of the poem. Bernier's attraction for Southey resides evidently in his sceptical and anti-institutional slant though Southey himself had turned from a radical position in the 1790s to a far more conservative one by this point. While Bernier's criticisms of Brahminical priestcraft would appear compatible with a radical or dissenting outlook in post-revolutionary Britain, in fact Southey uses it to *displace* his earlier radicalism focusing it on the distant location of India, while turning to a more strongly establishment position at home.

Despite Southey's evident and professed obligation to Bernier, it should be noted that his use of Bernier is carefully selective and dispenses with aspects of Bernier's critique, which do not suit him. For instance, Bernier's comment that

the Mahumetans, that bear sway at present in Indostan, are enemies to that barbarous custome, and hinder it as much as they can; not opposing it absolutely, because they are willing to leave their idolatrous people, who are far more numerous than themselves, in the free exercise of their Religion, for fear of some revolt: but by indirectly preventing it, in that they oblige the Women, ready to burn themselves, to go and ask permission of the respective Governors, who send for them, make converse with their own Women, remonstrate things to them with annexed promises, and never give them this permission, but after they have tried all these gentle ways, and till they find them fixt in their sottish resolution.[20]

On the other hand Southey quotes the *Commentaries* of Alboquerque: 'Let it suffice to mention one important historical fact: when the great Alboquerque had established himself at Goa, he forbade these accursed sacrifices, the women extolled him for it as their benefactor and deliverer (*Commentarios de Alb.* ii. 20) and no European in India was ever so popular, or so revered by the natives.'[21] Southey ignores the more recent evidence of the Mughal containment of *sati*, to invoke the fifteenth-century figure

19. Southey, *The Curse of Kehama*, p.195.
20. Bernier, *A Continuation*, p.114-15.
21. Southey, *The Curse of Kehama*, p.195.

of the Portuguese governor of Goa, Alfonso de Alboquerque (1453-1515), who proffers a more suitable example for Southey's colonialist and evangelical position, being European and Christian – if not quite English and Protestant. Furthermore Bernier's suggestion that the Mughal rulers dealt cautiously with such customs for fear of reprisals, clearly does not fit with his strongly interventionist thinking. Bernier's depiction of *sati* makes no claims for European involvement in the matter. Far from being supportive of Hindu practices, the Islamic Mughal rulers are shown to be cautious and sensitive in their handling of such cases. On the other hand, the credulous Hindu population manipulated or swayed by Brahminical wile are seen as the originators of the custom. Retaining Bernier's sympathy for the women (a standard feature of several European en-gagements with *sati*), Southey turns it into a critique of East India Company governance in India, which was represented as being too much in league with native ruling elites and practices.

Southey's admiring reference to Portuguese rule in Goa, provides a convenient transition to the second text we shall examine in relation to Bernier: Sydney Owenson's novel, *The Missionary*, published in 1811. Although Owenson published her novel only a year after *The Curse of Kehama*, directing her work to a similar context of debate regarding evangelical activity in India, she chose to set her novel in seventeenth-century Goa rather than the more immediate milieu of British India. Even more particularly, Bernier appears as a fictional figure in her text, functioning as a philosophical observer if not actually participating in the events of the novel. Owenson's story of the zealous Franciscan monk, Hilarion, whose grand attempts to bring the Hindu population of India to Christianity through his conversion of the Brahmin priestess, Luxima, quickly – and somewhat predictably – develops into a romance between the central characters of Hilarion and Luxima. Owenson returns specifi-cally to the seventeenth century of Bernier's India to place her novel within the context of emerging European ambitions for the domination of India. At a critical juncture, the missionary Hilarion discovers the true nature of his less-than-Platonic love for Luxima through the appearance of a potential rival, the Moghul prince Solyman Sheko, Aurangzeb's nephew, drawing an obvious parallel with contending European and Mughal perspectives with regard to the 'native' Indian population which is premised as Hindu.[22] Here, the Hindu woman, Luxima, represents India in terms of a feminised Eastern other, while Hilarion, the am-bitious missionary, represents a masculine and 'commanding' view of the West. Their meeting represents, at first sight, a polar encounter between

22. Michael J. Franklin has convincingly traced Owenson's portrayal of Solyman Sheko to Alexander Dow's *History of Hindostan*. See Franklin, 'Radically feminizing India', in Franklin (ed.), *Romantic representations*, p.171-72.

East and West: 'she like the East, lovely and luxuriant; he, like the West, lofty and commanding'.[23]

Owenson's interpolation of a rival contender for Luxima's affections in the character of the haughty Muslim nobleman complicates however the binary opposition between East and West which the relationship between Hilarion and Luxima suggests. Placing the action of the novel prior to the widespread colonisation of India which the Company had effectively embarked upon from 1757 (the Battle of Plassey), Owenson draws attention to a period in history when the European presence in India was relatively insecure and unclear as to its future. Offering his hand to Luxima, Solyman compares his pretensions with those of Hilarion: 'With me thou mayst one day reign upon the throne of India, and yet become the empress of thine own people; what he can proffer thee, besides his love, I know not.' The masculine and imperial attitudes of Christians and Muslims are simultaneously opposed to the feminine and subjugated attributes of the Hindu population. Owenson's depiction of the allegedly credulous Hindu population of India – at one level simple, hospitable and unassuming in nature – but controlled by a sinister and somewhat cynical Brahminical religious establishment, clearly owes much to Bernier, producing consequentially a similar polarisation to Southey's between the priestly caste and the common folk.

Despite these continuities between the three texts however, Owenson's position regarding missionary intervention on the part of the British is strikingly different from Southey's. As Julia Wright points out in her edition of *The Missionary*, Portugal's domination of Goa evokes, for the author of *The Wild Irish girl*, the English colonisation of Ireland and the restive nature of Irish politics in the wake of the Union of 1800. In the context of repressive legislation against Catholics and dissenters in Ireland prior to Catholic emancipation in 1829, incidents such as the Vellore massacre of 1806 recall the spectre of the Irish rebellion of 1798 and further uprisings such as that of 1803.[24] The impatient and angry mood of the populace in Goa which Owenson describes as a 'sullen gloom [...] the brooding of a distant storm' is excited by the sight of Luxima entering 'a convent of Dominican nuns, led by an officer of the Inquisition, and surrounded by Dominican and *Jesuit priests!*' Owenson adds a footnote referring to the Vellore 'mutiny' of 1806 which was followed by another uprising in Nandidurg and Bangalore: 'both were supposed to have originated in the religious bigotry of the natives, suddenly kindled by the supposed threatened violation of their faith

23. Sydney Owenson, *The Missionary*, ed. Julia Wright (Peterborough, Ontario, 2002), p.109.
24. Owenson, *The Missionary*, p.19-29.

from the Christian settlers.'[25] Here, it would appear that the more circumspect approach of the Mughal rulers cited by Bernier would be far more efficacious than the uncompromising intervention recommended by supporters of the evangelical wing of the East India Company. In the tragic denouement of the novel, Luxima attempts to commit *sati* at the *auto da fe* intended for Hilarion who falls foul of the Spanish Inquisition on account of his relationship with the Brahmin priestess. In the mêlée caused by the popular insurrection that follows both Hilarion and Luxima are wounded but manage to escape, though only for Luxima to die later from her injury. With her dying breath she exhorts Hilarion to preach tolerance to the Christians: 'that the sword of destruction, which has been this day raised between the followers of thy faith and mine, may be for ever sheathed!'[26] Owenson's conflation of the *sati* with the *auto da fe* provides a fitting culmination to the series of parallels which Owenson draws between Christian and Hindu beliefs and practices through the novel.

Yet the story does not end there. Bernier makes one final appearance in the novel. In the aftermath of the events described in the novel, twenty years later, as specified by Owenson, the emperor Aurangzeb, representative of 'the most powerful and despotic dynasty of the earth' visits Kashmir. 'In the immense and motley multitude which composed his suite, there was an European *Philosopher*, who highly distinguished by the countenance and protection of the emperor, had been led, by philosophical curiosity and tasteful research, to visit a country, which more celebrated than known, had not yet attracted the observation of genius, or the inquiry of science.'[27] Among the many wonders of Kashmir, this philosopher is shown *one* object only, as Owenson specifies, which evokes an '*interest of sentiment*':

> It was a sparry cavern, among the hills of Srinagar, called, by the *natives* of the valley, the '*Grotto of congelations!*'* They pointed it out to strangers as a place constructed by magic, which for many years had been the residence of a recluse! A stranger, who had appeared suddenly among them, who had been rarely seen, and more rarely addressed, who led a lonely and innocent life, equally avoided and avoiding, who lived unmolested, awakening no interest, and exciting no persecution – 'he was', they said, 'a wild and melancholy man! Whose religion was unknown, but who prayed at the confluence of rivers, at the rising and setting of the sun; living on the produce of the soil, he needed no assistance, nor sought any intercourse; and his life, thus slowly wearing away, gradually faded into death.

> * Monsieur de Bernier laments, in his interesting account of his journey to Cashmire which he performed in the suite of Aurengzebe, that circum-

25. Owenson, *The Missionary*, p.241.
26. Owenson, *The Missionary*, p.257.
27. Owenson, *The Missionary*, p.260.

stances prevented him from visiting the grotto of congelations, of which so many strange tales were related by the natives of the valley.[28]

This philosopher, who is identified in Owenson's footnote as Bernier, provides the perspective which frames Owenson's narrative, even as the romance of the ill-fated missionary enters Indian folklore. The tolerant and all-absorbing capacity of Hindu mythology renders the missionary's story a sentimental narrative which blends into the 'strange tales related by the natives of the valley'. Owenson's meticulous citation of Bernier signals the sceptical and critical view he denotes which might be expected of the European reader confronted by such tales.

Owenson's unexpected fictionalisation of Bernier's figure in the penultimate paragraph of her novel directs us to the deeper obligation that her own text registers with regard to his work. Although she quotes a number of orientalist authorities, Bernier is uniquely given a fictional existence in her own text. Furthermore, Owenson's setting of the novel in seventeenth-century India and her use of Kashmir as a significant locale, denoting a sensual and paradisiac East, point to her conscious and substantial reworking of Bernier's *Travels* which she quotes from in both the French and English versions of the text. As with Southey, these citations of his text, bearing an objective and authoritative tone, appear to conform remarkably to her own purposes. Luxima's extraordinary beauty, a significant aspect of her popular appeal, is portrayed, citing Bernier, as a heightened form of what is typical to the women of that region: '"Certainly", says De Bernier, "if one may judge of the beauty of the sacred women by that of the common people, met with in the streets, they must be very beautiful".'[29]

From the page number of the edition she uses it is evident that Owenson quotes from the 1672 English translation of Henry Oldenburg.[30] A close comparison of the texts reveals however that her phrasing departs significantly from her source in some details. Page 96 of the 1672 translation by Oldenburg in fact reads: 'And certainly, if one may judge of the Beauty of the retired women by that of the Common People, met with in the Streets, and seen up and down in the Shops, we must believe, that there are very handsome ones.'[31]

---

28. Owenson, *The Missionary*, p.260. Michael Franklin identifies the 'grotto of congelations' as the cave of Amarnath, a famous natural shrine dedicated to Shiva; however it should be noted that whereas Owenson attributes the local name for the grotto to 'the splendour of the stalactites that hung like glittering icicles from its shining roof' (p. 107), the Amarnath cave in Srinagar is famed for the single massive stalagmite that forms on its floor and is worshipped by Shaivites as a *lingam*. See Franklin, *Romantic representation*, p.169.
29. Owenson, *The Missionary*, p.97.
30. Wright's otherwise helpful edition fails to note the edition used.
31. Bernier, *A Continuation*, p.96 (t.4).

Apart from the more emphatic tone achieved by abbreviating the second half of the quotation ('we must believe' is subtly altered to read 'they must be'), the 'retired women' of Bernier's text are substantively replaced by Owenson's 'sacred women'. Thus, Bernier's comment regarding Kashmiri women in *purdah*, a common feature of *Muslim* culture across India, is used to justify the beauty of the *Brahmin* priestess, Luxima. Owenson's lack of familiarity with Indian culture may be partly to blame for this transferral; however the effect is in fact deeply significant in shifting Bernier's admiration for the fairer-skinned Muslim women of Kashmir (whom he finds to be European in appearance and complexion) to the wholly invented category of the 'sacred women' of the Brahminical caste.

Owenson's deliberate reworking of Bernier's text clearly serves her own artistic purposes. By inventing the character of the 'Brahmin priestess',[32] Owenson introduces a feminine aspect to the male-dominated culture associated with the Brahmins (of which the practice of *sati* was an integral part), and suggests a means of reforming that culture from within. Moreover, her text levels a feminist critique of the masculinity, not only of the patriarchal Brahminical culture that was under scrutiny in the wake of evangelical criticisms of Hindu practices, but also, crucially, of the (mostly male) Christian missionaries who sought conversion in India through forceful means. It is worthwhile contrasting Owenson's position with Southey's who argued instead that: 'by an absurdity unparalleled in any other system, the religion of a Hindoo does not depend upon himself; it is something independent of his thoughts words, actions, understanding, and volition, and he may be deprived of it by violence, as easily as of his purse or his wallet'.[33] By separating religious affiliation from volition, Southey suggests that Hindus might be saved from the pernicious effects of their own religion by conversions effected through violence or guile, just as one might deprive a person of his wallet by mugging or pickpocketing him. By the perverse logic of Hindu belief – how does one argue against irrationality? – such conversions (if one follows Southey) were more likely to be efficacious than intellectual or spiritual means of persuasion.

Given the diametrically opposite views arrived at by Southey and Owenson with regard to missionary activity in India despite their respective uses of Bernier's work to support their positions, the question arises as to which of them might be regarded as more faithful to Bernier.

32. Within the traditions of Brahminical Hinduism, officiating priests are normally male. Women are generally proscribed from officiating at sacred rituals except in more popular forms of Hinduism.
33. Robert Southey, 'Periodical accounts relative to the Baptist Missionary Society', *Quarterly review* 1 (1811), p.208.

It is interesting therefore to return to Bernier's work, and to note the
French philosopher's view of European missionaries and Christian conversions in India. While ostensibly applauding the missions and
favouring 'pious and learned missionaries', in his Letter to his friend
and fellow-philosopher, Monsieur de la Mothe le Vayer, Bernier warns
particularly against certain other missionaries in India who fail to
practice their faith properly, 'who therefore would do better to keep
themselves close in their convents, and not come hither and give us a
masquerade of their religion, and by doing so, and by their ignorance,
jealousie, loosness, and the abuse of their authority and character,
become a stumbling-block to the Law of *Jesus Christ*'. Among the 'good
missionaries' in India, Bernier gives particular praise to the Jesuits and
Capucins who 'charitably entertain the Christians of the country in their
religion, whether they be Catholicks, or Greeks, or Armenians,
Nestorians, Jacobites, or others'.[34] On a pragmatic note, he adds that
European missions should not seek to fund their existence through local
means in India, but rather should be independently funded: 'Our
Christians of Europe ought to wish, and even to employ their power,
care and charity, that missionaries may be sent over all, such as may be no
charge to the people of the country, and whom want may not induce to
do mean things.'[35]

Yet Bernier holds out little hope for the kind of mass conversion of
India about which zealous missionaries dreamed, the specific ambition of
Owenson's missionary which forms the basis of her narrative. Dispelling
rumours put about by unscrupulous missionaries that India was open to
large-scale conversions, Bernier advises his correspondent 'not [...] to be
so easily perswaded of so many stories, and not to believe the thing to be
so facil as some make it' (p.90-91). Emphasising the veneration accorded
to Christ in Islamic thinking (which accepts the notion of his miraculous
birth from a virgin mother but only stops short of accepting his divinity),
Bernier adds with notable ambiguity: "Tis not to be hoped that they will
approve the rest of our religion, so as to abandon theirs in which they
were born, and their false prophet to embrace ours.'[36] Clearly, Bernier's
distrust of bigotry and sectarianism in the church, and his insistence that
missionary activity should not be achieved through revenues raised
among non-Christian peoples, map onto post-Unionist Catholic concerns in Ireland regarding evangelisation and taxation in support of the
established Anglican church. However, while Bernier's cautious attitude

34. Bernier, *A Continuation*, p.88, (t.3).
35. Bernier, *A Continuation*, p.90, (t.3).
36. Bernier's text contains the same ambiguity in French: 'en sorte qu'ils quittent la leur, dans
    laquelle ils sont nés, et leur faux Prophete, pour embrasser la nostre' (*Voyages de François
    Bernier* (Amsterdam, Paul Marret, 1709), p.86).

to European missions accords well with the critical perspective offered by Owenson in *The Missionary*, it is worth noting that she softens and feminises his depiction of Hinduism considerably through her invention of Luxima's character. On the other hand, although Bernier's antipathy to what he regarded as Hindu superstitions and Brahminical cunning is far more powerfully developed in Southey's poem than in Owenson's work, Southey's remarkably hardline position regarding the conversion of Hindus would have been utterly incompatible with Bernier's attitude regarding the proper conduct of missionaries. Moreover, neither the English writer nor the Irish one had any direct knowledge of India except through books, whereas Bernier's work was based on personal enquiries and observation, often sceptical of or at odds with earlier European reports on India.

A close analysis of Bernier's work in relation to Southey and Owenson thus exposes the considerable disparities that inform their texts and their attitudes to India. Examined in detailed conjunction with each other they undoubtedly reveal the opposed and conflicting views which orientalist texts often bore to each other. On the other hand, *pace* Said's argument, it is worth reminding ourselves that all three texts were directed specifically to European audiences, seeking to influence official policy and public opinion in significant ways with regard to India. While Southey quotes Bernier as a proto-Enlightenment castigator of priest-craft, he ignores Bernier's cautionary subtext with regard to the possibilities of insurgency drawn from his experience of Mughal rule in India, a subtext that reflects on European as well as Asian forms of despotism. Owenson on the other hand draws Bernier into her text directly, paying greater attention to his scientific and philosophical outlook which frames her sentimental narrative accordingly. Owenson is probably closer in spirit to Bernier than Southey in her citation of his work; though both later writers direct his text to a significantly altered moment in British colonial/Indian history, and one that Bernier could not have anticipated in any exact sense. Both Owenson and Southey read Bernier in a tendentious way, interpreting his account of Mughal decline as a prophetic vision of European imperialism and appropriating his text to their changed ends. Furthermore, Bernier is only one source – though certainly an important one – among many that they draw upon. Writing in the aftermath of new directions in Indo-orientalism based on Sanskrit and Hindu sources, and led by British Indologists such as William Jones and Charles Wilkins, Southey and Owenson show far greater awareness of Hindu culture – romanticising and feminising it through their characterisation of sympathetic though also victimised female figures such as Kailyal and Luxima – than Bernier's view of Mughal-dominated view of India might have allowed. Though all three writers – French,

English and Irish – view India through the lens of early to late Enlightenment superiority (none of them can operate outside its parameters of
rationality and judgement), and to this extent may be viewed as contributors to the textual edifice of orientalism, it would considerably
distort their individual perspectives and historical specificity to assimilate their texts within the supposedly unifying ideology of a western gaze.

Intellectual history as global history: Voltaire's *Fragments sur l'Inde* and the problem of enlightened commerce

FELICIA GOTTMANN

In recent years the concepts of 'interconnected' or 'global' history have made significant inroads into several historical disciplines, including amongst others economic, social and material history, history of science and the history of consumption. They have not yet, however, significantly impacted on the history of ideas, and, with the odd exception, are rarely considered in the realm of political economy.[1] This essay aims to contribute to this project by presenting a case study that proves the importance of India in the later eighteenth-century French evaluation of commerce.

It is a general consensus amongst scholars of French eighteenth-century political economy to posit a caesura around mid-century after which a younger generation of *lumières*, *philosophes*, or enlightened men of letters were said to have taken over. Some mark it with the publication of Montesquieu's *Esprit des lois* in 1748, some with that of Rousseau's first discourse in 1750, but most depict the period of the 1750s as a transition from a general optimism amongst the enlightened elite about the beneficial powers of commerce and luxury to greater nuance and scepticism, or from a period of a theoretical defence of trade and consumption, to a more critical interest in its practical implementation.[2]

One very prolific writer however, spans both sides of the divide:

1. A notable recent exception is Paul Cheney, *Revolutionary commerce: globalization and the French monarchy* (Cambridge, MA, 2010).
2. Hont considers the publication of the *Spirit of the laws* the end point of the early period of the debate: Istvan Hont, 'The early Enlightenment debate on commerce and luxury' in *The Cambridge history of eighteenth-century political thought*, ed. Mark Goldie and Robert Wokler (Cambridge, 2006), p.379-418. Sonenscher begins his account where Hont ends, with Montesquieu: Michael Sonenscher, *Before the deluge: public debt, inequality and the intellectual origins of the French Revolution* (Princeton, NJ, 2007). For Shovlin, change occurred from the 1750s onwards, when both public and elite interest began to focus on reform and political economy: John Shovlin, *The Political economy of virtue: luxury, patriotism, and the origins of the French Revolution* (Ithaca, NY, 2007). In her classic account Meyssonnier differentiates between three periods, which however still presume a bifurcation into a period of theory and one of practical reform. Simone Meyssonnier, *La Balance et l'horloge: la genèse de la pensée libérale en France au XVIIIe siècle* (Montreuil, 1989).

Voltaire's first publications on the subject of commerce date from the 1720s, his last from the mid-1770s. His intervention, and the role of India in it, will be our case study.

Together with Melon and the young Montesquieu, Voltaire was one of the first authors to propagate the Whiggish defence of commerce in France. Inspired by his stay in England (1726-1728), his contacts there with the merchant community and his readings of Mandeville and the *Spectator*, he openly extolled luxury and commerce from the 1730s onwards. Importantly, his optimism about their beneficial impact explicitly included India.

In his increasingly sophisticated defence of luxury and trade, Voltaire shared the views of several Enlightenment political economists on both sides of the Channel. These can be broadly classed into four interlinked arguments. Firstly, following Mandeville, almost all defenders of luxury adopted his assertion that there can be no clear and stable definition of what constitutes luxury; that it cannot be clearly differentiated from the necessary and is historically relative.[3] Secondly, they link commerce to man's original sociability, so that commerce, sociability and mutual benefit become inseparable from each other.[4] Thirdly commerce is associated with peace, both internally and through international co-operation; prosperity, by giving employment to the masses and banishing idleness; and with greater liberty, both political and personal; as well as with urbanity, softer manners, refinement, taste through the increased influence of women; and with a defence of modernity in general. It is thus opposed to barbarism, violence, bloodshed and poverty, and has all the connotations Albert O. Hirschman has summarised as the 'doux commerce' thesis.[5] Finally, with the advent of the 'caesura' or the 'second generation', we also see a greater nuance, in the form of a

3.   Bernard Mandeville, 'Remark L', in *The Fable of the bees or Private vices, publick benefits*, ed. F. B. Kaye, 2 vols (Oxford, 1924) I, p.107-23. Like Jean François Melon, Voltaire first makes this point in the 1730s and continues to do so throughout his career. See for instance 'Luxe' in both the *Dictionnaire philosophique* (1764) and the *Questions sur l'Encyclopédie* (1770-1772). See also Jeremy Jennings, 'The debate about luxury in eighteenth- and nineteenth-century French political thought', *The Journal of the history of ideas* 68 (2007), p.79-105 or Philippe Perrot, *Le Luxe: une richesse entre faste et confort, XVIIIe-XIXe siècle* (Paris, 1995).

4.   On theories of commercial sociability in France during the first half of the eighteenth century, see Henry C. Clark, *Compass of society: commerce and absolutism in old-regime France* (Lanham, MD, and Plymouth, 2007), p.75-108, p.75-108 and for the later developments his 'Commerce, sociability, and the public sphere: Morellet vs Pluquet on luxury', *Eighteenth-century life* 22 (1998), p.83-103. On Voltaire's adoption of this view see Felicia Gottmann, 'Du Châtelet, Voltaire, and the transformation of Mandeville's fable', *History of European ideas* 38.2 (2012), p.218-32.

5.   The best-known account of this remains Albert O. Hirschman, *The Passions and the interests: political arguments for capitalism before its triumph*, 20th anniversary edn (Princeton, NJ, 1997), p.56-87. However, see also Christopher J. Berry, *The Idea of luxury: a conceptual and historical investigation* (Cambridge, 1994).

widely-accepted differentiation between a 'good' and a 'bad' kind of luxury. This is most familiar to historians from the writings of Hume and in Saint-Lambert's *Encyclopédie* article 'Luxe',[6] but Voltaire also developed this view and – especially in his great histories of the 1750s, the *Essai sur les mœurs* and the *Siècle de Louis XIV* – differentiated between a positive, 'bourgeois' type of luxury and a noxious, 'feudal' type. The latter was associated with ostentation and a type of society in which the luxury of the few was paid for by the misery of the masses. The modern kind of luxury however, was associated with private bourgeois consumption and based on personal enjoyment and good taste. It retained all the positive connotations of commerce and luxury outlined above. Voltaire's concept of modern, bourgeois commerce thus became central to his depictions of progress, civilisation and Enlightenment.[7]

India figures in Voltaire's defences of modern commercialism from the very beginning. In the 1734 *Lettres philosophiques* for instance, Voltaire writes: 'un négociant [...] enrichit son pays, donne de son cabinet des ordres à Surate et au Caire, et contribue au bonheur du monde.'[8] A similarly positive statement occurs in *Le Mondain* (1736), this time adding the further dimensions of increased union and world peace to the notion of happiness:

> Le superflu, chose très nécessaire,
> A réuni l'un et l'autre hémisphère
> Voyez-vous pas ces agiles vaisseaux
> Qui, du Texel, de Londres, de Bordeaux,
> S'en vont chercher, par un heureux échange,
> De nouveaux biens, nés aux sources du Gange?[9]

In these earlier instances India serves but as a shorthand for the global dimension of the benefits of commerce. It is never more than a signifier

---

6. Hume, whom Voltaire read and admired, differentiates between an 'innocent' and a 'pernicious' kind of luxury: David Hume, 'Of luxury', in *Essays and treatises on several subjects*, 4 vols (London and Edinburgh, Millar and Kincaid, 1753-1756), IV, p.20-35, reprinted under its later title 'Of refinement in the arts' in David Hume, *Political essays*, ed. Knud Haakonssen (Cambridge, 1994), p.105-14. Saint-Lambert's entry 'Luxe' was included in volume nine of the *Encyclopédie* in 1764 and later published as a separate essay. It should be noted that Saint-Lambert relies on Forbonnais, who himself heavily relies on Hume.

7. This is especially prominent in his later historiographical writings. On this, see particularly O'Brien, *Narratives of Enlightenment*, p.11-12 and 21-55; John Robertson, 'Preface', *Essai sur les mœurs et l'esprit des nations II, avant-propos*, ch.1-37, *OCV* vol.22, p.xxxvii-xliii; and Pomeau's introduction to his edition of the *Essay*: 'Introduction', in *Essai sur les mœurs et l'esprit des nations et sur les prinicpaux faits de l'histoire, depuis Charlemagne jusqu'à Louis XIII*, ed. René Pomeau, 2 vols (Paris, 1963), p.I-LXVI.

8. Voltaire, *Lettres philosophiques*, ed. Frédéric Deloffre (Paris, 1986), p.76. The Gujarati city of Surat was an important commercial centre for all European East India Companies, although by this time its significance was already waning in favour of Bombay.

9. Voltaire, *Le Mondain*, ed. Haydn T. Mason, *OCV*, vol.16, p.295-313 (296).

and in itself is never central to the argument. In a later text, however, European trade with India is a main preoccupation: the *Fragments sur l'Inde et sur le général Lally*. Written and published in 1773-1774, *Fragments* brings together, apparently unlinked, remarks on the European powers in India; an exposé of Indian culture, history and religions; and a defence of the French general Lally, who, after an unsuccessful campaign in India during the Seven Years War, was brutally executed on trumped-up charges of high treason in 1766. The Lally case was, after the more famous examples of Calas and Sirven, Voltaire's last great campaign.

In the text Voltaire still depicts commerce as a central and crucial force for change. 'Ce sont des marchands', he writes, 'qui ont changé la face du monde'.[10] But the work also represents a complete rejection of all of the assertions about commerce outlined before, which for decades had been central to Voltaire's concepts of Enlightenment and civilisation.

Whereas before Voltaire saw commerce as promoting peace, prosperity and happiness, as well as liberty and thus human dignity, he now linked it to war, carnage and misery. The work opens with the following remarkable passage:

Dès que l'Inde fut un peu connue des barbares de l'Occident et du Nord, elle fut l'objet de leur cupidité; et le fut encore davantage, quand ces barbares, devenus policés et industrieux, se firent de nouveaux besoins. [...] Les Albuquerques et leurs successeurs ne purent parvenir à fournir du poivre et des toiles en Europe que par le carnage. Nos peuples européens ne découvrirent l'Amérique que pour la dévaster, et pour l'arroser de sang; moyennant quoi ils eurent du cacao, de l'indigo, du sucre.[11]

The condemnation seems an echo of that expressed by the mutilated Negro slave in *Candide*, who pays the price for the Europeans' enjoyment of sugar. As with sugar, the objects in question are typical of the international luxury trade at the time. They link the fate of India and the East Indies to that of America and the West Indies in one sweep: at this time most of the cocoa and sugar consumed in Europe came from Central and South America and the West Indies, whilst indigo, spices, pepper in particular, as well as fine fabrics, silks and calicoes (high-quality printed cottons) were imported from India and the East Indies.[12] What links all these places is that they suffer so that Europe can enjoy. The stress is not laid on the pleasures and sophistication resulting from luxury, but instead on the pain it causes, on greed and violence. Luxury

10. Voltaire, *Fragments sur l'Inde et sur le général Lalli*, p.55-262 (61).
11. Voltaire, *Fragments sur l'Inde*, p.59.
12. See for instance the classic account by J. H. Parry: *Trade and dominion: the European overseas empires in the eighteenth century* (London, 1974), p.59-61, 66-70, 92-100 and 374.

objects are not gained by commerce but by war, the produce in question is 'bought' by devastation and bloodshed. Trade is no longer a 'heureux échange' as in the *Mondain*, it is no longer based on sociable mutuality and mutually beneficial. The injustice is exacerbated by the fact that these are 'nouveaux besoins', they are not necessary for survival, only sought out of greed. Human life and happiness are 'traded in' for trivial consumer goods, the barbarity of which is underlined by the contrast of blood and devastation with sugar and cocoa. The divide between civilisation and barbarism, so crucial to the defence of luxury and commerce, has completely collapsed.

For Voltaire, the blame for this does not lie with the few 'Albuquerques' of this world, but squarely with those who benefit from luxury, either through the profits from selling it, or through desiring and enjoying it: 'Presque tous ces vastes domaines, ces établissements dispendieux, toutes ces guerres entreprises pour les maintenir, ont été le fruit de la mollesse de nos villes et de l'avidité des marchands, encore plus que de l'ambition des souverains' (p.60). The condemnation falls on the same bourgeois luxury with its traditional links to urbanity, 'mollesse' and merchants, that Voltaire had previously extolled. In what seems a complete volte-face from Voltaire's earlier position, the merchant no longer 'contribue au bonheur du monde' as he had done in the *Lettres philosophiques* but to global misery, to war, devastation and enslavement:

> Les successeurs des bracmanes, de ces inventeurs de tant d'arts, de ces amateurs et de ces arbitres de la paix, sont devenus nos facteurs, nos négociateurs mercenaires. Nous avons désolé leur pays, nous l'avons engraissé de notre sang. [...] Nos nations d'Europe se sont détruites réciproquement dans cette même terre où nous n'allons chercher que de l'argent, et où les premiers Grecs ne voyageaient que pour s'instruire. (p.62)

Unlike in the earlier defences of commerce, in which Voltaire depicted it as fostering peace, liberty and the arts and sciences, it is now divorced from all three, indeed directly opposed to them: luxury and trade, here in the guise of money, are explicitly contrasted to the arts and sciences or progress towards enlightenment, here summarised in the reference to 's'instruire'. The successors of the *bracmanes* have to give up the arts and love of peace to accept a position of servitude in commerce, and engaging in trade destroys their independence and liberty, indeed alienates them from themselves: they become '*nos* facteurs', '*nos* négociateurs'. The engagement in commerce which Voltaire had advocated as a certain way to personal independence and development during his English years, had turned into the very opposite.

The anti-luxury argument is made most strongly in the following section:

C'est pour fournir aux tables des bourgeois de Paris, de Londres et des autres grandes villes, plus d'épiceries qu'on n'en consommait autrefois aux tables des princes: c'est pour charger des simples citoyennes de plus de diamants que les reines n'en portaient à leur sacre: c'est pour infecter continuellement ses narines d'une poudre dégoûtante, pour s'abreuver, par fantaisie, de certaines liqueurs inutiles, inconnues à nos pères, qu'il s'est fait un commerce immense toujours désavantageux aux trois quarts de l'Europe; et c'est pour soutenir ce commerce que les puissances se sont fait des guerres, [...] nous n'avons jamais réfléchi que le plus grand et le plus rude des impôts est celui que nous imposons sur nous-mêmes par nos nouvelles délicatesses qui sont devenues des besoins, et qui sont en effet un luxe ruineux, quoiqu'on ne leur ait point donné le nom de luxe. (p.61)

Voltaire had given luxury and commerce critical connotations before, in the *Essai sur les mœurs* for instance, but previously that was always because they were the wrong type of luxury, the noxious, feudal kind, not the beneficial, bourgeois luxury of enjoyment which spread universal opulence. This is not the case here. For the first time Voltaire attacked the very type of bourgeois, progressive luxury which he had extolled for over four decades: the kind that had passed from the exclusive domain of 'princes' and 'reines' to the 'bourgeois' and 'citoyennes', a development outlined in the *Essai sur les mœurs* and the *Siècle de Louis XIV*. Even though some of the above examples, such as jewellery, is perhaps ostentatious luxury, some is clearly the luxury of comfort and enjoyment: condiments, tobacco and the new drinks of tea and coffee, the type that is 'superflu', or as it is put here 'inutile', but which engenders both sensual pleasure and immense commercial activity; just what Voltaire had applauded in the *Mondain*.

Indian commerce is thus highly problematic. Colonial trade, involving slavery and forced labour, could be seen not to constitute 'true', that is, mutual commerce and thus, whilst to be strongly condemned, it did not necessarily threaten Voltaire's thought on commerce as civilisation. India however, as an ancient civilisation, a sovereign power which had traded internationally for centuries, ought to have been an illustration of the benefits of commerce as pointed to in the *Mondain* and the *Lettres philosophiques*. Instead, the *Fragments* nullifies all four arguments that had marked the optimistic thought on commerce: luxury now exists as its own category and is to be condemned; this condemnation is comprehensive: there is no longer any differentiation between an advantageous and a noxious kind of luxury; commerce is now divorced from mutuality, sociability, peace and liberty; and instead of promoting civilisation and Enlightenment, it is now a force for their opposite, violence and barbarity.

This utterly destroyed decades of Voltaire's own arguments about commerce which had made it absolutely central to his view of society, civilisation and ultimately of 'Enlightenment'. So the obvious question is why? Why did he threaten his entire edifice of Enlightenment social thought?

Strategic rhetoric can provide part of the answer: the *Fragments* is, after all, at least partly intended to exculpate Lally; and if it could be shown that his hand was forced by a criminally unjust system for which the entirety of French society bore responsibility, Lally would have to be absolved since he could not be judged by a society that was party to the offence. This cannot, however, account for the absoluteness of Voltaire's about-turn: he could, for instance, easily have made the same argument by invoking noxious luxury and thus could have left his defence of bourgeois commerce and luxury intact.

Instead I would suggest that the solution to this puzzle is twofold. It lies on the one hand in Voltaire's acute awareness of the state of, and shifts in, public opinion and debate, and on the other in a specific aspect of his own Enlightenment project: in its focus not only on political economy but also on a genuine cosmopolitanism, or, to put it into what it is now called, 'globalism'. Thus, to begin to solve the puzzle, *Fragments* needs to be seen in its historical context. It is published at a moment of intense debate in France, both about the nature and future of France's economy in general and the French East India Company in particular, and of commerce, consumption and commercial society as such.

Recent scholarship has dwelt at length on the burgeoning interest in political economy and the increasing hostility towards commerce in public debate in France from the 1750s onwards, which is generally explained by the public perception of a need for fundamental reform after France's dismal performance in the wars of the 1740s and 1750s. Michael Sonenscher has analysed the various attempts by eighteenth-century French intellectuals to reconfigure the French and European economies in order to solve the war-debt nexus. John Shovlin found that the increasing preoccupation with patriotism and agrarianism went hand in hand with a rejection of luxury-based commerce; and in his neo-Tocquevillian account, Henry C. Clark also narrates how a more positive view of the British-inspired model of commercial society endorsed by Melon, Voltaire and the Gournay circle amongst others, came, by the end of the Seven Years War, to be rejected in favour of a more agrarian-based solution to the nation's need for reform, as advocated by the Physiocratic movement amongst others.

Voltaire, attuned to public opinion and able to manipulate it like no other, was certainly aware of this shift or caesura, and both endorsed and encouraged it. Not only was he amongst the first to differentiate between different kinds of commerce, a good bourgeois and a noxious feudal kind, he also took a more agrarian stance himself. His appropriation of the figure of the patriarch of Ferney, which he linked to the agrarian overtones of his associated, Candidean motto 'il faut cultiver notre jardin' and expressed in media as varied as his poetry (the *Epître à Madame Denis sur l'agriculture* (1761) and the *Epître à Horace* (1772) amongst others), his letters, and the entries 'Economie', 'Blé', and 'Agriculture', in his *Questions sur l'Encyclopédie* (1770-1772), represent a clear attempt to associate himself with this shift. Taking a more agrarian position – which, more often than not, was in the discourse of the time associated with a rejection of luxury – could, eventually, facilitate a critique of commerce. However, whilst it would permit such a move, it does not explain it. For this, we need to take into account another contemporary debate: that on French-Indian trade.

The French East India Company had become nearly extinct after the Seven Years War and the government considered abolishing its monopoly. To justify this, the then controller general, Maynon d'Inveau, asked the *philosophe* and economist André Morellet to write a treatise against the monopoly in 1769, which he duly did. The *Mémoire sur la situation actuelle de la Compagnie des Indes* was written in the tradition of the economically liberal Gournay circle to which Morellet belonged, and even contained an essay by Gournay himself as an annexe. It provoked myriad responses and contributed to the abolition of the Company's monopoly in the same year, revealing widespread dissatisfaction with the Company. When Morellet's intervention came under fire, the Physiocrat Du Pont de Nemours wrote to support the pro-abolition stance. His *Du Commerce et de la Compagnie des Indes* which was also published in 1769 argues for France to cease all direct trade with India.

Once again this was a debate to which Voltaire paid close attention. He was an admirer of Gournay, a friend of Morellet and applauded the *Mémoire* which he saw as having justly killed off the company.[13] And, despite his general rejection of the Physiocratic movement, Voltaire maintained a friendship with the Physiocrat Du Pont de Nemours whose views and works he openly endorsed.[14] This debate again in some way

13. On Gournay, Voltaire wrote: 'C'est un homme dont je fais grand cas. Je crois que personne n'entend mieux le commerce en grand et ne méritait mieux d'être écouté' (D7724 Voltaire to Tronchin, 5 May 1758 in: Voltaire, *Correspondence and related documents*, ed. by Theodore Besterman, *OCV*, vols 85-135). Morellet and Voltaire were friends and correspondents of long standing. On his praise for Morellet's writings against the Company monopoly see D15812 and D15852 and to Joseph Audra (August 1769). Voltaire owned a copy of Morellet's *Mémoire* and its subsequent defences, all of which show signs of having been read: *Corpus des notes marginales*, ed. Natalia Elaguina et al. (Berlin and Oxford, 1979-), V, p.784-85.

14. Their correspondence was extensive and regular, especially after Dupont visited Voltaire in Ferney in 1768. See especially D16525 (Voltaire to Pierre Samuel Du Pont de Nemours, 16 July 1770), which links his efforts in agriculture to the writings of Du Pont and his

explains how Voltaire – ever sensitive to public opinion, which had turned against the monopoly trade in the service of which Lally was finally executed – could easily endorse a stance critical of French-Indian commerce. Yet again, it does not sufficiently explain why he chose to do so. The explanation lies in the merging of the two debates on the shape of the French economy and on the future of the French East Indian trade.

Whilst the European context, in particular the Anglo-French rivalry, for the debate on French economic reform and national regeneration is readily studied and acknowledged, the global dimension that it clearly held for contemporaries is lacking in current scholarly analyses. This global dimension lay largely in the East, in India; and this is where it also intersects with the debate on the French East Indian trade. Once again, Voltaire was fully cognisant of this. Marsh??

For France one of the most devastating outcomes of the Carnatic and Seven Years Wars was the almost complete loss of French power in India. India had held the interest of Europe's educated elite for several decades already, and Voltaire was once again at the forefront of this. He maintained personal acquaintances and a vast network of correspondence with scholars, natives, military men and servants of different national companies. He also read and owned numerous texts on India. As the century progressed, travel narratives and missionary reports (which Voltaire distrusted) began to be complemented by more scholarly works on India (which Voltaire relished), Dow and Holwell's in particular. It must be from his more detailed information on Indian culture, history and especially nature, climate and geography, that he came to see India as so blessed by nature as to be self-sufficient, that is, not in need of international trade.[15] This is not to say that Voltaire was therefore

---

Physiocrat colleague, Roubaud, with whom he signals agreement. In the same letter he expresses great interest in Du Pont's recent work on the French East India Company which he had read.

15. For an exhaustive list of all the works on India in Voltaire's library, see D. S. Hawley, 'L'Inde de Voltaire', *SVEC* 120 (1974), p.139-78. His main contacts in India were an old school friend from Louis le Grand, Maurice Pilavoine, who had been born in Surat and returned to India from whence he contacted Voltaire in 1758 (D7635); a mutual acquaintance of both, the Chevalier Baudoin de Soupir who had visited Voltaire in Geneva and who corresponded with him from India (see D7635, D7724, D8871); and especially Louis Laurent Fayd'herbe, the comte de Maudave, an adventurer, man of letters, military man, governor for the Company and failing projector, who put Voltaire in touch with an Indian Brahmin who then sent Voltaire a copy of the Eizourveidam. On other visitors see D9325 which mentions that 'un commodore anglais et un directeur de la factorerie anglaise de Surate sont venus diner chez moi' (Voltaire to Tronchin, 17 October 1760) and D19795 which states that Voltaire was in touch with George Pigot, governor of the English East India Company, who had also visited him in Ferney. Voltaire was also in close contact with Simon Gilly, one of the French Company syndics (see

unsupportive of India's trade. On the contrary: an extremely shrewd and
successful investor, he had bought into the French East India Company
by the 1720s already and continued to do so over the following decades,
further investing in private expeditions to India after the liberalisation
of the trade.[16] He was therefore particularly aware of the importance of
this trade to the French, and his correspondence during the Seven Years
War reveals his increasing worries on this account, which climax in the
smugly desperate letter to the comte d'Argental in 1761, after the British
conquest of the main French trading post in India, Pondicherry, which
reads: 'Enfin donc ce que j'ay prédit depuis deux ans est arrivé. Je criais
toujours Pondicheri ou Ponticheri et dans touttes mes lettres, je disais
prenez garde à Ponticheri. Ceux qui avaient partie de leur fortune sur la
compagnie des Indes n'ont qu'à se recommander aux directeurs de
l'hôpital.'[17] Indeed, France never again regained any significant foothold
in the Indian trade and Voltaire knew better than most that the 'quelques
arpents de neige' in North America could never make up for this loss.
The importance accorded to this commerce in eighteenth-century economic thought, means that its near loss must have added further weight
to the sentiment that urgent reform was needed within France.

Yet Indian trade played a more complex role in the French debates
about reform than simply that of instigator. Instead the French debates
about commerce and reform had a distinctly global dimension which lay
in their connection to the potential future of Indian trade: it is in this
connection that we can find the answer to the puzzle of Voltaire's
rejection of the international luxury trade.

If, as Sonenscher claims, the recent wars had led to intense speculation
on how to remedy the seemingly fatal link between commerce and war,
and if, as Shovlin claims, the wartime losses drove the French public to
intense debates about political economy, the resulting reform projects
had a global, not only a national or European dimension. To understand
fully the intellectual history of later eighteenth-century French political
economy debates, we must bear in mind their global context.

D11331 and D11355), and corresponded with a certain Bourcet de La Saigne who was
stationed in Pondicherry at the time (D19896, Pierre Jean Bourcet de La Saigne to
Voltaire, 1 February 1776).

16. On Voltaire's investments most details can be found spread throughout René Pomeau's
Voltaire en son temps, 2 vols (Paris and Oxford, 1995). A work specifically dedicated to the
topic is the strongly partisan *Voltaire financier* by Léon Kozminski (Paris, 1929). His
investments in the French East India Company are set out in D104, D210, and especially
in D.app74, 94, 299, 315 and 469. On his sending, in the early 1770s, a ship called *L'Hercule*
to India (Bengal), together with a consortium of investors, see D18537, D18856, D19365,
and D20505. Apparently the ship was struck by thunder and the captain, a certain Bérard,
absconded with their money.

17. D9925 Voltaire to the comte d'Argental, 2 August 1761.

The most striking early examples of this global dimension can be found in the 1769 monopoly debate. Both Morellet and Dupont's contributions link the future of France to that of India. Both Morellet and the Gournay circle, as well as Dupont and the Physiocrats promoted a liberal and proto-utilitarian economic agenda at home that sought to abolish guilds and other barriers to free trade internally. Both argued that the same policies ought to be implemented, unilaterally if need be, on the international level. Morellet is most explicit on this, believing the benefits of freed human agency as equally applicable to the national and to the international levels. Private interest, according to Morellet, gives rise to individual exertions, to trade, industry and the arts and sciences. As long as this is allowed to continue unhampered, its benefits will spread around the globe.[18] This is interesting to us, as it emphasises the intentionally transnational and universal nature of this strand of Enlightenment economic thought.

Du Pont also saw the future of France and the future of the Indian trade as fundamentally interlinked. Like Morellet, he holds that as a general principle, monopolies are unjust in that they oppose the fundamental principle of equality and thus 'viol[ent] les droits de la Société'.[19] He goes even further than Morellet, by positing a direct link between the current model of Europe-Indian trade and international warfare.[20] Like Morellet's, the Physiocratic solution is universalist and global, applicable both on the national and international level. France is to be regenerated through its agriculture and an intricate division of labour between agricultural producers, manufacturers and traders which would ensure economic health and co-operation within the country. The same principle however also applies on the global scale: the division of labour amongst countries, namely amongst the producers, which will be primarily agricultural like France, and the traders, which will be transporting and exchanging the agricultural produce of others like the Netherlands, will ensure a peaceful co-operation and free trade on a truly global scale. Whilst ostensibly addressing only the nature of French-

18. Abbé André Morellet, *Mémoire sur la situation actuelle de la Compagnie des Indes* (Paris, 1769), p.154-56.
19. Du Pont, *Du Commerce et de la Compagnie des Indes*, 2nd edn (Paris & Amsterdam, 1769), p.3.
20. Du Pont, *Du Commerce et de la Compagnie des Indes*, part I, ch.4, §1, 'Que la guerre lointaine est inséparable du commerce immédiat'. Voltaire had made a similar point a few years earlier: 'l'administration dans l'Inde a été extrêmement malheureuse, et je pense que nôtre malheur vient en partie de ce qu'une compagnie de commerce dans l'Inde, doit être nécessairement une compagnie guerrière. C'est ainsi que les Européens y ont fait le commerce depuis les Albuquerques. Les Hollandais n'y ont été puissants que parce qu'ils ont été conquérants. Les Anglais en dernier lieu ont gagné les armes à la main des sommes immenses que nous avons perdues, et j'ai peur qu'on ne soit malheureusement réduit à être oppresseur ou opprimé.' (D11355) Voltaire to Simon Gilly, 12 August 1763.

Indian trade, these two texts are of much wider importance in that they reveal the truly global vision of these Enlightenment economic philosophies.

Voltaire shares this universalising approach to French and Indian commerce. Like Morellet and Du Pont, he finds that the current system of European trade with India favours exploitation and short-term gain over justice and long-term public interest. It is at the root of the injustices committed against Lally in France and against the Indian people in Asia and must therefore be condemned. He goes further than Morellet and Du Pont however: while their vision is clearly global, their point of view is self-consciously national.[21] Neither of them seeks to adopt, for instance, an Indian perspective or invoke evidence that touches on any nation other than France. Consequently, their critique is limited to the *nature* of the trade, in Morellet's case the fact that it was conducted under a monopoly, in Du Pont de Nemours' that it was conducted directly, whilst he considered it best conducted indirectly by France and mediated by potential future trading nations. Neither Dupont nor Morellet ever condemn all European-Indian trade as Voltaire does. Instead they believed it to bring legitimate enjoyments to Europeans and to benefit to both parties involved, both having a mutual need of it.[22] Voltaire on the other hand attempts to adopt an Indian perspective, dwelling on Indian culture, Indian history, Indian religion and the state of India with the European presence. His perception of 'Enlightenment' was universalist and therefore had to embrace a truly cosmopolitan stance. The *Fragments* is such an attempt: in it, Voltaire rejected a patriotic point of view – if trade with India benefited France it was to be continued – in favour of a genuinely cosmopolitan or enlightened one; if trade was harmful to either party it was in contravention of the principles of mutuality, peace and progress of civilisation that should mark true commerce. Regardless of whether the injured party was one's *patrie* or not, such trade must be condemned and thus discontinued.

21. Du Pont, *Du Commerce et de la Compagnie des Indes*, p.19-20: 'Il me semble que ce n'est pas tant relativement à l'Europe en général que je dois me proposer de discuter les effets attachés à la nature du commerce de l'Inde, que par rapport à la France en particulier. Les circonstances paraissent me prescrire la Loi de borner ici mes réflexions à l'utilité et aux inconvénient que ce commerce peut avoir pour ma patrie.' Morellet investigates the French-Indian trade from two vantage points: from the point of view of the shareholders, and in terms of national or state interest.

22. Morellet, *Mémoire*, p.187: 'Tout commerce est fondé sur un besoin réciproque et égal. Les Indiens ont autant de besoin de notre argent et de notre or, que nous avons besoin de leurs toiles.' Du Pont, *Du commerce et de la Compagnie des Indes*, p.20: 'L'Inde étant une fois *connue*, et ses productions ainsi que ses marchandises *reconnues* pour propres à nous procurer des jouissances, il serait absurde et injuste de nous en interdire l'usage. Toute loi prohibitive est mauvaise, parce que toute loi prohibitive viole le droit que tous les hommes ont à se procurer des jouissances, et à rendre leur sort le meilleur possible'.

Cosmopolitanism marked Enlightenment thought as strongly as did political economy and Voltaire was by no means the only writer to combine the two. It has already been said that Morellet and Du Pont's adopted viewpoints were *self-consciously* national: in its general vision for the world economy Du Pont's Physiocracy was genuinely cosmopolitan. But there is another contemporary work which shows more similarities with Voltaire's stance than the Physiocrats ever did: Raynal's *Histoire philosophique et politique des établissements et du commerce des Européens dans les deux Indes*, whose first edition Voltaire bought and read at some point between May and September 1772.[23] Aligning Voltaire with Raynal might not be immediately convincing, given that it is well known that Voltaire was less than impressed with the work. He attacked it for historical inaccuracies in several letters as well as in an article in his *Questions sur l'Encyclopédie* (1770-1772).[24] And whilst he was acutely embarrassed and apologetic when he learnt that the work's author was a fellow-*philosophe* he esteemed, his comments written in and on volumes three and four are not entirely favourable: 'histoire lamentable execrable incroiable, écrite d'un stile si admirable qu'on n'y trouve pas un mot de raison[n]able'; for which he suggested as a subtitle 'ou déclamation des erreurs mal entassées'.[25] However, a more careful reading of Voltaire's comments reveals that he most strongly disagreed with the volumes on the Americas which bear the two comments. In the first volume on India, his complaints were limited to the depictions of Louis XIV and Peter the Great of Russia. Because apart from these, the arguments in those books were so similar to views he had himself expressed, especially in the *Essai sur les mœurs*, that he even pointed that out in his copy.[26]

What Voltaire could also have pointed out was that, in this first edition at least, Voltaire's stance proved to be more radical than Raynal's and Diderot's. In their similarity to Voltaire's earlier arguments, the first five books of their *Histoire* do condemn European cruelty and warfare in India, but still defend Indian commerce and the luxuries of which it consists, very much along the lines of Voltaire's earlier apology of luxury. Chapter 23 of book 5 of the *Histoire*, entitled 'L'Europe doit-elle continuer son commerce avec les Indes?' begins by asserting the relativity of any concept of luxury: 'Comment fixer les limites du nécessaire, qui varie avec sa situation [de l'homme], ses connoissances et ses desirs? A

23. In a letter to Condorcet dated 11 May 1772 he announces that he will order a copy, and in a letter to Catherine II of Russia from 29 September 1772 he cites the work: D17737 and D17942.
24. Article 'Ana, Anecdotes', in *Questions sur l'Encyclopédie A - Egalité*, ed. Nicholas Cronk and Christiane Mervaud, *OCV*, vol.38-40, vol.38, p.281-87.
25. Voltaire, *Corpus des notes marginales*, *OCV* vol.142, p.268 and 271.
26. Voltaire, *Corpus des notes marginales*, *OCV* vol.142, p.263.

peine eut-il simplifié par son industrie les moyens de se procurer la subsistance, qu'il employa le tems qu'il venoit de gagner, à étendre les bornes de ses facultés et le domaine de ses jouissances.' It then makes the link between commerce, unity and peace: 'L'alliage des nations fondues ensemble par le feu des combats s'épure et se polit par le commerce. Dans sa destination, le commerce veut que toutes les nations se regardent comme une société unique'; and between commerce, sociability and liberty: 'Dans son objet et ses moyens, le commerce suppose le désir et la liberté concertée entre tous les peuples, de faire tous les échanges qui peuvent convenir à leur satisfaction mutuelle. Désir de jouir, liberté de jouir; il n'y a que ces deux ressorts d'activité, que ces deux principes de sociabilité, parmi les hommes.'[27] All of these statements could have been taken from Voltaire's earlier works, and none of them match the newly uncompromising nature of his critique. However, both works do indeed share a standpoint that combines Enlightenment cosmopolitanism with an acute interest in political economy when discussing European-Indian relations, and by the *Histoire*'s third edition of 1780 Diderot and Raynal would have overtaken Voltaire's radicalism to propose a wholly new system of global commercial relations.

India and Indian trade thus play a crucial role not only in Voltaire's changing philosophy of commerce. Their inclusion in Voltaire's political economy proves two arguments at once: John Robertson's case about the centrality of political economy to the Enlightenment project,[28] and Karen O'Brien's argument about the strongly cosmopolitan character of the Enlightenment. However, in O'Brien's definition Enlightenment cosmopolitanism 'simultaneously encapsulates an attitude of detachment towards national prejudice [...] and an intellectual investment in the idea of a common European civilisation'.[29] While Voltaire's intervention clearly expresses the former part, it transcends the latter: rather than just European, for Voltaire, as for Raynal and Diderot, the community of civilisation is universal and global. If in their absolute commitment to humanism over barbarism the latter is revealed to ally

---

27. All quotations are taken from the 1770 edition which Voltaire owned and read: Guillaume-Thomas Raynal, *Histoire philosophique et politique des établissements et du commerce des Européens dans les deux Indes*, ed. Anthony Strugnell *et al.*, 5 vols (Ferney-Voltaire, 2010-), vol.1, p.567-68. For a good overview analysis of Raynal's philosophy of commerce see Marian Skrzypek, 'Le commerce instrument de la paix mondiale', in *Raynal, de la polémique à l'histoire*, ed. Gilles Bancarel and Gianluigi Goggi, *SVEC* 2000:12, p.243-54.

28. In *The Case for the Enlightenment: Scotland and Naples 1680-1760* (Cambridge, 2005), John Robertson argues that that 'the intellectual coherence of the Enlightenment may still be found [...] in the commitment to understanding and hence to advancing, the causes and conditions of human betterment in this world' with political economy as a central element in this study of the progress of civilisation (p.28-29).

29. O'Brien, *Narratives of Enlightenment*, p.2.

itself with commerce and luxury in any region of the globe, then commerce must be struck off the register of enlightened practices. It is thus highly probable that the advent of something resembling a caesura in the Enlightenment's appreciation of luxury is due to an increasingly supra-national perception of the consequences of Europe's commercial expansion globally. Eighteenth-century *philosophes* and political economists did not limit their purview to Europe alone. Nor then should we: if for the Enlightenment political economy and the linked fields of ethics and social philosophy are global, then so must be our study of them. Therefore Voltaire's *Fragments sur l'Inde* is but one case that clearly demonstrates the importance of a 'global' or indeed 'interconnected' approach to the study of intellectual history.

Fictions of commercial empire, 1774-1782

JAMES WATT

In the period between the parliamentary investigation of Robert Clive and the impeachment of Warren Hastings, accounts of the 'scandal of empire' (in Nicholas Dirks' phrase) commonly made global connections, paralleling British activities in the East and West Indies, while also suggesting that it was the experience of Indian empire that made Britain despotic in America.[1] If transnational commerce was still widely regarded as having the potential to foster a mutually civilising interconnection between the peoples of the world, many commentators in the 1770s and 1780s focused primarily instead on the way in which the actual operations of the East India Company belied any such idealised reciprocity. This essay will begin by discussing Richard Clarke's representation of Company servants concerned only with their own enrichment, in his poem 'The Nabob, or Asiatic plunderers' (1773), before considering the significance of Adam Smith's more dispassionate argument, in book IV of *Wealth of nations* (1776), that such men yield to the temptations facing them because it would be almost impossible not to do so. In the light of Smith's refusal to criticise the conduct of individuals and his attempts to recuperate the progressive possibilities of global commerce, the main part of this chapter will then examine three novels from the period, the anonymous *Memoirs of a gentleman, who resided several years in the East Indies* (1774), Helenus Scott's *The Adventures of a rupee* (1782), and Robert Bage's *Mount Henneth* (1782). These works are especially interesting, I shall argue, because while they sometimes rehearse particular forms of anti-Company polemic, they also provide counternarratives to the familiar story about the callousness and corruption of nabobs, whether by depicting characters acting 'naturally' as men or by presenting British interests in India as the function of a similarly 'natural' circulation of people and things. If these novels in different ways invoke the metaphor of circulation as a means of apprehending global connections as well as of rethinking British identity, however, they are

1. Nicholas Dirks, *The Scandal of empire*; on the tracing of connections between British activities in India and America in this period, see for example Tom Paine's essay 'Reflections on the life and death of Lord Clive', published in the *Pennsylvania magazine* in 1775.

(unsurprisingly) unable to represent an India 'civilised' by commerce, and they generally eschew the sentimental tropes that other contemporary works mobilised in an attempt to negotiate spatial distance.[2] As a result, I will suggest, they draw attention to the fictionality of their fictions of commercial empire, while rendering India – though also the scandal of empire – still more remote for their metropolitan readers.

'The Nabob, or Asiatic plunderers' (1773) can be read as a work that is at once inspired by, and critical of, Samuel Foote's well-known play *The Nabob* (1772), accentuating the ruthlessness of the newly rich caste of men exemplified by Foote's Sir Matthew Mite, but at the same time eschewing Foote's memorable caricature of their deviancy.[3] Clarke's poem pits gravity against levity, for it repudiates the idea of '*laughing* Satyr', which it associates with Foote's play, and instead states its intent to 'perpetuate an honest indignation' against nabobs: 'The Muse must be serious', the preface declares, 'or the impression will be lost'.[4] The poem takes the form of a philosophical dialogue between an 'Author' and his 'Friend', and it makes the latter a kind of devil's advocate who challenges his companion to explain why he is interested in Indian affairs: 'Concerns it you who plunders in the East,/In blood a tyrant, and in lust a beast?/When ills are distant, are they then your own?/Saw'st thou their tears, or heard'st th'oppressed groan?' (p.3). In response, the Author declares that the crimes of nabobs are comparable to those of the Spanish conquistadors, and he appeals to an expansive understanding of human commonality. '[A]s man, I feel for man', he states: 'My country's honor has receiv'd a blot,/A mark of odium ne'er to be forgot:/A larger country still I boast: embrace/With a warm heart all *Adam*'s wretched race' (p.4).

Just as Foote's Lady Oldham accuses Mite both of importing the vices of the East and of being an agent of ruin in India, so Clarke's Author presents 'Asia' as capable of corrupting others even as it is plundered by them: 'In *Asia*'s realms let slavery be bound', the Author states at one point, 'Let not her foot defile this sacred ground' (p.38). The poem alludes again to the threat of oriental contagion in a footnote on the final page, suggesting that Britain is on the way to emulating the 'great wickedness' of Babylon because of the 'inundation of luxury introduced by trade' (p.42). 'The Nabob' combines this appeal to a generalised

2.   On the use of sentimental tropes for the purpose of imagining relations with distant people, see Lynn Festa, *Sentimental figures of empire in eighteenth-century Britain and France* (Baltimore, MD, 2006).

3.   For a richly contextualised account of 'macaroni' masculinity in *The Nabob*, see Daniel O'Quinn, *Staging governance: theatrical imperialism in London, 1770-1800* (Baltimore, MD, 2005), p.66-73.

4.   Richard Clarke, *The Nabob: or, Asiatic plunderers: a satirical poem, in a dialogue between a friend and the author* (London, 1773), p.iii and v. Page references follow in the text.

Asiatic despotism not only with its sentimental portrayal of Indian
victims of British cruelty, but also with a brief reference to more literal
forms of slavery in the West Indies, represented – like the irreligion of
'our traders' in India – as 'the fruit of commerce', which 'refines [...]
manners, but always corrupts morals' (p.42). In thus delineating the
effects of global commerce, then, 'The Nabob' clearly repudiates any
notion of its potentially civilising agency. If it was a commonplace that
the Company imported oriental despotism and so corrupted British
politics and society, it was also frequently argued that Britons were
themselves the exporters of slavery to India.[5] Up until the trial of Warren
Hastings at least, numerous poems paralleled the activities of the
Company with those of slave-owners and traders, presenting, as in
Timothy Touchstone's 'Tea and sugar' (1792), an essential kinship between nabobs and creoles, said to be jointly responsible for tyranny and
exploitation abroad, and the sowing of 'base corruption's ready-growing
seed' at home.[6]

While the footnote referred to above declares that Britons' pursuit of
their interests in the East and West Indies exposes their Christianity as
merely nominal, however, the poem itself closes with an anecdote of
'what a father taught a son' that concedes the futility of any such moral
critique. The Author sets up a scenario – 'a still evening's walk, life's
calmest hour' – in which a venerable 'grey Sire' addresses his 'dearest,
only Child' (p.39) prior to his departure for India, but this familiar
seeming set-piece is subverted when the wisdom that the aged parent
imparts to his son turns out simply to be that 'man's a cypher, if not
crown'd with wealth'. After repeatedly telling his Friend that his own
fellow-feeling knows no bounds, Clarke's Author here rehearses what he
takes to be the dominant 'maxims of the world's school': 'Friendship's a
name; be first thy own dear friend,/Let friendship here begin, here let it
end' (p.40). The Author's interlocutor in turn comes to be vindicated, for
if his claims sometimes seem to partake of the worldly cynicism of
Foote's Nabob, he also provides evidence to substantiate his assertion
that 'conscience in some, and moral sense is dead' (p.26), referring to
recently published exposés of the Company such as William Bolts's
Considerations on Indian affairs (1772).[7] Finally acknowledging that nabobs
'dread no spectres of the famish'd dead' (p.31), the Author calls for the

5.   See for example, Edmund Burke's claim that the Company was 'forging new chains for the
     wretched natives of [Bengal]' in his July 1784 'Speech on Almas Ali Khan', *The Writings and
     speeches of Edmund Burke, vol.5: India: Madras and Bengal 1774-1785*, ed. P. J. Marshall (Oxford,
     1981), p.466.
6.   Cited in Kate Teltscher, *India inscribed*, p.173.
7.   On the self-interestedness of Bolts's opposition to Clive, see Dirks, *The Scandal of empire*,
     p.250-55.

hanging of such 'odious murderers' for the 'public good', in case their crimes 'should be too soon forgot' (p.32), and so as to strike fear into those who would otherwise be tempted to imitate them. In the very process of attempting to 'hand down the Memory of the Oppressors to the latest Posterity' (p.iii), then, the Author actually registers the possibility, even the likelihood, that Britons might develop an amnesia regarding the evils perpetrated by 'Asiatic plunderers', if they were ever aware of them in the first place. Though the Author initially strives to bring home what his Friend represents as distant ills, his righteous vision of the spectacular punishment of 'guilty greatness' (p.32) appears to proclaim the failure of his efforts to establish a community of feeling between Britons and the nameless and voiceless victims of the recent famine in Bengal.

Adam Smith recognised the destructive impact of the Company – and may have alluded to the Bengal famine – when he suggested that, to the newly rich Company servant on his way home from India, it would be a matter of indifference if the country he left behind were 'swallowed up by an earthquake'.[8] One explanation for Smith's refusal to 'throw any odious imputation upon the general character' (p.372) of Company men is that *Wealth of nations* offers a structural analysis of the Company's monopolistic practices, and is therefore most concerned with issues of institutional organisation and culture. This reluctance to criticise individuals perhaps also converges with the 'accommodationist' position eventually accepted by Clarke's Author, however, since Smith presents any moral objection to the fortune-seeking activities of Britons in India as the result either of bad faith or naivety. In presenting the conduct of such men as an inevitable consequence of 'the system of government' under which they operated in Bengal, for example, Smith argued that 'they who have clamoured loudest against them would, probably, not have acted better themselves' (p.372).[9] He even more pointedly refrained from criticising Company servants when considering the contentious issue of individuals engaging in private trade for personal gain, stating that

> Nothing can be more compleatly foolish than to expect that the clerks of a great counting-house at ten thousand miles distance [...] should, upon a single order from their masters, give up at once doing any sort of business upon their own account, [and] abandon for ever all hopes of making a fortune, of which they have the means in their hands (p.370).

8. Adam Smith, *Wealth of nations*, ed. Kathryn Sutherland (Oxford, 1993), p.372. Page references follow in the text.
9. Smith here echoes Clive's self-defence that 'The servants of the Company yield only because they are men', cited in O'Quinn, *Staging governance*, p.49.

In a passage such as this, *Wealth of nations* frames the individual quest for wealth in India as the product of a rational single-mindedness rather than a lack of sensibility. Smith defended private trading in the name of free trade, and it was free trade, he argued, which offered a means of redressing the 'dreadful misfortunes' that had been occasioned by 'the uniting [of] [...] the most distant parts of the world' (p.364) at the end of the fifteenth century. 'The discovery of America, and that of a passage to the East Indies by the Cape of Good Hope, are the two greatest and most important events recorded in the history of mankind' (p.363), Smith famously declared, supplementing this statement with the observation that 'Their consequences have already been very great', though impossible to determine in their 'whole extent'. Smith went on to consider both the immediate and long-run – yet to be realised – consequences of this period in world history, acknowledging the exploitation of 'the natives [...] of the East and West Indies' that resulted from the European voyages of exploration, but also signalling his optimism regarding 'that mutual communication of knowledge and of all sorts of improvements which an extensive commerce from all countries to all countries naturally, or rather necessarily, carries with it' (p.364). If he recognised that non-Europeans understood the establishment of global connections in terms of the 'misfortunes' rather than 'benefits' that resulted, therefore, Smith nonetheless argued for the equalising potential of a transnational commerce that operated independently of chartered corporations such as the East India Company, and which for that reason genuinely created and circulated wealth.

While he was strongly critical of the Company, Smith 'sidestepped the question of what Britain's relations with India ought to be, and indeed whether British rule of India could be justified'.[10] A number of contemporary fictions of British India, however, more directly invoked the fantasy of a commercial empire from which Britain and India mutually benefited, while also sometimes suggesting that it was the Company that actually guaranteed this state of affairs. These fictions acknowledged the taint of scandal surrounding the Company's recent operations, but rather than emphasise the corrupting agency of returning East Indians who had themselves been corrupted by their experiences overseas, in the manner of Foote's play, they countered this critique of nabobery by (implicitly at least) engaging with and reframing some of its principal terms and tropes, most notably the idea of colonial adventure. These works in turn provided metropolitan readers with an importantly different set of 'Indian' reference points, bypassing the Bengal famine,

10. Jennifer Pitts, *A Turn to empire: the rise of imperial liberalism in Britain and France* (Princeton, NJ, 2006), p.55.

which for many continued to symbolise the ruthlessness of Company rule, and instead organising themselves around alternative (and earlier) episodes or events such as the Black Hole of Calcutta and the Battle of Plassey. Even as the novels that I shall discuss sometimes undercut their own claims about mutually beneficial colonial commerce, they also sought to legitimise Indian empire as well as – in the case of *Adventures of a rupee* and *Mount Henneth*, especially – to stabilise the meaning of British liberty.

One of the first 'Indian' fictions published in Britain, *Memoirs of a gentleman, who resided several years in the East Indies* (1774), by 'C. W.', appears to present itself as the 'back-story' of an unscrupulous nabob now returned home. The narrator of the work is a fortune-seeking German surgeon (nonetheless known as 'the English doctor') who sails for Bengal after failing to get ahead in the Dutch East India Company settlement of Batavia.[11] Finding employment with a 'Rajah' (p.95), he is soon involved in rescuing the widow of the Rajah's brother from *sati*, a practice which is said to provide 'A most shocking instance [of] how far men will proceed in wickedness, when they have once deviated from the truth' (p.98). Rather than dwell on this, however, the narrator emphasises the way in which the nameless 'Gentoo lady' (p.105) that he saves subsequently becomes attached to him, such that she harbours a passionate jealousy towards the numerous other women that he encounters. Across the work as a whole, the narrator styles himself as more of a libertine than a liberator, describing at a later stage how he and a Danish doctor together procured and enjoyed 'as many black women as we could find' (p.143). *Memoirs of a gentleman* concludes with a brief account of its protagonist's infatuation with a Frenchwoman of English descent (with 'extremely white' [229] skin) who in turn takes him for 'an English gentleman' (p.230), and such a resolution might be seen to prepare the way for the narrator's reform and return to respectable society. At the end of the preceding chapter, nonetheless, the narrator unequivocally celebrates his lifestyle of sexual adventurism, stating that 'I was never so happy while in the East Indies, as when in company with the fair sex, who were always very obliging to me' (p.221).

When reissued in 1780 under the more novelistic title of *The Indian adventurer, or History of Mr Vanneck*, the work was condemned by the *Monthly review* as 'insipid and vulgar, and withal insufferably coarse and indelicate'.[12] According to this reader, clearly, the behaviour of the protagonist was straightforwardly deviant and immoral, and could not in any way be licensed or condoned. If *Memoirs of a gentleman* may have

---

11. *Memoirs of a gentleman, who resided several years in the East Indies* (London, for J. Donaldson, 1774), p.121. Page references follow in the text.
12. *The Monthly review, or Literary journal* 63 (1780), p.233.

been read as a story of individual depravity that bore out popular suspicion of the conduct of nabobs in India, however, it is noteworthy that the work says nothing about the scandal of empire, and that it instead attends to the circumstances in which the Company came to establish its sovereignty. The vicissitudes of the narrator's life make him a spectator on what the work's subtitle refers to as 'the late revolutions, and most important events in that part of the world', so that, for example, after fleeing with the Indian widow whom he rescues, he and his new companion are apprehended by 'English Seapoys' (p.113) and held as prisoners in Calcutta; this experience of captivity in turn prompts brief references to the horrors of the Black Hole, to Clive's defeat of Siraj ud-Daula and to the rapid succession of native rulers that followed thereafter. In his 1783 'Speech on Mr Fox's East India Bill', Burke sketched the recent history of 'bargains and sales' over which the Company had presided in Bengal and elsewhere, presenting the Company's clients as little more than pawns in the hands of a power that had broken every treaty into which it had entered: 'Seraja Dowla was sold to Mir Jaffier; Mir Jaffier was sold to Mir Cossim; and Mir Cossim was sold to Mir Jaffier again.'[13] *Memoirs of a gentleman*, by contrast, presents the figure of 'Meer Cossim' as a scheming despot, who, having 'insinuated [...] that his father-in-law was not properly qualified for the sovereignty' (p.118), and 'exacted such exorbitant taxes from the people' (p.119) once installed in power, then attempts to involve the narrator in soliciting the Dutch to ally with him against the British. The narrator offers personal testimony as to the untrustworthiness of Meer Cossim, and this characterisation of him is then followed by an account of his attack on the Company garrison in Patna and the subsequent defeat of his combined forces at the 1764 battle of Buxar, a conflict that decisively secured British authority in Bengal and paved the way for the Company's assumption of *diwani* rights in the following year.

It is significant that the author of *Memoirs of a gentleman* opted to rehearse this narrative of recent events in Bengal at a time when the reputation of the Company was at a nadir. Nabobs, in the novel's terms, are not the villains identified by Foote or Clarke, but rather the 'East India Princes' (p.114) they were thought to imitate, figures whose essential 'character' the narrator resolves – just before detailing the 'exploits' of Siraj-ud-Daula – to 'set [...] in the clearest light' (p.115). While the work makes no direct reference to the parliamentary investigation of Company affairs that took place immediately prior to its publication, it nonetheless counters the charge that Company servants were solely

13. Burke, 'Speech on Fox's India Bill', in *The Writings and speeches of Edmund Burke*, vol.5, p.394, 393.

interested in their own gain, at the same time offering an implicit
defence of private trading. The narrator of the *Memoirs* is alive to
commercial as well as sexual opportunity, therefore, but he also presents
himself as scrupulously honest in all his dealings, such that in the opinion
of one native merchant community, he claims, he was among 'the most
humane Europeans they had ever met with' (p.177). By thus pointing to
the continuity between commercial and sexual opportunism, *Memoirs of a
gentleman* might be seen at once to rehearse and contain the popular
critique of men with Indian fortunes, for though the narrator displays
some of the same characteristics that were projected onto 'nabobs', real
and fictional, his libidinal energies are to some extent 'networked', and
channelled into honourable pursuits.[14] The narrator's account of his
private trading activity does not simply demonstrate his honesty, however, since the all but ceaseless mobility that this activity entails also
serves to convey an ideologically powerful impression of the state of flux
pertaining, until recently, 'in that part of the world'. The 'late revolutions' of the *Memoirs* subtitle are presented as internally generated as
much as they are the product of any external agency, and the novel can
thus be seen as helping to circulate the enduring story of Mughal
implosion that, according to so many later histories of empire, served
to clear a space for, and legitimise, British intervention in India.[15]

The object-narrator at the beginning of Helenus Scott's novel *The
Adventures of a rupee: wherein are interspersed various anecdotes Asiatic and
European* (1782) establishes the idea of Indian lawlessness in a similar
fashion to *Memoirs of a gentleman*, by initially describing its time in the
hands of a corrupt fakir (who 'prayed to Brama, and *preyed* upon his
neighbour'), then imagining a different life in England on the basis of the
reputation enjoyed by 'that great East India Company' in Bengal.[16] In
stating that the Company is able to 'keep black men in such good order at
so great a distance' (p.13), the rupee at once alludes to and circumvents
the problem of remotely exercised authority that was raised by Smith,
Burke and many others. Shortly after this, the novel incorporates the
'History of Miss Melvil', whose account of her father's final words to his
Eastbound son reworks the scene of paternal advice at the end of 'The
Nabob': 'Your particular province is to protect the trade of your country,

14. Contrast Foote's representation of Sir Matthew Mite's plan to establish a seraglio in
    London. On Mite's deviance, see O'Quinn, *Staging governance*, p.70-73.
15. See for example, T. B. Macaulay's 1840 essay on Clive, in *Prose and poetry*, ed. G. M. Young
    (Cambridge, MA, 1970), p.312-17.
16. Helenus Scott, *The Adventures of a rupee: wherein are interspersed various anecdotes Asiatic and
    European* (London, for J. Murray, 1782), p.13. Page references follow in text. Critical
    accounts of this work that I have found especially useful include the essays by Liz Bellamy
    and Aileen Douglas in *The Secret life of things: animals, objects, and it-narratives in eighteenth-
    century England*, ed. Mark Blackwell (Lewisburg, PA, 2007).

against the insults of European powers, or of the Indian nations, who ignorant of the blessings that commerce diffuses, even to themselves, are often disposed to interrupt its equitable course' (p.59). Whereas Burke famously declared that 'Every rupee of profit made by an Englishman is lost forever to India', Scott's work here rebuts any such claims about the Company extraction of Indian wealth, suggesting that the equality of commerce wishfully imagined by Smith might already prevail.[17]

This opposition between, on the one hand, the state of anarchy in which the fakir's band flourishes, and on the other the conditions of stability provided elsewhere by the Company, is complicated by the novel's initial presentation of Hyder Ali, the Sultan of Mysore, as an additional lawgiving force. The seemingly positive depiction of Hyder in *The Adventures of a rupee* is especially noteworthy since at the time of its publication, as Scott records, the state of Mysore (in alliance with France) had been at war with the Company for nearly two years. Hyder is described as a distinguished general who instils a European-style military discipline among his troops, and he is further presented as a distinctly humane figure, capable of feeling for others.[18] Although he is said to keep a seraglio, and to preside over 'scenes, which in this country are but little known' (p.42) ('Happy women of England', the narrator interjects, 'whom custom and religion have made the equals of men!' [43]), Hyder is in other respects the antithesis of a sexual despot, for he acts as the protector of the Scottish Miss Melvil, whom his forces had captured at Arcot shortly after she joined her enlisted lover, and her brother. Maria Melvil refers to her temporary guardian as 'illustrious Hyder', and she speaks warmly of 'the gentlest usage, and the most fatherly affection' (p.87) which she receives in his custody, before she is finally returned to her betrothed 'in her native innocence' (p.91).[19]

Critics of the Company in the early 1780s often invoked the potency of Hyder Ali against the military expansionism that they associated with Warren Hastings, Governor-General of Bengal: in his 'Speech on Fox's East India Bill', for example, Burke referred to 'the mighty strength, [...] and the manly struggle' of the late Sultan in his contest with Company forces.[20] The scene of fatherly counsel referred to above similarly alludes

17. Burke, 'Speech on Fox's East India Bill', *The Writings and speeches of Edmund Burke*, vol.5, p.402.
18. Contrast Eliza Fay's representation of imprisonment by Hyder in her *Original letters from India* (published in 1817). On Mysore captivity narratives, see Linda Colley, *Captives: Britain, empire and the world 1600-1850* (London, 2002), p.269-95.
19. The story of Maria's quest for her lover may have been drawn upon by Sir Walter Scott in his historical novella *The Surgeon's daughter* (1827), which revisits the period leading up to the second Mysore war.
20. Burke, 'Speech on Fox's East India Bill', *The Writings and speeches of Edmund Burke*, vol.5, p.401.

to contemporary debates about the proper business of the Company, since while Mr Melvil tells his son that the protection of commerce constitutes a particularly 'glorious' calling, by which unspecified past 'abuses' may be rectified, he acknowledges that others have with justification 'cursed our rapacity' (p.60). This sense of a general unscrupulousness among Company servants is clearly signalled by the title of the chapter in question, 'A father's advice to his son on going to India, I am afraid, somewhat unlike that of every modern one' (p.47). Elsewhere, however, *The Adventures of a rupee* moves away from any such implicit criticism of the Company and, shortly after recounting the story of Maria Melvil's captivity and release, it shifts its focus back to Britain, when the rupee narrator comes into the possession of 'an English common sailor' (p.93), and is thus finally granted its wish to travel to England. Here too the novel might be seen to attempt the negotiation of troubling realities, but it now more clearly appears to address the repercussions of Britain's conflict with its American colonies.

According to the anonymous 'Memoirs of the author' that prefaced the second edition of the novel, Scott's 'passionate admiration of liberty and of great men struggling for its preservation called his notice to America', inspiring him with a desire 'to make [...] the offer of his sword' to George Washington; 'from this youthful sally, in which he consulted chiefly the vivacity of his temper', however, 'he was diverted by the prudence of his friends', who were able to obtain him a Company cadetship in India.[21] Scott's apparent support for the American revolutionary cause, represented here as a quixotic display of enthusiasm, makes his novel's lack of reference to America all the more intriguing. The work's engagement with the ramifications of this conflict is nonetheless evident when sailor Jack gives up his Indian souvenir to a pawnbroker, and the rupee then refers to the different customers that come into the pawnbroker's shop. Shortly after describing an 'old warriour' (p.142) who 'left his legs in Germany' (p.143) and now pawns his sword for cash so that he is able to carry on drinking the King's health, the narrator observes the entrance of a 'powdered and scented' young gentleman-officer, 'with a belly somewhat prominent, a certain sign of ease'. This man comes to purchase rather than pledge, acquiring 'a breast-pin set with diamonds' (p.163), which he fixes to his shirt before admiring himself in a mirror and strutting out. The novel later describes the same figure as representative of 'many of our military youths', '[w]ithout science, without the capacity of acquiring any, with no knowledge of war, and with no predilection for the army that reason can

21. Scott, *The Adventures of a rupee: wherein are interspersed various anecdotes Asiatic and European, a new edition. To which are prefixed, memoirs of the life of the author, and to which are annexed his remarks concerning the inhabitants of Africa*, 2nd edn (London, for J. Murray, 1782), p.iii.

justify' (p.243), and it becomes clear here that it participates more broadly in the denunciation of an effeminate and ineffectual officer-caste. Scott employs a form of class critique that sometimes overlapped with the censure of an 'aristocratic' nabobery but which in this episode alludes in particular to the incompetence of those associated with the disastrous conflict in America.

The social survey facilitated by the rupee juxtaposes poverty and luxury, nowhere more overtly than when – again at the pawnbroker's – a young chimney-sweep tells of how his mother sold his teeth to an 'old lady of quality', who was unable to 'retain [her] property' because her gums were 'rotten with disease and sweetmeats' (p.214). In contrast to such graphic representation of dissipation and decay the novel presents the moral example of figures such as a Welsh parson, whose primitive Christianity contrasts with the sham austerity of the fakir, the rupee's first owner. Together with sailor Jack and others, the parson embodies the resources of a scarce yet enduringly active national virtue. That the novel offers a remedial response to the corruption that it diagnoses is perhaps clearest though when it introduces Signor Antonio, a political refugee from Venice who in a chance encounter meets his old friend Signor Tedeschi, now contentedly settled in Britain. Just as Scott's work uses 'the most objective of sources: the object itself' to praise the effectiveness of Company rule, so it uses Signor Tedeschi to remind Britons of their own privileged birthright: 'This happy land shall shine for ever in the historian's page, a glorious instance of the blessings that freedom bestows. Though I am an Italian [...] my greatest boast shall be, that as a Briton, I can feel my heart beat at the very name of liberty' (p.197).[22] 'Blest country', Signor Antonio replies, 'the refuge of mortals from oppression. Surely Britons cannot know the extent of their own happiness, which experience enables me to see from comparison in its strongest colours!' (p.198).

In claiming that a native spirit of British liberty remains uncompromised (and that it will indeed 'shine for ever', p.197), Scott's Venetians sidestep the fact that American revolutionaries had invoked the very same heritage in their resistance to British colonial rule. That Scott himself sought at the least to pass over his own earlier support for that cause is suggested by a subsequent episode, in which the rupee comes into the hands of a nurse employed in 'taking care of the lovely children of the greatest King' (p.223). As this reference makes plain, Scott's work absolves the monarchy of any responsibility for the American debacle, while at the same time distancing itself from the Whig campaign against the Company's conduct in India (which, es-

22. Festa, *Sentimental empire*, p.122.

pecially after the fall of the Fox-North coalition at the end of 1783, presented George III as a despotic figure). The favourability of the immediate impression that the King creates – he is exalted above his subjects in 'merit' as well as 'dignity' – is heightened by the fact that, as the narrator explains, 'Hyder Alli was the only potentate I had before visited'. Invoking an ability to read people's thoughts, the rupee now tempers its earlier account of the Sultan, presenting him as a man whose mind was 'perpetually on the rack [...] [with] forming dark designs to accomplish his bloody purposes'. Hyder dreams of 'that glorious day, when I can wreck my vengeance on these white men that infest our country', whereas 'Britannia's queen [...] wishes well to all mankind' (p.230). Her husband, meanwhile, is said to be preoccupied with 'holding in his hands the scales in which mighty Kingdoms were weighed', remaining the embodiment of justice in proud defiance of the European nations that had recently 'taken up arms against his sea surrounded land' – additional but also reassuringly familiar adversaries. The narrator goes on to assert that the 'impotent efforts' of these nations 'will expose them to contempt, while Britain shall remain the admiration of future times', and the rupee further prophesies that George III's 'free born subjects' (p.231), wherever they subsequently go, will 'carry in their hands both victory and law!' (p.232).

The work briefly reasserts the compatibility of British liberty and Indian empire when the 'young princess' (p.223) who had been given the rupee by her nurse loses the coin in St James's Park, and it comes into the possession of a soldier named Bob. The soldier's story is a pathos-laden one, in that his preparation to go abroad 'in the service of his country' (p.226) separates him from his sweetheart, but at the same time this story enables Scott to reflect on 'the great success of the India Company', which Bob attributes to the apparently meritocratic means by which 'their officers attain a high command': 'It is not because a man is of a noble family, or has a weighty purse', the narrator states, channelling Bob's thoughts, 'it is known abilities and former services that entitle him to a distinguished rank' (p.244). Although this idealised image of the Company has to be read in part as a function of its author's quest for professional advancement – Scott was about to be commissioned as an assistant surgeon when he wrote the novel – it significantly bypasses the history of scandal that Mr Melvil had earlier invoked. As in *Memoirs of a gentleman*, the critique of Company rapacity is therefore countered by the fiction that Britain's Indian empire remains benignly commercial in character. Scott referred to the slave trade as a 'detestable commerce' in his 'Remarks concerning the inhabitants of Africa', appended to the second edition of the work, and in doing so he clearly interrogated the eighteenth-century ideology of commerce that saw it as the means 'by which happiness and knowledge are [...] generally diffused': for Africans, Scott declared, contact with Europeans had brought only 'ignorance and distress.'[23] As in the scene where Mr Melvil offers advice to his son, however, the novel insists on the progressive agency of commerce, in the form of the mutual interdependence that it generates. The potential for harmonious and sociable relations between people of different 'kingdoms' is signalled again, in a domestic context, at the end of the work, when Bob refers to his friend Moses (said to be renowned for his 'extreme application to business', p.248), and states that the 'similarity of sentiment' that unites the two men overrides and renders irrelevant 'distinctions, which neither of us can help' (p.246).

It is significant, however, that if Bob and Moses are presented as belonging to different kingdoms, the friendship between the pair is nonetheless one that is established in Britain itself. While the 'it-narrative' genre appears to be especially hospitable to the staging of circulation and the enacting of relations between peoples and places, as Deidre Lynch has shown, *Adventures of a rupee* does not depict any diffusion of the blessings of commerce taking place in India.[24] Instead, the rupee narrator spends most of its time in Britain, where it is 'a kind of curiosity' (p.103), but where – since it is not legal tender – it is at the same time in effect out of circulation; while in the pawnbroker's shop, the rupee is a static rather than mobile observer. The rupee's distance from actual processes of commercial exchange is emphasised again at the end of the work, when it speaks of being 'safely laid up in the storehouse of a company of antiquarians, [...] with medals, busts, inscriptions, and others of my learned brethren' (p.260). In this company, the rupee tells of how 'Cato gave us a long oration [...] against the vices of the age', speaking 'with much severity against corruption, from which he naturally passed to censure the British parliament' (p.263). This brief reference to parliamentary corruption is striking in view of the work's earlier praise of George III, so often accused at this time of encroaching upon the powers of parliament. That the figure of Cato more or less has the final word in *The Adventures of a rupee* is especially interesting when the work's engagement with the politics of empire is taken into account, since as in the influential and much reprinted text *Cato's letters* (1720-1723), the historical Cato was widely associated with opposition to territorial dominion. This final allusion to Cato is so resonant because, implicitly at least, it at once provides a reminder of the revolutionary argument against British authority in America and a warning about the future development of British power in India.

23. Scott, *Adventures of a rupee*, 2nd edn p.251.
24. Deidre Shauna Lynch, *The Economy of character: novels, market culture, and the business of inner meaning* (Chicago, IL, 1998), ch.2.

To finish, I shall briefly refer to another work of 1782, Robert Bage's epistolary novel *Mount Henneth*, which similarly appears to engage both with Britain's defeat in America and the tarnished reputation of the East India Company, but which still more clearly than *Adventures of a rupee* draws attention to the wishfulness of its remedial ideological investment in commercial empire.[25] Numerous characters in the novel clearly express their opposition to the American war – 'this plague and pestilence of Britain', in the words of one – on the basis of its impact upon their personal stakes in transatlantic commerce, and at the very outset Tom Sutton laments 'the wound given to this country, by its breach with the colonies'.[26] Before he becomes a steward to James Foston (the new owner of the Henneth estate), Sutton also considers the prospect of service with the East India Company, an idea which prompts his sister Nancy to tell him that the quest for an Indian fortune will take him to 'tainted regions, where war and desolation reign; to become an adept in the murder of mankind' (vol.1, p.57).

Bage's novel appeals to the familiar terms of anti-nabob rhetoric on a number of occasions, coupling America and India, and appealing to a general sense of the 'mercantile or military oppression, for which our generous countrymen are at present famous' (vol.1, p.29). When another character contemplates what lies ahead for Sutton, however, he expresses a wish that Sutton follow the early career of Foston, who, we are told, 'went out a writer in the service of the East India Company, but was a lieutenant under Col. Clive, when the chapter of accidents, and the exercise of all the virtues of humanity, gave him possession of a fortune, that exceeded his wishes, almost as much as it exceeded his hopes' (vol.1, p.34). As it is later recounted by Sutton, the story of Foston might be read as a rewriting of the recent history of the Company that elides the 'chapter of accidents' by which Foston attained his Indian fortune with a Seeley-like account of how Britain began all but absent-mindedly to acquire its Indian empire.[27] Such an interpretation seems persuasive in part because Foston so clearly represents himself at the beginning of his narrative as an unreconstructed figure, who for two years – like the narrator of *Memoirs of a gentleman* – exploits every possible opportunity for sexual conquest as well as self-enrichment. As Foston relates, the first stage of his career in India culminates in him drunkenly spitting at and

---

25. For a fuller account of Bage's fiction in the context of the politics of empire in the 1780s, see James Watt, '"The blessings of freedom": Britain, America, and "the east" in the fiction of Robert Bage', *Eighteenth-century fiction* 22.1 (2009), p.49-70.

26. Robert Bage, *Mount Henneth*, 2 vols (New York, 1979), vol.1, p.97-98 and vol.1, p.13. Page refs follow in text.

27. According to Seeley in *The Expansion of England* (1883), India in the late eighteenth century 'lay there waiting to be picked up by somebody'. Cited in Dirks, *The Scandal of empire*, p.316.

then striking a 'wooden deity' (vol.1, p.205) attached to a village temple, following which he is seized and 'fairly and speedily plumpt' in the Ganges, for 'the river god, to drown, or purify [...] as he thought fit' (vol.1, p.206).

Bage's novel does not press the symbolic significance of this moment of cleansing, nor does it really dwell upon Foston's subsequent encounter with 'the venerable old priest' (vol.1, p.208) who had witnessed the whole sequence of events. Foston's contact with the Hindu priest nonetheless assumes a pivotal status within his narrative, since it helps him to get rid of 'a [great] quantity of coxcombry', and also to begin to acquire 'true wisdom' and 'a more liberal cast of mind' (vol.1, p.213). The process of purification that Foston undergoes initially renders him vulnerable, first to fever then to robbery, but it also makes him a righteous figure, eager to avenge 'the well-known horrible catastrophe of the black hole' (vol.1, p.215), in which one of his friends had perished, and to hunt down Siraj ud-Daula after the defeat of his forces at the Battle of Plassey. As this reference to the Black Hole of Calcutta shows, Bage's representation of Foston's redemption helps to establish some different 'Indian' reference points from those – such as the Bengal famine – invoked by the anti-Company polemic that the novel earlier rehearses. In a particularly direct engagement with this rhetoric, the novel presents the second stage of Foston's Indian career culminating in his summary execution of two soldiers from Siraj's army, after catching them in the act of raping the daughter of a Persian merchant. The predation of 'Asiatic plunderers' (in Clarke's phrase) was frequently figured in terms of the rape of Indian women, as is well known, but what is obvious here is that the perpetrators of rape are themselves Indian, their violence the occasion for Foston to demonstrate his new sense of himself as a moral agent. Bage has the victim, Caralia, declare that 'No author has yet been so bold as to permit a lady to live and marry, and be a woman, after this stain' (vol.1, p.233), but her father, Duverda, ignoring these protestations, subsequently pledges her hand, along with 'all his effects in all the formalities of the Hindostan law' (vol.1, p.257), to their joint rescuer.

As Betty Joseph suggests, Caralia's minimal role in Foston's story serves to highlight the larger narrative function that she performs, which is to prove that Foston's redemption is genuine, and then to reward him for it, by setting in motion the 'laundering' of colonial wealth by which her father's fortune ends up being used to purchase a landed retreat in rural Wales.[28] Further to this, however, the description of Foston's encounter

---

28.　Betty Joseph, *Reading the East India Company, 1720-1840: colonial currencies of gender* (Chicago, IL, 2004), p.74.

with Caralia and Duverda might also be seen to strive for a more secure meaning for the idea of British liberty which, for supporters of the American cause such as Bage, had been radically called into question by Britain's treatment of its American colonies. When Duverda tells Foston of how he made his money from trading with 'European factories', for example, he details the peculiar 'sense, knowledge and virtue' of the English merchants that he had dealt with, and goes on to present their conduct as a shining alternative to the despotism, lust and violence that Siraj ud-Daula embodies, and which in fact reign 'All over the East' (vol.1, p.239). Pledging that his daughter will never find a partner 'amongst the sons of slavery or rapine', Duverda entreats Foston to carry Caralia to Britain so as to 'shew her the blessings of freedom' (vol.1, p.256). In a similar way to both *Memoirs of a gentleman* and *Adventures of a rupee*, therefore, *Mount Henneth* here presents a seemingly objective 'external' view of virtuous commerce and of the generalised sense of British liberty of which it is understood to be a manifestation.

If the resolution of Bage's 'India plot' might be seen to allegorise the wealth of Bengal as something that is gifted to – rather than expropriated by – the British, the function of this episode nonetheless seems to have at least as much to do with closing off the novel's more complicated and extensive 'America plot' as with attempting any larger vindication of the Company and its servants; if *Mount Henneth*'s brief account of conflict in Bengal in the 1750s perhaps encouraged readers to support military campaigns elsewhere in India in the early 1780s, it is significant that the novel makes no acknowledgement of the ongoing second Mysore war to which *The Adventures of a rupee* alludes. Even more than *The Adventures of a rupee*, *Mount Henneth* demonstrates the difficulty, or perhaps the implausibility, of representing the equal and widespread distribution of Smith's commercial 'benefits' in India. Bage's vision of a virtuous community in Britain, centred on the Henneth estate, is at the same time considerably more modest and inward-looking than that of Scott's account of George III and his 'free born subjects'. If *Mount Henneth* offers a rewriting of anti-Company polemic, therefore, Foston's retreat to Wales, even as it is funded by Indian wealth, represents an emphatic retreat from India too. To return in conclusion to the idea of the 'scandal of empire' considered at the outset, Dirks argues that the ruthless operations of the East India Company were publicised yet also all but written off by the Hastings trial, which ultimately effected a forgetting of scandal that in turn enabled 'the regeneration of the imperial idea'. Although there is no space here to address the significance of this much written about event, 'the greatest spectacle of late-eighteenth-century Britain', Dirk's suggestive claims about the longer-term impact of the trial may help to illuminate the ideological work performed by the novels under discussion in this essay.[29] As I have argued here, their function may have similarly been to contain scandal, in part by circulating fictions of commercial empire which, while they avowed their fictionality, perhaps additionally helped to make possible a kind of national amnesia regarding the recent history of how the Company had established its authority in Bengal and beyond.

29. Dirks, *The Scandal of empire*, p.85.

The Spanish translation of Bernardin de Saint-Pierre's *La Chaumière indienne*: its fortunes and significance in a country divided by ideology, politics and war

GABRIEL SÁNCHEZ ESPINOSA

Bernardin de Saint-Pierre's original texts enjoyed a significant, early and varied reception in Spain during the reign of Charles IV (1788-1808). An episode in *Paul et Virginie* (1788), seems to have inspired Goya for his cabinet painting *Naufragio* while convalescing in Cadiz in 1793.[1] During his banishment in Gijón Gaspar Melchor de Jovellanos noted in his diary in April 1794 his reading of *Paul et Virginie*, and his efforts to put it into Spanish, adding that if the results were good, it could be printed for the benefit of his recently established Asturian Nautical and Mineralogical Institute.[2] We do not know if the translation was ever completed, since no trace of it has survived. Jovellanos's friend, the poet and magistrate Juan Meléndez Valdés, while banished to Medina del Campo and Zamora in the final months of 1798, bought three copies of *Paul et Virginie*, at a cost of 12 *reales* each, probably to give away among his new circle of friends and acquaintances.[3] However, the first Spanish translation of *Pablo y Virginia*, by the cleric José Miguel Alea, advertised for the beginning of 1796, was held up by an unexpected legal investigation, after being denounced by a rival translator to the Council of Castile, which ordered a comparison of both translations. After being awarded the exclusive privilege to publish it on 1 July 1798, Alea's *Pablo y Virginia* was printed by Pantaleón Aznar later in the year in a compact duodecimo edition with an elegant title-page in the Romantic style.[4]

---

1. See Mercedes Águeda, 'Goya y Bernardin de Saint-Pierre', *Cuadernos de arte e iconografía* IV.8 (1991), p.167-74.
2. The comments date from the week 6-13 April 1794. Jovellanos read *Paul et Virginie* in the edition included in Bernardin de Saint-Pierre's *Etudes de la nature* (Paris, P.-F. Didot le jeune, 1790). See Jovellanos, *Diario 1* in vol.6 of his *Obras completas* ed. J.-M. Caso González (Oviedo, 1994), p.568-71.
3. According to the accounts kept by his administrator Bernardo González for the period June 1799-December 1803. See Georges Demerson, *Don Juan Meléndez Valdés y su tiempo* (Madrid, 1971), vol.1, p.394.
4. Jacques-Henri Bernardin de Saint-Pierre, *Pablo y Virginia* (Madrid, por Pantaleón Aznar, 1798). Alea dedicated his translation to the all-powerful minister Manuel Godoy, to whom

The Spanish translation of *La Chaumière indienne* (1791) was first published in Salamanca in 1803 by Francisco de Tójar under the title *El inglés de la India, ó la cabaña indiana.*[5] Born in Granada, the printer-bookseller Tójar associated himself with the literary circle surrounding his brother-in-law the poet José Iglesias de la Casa and the periodical *Semanario de Salamanca* that he directed for a year in the mid-1790s. He acquired a name for himself through editions of exotic novellas in small formats, all translated from the French, among them the *Colección de cuentos morales* by Saint-Lambert (1796), the *Colección de historias, apólogos, y cuentos orientales* (1804) and *Zadig ó el destino* (1804), published without indicating Voltaire's authorship.[6] Its translator, disguised on the title-page by the initials D. M. L. G., is Don Mariano Lucas Garrido, personal secretary to the poet Meléndez Valdés, who only years later, during the Trienio Constitucional (1820-1823), would reveal his authorship in an end-note to the text of his 1821 translation of the *Eponine* by J. Delisle de Sales.[7] Garrido, a progressive cleric like Alea, whom he knew from his

---

he was indebted for a grant to pursue abroad studies in ichthyology. His version of *Pablo y Virginia* was frequently reprinted: Philadelphia, 1808 and 1810; Palma de Mallorca, 1814; Valencia, 1816, are the first of these reprints. See Jean Sarrailh, 'Paul et Virginie en Espagne', in *Enquêtes romantiques* (Paris, 1933), p.3-39.

5.   Bernardin de Saint-Pierre, *El inglés de la India, ó la cabaña indiana. Traducida del francés por D. M. L. G.* (Salamanca, Francisco de Tójar, 1803), 12°, 132p. The work enjoyed a very early European success. Two different translations of *The Indian cottage* were printed in London in 1791 (one printed for John Bew, and the other for W. Lane). That same year, the translation printed for Bew was reprinted in Dublin (printed for J. Parker *et al.*). The first German translation, by Schröder, also appeared in 1791 under the title *Die indianische Strohhütte* (Neuwied und Leipzig, Johann Ludwig Gehra, 1791). The first Italian translation, entitled *La Capanna Indiana*, undertaken by A. Bruner, was published in Paris in 1796 (nella Stamperia di Honnert).

6.   *Coleccion de cuentos morales que contiene El Zimeo, novela americana; Las fabulas orientales y el Abenaki los da a luz traducidos del frances D. Francisco de Toxar* (Salamanca, en la imprenta del editor, 1796); *Colección de historias, apólogos y cuentos orientales traducidos del frances por D.**** (Salamanca, por D. Francisco de Toxar, 1804); [Voltaire], *Zadig ó El destino: historia oriental publicada en frances por Mr. De Vadé; y traducida al español por D.**** (Salamanca, por D. Francisco de Toxar, 1804). For an overview of Tójar's career as printer and editor, see the introduction by Joaquín Álvarez Barrientos to his edition of *La filósofa por amor* (Cadiz, 1995).

7.   J. Delisle de Sales, *Eponina. Traduccion libre del frances por don M. L. G.*, 2 vols (Madrid, 1821): 'El pensamiento de este capítulo sobre el encuentro del salvaje y su contestacion á las preguntas que le hace nuestro filósofo, está imitado de la obrita de la Cabaña indiana de Bernardino de san Pedro [...] La mencionada obrita es muy digna tambien de leerse, y suministra no pocas lecciones muy provechosas sobre el punto de felicidad que se ventila en la presente. Yo la publiqué traducida al castellano en el año 1803 en Salamanca con el título de = *El Inglés en la India, ó La Cabaña Indiana, por D. M. L. G.*' [In this chapter, the idea of the encounter with the savage and his reply to the questions of the philosopher, are taken from the novella *La Chaumière indienne* by Bernardino de san Pedro [...] It is a work most worthy of being read, since it provides many invaluable lessons on the subject of happiness, which is discussed in detail in *Eponina*. I published the Spanish translation in

contacts with the circle of the poet Quintana, editor of the journal *Variedades de Ciencias, Literatura y Artes*, would ally himself with the cause of Joseph Bonaparte during the Peninsular War, as did his mentor Meléndez Valdés, fleeing into exile after the battle of Vitoria, in June 1813.[8]

El inglés de la India, ó la cabaña indiana, advertised in the *Gaceta de Madrid* on 8 July 1803, would be sold for four *reales* in paper wraps or for six bound in a Spanish marbled leather binding.[9] Its compact format was designed to be taken anywhere, in the pocket of a coat or hidden between the pleats of a dress, in order to be read outside the home: on walks, in the garden, in a coach or while waiting to be received. It corresponds to a habit of intense reading, as the books that one takes outside are carefully chosen, books that are thought of as companions and which become faithful friends.[10] Tójar, perhaps following the example of the first French edition of *La Chaumière indienne* printed by Pierre-François Didot le jeune, gives it an elegant appearance with delicate types in which the words are characteristically more spaced than usual.[11] The Spanish title *El inglés de la India, ó la cabaña indiana*, is not the original one, it has been expanded either due to the influence of bipartite titles in contemporary translations of novels by Fielding and Richardson,[12] or to take advantage of the effect of recent news in the

---

Salamanca in 1803, under the title *El Inglés en la India, ó La Cabaña Indiana, por D. M. L. G.*], in n.8, vol.2, p.244-45.

8. Manuel Lucas Garrido, prebendary of Villafranca and high-ranking employee in the Ministry of Religious Affairs under Joseph I, went into exile as an *afrancesado*, residing in Auch, Toulouse and Montpellier. Later, during the Trienio Liberal, he was successively in 1821-1823 professor of Natural Law in the College of San Isidro, secretary of the Committee for the freedom of the press and temporary professor of Moral Doctrine and Natural Law in the Universidad Central.

9. See *Gaceta de Madrid* (Friday 8 July 1803), p.592. In Madrid this duodecimo volume was sold by Ramos in his bookshops in the Carrera de San Jerónimo and the calle Carretas. Subsequent advertisements appeared in the bimonthly journal *Variedades de Ciencias, Literatura y Artes* 19 (1804), p.63, and the daily *Diario de Madrid* (Monday 25 August 1806), p.234, that now indicates its price in paper wraps having risen to 5 *reales*.

10. Russell P. Sebold, 'Novelitas de faltriquera', *ABC* (Friday, 1 September 2000), p.58. For different habits and ways of reading in Spain at the end of the eighteenth century, see Gabriel Sánchez Espinosa, 'Gaspar Melchor de Jovellanos: un paradigma de lectura ilustrada', in *El Libro ilustrado: Jovellanos lector y educador*, ed. by Nigel Glendinning and Gabriel Sánchez Espinosa (Madrid, 1994), p.33-59.

11. *La Chaumière indienne par Jacques-Bernardin-Henri de Saint-Pierre* (Paris, Imprimerie de Monsieur [that is, Count of Provence, the future Louis XVIII] chez P. Fr. Didot le jeune, 1791, 18°). Saint-Pierre was married to Félicité Didot, daughter of P.-F. Didot le jeune (1732-1795). Concerning Didot's small format editions of *Paul et Virginie* and *La Chaumière indienne* (1791), see Daniel B. Updike, *Printing types: their history, forms, and use* (Cambridge, MA, 1937) vol.1, p.227.

12. The mid-1790s saw the simultaneous publication in Spain of several of the main English

public mind, particularly that of English victories over Tipu Sultan,[13] or because the editors wanted to highlight the equal significance of the two main characters (Fig.3, p.179).

The first review of the Spanish translation appeared in January 1804 in the periodical *Memorial Literario ó Biblioteca Periódica de Ciencias y Artes*, then edited by Pedro María de Olive, a cultural publication closer to the Neoclassical literary circle of Moratín, Estala and Melón, than to the progressive and pre-Romantic group around Quintana and Cienfuegos. It was an ambiguous review, combining the customary praise of the gentle, delicate style of its French author, criticism of his scientific theories, a positive judgment on the Spanish translation that appeared 'to have been done with care and intelligence', with an unequivocal misunderstanding of the ultimate intention of the work, that seems to be underestimated by the reviewer: 'But somebody might say, what is the point of this little tale for us in Europe, and what meaningful truths can we discover in it? Because if the intention is to modify the fate of the unlucky pariahs or to show the errors of the Brahmins, it should be printed and published in Benares or Calcutta.'[14] But even before it was advertised in the *Gaceta de Madrid*, in a letter written in Granada on 1 June 1803, the Franciscan theologian Fr Gonzalo de Arenas denounced the work for favouring 'the heathen system of Deism', and a few weeks later, on 16 July, Fr José de San Jerónimo, stressed the 'outrageous and scandalous doctrines, bordering on error' of the novella, that delivers

> the pills of scepticism and libertinism in the disguise of some of the Pariah's responses that have a Catholic flavour mixed with the novelty of enthusiasm, adorned with the variety of its descriptions and portrayals, and improved with the sweetness and pathos of its style. Step by step it disposes the spirit of the readers in a way that, with their understanding bewitched, their will is blindly overpowered, to the point of embracing its wretched principles.[15]

---

eighteenth century novels, mostly translated from the French. Among others *Pamela Andrews, ó La virtud recompensada...* (Madrid, 1794) and *Tom Jones ó El exposito...* (Madrid, 1796). See Philip Deacon, 'La novela inglesa en la España del siglo XVIII: fortuna y adversidades', in *Actas del I congreso internacional sobre novela del siglo XVIII*, ed. Fernando García Lara (Almería, 1998), p.123-39.

13. Public curiosity was initially fed by Calzada's translation of Antoine-Etienne-Nicolas Fantin Desodoards' *Memorias de Typoo-Zaïb, Sultan del Masur ó Visicitudes de la India en el siglo XVIII... escritas por dicho Sultan; y traducidas al frances del idioma malabar; publicadas por... Desodoards*, 2 vols (Madrid, 1800, 8°). On 1 January 1806, the three-act heroic melodrama *Tipóo-Saib o la Toma de Seringapatam* was premiered in Madrid.

14. *Memorial Literario ó Biblioteca Periódica de Ciencias y Artes* 5 (January, 1804), p.16-21. Translations from Spanish into English are my own. See Inmaculada Urzainqui, 'Los redactores del *Memorial literario* (1784-1808)', *Estudios de Historia Social. Periodismo e Ilustración en España* 52-53 (1990), p.501-16.

15. See the Inquisition's file on the 1803 edition in Madrid, AHN Inquisición, leg.4461 (8).

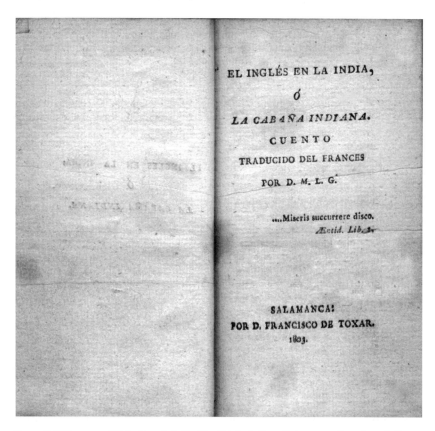

EL INGLÉS EN LA INDIA,

ó

LA CABAÑA INDIANA.

CUENTO

TRADUCIDO DEL FRANCES

POR D. M. L. G.

....Miseris succurrere disco.
Æntid. Lib. 1.

SALAMANCA:
POR D. FRANCISCO DE TOXAR.
1803.

Figure 3: Title-page of *El Inglés en la India, ó La Cabaña Indiana* (Salamanca, Francisco de Toxar, 1803).

After its denunciation, the novella was sent to the Inquisition in Madrid on 13 September 1804, where it was examined by the Minor Clerks Regular Juan de Montoya and Vicente Cea Gil who, in contrast with the opinions of the Granada friars, concluded that

> even if this novella is useless [...] and will be read with delight only by present-day young people, it does not contain propositions that merit theological censure [...] If we pay attention to the fact that it portrays the customs that travellers describe in their reports, it seems that it does not resist or oppose wholesome, true Catholic doctrine; it merely describes the habits, rites and ways of living of the various inhabitants of this Earth; so it is clear that if it merely tells us what others do, without saying more, it does not offend Catholic belief.

This detailed explanation was endorsed on 3 May 1805 by Dr Pascual Moreno y Canto, and as a result it was decided that publication would not be forbidden. Curiously, very soon afterwards, the Holy Office prohibited, through a Decree of 20 September 1806, a collection of sermons translated from the French by the same Mariano Lucas Garrido, that had been published two years earlier by Francisco de Tójar.[16]

The second Spanish edition of *La cabaña indiana* was printed in Valencia in the midst of the Peninsular War, in the spring of 1811. We know of its availability in Palma because of an advertisement in the *Diario de Mallorca* of 16 July.[17] The edition was funded by the Valencian booksellers Mallén, Salvá y Compañía, whose bookshop in the Calle San Vicente, next to the church of San Martín, was renowned as one of the best in Spain. Notwithstanding the indication that the translation – still attributed to 'D. M. L. G.' – had been corrected for this edition, it is basically the same as the one edited in 1803 with only slight modifications in spelling and punctuation, and a few other minor variants. A key feature of the reprint is the inclusion of an additional short story by the author, 'El café de Surate, translated into Spanish by Doña M. J. P.' – a female translator whose identity is unknown – a text that from then on accompanies *La cabaña indiana* in all subsequent editions. The new volume reverts to the original title, without the unnecessary expansion of the first Spanish edition, and includes an attractive and significant illustration facing the title-page, drawn by the artist Francisco Llácer and

---

16. In a reference to E. S. Reybaz's *Sermones de Mr ... precedidos de una carta sobre el arte de la predicacion; traducidos del Frances por D. Mariano Lucas Garrido*, 2 vols (Salamanca, en la Oficina de D. Francisco de Toxar, 1804). The original French edition, printed in Paris in 1801, was then also forbidden.

17. Bernardin de Saint-Pierre, *La cabaña indiana y el café de Surate, Cuentos de Santiago Bernardino Henrique de Saint-Pierre* (Valencia, por José Ferrer de Orga y Comp., 1811), 16°, 141p. According to the *Diario de Mallorca* (16 July 1811), p.760, it could be obtained in Carbonell's bookshop in Palma's Plaza de Cort.

engraved by Francisco Jordán.[18] The illustration depicts the family of the pariah as a paradigm of domestic love:

> Admiraba despues el Doctor la tranquilidad del Indio y su muger, que meciendo con el pie la cuna, en que dormia su hijo, negro y reluciente como el ébano, se entretenia en hacerle un collar con guisantes de Angola encarnados y blancos, mirando de quando en quando el Paria con ojos de interes y ternura ya á la una, ya á el otro. En suma, hasta el perro parecia tener su parte en la felicidad comun, y echado con un gato junto a la lumbre, abria de tiempo en tiempo los ojos, y miraba á sus amos, dando blandos ahullidos. (1803, p.54-55)[19]

It is an image that presents us with the double exoticism, each in varying degrees, of the two protagonists of the story: a pariah with oriental eyes and a Chinese air about him,[20] and an English traveller who has been portrayed in all probability in the image of one of the contemporary Englishmen attached to Wellington's expeditionary force in the Peninsula: dressed in his riding mantle, breeches and top boots, wearing a top hat with saddled brim, and seated on a travel bag, on top of which rest two pistols. The pariah's Brahmin wife, in her combination of modesty and sexual allure, might be modelled on representations of Mary Magdalene in Spanish Baroque painting (Fig.4, p.182).

Despite the fall of Valencia into French hands in early January 1812 and the subsequent move of the enterprising editor-bookseller Vicente Salvá to Palma de Mallorca,[21] an island free of foreign occupation for the

18. The engraving, inscribed *Franᶜᵒ Llazer lo invᵗᵒ y dibᵖ Franᶜᵒ Jordan lo grᵒ*, measures 72 x 47 mm. Both Francisco Llácer y Valdemont (1781-1857) and Francisco Jordán (1778-1832) studied in the Valencian Academia de San Carlos, where they were disciples and enjoyed the protection of the painter Vicente López.

19. 'Le docteur admiroit autour de lui le calme de l'Indien et de sa femme, encore plus profond que celui des élémens. Leur enfant, noir et poli comme l'ébène, dormoit dans son berceau: sa mère le berçoit avec son pied, tandis qu'elle s'amusoit à lui faire un collier avec des pois d'angole rouges et noirs. Le père jetoit alternativement, sur l'un et sur l'autre, des regards pleins de tendresse. Enfin, jusqu'au chien prenoit part au bonheur commun; couché avec un chat, auprès du feu, il entr'ouvroit de temps en temps les yeux et soupiroit en regardant son maître.' (Paris, Didot, 1791), p.54-55.

20. The only Indian visitors to Spain at the end of the eighteenth century that I have been able to trace, are the two Malabar mahouts who attended the Indian elephant that came to Madrid in the autumn of 1773, destined for Charles III's menagerie. Their Christian names were José Espino and Francisco de la Cruz. See Gabriel Sánchez Espinosa, 'Un episodio en la recepción cultural dieciochesca de lo exótico: la llegada del elefante a Madrid en 1773,' *Goya* 295-296 (2003), p.269-86.

21. On 30 August 1809 Vicente Salvá Pérez (Valencia, 1786, París, 1849), had married Josefa Mallén, daughter of the Franco-Spanish bookseller Diego Mallén (d.1799), of Dauphinois origins, son of Juan Antonio Mallén, a bookseller already active in Valencia in the mid-1750s, and a correspondent of the Genevan booksellers Cramer and Grasset. Salvá's marriage led to a partnership with his brother-in-law Pedro Juan Mallén under the name Mallén, Salvá y Compañia. The Peninsular War led to his move to Mallorca, where he

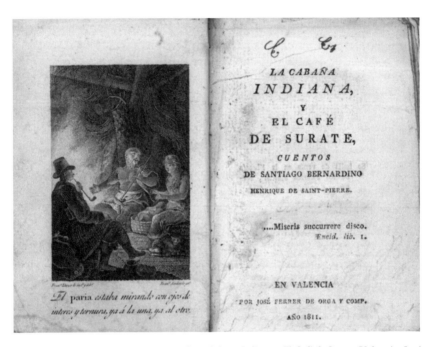

Figure 4: Frontispiece and title-page of *La Cabaña Indiana y El Café de Surate* (Valencia, José Ferrer de Orga, 1811)

duration of the war, the print run of the second edition of *La cabaña indiana* was sold unhindered in the capitals of loyalist and *afrancesado* Spain. Thus, we find it advertised at the beginning of December 1811 and in mid-March 1813 in the *Diario de Madrid*, the official periodical of Joseph I Bonaparte's state.[22] In parallel, the Cadiz anti-liberal periodical *El Procurador General de la Nación y del Rey*, a publication whose editorial staff were members of the *tertulia* of the Count of Torre Muzquiz, included *La cabaña indiana* on 2 June 1813 in a list of books and brochures of supposedly subversive character that could be found and read in the patriot capitals of Cadiz and Mallorca and whose reading was considered 'extremely harmful':

1. The *Social Contract* by Rousseau translated into Spanish, printed in Valencia, and disguised under the title: *Principles of political law*.
2. *La Cabaña indiana*, originally in French by Henrique de St. Pierre, translated and printed in Valencia.
3. The *Diccionario crítico-burlesco*, printed in Cadiz and banned by almost all the reverend Bishops of Spain.
4. The pamphlet entitled *Bread and bullfights*.
5. *The Eusebio*, and the *Letters of Abelard and Heloise*.
6. The periodical *La Aurora*.[23]

The editors and distributors of these texts sought 'the ruin of the Church', according to the sonnet that the anonymous anti-liberal journalist dedicated to them. He cannot avoid the facile rhyme galicistas-jansenistas, and shows himself to be a believer in a conspiratorial vision of history and of the current Spanish civil conflict. He assures them 'eternal fire, eternal suffering'. The denunciation was, no doubt, linked to the inspection of Palma de Mallorca's bookshops on 4 May 1813 that provoked the public complaint in the *Diario de Palma* of 21 November of the Mallorcan bookseller Miguel Domingo:

> without myself judging the legitimacy of that act, that some [that is, Liberals] will think contrary to article 306 of the Constitution (and that I, in order to excuse the city councillors, explain due to the difficulty of the circumstances

---

published in 1812-1813 in association with Isidoro Antillón the periodical *Aurora Mallorquina* that caused his exile to France and Italy after Ferdinand VII's restoration. Salvá returned in 1818 and in 1822 was elected to parliament as deputy for Valencia. After the fall of the Liberal régime in 1823, he emigrated to London where he opened the Spanish and Classical Library bookshop at 124 Regent Street. He transferred to Paris in 1831, where he again worked as a bookseller. See Carola Reig Salvá, *Vicente Salvá, un valenciano de prestigio internacional* (Valencia, 1972).

22. In *Diario de Madrid* (Wednesday 4 December, 1811 and Wednesday 10 March, 1813), p.635 and p.279-80, respectively. In the first instance it was sold in Pérez's bookshop, in the second in Alejandro Rodríguez's bookstore, both situated in the Calle Carretas.
23. *El Procurador General de la Nacion y del Rey* (2 June 1813), p.2019-20.

brought about by fanatics), I wish to state that the inspectors only found in my bookshop 4 copies of *La Cabaña indiana*, which they took with them and haven't returned to me, notwithstanding my just reclamations to this end. *La Cabaña indiana* was translated into Spanish many years before our glorious uprising, and was never forbidden by the Inquisition, as asserted by the ill-intentioned Father Manzaneda [...] The fact that it was originally written by Saint Pierre is not a justifiable reason for considering it banned, as everyone can see from *Pablo y Virginia* by the same author, a work in the hands of everybody. In order to convey to Father Manzaneda and his followers my final response on this matter, I would like to announce that the same short story, one which truly merits the appreciation of the public, can be bought in my bookshop for 8 reales, and I beg the Mayor Don Gaspar Coll, to return to me the 4 copies that, unjustly, he still retains.[24]

At the end of March 1814, Ferdinand VII returned to Spain after his not uncomfortable confinement at Valençay. On 16 April, sixty-nine traditionalist members of parliament handed him the so-called *Manifesto of the Persians*, requesting that the king rule as an absolute monarch and abolish the Cadiz Constitution of 1812 and the system of constitutional monarchy. Ferdinand VII was more than ready to oblige and annulled the Constitution on 4 May 1814, proscribed the followers of the French, re-established the Inquisition and began the repression of Liberal patriots who had helped him regain his crown in his absence.[25] Among the repressive measures enacted was the prohibition of selling, owning and reading many of the publications of the previous Liberal period and even some published from before the war. On 22 July 1815 an inquisitorial decree was issued, listing works against religion and state to be withdrawn from circulation:

[A]mong the evils brought about by the enemy invasion in 1808 [...] not least was the freedom to think and write with such excess and extravagance that in a period of five years our pious and Catholic nation was flooded with all kind

---

24. *Diario de Palma* (21 November 1813), p.307-308. Father Manzaneda, the instigator of this oppressive inspection of bookshops, is here described as a preacher 'in the style of Isaiah [...] disobedient to the instructions of the diocesan prelate'. Article 306 of the 1812 Cadiz Constitution established that 'the home of any Spaniard cannot be raided, except in those cases determined by the Law for the good order and security of the State'.

25. Francisco de Goya's print *Disparate de Bestia*, etched between October 1816 and January 1820, for his *Disparates* series, could be interpreted in relation to the unstable political context that had arisen after the restoration of Ferdinand VII. Four oriental-looking figures, perhaps Turks or Moors, are trying to get the attention of a tuskless Indian elephant standing in an illuminated ring – perhaps a distant memory of those seen by the artist in Madrid in 1773 or in the autumn-winter of 1806-1807. They are showing him a large-format opened book and some bell trappings. The orientals in the print would be the Persian members of parliament. The elephant, representing the Spanish people, is exposed to the risk of being duped by the advocates of Absolutism. See Gabriel Sánchez Espinosa, 'Un episodio...', p.269-86.

of perverse pamphlets, periodicals, brochures and books that could be read by anyone, bringing about the ruin of their souls.[26]

An extensive list of 150 works, ordered to be 'expressly confiscated with the approval of His Majesty' and comprising books, pamphlets and periodicals, is attached to the decree. In alphabetical order, the list includes such literary milestones as the comedy *El sí de las niñas* by the *afrancesado* playwright Leandro Fernández de Moratín, the *Poesías patrióticas* and tragedy *La viuda de Padilla* by the Liberal writers Manuel José Quintana and Francisco Martínez de la Rosa, alongside *La cabaña indiana* in the Valencian edition of 1811. The list ends with an ominous 'to be continued'.[27]

The omission of the 1803 Salamanca edition, textually identical to the Valencian one of 1811, can be explained by the difference in title and the urgent need to repress a type of literature that, according to the conspiratorial mindset of Absolutist thinkers, aimed to bring about a change in mentality as a prelude to an irreversible social and political change: 'The customs of the Spaniards had to be altered, corrupted, transformed, so that reform could multiply its triumphs.'[28] But it is still remarkable that in their attacks, the apologists of monarchy and the church never fail to target with extreme antipathy and hate from among the variety of contemporary pocket-books, *La cabaña indiana*:

Spaniards swore to uphold the Constitution, but a Constitution that would protect their religion, the Church, their faith, their general discipline, their institutions, customs and universal practices; not some laws that, with the pretence of defending these, would do the opposite; not some laws that would serve as a pretext to wage war on our religion and would authorise the greatest scandals; not some laws like the one on asylum which will open Spain to Protestants, heretics, Jews and all kind of enemies of our faith; that under the cover of press freedom have flooded the nation with the works of *Rousseau, Montesquieu, Filangieri, Millot* and have allowed to circulate unpunished the spurious letter from *Talleyrand to the Pope*, the *Ruins of Palmyra*, the

26. The edict is collected in Fermín Martín de Balmaseda, *Decretos del Rey Don Fernando VII. Año segundo de su restitucion al trono de las Españas. Se refieren todas las reales resoluciones generales que se han expedido por los diferentes ministerios y consejos en todo el año de 1815* (Madrid, 1819), vol.2, p.503-16.
27. Leandro Fernández de Moratín (1760-1828), *El sí de las niñas* (Madrid, 1805); Manuel José Quintana (1772-1857), *Poesías patrióticas* (Madrid, 1808); Francisco Martínez de la Rosa (1787-1862), *La viuda de Padilla* (Madrid, 1814). The list of 150 works is prefaced by a shorter one of just 17 containing works especially hated by the Absolutist monarchy and its ally the Spanish Catholic church, among which stands out the widely read *Diccionario crítico-burlesco...* (Cadiz, 1811), by the Liberal satirist Bartolomé José Gallardo (1776-1856).
28. Fray Rafael de Vélez, *Apología del Altar y del Trono ó Historia de las reformas hechas en España en tiempo de las llamadas Cortes, e impugnacion de algunas doctrinas publicadas en la Constitucion, diarios, y otros escritos contra la Religion y el Estado* (Madrid, 1818), vol.I, p.165.

Citador, La cabaña indiana, Ovid's *Art of love*; and especially those volumes in twelvemo format, which in their illustrations corrupt all our young people.[29]

The omitted first edition was, however, denounced in early 1816 in Barcelona.[30] New proceedings were opened, detailed opinions and assessments of censors were gathered and finally, in a decree of 29 May 1819, the Inquisition included it among books forbidden *in totum* for those without a licence to read forbidden books 'No. 25. The pocket-book in 8° entitled *El Ingles en la India, ó la Cabaña indiana,* a short story translated from the French by D. M. L. G., and printed in Salamanca by Don Francisco de Tojar, in the year 1803: for fomenting deism and materialism'.[31] The prohibition would be short-lived, since on 1 January 1820 an army revolt in Cabezas de San Juan led by Colonel Rafael de Riego would start the Trienio Constitucional, one of whose first measures was the abolition of the Inquisition, this time definitively. With the recovery of liberty, new editions of *La cabaña indiana* ensued.

It was printed twice in Valencia in 1820 by the Liberal editor-book-seller Vicente Salvá, the first being an edition in two volumes comprising the *Votos de un solitario y su continuacion, El café de Surate y La cabaña indiana.*[32] The translation of the latter work, revised and corrected by Salvá, is not the same as that of 1803 and 1811 by Mariano Lucas Garrido, though for *El café de Surate* Doña M. J. P.'s translation, with minimal spelling and punctuation changes, was used. Shortly afterwards, 'with the intention of pleasing those that would like to own *La Cabaña indiana* and the *Café de Surate* in one volume', that is to say without the *Votos*, Salvá issued an edition that reproduced the two texts and all other elements of the two-volume one.[33] Also from 1820 is an edition that according to its title-page was printed in Madrid, but that seems in reality to have been

29. [Fray Rafael de Vélez], *Apéndices á las Apologías del Altar y del Trono. Confrontacion de las citas que de la Apología del Trono hace el C. Vern... en sus Observaciones con la letra de aquella obra. Hacíala el autor de las Apologías* (Madrid, 1825), p.22.
30. See the file in Madrid, AHN Inquisición, leg.4501 (12).
31. According to the transcription of the 29 May decree published in the *Diario de Madrid* (Saturday 5 June 1819), p.778-80.
32. Bernardin de Saint-Pierre, *Votos de un solitario y su continuacion, El café de Surate y La cabaña indiana,* 2 vols (Valencia, [colophon: en la imprenta de Oliveres, ántes de Estevan], 1820), 12°. *El café de Surate* and *La cabaña indiana* are printed in vol.2, p.105-17 and 119-207, respectively. The engraving facing the title-page is taken from the 1811 Valencian edition, although here inserted in an ink frame. Confirmation about the revision and correction by V. Salvá of the previous translation – in reality a completely new one – can be found in Pedro Salvá y Mallén, *Catálogo de la biblioteca de Salvá* (Valencia, 1872), vol.2, p.179.
33. Bernardin de Saint-Pierre, *La cabaña indiana y el café de Surate: Cuentos de Santiago Bernardino Henrique de Saint-Pierre* (Valencia, [colophon: en la imprenta de Oliveres, ántes de Estevan],1820), 12°, XXVI + 108p. The *Gaceta de Madrid* (Tuesday 30 January 1821), p.136, advertised its availability in the Madrid bookshops of Bailo and the Viuda de Barco López.

printed in Lyons by the editors-cum-booksellers Cormon y Blanc.[34] This edition triggered off a new series of editions printed in France in Spanish that were destined both for the Peninsular market and for those recently opened up in the new South American republics.[35] In 1821 it was produced in Bordeaux by the printer Pedro Beaume;[36] there was another Bordeaux edition in 1822, perhaps by the same printer.[37] In 1822, the firm Cormon & Blanc published it in Lyons with a print run of a thousand copies.[38] In the same year, it was published in Paris, jointly with Chateaubriand's *Atala* and *René*,[39] with a print run of two thousand copies.

At this point, we might ask ourselves what were the reasons which would explain the uninterrupted and unexpected editorial success of *La cabaña indiana* among the Spanish reading public in the eventful first decades of the nineteenth century. The coincidence of a period of extreme outpouring of sentiments of national identity – culminating in the proclamation of the Cadiz 1812 Constitution – with a growing interest and curiosity for the exotic should not surprise us, as it represents only an apparent paradox.[40] After the partial integration of Spanish America following the unprecedented efforts of the first Bour-

34. Bernardin de Saint-Pierre, *La cabaña indiana y el café de Surate. Cuentos de...* (Madrid, 1820), 12°, 129p. The edition reproduces the translations carried out, respectively, by Mariano Lucas Garrido y doña M. J. P. with very minor changes in spelling and punctuation.

35. For an inventory of and a commentary on these works, all overtly associated with Liberal and progressive ideas, see Aline Vauchelle-Haquet, *Les Ouvrages en langue espagnole publiés en France entre 1814 et 1833* (Aix-en-Provence, 1985). In 1826, during the blackest period of the *década ominosa* in Spain, the French police, under pressure from the Spanish government, confiscated some editions in Spanish from the Parisian bookshops of Rosa and Seguin and from Jean Alzine's bookshop in Perpignan. Books by the former Inquisitor J.-A. Llorente, memoirs by *afrancesados*, anticlerical works and various translations of Rousseau, Constant, Destutt de Tracy were seized, likewise Spanish editions of *Faublas*, *Les Liaisons dangereuses*, *Julie ou La Nouvelle Héloïse*, *Bélisaire*, *Les Incas*, the *Lettres persanes* and *La Chaumière indienne*. See Vauchelle-Haquet, *Les Ouvrages*, p.75 and 76-77.

36. Bernardin de Saint-Pierre, *La Cabaña Indiana, y El Café de Surate, Cuentos de Santiago Bernardino Henrique de Saint-Pierre* (Burdeos, 1821), 12°, 132p.

37. Bernardin de Saint-Pierre, *La Cabaña Indiana, y El Café de Surate* (Burdeos, 1822), 18°.

38. It was advertised in the *Bibliographie de la France* on 16 March 1822: Bernardin de Saint-Pierre, *La cabaña indiana y el café de Surate. Cuentos de Santiago Bernardino Henriago de Saint-Pierre* (Lyon, chez Cormon & Blanc, 1822), 18°. Listed as no.171 in Vauchelle-Haquet's inventory.

39. François-René de Chateaubriand and Bernardin de Saint-Pierre, *Atala y René por Chateaubriand, Cabaña indiana y El café de Surate por Bernardin de Saint-Pierre; bajo la dirección de José René Masson* (París, Masson e Hijo, calle de Erfurth n° 3, 1822), 18°, 317 p. The requisites of the *Dépôt légal* were completed on 25 July 1822. It was advertised in the *Bibliographie de la France* on 3 August 1822 and is catalogued as no.192 in Vauchelle-Haquet's inventory. It reprints the 1803 translation of *La cabaña indiana*; the version reprinted of *El café de Surate* is the one by *doña* M. J. P., with minor adjustments in spelling and punctuation.

40. See Francisco Lafarga, 'Territorios de lo exótico en las letras españolas del siglo XVIII', *Anales de literatura Española* 10 (1994), p.173-92.

bons to modernise governance and commerce between the Spanish mainland and its colonies, and to study and control those territories through a string of state sponsored scientific expeditions, true exoticism would be sought in unexpected geographical and cultural locations, such as the Levant, China-Japan, Africa, the Quaker colonies, the indigenous tribes in North America and the recently discovered Pacific Islands.[41] In quantitative terms, the presence of India among these territories of what was culturally exotic for Spain was very minor, no doubt due to the practically non-existent contact between Spain and the Indian subcontinent throughout the eighteenth century.[42]

The text of *La cabaña indiana* is distinguished by a wide range of motifs deriving from Indian culture whose exotic nature elicits the interest and attention of the reader and sustains the tension implicit in the act of reading, motifs that, notwithstanding their cultural distancing effect, could still be recognised by the Spanish reader. Among the most characteristic, we might highlight the caste system with the figure of the pariah, the ritual of *sati*, the description of Hindu religious ceremonies centred on the Jagannath temple on the coast of Orissa and the occasional allusion to the *bayadères*. In addition the text's descriptions of landscapes, both urban and rural, exert a compelling evocative power. Among these descriptions, as viewed by the solitary figure of the pariah, the vision of nocturnal Dehli as a multicultural and multi-religious space stands out. The Spanish translation is flavoured by exotic words from Hindi and Urdu accompanied by their Spanish equivalents: '*frangui, ó impuro*' (1803, p.32), '*Dsandhem ó bandolera*' (1803, p.36) or '*Kaber-dar, alerta*' (1803, p.79). Most of the endnotes to the text, all supplied by the Spanish translator, have a specific botanical character, relating to Indian trees mentioned in the text, and make a point of indicating their nutritional, medical and commercial usefulness, reflecting the fact that botany was probably the science most directly and effectively championed in Spanish Enlightenment culture.[43]

---

41. Gabriel B. Paquette provides an effective synthesis of the transformation experienced by the Spanish Atlantic Empire in the fifty year period prior to its independence, in *Enlightenment, governance, and reform in Spain and its empire, 1759-1808* (Basingstoke, 2008). For a comprehensive summary of Spanish eighteenth-century scientific expeditions, see Javier Puerto's 'El modelo ilustrado de expedición científica', in *Ilustración, ciencia y técnica en el siglo XVIII español*, ed. Enrique Martínez Ruiz and Magdalena de Pazzis Pi Corrales (Valencia, 2008), p.129-51. For more detailed analysis on specific expeditions, see the recent studies by Miguel Ángel Puig Samper, Juan Pimentel and Daniela Bleichmar, too numerous to list.

42. For the very rare Spanish commercial ventures in India undertaken from the Philippines, see Salvador P. Escoto, 'Haidar Alí: un intento frustrado de relación comercial entre Mysore y Filipinas, 1773-1779', *Revista Española del Pacífico* 10 (1999), p.45-75.

43. In comparison with the rest of Bernardin de Saint-Pierre's work and more specifically

But under its enticing exotic apparel, *La cabaña indiana* was intended as a focus for social and philosophical criticism, and as such it was understood by its first readers across the whole spectrum of Spanish society, then immersed in a process of accelerated transition between the *ancien régime* and a new class-based society.

There were already precedents for an allegorical reading of those few texts which inhabited a space halfway between the narrative and the factual-geographical in their relationship with the Indian subcontinent, texts that had been published in the Spanish periodical press just a decade earlier. For example, the article, or tale, 'Apuntes para formar la idea de la ciudad de Caalla, distante seis leguas de la Corte de Dradmi, reino de Naaspe, en los senos más reconditos de la India', published in November 1790 in the *Correo de Madrid*, gave rise to a long footnote signed by *Quiquendam* that assimilates the Indian to the Spanish context and makes a passionate plea against a parasitic hereditary nobility which is useless to their homeland, and in favour of the ennoblement of those who merit it for their services;[44] and in 'Teruna-Malli en la Costa de Malabar. Descripcion de una fiesta religiosa, sacada de una carta dirigida à Europa últimamente', published in April 1788 in *Espíritu de los mejores diarios literarios que se publican en Europa*, a perfect opportunity for anti-clerical satire is exploited when, portraying the hypocrisy of certain Indian religious men, they are referred to as 'frailes', a term that presents an unequivocal nod to the Spanish reader, who will then apply the relevant criticism to his own context at a moment when enlightened figures collaborating with a reformist government are pushing in their reports and white papers for the introduction of legislation and procedures which would limit the excessive, uncontrolled numbers of friars and convents, and eventually reduce the excessive economic power of the Spanish Catholic church:

> At this time I saw a row of all manner of friars, in different attitudes, and dressed in a very strange manner, who proffered copper collection plates to all passers-by, saying: *give alms, and go to Heaven*. Others sat in the chapels,

---

with the massive critical attention paid to *Paul et Virginie*, studies devoted to the commentary and analysis of *La Chaumière indienne* are scarce; the following should be highlighted: Roseann Runte, '*La Chaumière indienne*: a study in satire', *The French review* 53.4 (1980), p.557-65, Binita Mehta's chapter 'The untouchable as noble savage: Bernardin de Saint-Pierre's *La Chaumière indienne*', in her *Widows, pariahs, and bayadères: India as spectacle* (Lewisburg, PA, 2002), p.114-22, and Malcolm Cook, 'Bernardin de Saint-Pierre, lecteur de Voltaire', in *Voltaire et ses combats*, ed. Ulla Kölving and Christiane Mervaud (Oxford, 1997) vol.2, p.1079-84.

44. 'Apuntes para formar la idea de la ciudad de Caalla, distante seis leguas de la Corte de Dradmi, reino de Naaspe, en los senos más reconditos de la India', in *Correo de Madrid* 409 (24 November 1790), p.52-54.

offering blessings and praises to their gods, describing their attributes and principal deeds, and recommending their devotions; without failing from time to time to glance at their plates, that were gradually being filled.[45]

Similarly, allusions in *La cabaña indiana* to 'los campos abandonados, que tan comunes son en la India' – deserted fields, so common in India, 'la ruina de sus cultivadores' – the ruin of its farmers and 'las ruinas de la agricultura' – the ruins of its agriculture (1803, p.75, 102), would have obvious parallels for Spanish readers, used to encountering similar phrases, time and time again, in the reformist agrarian texts of the Spanish Enlightenment.

A text like *La cabaña indiana* that, in an Indian environment, rejects organised religion, associated here with superstition, that raises questions about priestly authority and champions a natural spirituality without intermediaries, that denounces the abuses derived from entrusting children's education to a priestly caste, that berates their hypocrisy and censures the exploitation for their own social and economic benefit of the spiritual and moral control that they exert over the consciences and habits of their followers; a text that, in short, allows the reader through a *Verfremdung* technique to relativise the principles and prejudices of his or her own religion – for example, the pariah's infamy finds an echo in the notion of the original sin of the Catholics – could not fail to be perceived by the inquisitorial censors as a direct threat to the monopoly exercised by the Catholic church in Spain. This led to the persistent persecution of the work with a view to its suppression, in a fashion similar to the emasculation suffered a few years before by Pedro Montengón's didactic novel *Eusebio* (1786-1788), set among the Quakers of Pennsylvania, which in its revised, Inquisition-amended second edition (1807-1808), was shorn of most of its radical religious implications.[46]

The parallel editorial success during the first decades of the nineteenth century of *La cabaña indiana* with the *Noches lúgubres*, a prose work of hotly debated generic classification and contrasting interpretations, composed by José de Cadalso in 1770-1771, does not seem fortuitous or

---

45. 'Teruna-Malli en la Costa de Malabar. Descripcion de una fiesta religiosa, sacada de una carta dirigida à Europa últimamente', in *Espíritu de los mejores diarios literarios que se publican en Europa* 118 (5 April 1788), p.13-14 – from which the quotation derives – and 119 (7 April 1788), p.19-20. The translator of *La cabaña indiana* in his footnote to the religious festival in the Jagannath Temple makes frequent use of the Spanish Catholic term 'procesión' (1803, n.2, p.122); in his description of Dehli he mentions the 'campanarios de las mezquitas' (1803, p.85). This practice contributes, no doubt, to the reader's identification of the fictional India with Spain.

46. See Maurizio Fabbri, 'Observaciones sobre las dos redacciones del *Eusebio* de Montengón', in *El siglo que llaman ilustrado. Homenaje a Francisco Aguilar Piñal*, ed. Joaquín Álvarez Barrientos and José Checa Beltrán (Madrid, 1996), p.317-25.

unrelated.[47] First published posthumously in instalments in the periodical *Correo de Madrid* in 1789-1790 and reprinted in a miscellaneous collection in 1792, the *Noches lúgubres* was re-issued on three occasions between 1802 and 1804, once as part of the *Obras de Don Joseph Cadalso*.[48] After a few years of editorial silence, from 1815 onwards, it would be continuously reprinted,[49] and up to the beginning of the 1830s, besides its inclusion in the 1818 Madrid edition of Cadalso's collected *Obras*, it was published on its own in Spain on at least eleven different occasions. In France there were four separate editions printed in Paris, and three more edited in Bordeaux alongside Jovellanos's *El delincuente honrado*, a bleak *comédie larmoyante* written in prose in the early 1770s. An extensive fragment of the *Noches lúgubres* was included in a two-volume anthology of literary models edited for a Spanish school in Bordeaux, and its first French translation was printed in Paris in 1821. In 1829 the *Noches lúgubres* appeared in New York, again alongside Jovellanos's play. Most of the editions are in small formats, ranging from twelvemo to thirty-twomo.

The similarities between *La cabaña indiana* and the *Noches lúgubres* – works created autonomously in very different circumstances, but that undoubtedly satisfied the needs and expectations of a similar reading public who did not tire of reading them over and over again – are very striking, and we will only point out the most evident of them here. The protagonists of both works have no name or are designated by a generic name.[50] Both narratives are situated at night-time, a feature which lends itself to the unfolding of terror and the sublime – the main episode in *La cabaña indiana* takes place during the long dark evening in which the pariah takes the English doctor into his hut. Both texts acknowledge

47. The critical debate surrounding the *Noches lúgubres* can be followed in the major editions by Nigel Glendinning (Madrid, 1961 and 1993), Russell P. Sebold (Madrid, 1993 and 2000), and Emilio Martínez Mata (Barcelona, 2000), frequently reprinted. Colonel Cadalso was killed in combat during the siege of Gibraltar at the end of February 1782.

48. For a full reconstruction of the editorial history of the *Noches lúgubres* during these decades, it is essential to complete the bibliographical details listed in the editions mentioned above with the items catalogued by A. Vauchelle-Haquet, plus new data included in the *Catálogo Colectivo del Patrimonio Bibliográfico Español* online database.

49. The 1815 Madrid edition by Repullés, printed in a handy sixteenmo, provoked the opening in 1816 of an inquisitorial case against the *Noches lúgubres* in the Valladolid Inquisition that would bring about its final prohibition in 1819. See Miguel Ángel Lama, 'Todo es exagerado y falso hasta cierto punto: nota a una lectura de las *Noches lúgubres* de Cadalso', *Dieciocho* 33.1 (2010), p.47-54, who discusses the handwritten annotations by an unknown, but outraged and traditionally-minded contemporary reader in a copy of this edition.

50. For a discussion of this characteristic in relation to the *Noches lúgubres*, see Russell P. Sebold, 'José Cadalso: sus *Noches lúgubres*, su romanticismo', in *Historia de la literatura Española: siglo XVIII*, ed. Guillermo Carnero (Madrid, 1995), vol.2, p.740-41.

their debt to Edward Young's graveyard poetry,[51] and in both works the main characters find physical and spiritual consolation in cemeteries:

> para no morir de hambre, me veia forzado [speaks the pariah] a buscar mi sustento entre los muertos; es decir, á acudir á los cementerios, donde tomaba los manjares que deponia sobre los sepulcros la piedad de las familias. En estos lúgubres sitios me complacia en meditar, y extatico exclamaba: aquí es la ciudad de la paz; aquí han desaparecido el poder y el orgullo; aquí están en seguro la inocencia y la virtud; aquí diéron fin todos los temores de la vida, y aún el de la muerte; ésta es la hospederia, donde ha desuncido el carretero para siempre, y donde reposa el Paria. (1803, p.89-90)[52]

The atmospheric episode in the second of the *Noches lúgubres*, in which Tediato is detained as a murder suspect and thrown into jail to be interrogated and tortured, seems to be reflected in the situations experienced by the pariah during his nocturnal strolls through Dehli:

> Despues pasé junto a un grande edificio, que conocí ser una carcel por el ruido de cadenas que sonaban dentro, y mas adelante hallé un vasto hospital, del qual salian carros, llenos de cadaveres. Siguiendo mi camino, encontré ladrones, que huian azorados, patrullas de guardias, que iban en su alcance; pelotones de mendigos, que á pesar de los palos demandaban á las puertas de los palacios las sobras de los festines, y por todas partes mugeres que se prostituian para ganar su sustento. (1803, p.79-80)[53]

The pariah's nocturnal episode – since he is in danger of being killed, if discovered during the day – is abruptly ended by the terrifying fire of the Great Mughal's palace:

51. 'Yo [speaks the English doctor] te confieso que la mayor parte de las ciudades son mejor para vistas de noche; pero al cabo la naturaleza tiene sus bellezas nocturnas, que no son ménos peregrinas que las del día, y no ha cantado otras en verso un célebre poeta, compatriota mio.' (1803, p.91-92). '...croyez-moi [speaks the English doctor], la plupart des villes ne méritent d'être vues que la nuit. Après tout, la nature a des beautés nocturnes qui ne sont pas les moins touchantes; un poète fameux de mon pays n'en a pas célébré d'autres' (Paris, 1791), p.101-102.
52. 'Ne pouvant [speaks the pariah] donc trouver à vivre parmi les vivans, j'en cherchois parmi les morts: j'allois dans les cimetières manger sur les tombeaux les mets offerts par la piété des parens. C'étoit dans ces lieux où j'aimois à réfléchir. Je me disois: c'est ici la ville de la paix; ici ont disparu la puissance et l'orgueil; l'innocence et la vertu sont en sûreté: ici sont mortes toutes les craintes de la vie, même celle de mourir: c'est ici l'hôtellerie où pour toujours le charretier a dételé, et où le paria repose' (Paris, 1791, p.99-100).
53. 'Je [speaks the pariah] côtoyai ensuite un grand bâtiment, que je reconnus pour une prison, au bruit des chaînes et aux gémissemens qui en sortoient. J'entendis bientôt les cris de la douleur dans un vaste hôpital, d'où l'on sortoit des chariots pleins de cadavres. Chemin faisant, je rencontrai des voleurs qui fuyoient le long des rues, des patrouilles de gardes qui couroient après eux; des groupes de mendians qui, malgré les coups de rotin, sollicitoient, aux portes des palais, quelques débris de leurs festins; et par-tout, des femmes qui se prostituoient publiquement pour avoir de quoi vivre' (Paris, 1791, p.86-87).

salió repentinamente de las cocinas del Serallo una enorme pirámide de llamas, cuyos torbellinos de humo se confundian con las nubes, y su dorado resplandor, iluminando las torres de la fortaleza, sus fosos, la plaza, los campanarios de las mezquitas, se extendia por todo el horizonte. A punto tocaron á rebato con un espantoso ruido los gruesos timbales de cobre, y los *Karnas* ó grandes obúes de la guardia; y derramándose por toda la ciudad esquadrones de caballería, forzaban las puertas de las casas inmediatas al palacio, y obligaban á golpes á sus moradores á acudir al incendio. Yo mismo experimenté, quan perjudicial era á los miserables la vecindad de los Grandes, que semejantes á el fuego, abrasan hasta los mismos que le subministran el incienso, si se acercan demasiado. (1803, p.84-85)[54]

The fire motif in *La cabaña indiana* is highly significant, since it was probably understood by contemporary readers as the symbolic fire that was devouring the state in the *ancien régime*, and the image of the flames and destructive, uncontrolled fire, with its associated negative luminosity, is a sinister presence in the art produced in Spain at the turn of the century, especially around the years of the Peninsular War.[55] The violent clash of the historical and the private – 'Obligaban á golpes á sus moradores á acudir al incendio' – now perceived as a paradigm of human existence, will compel the pariah to abandon the city and human society for good.[56]

The first two decades of the nineteenth century were a period of intense anxiety for Spain, a time of crisis for all previously held truths, both those based on Catholic tradition as well as for those derived from the philosophical principles of the Enlightenment, whose social, political and cultural programme of reform was then thought to be a project of impossible practical implementation after the advances and retreats that characterised the reign of Charles IV, the ruthless civil conflict triggered

54. '...une longue colonne de feu s'éleva tout-à-coup des cuisines du sérail: ses tourbillons de fumée se confondoient avec les nuages, et sa lueur rouge éclairoit les tours de la forteresse, ses fossés, la place, les minarets de la ville, et s'étendoit jusqu'à l'horizon. Aussitôt les grosses timbales de cuivre, et les karnas ou grands hautbois de la garde, sonnèrent l'alarme avec un bruit épouvantable: des escadrons de cavalerie se répandirent dans la ville, enfonçant les portes des maisons voisines du château, et forçant, à grands coups de korahs, leurs habitans d'accourir au feu. J'éprouvai aussi moi-même combien le voisinage des grands est dangereux aux petits. Les grands sont comme le feu, qui brûle même ceux qui lui jettent de l'encens s'ils s'en approchent de trop près' (Paris, 1791, p.93-94).
55. Mention might be made of Goya's oil paintings *Incendio, fuego de noche* (1793-1794), *La Hoguera* (*c.*1808-1814), *Incendio de un hospital* (*c.*1815) and his print *Escapan de las llamas*, no.41 of the *Desastres de la guerra* series, produced immediately after the war.
56. Curiously, a similar conflict between public and private will be resolved in the apocryphal continuation contained in an 1817 edition – bearing no other imprint – of the *Noches lúgubres*, with Tediato setting fire to his house, where he had just brought the disinterred corpse of his lover. See John Dowling, 'Las *Noches lúgubres* de Cadalso y la juventud romántica del Ochocientos', in *Coloquio internacional sobre José Cadalso*, ed. Mario di Pinto *et al.* (Abano Terme, 1985), p.105-24.

by the French invasion, and the subsequent stagnation in all areas that
followed Ferdinand VII's restoration in 1814.

The representative of Enlightenment thinking in *La cabaña indiana* is
the English doctor participating in a scientific expedition – organised by
an institution equivalent to the Royal Society – to various parts of the
world with the purpose of bringing together the totality of human
knowledge. In spite of three years of travels that have taken him to India
and the assembling of a collection of manuscripts and rare imprints
composing ninety bales which weigh 9500 pounds, despite having accomplished his aim of answering 3500 questions given to each of the
expeditionaries, he cannot assuage his inner anxiety:

> lejos de haber ilustrado ninguna de las tres mil quinientas qüestiones, habia
> contribuido solo á multiplicar las dudas: y como todas estaban mútuamente
> enlazadas, lo insuficiente ó embrollado de una solucion destruia, ó hacia
> dudosa la evidencia de la otra [...] por manera que las verdades mas claras se
> habian hecho problemáticas, y era ya casi imposible distinguirlas en este
> vasto laberinto de respuestas y autoridades contradictorias. (1803, p.19)[57]

But the representatives of European Enlightenment in *La cabaña indiana*
and the *Noches lúgubres*, notwithstanding their conviction of the impossi-
bility of establishing a solid foundation for knowledge upon which to
build the Enlightenment's project, will keep their doubts and anxieties to
themselves, and in public still uphold its reformist ideals. The crisis of
Enlightenment in Spain, against the European backdrop of the
Napoleonic wars, will force the progressive thinkers to seek refuge –
real or symbolic – in nature, where, perhaps, it might still be possible to
develop some kind of social utopia. This explains why in December 1806
the poet Manuel José Quintana (1772-1857) urged Francisco Balmis
(1753-1819), leader of an official expedition to introduce Jenner's small-
pox vaccine to Spanish America, to remain paradoxically in the politically uncontaminated America.[58] In similar fashion, the English doctor in

---

57. '...que loin d'avoir éclairci aucune des trois mille cinq cents questions de la société royale,
il n'avoit contribué qu'à en multiplier les doutes; et comme elles étoient toutes liées les
unes aux autres, il s'ensuivoit, au contraire de ce qu'avoit pensé son illustre président, que
l'obscurité d'une solution obscurcissoit l'évidence d'une autre, que les vérités les plus
claires étoient devenues tout-à-fait problématiques, et qu'il étoit même impossible d'en
démêler aucune dans ce vaste labyrinthe de réponses et d'autorités contradictoires.'
(Paris, 1791, p.9-10).
58. Manuel José Quintana, 'A la expedición española para propagar la vacuna en América
bajo la dirección de Don Francisco Balmis': '... Balmis, no tornes, / no crece ya en Europa /
el sagrado laurel con que te adornes. / Quédate allá, donde sagrado asilo / tendrán la paz,
la independencia hermosa,' in *Poesías patrióticas*, p.7: 'Thou, Balmis! Never mayst return;
nor grows/in Europe now the sacred laurel meet/with which to crown thee. There in calm
repose,/where peace and independence a retreat/may find, there rest thee!', translated by
James Kennedy, *Modern poets and poetry of Spain* (London, 1852), p.158.

La cabaña indiana seeks refuge from the symbolic typhoon in the remote and primitive, but solid and welcoming, hut of the pariah.[59]

The dialogue between the disillusioned man of the Enlightenment and the natural man ('hombre de la naturaleza', 1803, p.69), as well as proposing new epistemological principles, with a revaluation of sentiment over reason and the call for a renewed establishment of our connection with nature, highlights, through the personal relationship emerging between the European and the outcast, the effective comfort provided by the revived value of fraternity. The sentiment of fraternity, full of contemporary Republican connotations, has its parallel in the transformed relationship between Cadalso's Tediato and the gravedigger Lorenzo reached at the end of the *Noches lúgubres*, or that manifested by the poet Nicasio Álvarez de Cienfuegos towards a proletarian representative in his ode 'En alabanza de un carpintero llamado Alfonso'.[60] The new basis of their relationship is symbolised in the pariah's rejection of the Englishman's gift, a valuable 'relox de oro, obra de Grenham, el mas celebrado fabricante de Lóndres, el qual tiene cuerda para un año' (1803, p.111) – a perfect example of the best European manufacture, but also in the end an instrument for the control of both nature and society – and the resulting exchange, as suggested by the pariah, of their more egalitarian smoking pipes instead.[61]

It would be difficult to find a more striking instance of the underlying programmatic character of *La cabaña indiana* than the composition in capital letters by its editor Tójar of the summary which contains the pariah's three answers concerning truth, answers that the English doctor keeps to himself, for his own benefit, and does not communicate to the president of the Royal Society (Fig.5, p.196). This is the authentic ideological core of the work, unequivocally situated at its conclusion. We may wonder why Tójar presented his text in this manner, as this was not the case in any of the first French editions of *La Chaumière indienne*, and the original 1803 layout would be copied in all Spanish editions during the first two decades, with the exception of the two Valencian editions of 1820 in which the capital letters are replaced by italics. It

59. 'Gozábase este [the English doctor] en contemplarse al abrigo de tan furiosa tempestad en aquella Cabaña sólida' (1803, p.54). 'Cependant le docteur jouissoit du plaisir d'être en sûreté au milieu de la tempête. La cabane étoit inébranlable' (Paris, 1791, p.53).

60. Nicasio Álvarez de Cienfuegos, *Obras Poeticas* (Madrid, Imprenta Real, 1816), p.161-74. The ode, posthumously published in 1816, hadn't been included in the 1798 first edition of his poems, but had been widely read in manuscript. Introduced by a quotation from Seneca, *Virtutem... invenies... callosas habentem manus*, in lines 20-22 we find the explicit '...¡Ó congojosa / Choza del infeliz! á ti volaron / La justicia y razon...' – Oh dreadful hut of the wretched man! Justice and reason found refuge in you.

61. 'cette montre d'or; elle est de Greenham, le plus fameux horloger de Londres; on ne la remonte qu'une fois par an' (Paris, 1791, p.124)

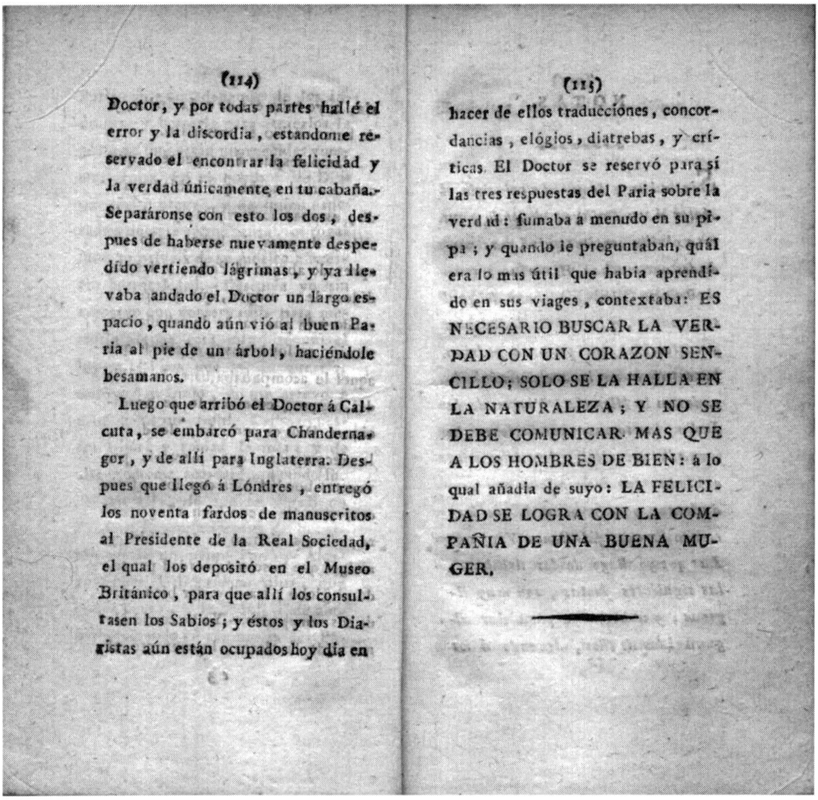

114

Doctor, y por todas partes hallé el
error y la discordia, estándome re-
servado el encontrar la felicidad y
la verdad únicamente en tu cabaña.
Separáronse con esto los dos, des-
pues de haberse nuevamente despe-
dido vertiendo lágrimas, y ya lle-
vaba andado el Doctor un largo es-
pacio, quando aún vió al buen Paria al pie de un árbol, haciéndole
besamanos.

Luego que arribó el Doctor á Cal-
cuta, se embarcó para Chanderna-
gor, y de allí para Inglaterra. Des-
pues que llegó á Lóndres, entregó
los noventa fardos de manuscritos
al Presidente de la Real Sociedad,
el qual los depositó en el Museo
Británico, para que allí los consul-
tasen los Sabios; y éstos y los Dia-
ristas aún están ocupados hoy dia en

hacer de ellos traducciónes, concor-
dancias, elógios, diatrebas, y crí-
ticas. El Doctor se reservó para sí
las tres respuestas del Paria sobre la
verdad: fumaba á menudo en su pi-
pa; y quando le preguntaban, quál
era lo mas útil que habia aprendi-
do en sus viages, contextaba: ES
NECESARIO BUSCAR LA VER-
DAD CON UN CORAZON SEN-
CILLO; SOLO SE LA HALLA EN
LA NATURALEZA; Y NO SE
DEBE COMUNICAR MAS QUE
A LOS HOMBRES DE BIEN: á lo
qual añadia de suyo: LA FELICI-
DAD SE LOGRA CON LA COM-
PAÑIA DE UNA BUENA MU-
GER.

Figure 5: Last page of *El Inglés en la India, ó La Cabaña Indiana* (Salamanca, Francisco de Toxar, 1803).

might be argued that the use of capital letters in the layout on the page of these sentences does truly monumentalise them; it converts them into an inscription to be read and re-read, memorised and espoused by its readers. With this original and unusual graphic device, the printer-bookseller Francisco de Tójar fired the starting signal for an intensive reading, both frequent and reiterated, of *La cabaña indiana*.[62] The text, with its questionings and new values presented in exotic attire, would be privileged by the generations of Spanish readers that lived through the extreme circumstances suffered by Spain in the first decades of the nineteenth century.

62. J. Dowling in the article referred to above, relates the case of intensive reading of the *Noches lúgubres* by a young man from Montilla (Córdoba) in the spring of 1819. According to his widowed mother, the young man abused his brothers and went as far as to lock himself up in a chamber of their house with a loaded pistol, threatening to kill himself. His brothers prevented it, and his mother snatched away the book that he was constantly reading from and handed it in to an inquisitor. He was reading the *Noches lúgubres* in the 1817 Valencia edition in 16mo by Cabrerizo.

Displaying its wares: material culture, the East India Company and British encounters with India in the long eighteenth century

JOHN MCALEER

The relationship between Britain and India in the long eighteenth century was mediated principally through the agency of the East India Company.[1] As a commercial organisation, it became one of the most successful the world has ever seen. It went even further in India, uniting, as Thomas Babington Macaulay told the House of Commons in 1833, 'the character of trader and the character of sovereign'.[2] The channels of commerce and communications opened up and facilitated by the Company's presence in India moulded representations and interpretations of the subcontinent in Europe, shaping British people's consciousness of India and its population. This chapter considers how the East India Company, its history and Britain's diverse encounters with India in the long eighteenth century can be understood through the production, collecting and public display of images, objects and artefacts.[3]

Recently, a century and a half after the demise of the East India Company, there has been more recognition of the fundamental role played by objects and material culture in shaping the history of the European encounter with India.[4] Material culture formed a crucial part of the Company's mercantile, corporate and political identities. One commentator has referred to the history of the East India Company as

[left margin handwritten note: Not included key reference (Tassran)]

---

1. There has been much scholarly debate about the role played by India in British culture generally. For two contrasting views, see P. J. Marshall, 'Taming the exotic: the British and India in the seventeenth and eighteenth centuries', in *Exoticism in the Enlightenment*, ed. G. S. Rousseau and Roy Porter (Manchester, 1990), p.46-65 (46), and Hermione de Almeida and George H. Gilpin, *Indian renaissance*, p.103.
2. Thomas Babington Macaulay, 'A speech delivered in the House of Commons on the 10th of July, 1833', in *Archives of empire, volume 1: from the East India Company to the Suez Canal*, ed. Barbara Harlow and Mia Carter (London, 2003), p.54-58 (54, 57).
3. For a collection of contemporary perspectives on a range of British encounters with the subcontinent, see Tim Keirn and Norbert Schürer (ed.), *British encounters with India, 1750-1830: a sourcebook* (Basingstoke, 2011).
4. P. J. Marshall, 'The great map of mankind', in *Pacific empires: essays in honour of Glyndwr Williams*, ed. Alan Frost and Jane Samson (Vancouver, 1999), p.237-50 (238).

'material evidence of a punishing encounter, driven by a desire for the smell, taste, colour and texture of exotic stuffs and essences'.[5] The East India Company was, at its most basic, an organisation interested in objects. Its main business involved the transportation of huge quantities of commodities – spices, tea, porcelain and a dazzling array of textiles – back to Europe for sale, fundamentally altering ideas of taste and fashion for millions of British people. Ironically, the tangible, material and physical items on which the East India Company based its commercial success were ephemeral and few examples have survived. But other artefacts – variously collected, commented upon and displayed by the Company and its officials – also had a significant impact on how British people understood India and Indians. In its own lifetime, the Company actively shaped European perceptions of the subcontinent, its people and their relationship to the Company. It commissioned artists and sculptors to make images of its principal settlements and to commemorate its representatives, their activities and successes. The recognition of its officials through presentation items and public monuments, as well as the architectural decoration of its buildings, also allowed the East India Company to present highly mediated views of India and Indians. Company officials in India encountered and remarked on the indigenous art and artefacts that they saw there. And, through the collecting activities of its servants and the establishment of the India Museum, the Company also influenced the development of museum collections and played a role in forging museum narratives of British imperial history. This study explores how these elements reflected prevailing attitudes to India and the perceived role played by the Company there.

The discussion moves beyond the lifetime of the East India Company itself, exploring how the Company's role in mediating British encounters with India in the long eighteenth century have subsequently been understood and interpreted using material culture in museums and exhibitions. In recent decades, there has been a revival of interest in this historical episode. With the decline of European empires following the Second World War, the changing demographics of British society and, more recently, the rise of India and China as global economic powers, the relevance of the East India Company and its history have become clearer than ever. The concerns of scholars, and the public more generally, in 'border-crossing, globalisation, and comparative, regional and transnational history' has also contributed to an upsurge of interest in the Company.[6] The chapter concludes, therefore, by considering how

---

5. Peter Campbell, 'At the British Library: review of *Trading places: the East India Company and Asia, 1600-1834* by Anthony Farrington', *London review of books* 24 (2002), p.31.
6. Philip J. Stern, 'History and historiography of the English East India Company: past, present, and future!', *History compass* 7 (2009), p.1148.

new research and changing historiographical trends have influenced the interpretation of the material culture legacy of the Company. In doing so, it suggests that the East India Company, its history and its material culture can act as a springboard for introducing British encounters with India in the long eighteenth century and broader themes about the history of the British Empire.

India and the East India Company in the long eighteenth century

To those living in late-medieval and early-modern Europe, the term 'India' conveyed a picture of a 'farre-distant' country rich in spices and gems, embracing much of Asia and part of Africa, which was invaded and conquered by Alexander.[7] Just before the Portuguese set off on their voyages to India round the Cape, Giulian Dati's *Il Secondo Cantare dell'India* was published in Rome in 1494. Illustrated with woodcuts, the book encapsulates the state of European knowledge at the time about the inhabitants and fauna of India: one-eyed, dog-headed and headless men vie for the reader's (and viewer's) attention with pygmies, men and women with large feet used as parasols, a winged snake, a flying panther and other strange beasts, birds and insects.[8] But, by the seventeenth century, Walter Raleigh suggested that India was becoming 'better known unto us in this age, by means of our late navigations in those parts'.[9]

This British familiarity with the subcontinent steadily increased with the growth of the East India Company and the consolidation of its power in India. By virtue of its royal charter, granting it a monopoly on all English (later British) trade east of the Cape of Good Hope, the Company was in a unique position to bring views of distant lands back to London and to influence British views of them in the process. It projected its commercial relationship with India through the buildings it constructed, the paintings and sculpture it commissioned and the cultural artefacts collected by its representatives. The East India Company was a trading concern, interested in maximising profit. But, in achieving this principal objective, it employed material objects to advertise its mercantile success, commercial importance and political power.

Some of the most impressive statements of the Company's commercial

7. Surendra Nath Mukherjee, *Sir William Jones: a study in eighteenth-century British attitudes to India* (Cambridge, 1968 and London, 1987), p.7. See also Donald F. Lach, *Asia in the making of Europe*, 3 vols (Chicago, IL, 1965-1993).

8. O. P. Kejariwal, *The Asiatic Society of Bengal and the discovery of India's past, 1784-1838* (Delhi, 1999), p.9.

9. Walter Raleigh, *The Historie of the world* (London, R. White and T. Basset, 1677), p.599.

success were made through the medium of architecture. While its
buildings performed important administrative and governmental functions, their grandeur and magnificence indicated the kind of relationship that the Company sought to establish with India. In London, the
Company had a number of headquarters or 'houses' over the course of its
existence. East India House, on Leadenhall Street, served the Company
at the height of its eighteenth-century commercial power.[10] Even then,
however, some commentators noted that the appearance of the building
was not commensurate with the success of the Company, 'whose servants
exercise sovereign authority in their Indian territories and live there in a
princely state'.[11] Perhaps piqued by such criticism, the directors ordered
a full-scale expansion and redevelopment of the building in the 1790s.
Following the purchase of several nearby sites in Lime Street and
Leadenhall Street, this work was carried out between 1796 and 1799
(Fig.6, p.203). The decoration of the new building was a bold statement of
the economic and mercantile relationship between Britain (in the guise
of the Company) and India. Sculptural decoration, high above the street,
projected the 'corporate message' of the people working inside the
building. The figural group in the pediment of the new façade, sculpted
by John Bacon, contained a personification of Asia pouring out her
treasure at the feet of the king, George III.[12]

If the exterior proffered successful commercial connections as the
principal glory of the Company (and by extension, Britain) in Asia, the
interior was also carefully designed to exude overtones of power, trading
wealth and commercial durability. This was particularly the case in the
Court Room (in effect, the Company boardroom). Here, a large marble
mantelpiece was commissioned from the Dutch sculptor John Michael
Rysbrack in 1728, and completed two years later. The large and elaborate
bas-relief overmantel, which was part of the decorative scheme, shows
Britannia on a rock receiving the riches of the East, while figures
representing Asia, India and Africa bring gifts of jewels and incense. In
the background, two East Indiamen, the ships that facilitated the
Company's success, are visible.[13] The theme of India offering her riches
to the representatives of Britain was one that recurred throughout the

10. See William Foster, *The East India House: its history and associations* (London, 1924).
11. James Noorthouck, *A New history of London* (London, R. Baldwin, 1773), p.663; quoted in
    Foster, *East India House*, p.133.
12. See Huw Bowen, "'The most illustrious and most flourishing commercial organisation
    that ever existed": the East India Company's seaborne empire, 1709-1833', in H. V. Bowen,
    John McAleer and Robert J. Blyth, *Monsoon traders: the maritime world of the East India
    Company* (London, 2011), p.91-125 (95-99).
13. Joan Coutu, *Persuasion and propaganda: monuments and the eighteenth-century British Empire*
    (Montreal and Kingston, 2006), p.273.

London. Printed for Bowles & Carver... No. 69. St Paul's Church Yard.

A View of the EAST-INDIA HOUSE, *Leadenhall Street*, London.

Richard Jupp Esq. Architect.

Published 16 Feb. 1802.

Figure 6: *A View of the East-India House, Leadenhall Street*, 1802 (National Maritime Museum, Greenwich; PAH2178).

building. In 1778, for example, Spiridione Roma was commissioned to paint the ceiling of the Revenue Committee Room with a similar scene.[14] The importance of trading success also extended to the paintings that adorned the walls. In November 1732, George Lambert was paid '£94.10s for six pictures of the Forts' for the Court Room. The commission was a collaborative effort, with Lambert painting the landscape elements and Samuel Scott painting the ships.[15] The cumulative effect of these architectural and artistic additions was to make East India House, in the words of Charles Lamb, the 'stately home of merchants'.[16]

The encounter with India was also represented beyond the threshold of the Company's headquarters. The Company and those who served it recognised the power of art, sculpture and architecture to shape public opinion in Britain about the Company's activities in India. In an indication of the weaving together of commercial and national interests, which had progressed steadily from the middle of the eighteenth century, many representatives of the Company were commemorated in stone for their success in war and battle. Two impressive monuments in Westminster Abbey – erected to the memory of Charles Watson and Eyre Coote, naval and military commanders respectively – encode subtly different representations of European encounters with India in their marble serenity.

Although Vice-Admiral Charles Watson served with the Royal Navy, his memorial was commissioned from James Athenian Stuart by the directors of the East India Company. In agreeing to pay over £1000 for the monument, the leaders of the Company were publicly acknowledging their reliance on, and gratitude towards, the British state. The monument incorporates a classically inspired sculpture of the Admiral, who was instrumental in assisting Robert Clive before the Battle of Plassey, between two subordinate figures: a seated pirate stares defiantly and a kneeling female personification of Calcutta offers her breast in a gesture of thanksgiving. Stuart provided the directors with a detailed account of the narrative focus of his work:

> The scene of this monument is composed of four palm trees set at equal distances, in the middle space is represented the Vice Admiral holding a palm branch, the symbol of Victory, in one hand, and extending the other towards a figure designed to represent Calcutta; he commands her to be freed; she appears loosed from her manacles, which are seen hanging on the

14. Barbara Groseclose, *British sculpture and the Company Raj: church monuments and public statuary in Madras, Calcutta, and Bombay to 1858* (Newark, NJ, 1995), p.50.
15. See Brian Allen, 'The East India Company's settlement pictures: George Lambert and Samuel Scott', in *Under the Indian sun: British landscape artists*, ed. Pauline Rohatgi and Pheroza Godrej (Bombay, 1995), p.1-16.
16. Quoted in Ray Desmond, *The India Museum, 1801-1879* (London, 1982), p.1.

palm tree behind her, and is returning thanks to her deliverer [...] on the right hand of the Admiral is a captive chain[e]d.[17]

The shields below the figures reiterate the Admiral's achievements: Ghereah was 'taken, February XIII, MDCCLVI', while Calcutta was 'freed, January XI, MDCCLVII'. Some thirty years later, in 1784, Thomas Banks was commissioned to immortalise General Sir Eyre Coote in the same location. Here, Coote's profile appears in a medallion being pinned by Victory to a palm tree at the base of which is an elaborate military trophy. To the right, as the inscription records, 'a province of the East, preserved to this country by the victories of Sir Eyre Coote', sits weeping with his head in his hand, neglecting an overflowing cornucopia, the only allusion to the material riches that Coote's victories brought.[18] In both examples, at the geographical and spiritual heart of the empire, the personifications of India suggest that the Company's commercial success requires military protection.

These marble representations were not the only means of realising the encounter between India and Britain for the British public. All manner of two-dimensional material culture, from Mughal miniature paintings to grand British history paintings, charted the relationship and revealed the self-image of the Company and its servants as political and diplomatic power-brokers in India. The East India Company's presence in India also encouraged artists to travel there speculatively.[19] Often the physical manifestations of these representations – narrative history paintings, portraits and popular prints – found their way into public circulation in Britain, further influencing and moulding public perception there. In the 1770s, a number of artists represented the newly acquired territorial and commercial power of the East India Company for the London public.[20] Tilly Kettle was the first professional painter to travel and work in India with Company approval. The success of his work encouraged Kettle to ship his paintings back to London where they were displayed at the exhibitions of the Society of Artists. Such metropolitan exhibitions provided a public space for the display of the Company's encounter with India and its local rulers, offering an insight into the ways in which it perceived itself and its role in Indian society. Kettle's group portrait of *Shuja-ud-daula, Nawab of Oudh, and four sons, with General Barker and military officers* (1772, Victoria Memorial Museum, Calcutta) was sent

17. Coutu, *Persuasion and propaganda*, p.140, 275.
18. Groseclose, *British sculpture and the Company Raj*, p.57.
19. See Mildred Archer and Ronald Lightbown, *India observed: India as viewed by British artists, 1760-1860* (London, 1982).
20. See Michael North, 'Production and reception of art through European company channels', in *Artistic and cultural exchanges between Europe and Asia, 1400-1900*, ed. Michael North (Farnham, 2010), p.89-107.

back to Britain for exhibition in 1775. It depicts Robert Barker, of Faizabad, completing a treaty of alliance with the Nawab of Oudh, whose hand he holds in a gesture of friendship. As Hermione de Almeida and George Gilpin point out, 'to the English viewer, the painting is both edifying and gratifying in its suggestions of English accomplishment and Indian substance'.[21]

Tilly Kettle was not the only artist to exhibit India-inspired images in London which served to reinforce the idea of the Company as a wise, benevolent and altruistic ruler. At some 14 feet wide by 10 feet high, Benjamin West's painting of *Lord Clive receiving the grant of the diwani* (*c.*1818, from an earlier version, *c.*1774-1795, India Office Records, London) demonstrates the sheer material presence of some of these images. It is a powerful and impactful object, its physical scale matching the significance of the event it depicts. The painting shows the moment on 12 August 1765 when the East India Company acquired the *diwani* for Bengal – the responsibility for collecting the revenues for the Moghul emperor. West chose to ameliorate the circumstances of the event, aggrandising the location (originally, the *diwani* was presented in Clive's tent), and ennobling the essentially financial transaction. The work was finished to mark the end of Warren Hastings's trial and was exhibited for first time at the annual exhibition dinner held in Hastings's honour. It acted, therefore, as an endorsement to all who saw it in London of the Company's greater economic and territorial control of Bengal as a result of the acquisition of the *diwani*.[22] Images such as West's portrayed the power, prestige, diplomatic influence and political authority acquired by the Company, and suggested the advantage to Britain of the Company's position in India.

But despite the Company's success, its advance across the subcontinent was neither smooth nor inevitable. The Sultans of Mysore were among the most successful in checking the Company's power. Initially led by Hyder Ali, the Mysoreans fought four wars against combined Company and British Crown forces, over successive generations, for control of southern India. In September 1780, at the beginning of the Second Anglo-Mysore War, Tipu Sultan, Hyder's son and successor, defeated Colonel Baillie at the Battle of Pollilur, killing some 3000 British troops in the process. Sir Hector Munro, whose son is shown in the grip of Tipu's mechanical tiger, described the defeat as 'the severest blow that the English ever sustained in India'.[23] As the ruler of an extensive empire, Tipu was one of the best-known obstacles to the advance of Company

---

21. De Almeida and Gilpin, *Indian Renaissance*, p.70.
22. De Almeida and Gilpin, *Indian Renaissance*, p.142-43.
23. Quoted in Susan Stronge, *Tipu's tigers* (London, 2009), p.14.

power in India: Edmund Burke called him 'this Marcus Aurelius of the East'.[24] It took a large concerted action, by a combined Crown and Company army, eventually to defeat Tipu in 1799, when Seringapatam finally fell.

Tipu's defeat immediately yielded material culture and inspired the production of a raft of images and objects in Britain, all of which combined to illustrate the overthrow of an apparently despotic tyrant but also to show the passing of his power into the benevolent arms of the East India Company. Tipu's legendary tiger-throne was dismantled in Madras so that it could be shipped to Calcutta (and thereafter back to London for display – or use – at Windsor Castle). The governor general, Richard Wellesley, Earl of Mornington, removed the golden bird ornament from the canopy of the throne to be dispatched to Henry Dundas and the Court of Directors in London, symbolising how power and authority had passed from Tipu's court to the Court Room of the Company in Leadenhall Street. The objects created in Britain to celebrate Tipu's defeat focused less on the transfer of control and more on the military power of the British forces in India. Robert Ker Porter's panorama, *The Storming of Seringapatam* (1800), is an indication of this trend. It was finished in six weeks, stretched to some 120 feet, covered 2550 square feet of canvas and contained several hundred figures. In depicting the moment when Tipu's fort was breached simultaneously in two places, it included twenty larger-than-lifesize portraits of British officers. The work was first exhibited at the Lyceum Theatre in London on 26 April 1800, before touring the provinces and Ireland (a lighted rotunda or polygon building was built specially for it in Belfast). After two years, and as a testament to the enduring fascination of the public with this oriental ruler and the Company's victory over him, it returned to the Lyceum for a further stint.[25]

The East India Company's presence in India also exposed its servants to indigenous Indian art. The display of this material could illustrate the enlightened, intellectual and scholarly approach of British government in the subcontinent. Aesthetic considerations may have played a part but the principal motivation for Europeans involved in these collecting activities was what they could deduce from these artefacts about India's past. In doing so, they initiated a long and fruitful relationship between European scholars and Indian material culture. Collectors often commissioned or sought to acquire Indian images and objects that would provide illustrations of religious beliefs, of Indian history or of types of people. In 1784, for example, Captain Alexander Allan brought several

24. Quoted in F. P. Lock, *Edmund Burke: volume II, 1784-1797* (Oxford, 2009), p.362.
25. De Almeida and Gilpin, *Indian Renaissance*, p.159-60.

sculptural pieces from Elephanta, as well as an entire Hindu temple from the Rohilla hill district in north-east India, back to Britain.[26] Charles Wilkins discovered, deciphered and translated inscriptions on a 'decapitated monumental column', which he came across in Buddal in Dinajpur.[27] In 1788, Alexander Davidson, the governor of Madras, provided evidence of Indo-Roman trade through the use of objects. He sent drawings of two Roman coins found at Nellore, about one hundred miles north-west of Madras.[28]

The portrait of Sir William Jones, painted by Arthur William Devis in about 1793 and now in the collection of the India Office at the British Library, neatly illustrates the connections between the East India Company's activities, academic scholarship and Indian material culture. Jones travelled to India in 1783 to take up an appointment as puisne judge to the Supreme Court of Bengal, but he is shown here as a philologist and scholar of ancient India, the activities for which he is best remembered. The painting also encapsulates how scholarship depended on the study of material culture. As founding president of the Asiatic Society of Bengal, Jones is depicted as a scholar. Displayed prominently on the table on which his right hand rests is a sculpture of the Hindu god, Ganesh, in his guise as patron of learning.[29] The East India Company facilitated not just the conducting of research into Indian material culture, but also its dissemination back in Europe. Objects were transported back to Britain on its homeward-bound fleets, as was other evidence of European intellectual engagement with India, its people and its past. In 1789, for example, Sir William Jones remarked to Charles Wilkins that the 'ships of this season will carry home seven hundred copies of our first volume of Transactions'.[30] By 1798, pirated editions of the transactions of the Asiatic Society of Bengal had appeared, and they were published in French in 1805.

As a result of this scholarship and collecting activity, the Company played an important role in the history of museums in Britain, their display of non-European material culture and their interpretation of the British engagement with the wider world. From the outset, the Company was an agent for museums, bringing objects, information and knowledge back for study and display in Europe. Robert Clive returned to Britain

---

26. De Almeida and Gilpin, *Indian Renaissance*, p.52.
27. Charles Wilkins, 'Inscriptions on a pillar near Buddal translated from the Sanskrit', *Asiatic researches* 1 (1788), p.131-45.
28. Alexander Davidson, 'Extract of a letter from Alexander Davidson', *Asiatic researches* 2 (1790), p.332.
29. C. A. Bayly (ed.), *The Raj: India and the British, 1600-1947* (London, 1990), p.213.
30. William Jones to Charles Wilkins, 27 February 1789; quoted in Kejariwal, *Asiatic Society of Bengal*, p.54.

with a large collection of ceremonial objects, including armour and many weapons. Warren Hastings came back with ivory furniture.[31] Lady Impey, wife of Sir Elijah Impey, Chief Justice of the Supreme Court of Calcutta, employed three Indian artists to paint specimens of flora and fauna, which are now in the Linnean Society Library in London. Richard Wellesley, governor general at Fort William from 1798 to 1805, collected nearly 3000 drawings, which are now in India Office Records at the British Library. They illustrate not only the flowers and creatures he observed on his tours of the country, but specimens that had been sent to him by naturalists from all over India and neighbouring countries.[32]

Self-interest led the Company to set up scientific institutions, make expert appointments, sponsor expeditions and subsidise publications. Since its servants' zeal had led to the accumulation of much valuable scientific data, the Company decided to establish a library and museum at its headquarters in London in 1801. Warren Hastings, the former governor general of Bengal and once one of the most powerful men in India, supported the foundation of a museum for the display of objects acquired by East India Company officials in the subcontinent. He believed that it was likely to enhance British prestige: 'A desire to add the acquisition of knowledge (and wonderful will be the stores which the projected institution under such auspices will lay open to them) to the power, the riches, and the glory which its acts have already so largely contributed to the British Empire and Name.'[33] When the India Museum was opened in 1801, its first curator, Sir Charles Wilkins specified three fields of collecting activity: 'A cabinet of natural productions', 'Artificial productions' and 'Miscellaneous articles.' The purpose of the library was to house manuscripts, books and drawings; while a 'cabinet of natural products' displayed specimens and objects. At the same time, the Company's daybooks began to record a steady flow of acquisitions. On 2 June 1802, for example, 'three chests containing a collection of insects, shells, minerals and other objects of natural history, made at Ceylon by M. Jonville accompanied by a memoir in French and sundry drawings' arrived in Leadenhall Street.[34] Descriptions of the museum and library give an indication of the eclectic nature of the items on display. A Chinese war-junk, Sumatran *proa*, Burmese musical instruments, indigenous weapons and hunting tools and 'Indian, Siamese, and Javanese

---

31. Marshall, 'Taming the exotic', p.51.
32. Mildred Archer, 'India and natural history: the role of the East India Company, 1785-1858', *History today* 9 (1959), p.736-43 (736).
33. British Library (BL), India Office Records (IOR), E/1/101/236, Warren Hastings to Stephen Lushington, 15 November 1799; quoted in Desmond, *The India Museum*, p.13.
34. Archer, 'India and natural history', p.742-43.

birds, Sumatran and Indian mammalia, besides, butterflies, moths, beetles, and shells' were all to be seen in the series of rooms that comprised the museum.[35] Chinese counting-machines, implements for writing, drawing and engraving on wood, Chinese weighing and measuring machines, a Chinese mariner's compass, Sycee silver and the shoe of a Chinese lady were also to be seen.[36] For *The Orientalist* of 1869, 'it is practically inaccessible and hid away out of sight, and when you get to it you find a bonded warehouse and not a museum in a straightforward airy order'.[37] But it fulfilled some specific educational purposes, drawing crowds of visitors, who were attracted to the bizarre and exotic mixture from India of impenetrable tablets, religious sculptures and elephant heads.[38] In this instance, the East India Company provided a physical and tangible view of India (and its own field of commercial activity) to the visiting public, shaping their perceptions of the subcontinent in the process.

Museum representation

In the case of the India Museum at East India House, the Company was a curatorial agent, actively selecting and arranging material to present a mediated representation of the subcontinent to visitors. However, even when it was still a going concern, the Company was itself the subject of display and interpretation. In other words, the Company's activities (and objects collected in the course of those activities) were used to comment upon or to evoke the nature of British engagements and encounters in India. The display of artefacts, and the interpretation of history through their juxtaposition, is one of the cardinal functions of museums. Such processes can provide powerful ways of explaining and exploring historical themes and debates. Michael Adas, for example, has argued that when two cultures meet, it is their material culture that is used to make judgements regarding their state of civilisation.[39] The possibility of engaging with other cultures and people through the medium of museums and their objects has long been recognised, not least in relation to the encounter between Britain and India. In recommending the India Museum, for example, Charles Knight promised his readers that a 'visit

35. J. C. Pratt, 'The East India House', in *London pictorially illustrated*, Charles Knight (ed.), 6 vols (London, 1841-1844), vol.5, p.63.
36. Pratt, 'The East India House', p.63.
37. Quoted in Jonathan Jones, 'Fugitive pieces', *The Guardian* (25 September 2003).
38. Jacqueline Yallop, *Magpies, squirrels & thieves: how the Victorians collected the world* (London, 2011), p.338-39.
39. Michael Adas, *Machines as the measure of men: science, technology and ideologies of Western dominance* (Ithaca, NY, 1989).

to this Museum is certainly calculated to render impressions concerning the East more vivid and striking'.[40]

One of the most remarkable objects in this regard is Tipu's Tiger, now in the Victoria and Albert Museum, London. This eighteenth-century automaton was created for Tipu Sultan of Mysore and makes use of his personal emblem of the tiger. The carved and painted wood casing represents a tiger savaging a near life-size European man, while mechanisms inside the object make one of the man's hands move, and emit a wailing sound from his mouth and grunts from the tiger. Ostensibly, this object embodies an episode in the history of the Company in India. But the evidence of its display and interpretation over the years also helps to trace the shifting and fluid nature of the ways in which museums have understood and presented that history to visitors. The tiger was found in Tipu's *Ragmahal*, a room devoted to his musical instruments, following the fall of his capital, Seringapatam, in 1799. The internal organ was a gift from his French allies, while the outer casing of the tiger and man were added later in Channapatna.[41] When it was removed from Seringapatam, the tiger was immediately recognised as a powerful and evocative object, capable of conveying a strong message about the nature of Tipu's rule as well as the British (and the East India Company) response to it. The governor general, Richard Wellesley, thought it would serve as an instructive reminder to the British public of the 'despotic' nature of Tipu's rule. He wrote to the Court of Directors in London: 'It is imagined that this characteristic memorial of the arrogance [and] barbarous cruelty of Tippoo Sultan may be thought deserving of a place in the Tower of London.'[42] Notwithstanding this advice, the tiger ended up in the India Museum, where it was first exhibited in 1808. It was transferred to the South Kensington Museum (which subsequently became the Victoria and Albert Museum at the turn of the twentieth century) in 1880, and remains an object of fascination for visitors.

The nineteenth-century legacy of the Company's encounter with India is perhaps best seen in the rise of museums. When the East India Company Museum was disbanded in 1879, much of the collection went on display in the Eastern Galleries of the South Kensington Museum. Once again, the objects attracted large numbers of visitors: nine rooms and an adjoining landing were given over to the display of architectural

---

40. Pratt, 'The East India House', p.64.
41. For a more detailed discussion of the display history of Tipu's Tiger, see Sadiah Qureshi, 'Tipu's tiger and images of India, 1799-2010', in *Curating empire: museums and the British imperial experience*, ed. Sarah Longair and John McAleer (Manchester, 2012), p.207-24.
42. Entry 212 in the original India Museum Accession Catalogue, Victoria and Albert Museum; quoted in Qureshi, 'Tipu's tiger and images of India', p.209.

fragments from Mughal palaces, models of Indian domestic scenes and religious festivals, and fabrics, carpets and homewares. So magnificent and popular were the displays that the travel publisher Baedeker even included a guide to the collection in its London itinerary.[43] Following the Company's demise, however, the link between the East India Company and Britain's encounters and engagements with India became somewhat submerged in broader imperial concerns. Jonathan Jones commented in 2003:

> The Indian Museum was [...] a phantom collection of a phantom orient, an India buried in London, skulking on Leadenhall Street, forgotten in Whitehall, lost near the Thames, displayed in South Kensington. [...] The India Museum has so completely vanished from memory that it seems hard to credit that there ever was such a place. Even the museums that inherited its collections make little of their debt.[44]

The use of material culture to present, explain and interpret Britain's encounter with India in the long eighteenth century is now being resurrected. The interpretation of the Company's rise to wealth, power and dominance can be set against the other effects of its presence in the subcontinent. Because the principal agent facilitating and mediating this encounter, the East India Company, inspired strong opinions – both then and now – its story seems particularly suited for treatment in museums. Less than three years after its demise, its legacy was assessed by the *Illustrated London news*. The popular newspaper concluded that the Company was 'the most celebrated commercial association of ancient or modern times'.[45] In the more recent past, critics and historians have labelled it variously as 'the Honourable Company' and 'the corporation that changed the world'.[46] As these comments suggest, the Company's history has all the classic ingredients – wealth, power, greed and corruption – to make it an intriguing subject for museum display. This history has the additional advantage (or perhaps dubious distinction), for today's museums, of encapsulating contemporary concerns about multinational business and the effects of globalisation. Peter Campbell, for example, has suggested that the commercial companies formed by 'the Great Nations of Europe' to trade with Asia 'gave the world an early taste of the pleasures and perils of globalisation'.[47] For a variety of reasons, then, the East India Company is a worthy and important subject for museum display, providing an intriguing gateway for exploring Britain's

43. Yallop, *Magpies, squirrels & thieves*, p.339.
44. Jones, 'Fugitive pieces'.
45. 'The East India House', *Illustrated London news* (3 August 1861), p.125.
46. See John Keay, *The Honourable Company: a history of the English East India Company* (London, 1993) and Nick Robins, *The Corporation that changed the world* (London, 2006).
47. Campbell, 'At the British Library', p.31.

various engagements with India. Since its abolition, but at an accelerated pace over the last few decades, there has been a desire to present new interpretations about the Company, its place in British history and its role in reflecting and mediating the relationship between Britain and India. This has arisen from new trends in academic research, new impulses and directions in museum interpretation and the generally fruitful, though sometimes fraught, connection between the two.

The first in a series of major temporary exhibitions to explore how the Company, Britain and India interacted was *The Raj: India and the British, 1600-1947*, held at the National Portrait Gallery in 1990. It was one of the first to confront the complexities of this history and the material culture it produced. The exhibition tackled themes of representation, charting the 'creation and projection of Indians and their lives, and of Indian images of the British' through the selection, display and juxtaposition of a range of paintings, miniatures and other objects.[48] At that time, it was the largest show ever mounted by the gallery. The then director, John Hayes, promised a suitably wide-ranging experience for visitors, focusing on 'the long relationship between the peoples of one of the great ancient civilisations of the East, [...] and the representatives of a vigorous Western trading nation'.[49] The sponsors of the exhibition were supporting 'a unique and timely contribution to our understanding of the complex and multi-faceted relationship which developed between India and Britain over three hundred and fifty years'.[50] The exhibition brought together objects that explained individual lives, both British and Indian, and their responses to the Company's presence in India. By contextualising different perspectives on the story, the National Portrait Gallery began the process of reassessing the Company for a twentieth-century audience.

In 2002, this trend continued when the home of the East India Company's archives mounted a major exhibition to showcase this material, which was accompanied by an illustrated companion history, public lecture series and a continuing online exhibition. The British Library's *Trading places: the East India Company & Asia, 1600-1834* also focused on the 'remarkable story' of the Company's history. But the organisers were keen to point out that this was not 'merely a history of the past'; rather, the exhibition sought to impress visitors with the 'lasting impression on life in both Britain and Asia' made by the Company and proclaimed that 'its legacy is a story of today'.[51] As a

48. Bayly (ed.), *The Raj*, p.11.
49. John Hayes, 'Foreword', in Bayly (ed.), *The Raj*, p.8.
50. Bayly (ed.), *The Raj*, p.7.
51. See http://www.bl.uk/onlinegallery/features/trading/exhibition1.html, last accessed July 2013.

commercial organisation, the Company's activities were meticulously recorded in ledgers, daybooks and letter books that stretch for miles on the shelves of the British Library's storage rooms. Much more than the self-defining adornment on its buildings, or the grand paintings it commissioned, the records of its business transactions provide a view on the reality of the Company's relationship with India. And in 2004, *Encounters: the meeting of Asia and Europe, 1500-1800* was held at the Victoria and Albert Museum. It sought to address the varied nature of the encounters, relationships and misunderstandings between Asians and Europeans in the period, again through the medium of material culture. The exhibition explored, 'from a broad perspective the way in which Asians and Europeans responded to one another'.[52] *Encounters* recognised that it was not just the material culture of the East India Company that explained the British encounter with India in the eighteenth century. Rather than repeating the message that the East India Company sought to present about itself, *Encounters* suggested that a range of material culture was required fully to comprehend and appreciate the ways in which the Company engaged with, and ruled over, India. As Oliver Impey pointed out, most of the objects on display powerfully demonstrated the fact that East and West were unusual, unfamiliar and, indeed, exotic to each other during the period.[53] All of these exhibitions, in some form or other, sought to explore the encounters between the Company (and, by extension, Britain) and India. They recognised that these encounters between a European trading concern and the Indian subcontinent was one of the most important aspects of the Company's history, but also one of the most fraught.

The National Maritime Museum's new permanent gallery, *Traders: the East India Company and Asia* and the collection upon which it draws, reflect the fact that aspects of the Company's history, ignored or skirted over in the past, can be retrieved by the use and display of material culture. This is the first permanent gallery dedicated to the history of the Company in its hometown. The Museum's collections allowed the gallery to chart the change in the Company's relationship with India, and its reliance on Indians for its maritime and military might. By exploring the nature of the Company's activities, present-day exhibitions can move beyond the

52. Anna Jackson and Amin Jaffer, 'Introduction: the meeting of Asia and Europe, 1500-1800', in *Encounters: the meeting of Asia and Europe, 1500-1800*, ed. Anna Jackson and Amin Jaffer (London, 2004), p.1-11 (5).

53. For a variety of reasons, the term 'exotic' is one that museums have increasingly eschewed in the recent past. *Encounters* was originally to have been called 'Exotic encounters'. One can only assume that the epithet was dropped by someone less familiar with the subject matter than those organising the exhibition and writing the catalogue. See Oliver Impey, 'Review of *The meeting of Asia and Europe*', *The Burlington magazine* 146 (2004), p.773.

simplistic, straightforward narratives presented in the architecture, painting and sculpture commissioned by the Company itself. The Company's is a story of commerce and conflict, trade and empire conjoined. As some of the earliest British critics of the East India Company observed, one of its distinguishing features was its combination of corporation and government in one institution. Or, as Philip Francis put it, the Company united 'the character of Sovereign and merchant, exercising the power of the first for the benefit of the second'.[54] As many commentators have observed since, there was a direct connection between the Company's developing commercial interests in India, and its expanding political and territorial interests. Another result of the Company's dominance of British trade with Asia was the increasing interdependence of the Company and British governmental concerns. In other words, the Company became an important organ of the British maritime and imperial state. Both of these themes – fundamental to understanding the rise and, ultimately, the downfall of the Company – can be illustrated powerfully through material culture in the National Maritime Museum's collection.

One of the most important expressions of the intertwining of trade and conflict (or the coercive power to prosecute it) was the development of the Bombay Marine. The Company established a separate maritime force, effectively a navy, to protect its shipping and other commercial interests. It first formed a 'Marine' as early as 1613. A local force of small boats, mounting between two and six guns each, was established to defend Company trade from Surat, and for convoying purposes. By 1669, trade at Bombay had been so much exposed to the attacks of Malabar pirates that three small, armed vessels were constructed. By 1716, its duties of convoying ships in trade cost £51,700 per annum and it consisted of one ship of 32 guns, four medium-sized 'grab-ships' (20 to 28 guns) and 20 small 'grab' and 'galivats' (5 to 12 guns).[55] In the eighteenth century, the Bombay Marine was mainly responsible for clearing the coasts of pirates. One such example of this is the action taken by Commodore Sir William James in 1755 (Fig.7, p.217). In that year, he captured Severndroog Fort, on the west coast of India, an event commemorated by Sir Joshua Reynolds's three-quarter-length portrait of 1784. James is shown, in the full-dress uniform of a commodore of the Bombay Marine, holding a plan of the stronghold of Severndroog in his hand. This was a principal base of Angrian marauders. Commodore James, in his flagship the *Protector* (44 guns), together with Maratha allies,

54. Robins, *The Corporation that changed the world*, p.122.
55. Charles Rathebone Low, *History of the Indian navy, 1613-1863*, 2 vols (London, 1877), vol. 1, p.90-91.

engaged in a four-hour bombardment of the fort, before a magazine in the fort blew up and most of the fleeing garrison were taken prisoner by the British ships.

The challenges and resistance to Company rule, as well as the use of indigenous troops to buttress its power, are also issues which help to explore and explain the relationship between Britain and Asia. New interpretations of this material help to present a historical narrative where the Company is one actor among many; one agent in a diverse range, influencing and shaping the British encounter with India in the eighteenth and early nineteenth centuries. Medals (Fig.8, Fig.9, p.218-19) awarded to sepoys serving in the East India Company's army during the long wars with France demonstrate that, without them, the Company could not have become an important military power in Asia. They show the extent of Company ambition in the entire Indian Ocean region, as they were presented to sepoys for service in Egypt and on the Ile de France (nowadays Mauritius) respectively. They highlight how India and the East India Company's presence there had become part of a bigger geopolitical picture, encompassing an entire hemisphere.

Similarly, a figurehead, supposedly representing Tipu Sultan, also provides a means of shifting the historical narrative of the Company's relationship with the subcontinent (Fig.10, p.220). As we have seen, Tipu quickly assumed celebrity status in Britain and was portrayed in all sorts of ways. This is another example: part of a ship's carving with a seated figure wearing a turban representing Tipu. He is riding a *roc*, a mythical bird of great strength. This, together with the umbrella he holds, symbolises his regal status. But, by virtue of its location in a museum context, as part of a new gallery on the history of the East India Company, it can provide new pathways into this historical episode. In a similar way to Tipu's Tiger, this figurehead represents elements of the historical engagement between Britain and India. It was carved in India in the early nineteenth century, in the decades immediately following Tipu's defeat. It was first on HMS *Seringapatam*, a 46-gun Royal Navy warship launched at Bombay Dockyard in 1819. But the meaning of the object has been transformed in its museum career. The carving was preserved when *Seringapatam* was broken up in South Africa in the 1870s. It was then located at Fire Engine House in Devonport Dockyard until 1937. In that year, the Admiralty transferred the object, along with a number of other figureheads, to the newly opened National Maritime Museum in Greenwich. In 1999, the object formed part of the Museum's *Trade and empire* gallery. That gallery was replaced in 2007 and the carving went into storage. In 2011, however, the figure embarked on a new chapter in its museum career, as part of the *Traders* gallery. In the context of the new gallery, the figurehead illustrates the Company's struggle for power and

Figure 7: *Commodore Sir William James*, by Sir Joshua Reynolds, 1784 (National Maritime Museum, Greenwich; BHC2801).

Figure 8a and 8b: Egypt Medal awarded by the Honourable East India Company, c.1801 (National Maritime Museum, Greenwich; MED0466).

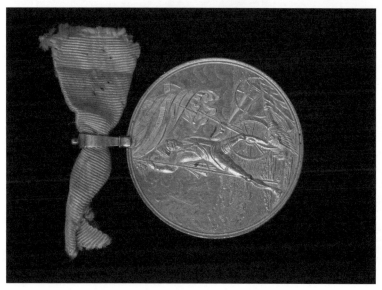

Figure 9a and 9b: Medal awarded by the Honourable East India Company for the capture of Ile de France, c.1811 (National Maritime Museum, Greenwich; MED0014).

Figure 10: Ship carving from HMS *Seringapatam*, 1819 (National Maritime Museum, Greenwich; FHD0102).

territory in the Indian subcontinent. Representing a local, 'Indian' empire-builder, the object is contextualised as part of a late-eighteenth-century struggle between many contending forces for the upper hand in the subcontinent. The interpretation of the object looks at who Tipu was, how he was represented in Britain during the Anglo-Mysore wars and how his legacy and commemoration have been used in the more recent past.

The figurehead encapsulates the British encounter with India in the long eighteenth century on a number of levels. It represents, in striking three-dimensional form, the expanding territorial power and ambition of the East India Company in the subcontinent at the time. But, through its subsequent museum history, the figurehead also illustrates the fluid and shifting nature of material culture and its interpretation over time. This object, then, reinforces P. J. Marshall's assertion that 'the British encounter with India was prolonged and intense'.[56] Throughout its long and varied career, the East India Company recognised and exploited the iconographical and political power of material culture to present the commercial, diplomatic and intellectual ties that it forged with India. By harnessing the versatility of objects, and by combining it with new scholarly insights, that history of encounter and exchange can be re-examined and reassessed for the twenty-first century public.

56. Marshall, 'Taming the exotic', p.46.

The Danish Asiatic Company: colonial expansion and commercial interests

MOGENS R. NISSEN

As in Britain, France, Sweden and the Dutch Republic, trade companies were established in Denmark during the early modern period to handle long-distance trade. Seen in a contemporary perspective they were unusual companies that were neither entirely private nor fully public. Depending on how one defines a 'trade company' at least twelve different Trade Companies were established in Denmark from the beginning of the seventeenth to the late eighteenth century. The companies operated in different geographical areas of the globe and traded with different types of goods. An important common characteristic was that the companies were financed by shareholders, and that they were based on a royal 'charter'. In these charters various privileges were given – usually with a monopoly as the most important privilege – as well as a series of responsibilities to the autocratic state.

This chapter focuses on the Danish Asiatic Company (Asiatisk Kompagni), which was the largest Danish trade company, and the company that existed for the significantly longest time. It was established in 1616 and ceased trading in 1843. However, it is the period from the early 1730s to the 1790s that is our main concern. It was during this period that the Company peaked financially, and it was in the latter half of the 1700s that the basis for private merchants' trade in Asia was formed. The focus is on economic and political interests in the Company. The perspective is Danish and concentrates on the Company in Copenhagen, while the Indian trade colonies are only briefly covered. It is an examination of the political debates regarding the Company's privileges and responsibilities, including a growing debate concerning a continuation of the monopolised trade or a liberalised free trade for all Danish merchants.

A principal source to illuminate this is the companies' charters and the internal management rules – the so-called 'conventions'. Ole Feldbæk's publication of sources including charters and conventions is used.[1] The content of this study is partly based on various Ole Feldbæk publications

1. Ole Feldbæk, *Danske Handelskompagnier 1616-1843: Oktrojer og interne Ledelsesregler* (Copenhagen, 1986).

on the Danish Asiatic Company. In addition, reference is made to Kristof Glahman's article on the period 1732-1772, and Rasch and Sveistrup's comprehensive study concerning the period 1772-1792. The parts relating to the shareholder composition are based on my own research. The Danish Asiatic Company is compared to the conditions and interests in the similar Swedish Asiatic Company (SEAC) in the same period, primarily based on the work of Leos Müller.

The East India Company and the establishment of the Asiatic Company

The Asiatic Company was established in 1732, when Christian VI signed the charter on 12 April and when the convention was adopted at the Company's general meeting on 30 July. Formally it was a new company, but it was definitely not a company that started from scratch. Already in 1616 Christian IV created the East India Company (Ostindisk Kompagni), and two years later the first ships were sent to India. During this first expedition Tranquebar on the Indian south-east coast was established as a Danish trade colony. From 1620 to 1845 it was the largest and most important Danish trade colony in India.

The first company had a company-like structure in which all interested, in principle, were free to invest money.[2] It was especially based on the experiences of the Dutch East India Company – Vereenigde Oost-Indische Compagnie (VOC) – that was established in 1603, which for instance can be seen in the fact that many words and terms in the 1616 articles are Dutch. It proved to be difficult to get the necessary funding, and the Crown chose to invest a substantial part of its capital.[3] The lack of interest in investing in the Company and the first expedition to India is related to massive uncertainties associated with the project, but it can also be linked with the fact that investors had almost no influence on the Company. The Crown inaugurated the management, who then had virtually unlimited power to make all business decisions without needing to gain support among the investors.[4]

In the first decades the Company experienced very difficult times, and in 1650 it was closed. Out of eighteen ships sent out in the period 1618-1639, only seven returned unscathed to Copenhagen with Asian goods.[5]

2. Feldbæk, *Danske Handelskompagnier 1616-1843*, p. 27, 1616-artikler, para.10.
3. Jan Rindom, 'Ostindisk Kompagni 1616-1650 – et spørgsmål om organisatorisk udvikling og interne magtkampe', *Handels- og Søfartsmuseet på Kronborg, Årbog* (2000), p.99-125 (101-103).
4. Feldbæk, *Danske Handelskompagnier 1616-1843*, p.26-30, 1616-artikler, para.3, para.16, para.17 and para.20.
5. Ole Feldbæk, 'Den danske Asienhandel 1616-1807: Værdi og volumen', *Historisk Tidsskrift* 15.5 (1990), p.104-52 (107).

It ruined the Company, and already from the early 1620s the king, Christian IV, was practically the sole owner, as he continuously converted loans granted the Company into shares.[6]

From 1639 to 1669 no ship arrived from Copenhagen in Tranquebar, but it still remained a Danish trading colony in India. That was the reason why the king – Frederick III – in 1668 equipped and sent a ship to India and when, in autumn 1670, it came back with pepper and other spices, a new company was created. In November and December 1670 the new king Christian V issued a charter and company conventions. The main content of the charter was that the Company had a forty-year monopoly on trade in Asia and with Asian goods.[7] In response to the royal privileges it was required that all ships be fitted out in Copenhagen, and that the ships return to the Danish capital. The Crown still had strong control over the Company, while the shareholders had very little input. The Crown appointed directors and controlled the Company conventions. Again, the directors had an almost total authority to make all business decisions, including demanding additional investments of the shareholders if necessary.[8]

There is limited knowledge concerning the development of the East India Company in the latter half of the 1600s, but apparently trade increased considerably at the end of the century during The Nine Years War (1688-1697). Gøbel has shown that at least ten ships were sent to India in the period 1677-1697, while nine returned to Copenhagen. Through the 1690s six ships returned to Copenhagen,[9] and in 1698 the Crown decided to extend the Company's charter a further forty years until 1750.[10] The reason was that at the time when the Company was in a good shape, the Crown wanted to signal to potential investors that there was a boom in the trade with Asian goods, which could be developed further.

During the Great Northern War (1709-1720) the Company suffered greatly. The ships risked being taken by Swedish privateers, and during the war the Company was forced to lend its money to the Danish state. Therefore, when the war was over the East India Company was financially crippled. To make matters worse the 1720s were characterised by shipwrecks and a number of difficult expeditions. Thus in 1729 the Company chose to return the charter and ceased business. It was a spoke in the wheel for the Danish Crown. In the period 1671-1727 a total of

6. J. Rindom, 'Ostindisk Kompagni', p.105-111.
7. Feldbæk, *Danske Handelskompagnier 1616-1843*, p.39, 1670-oktroj, para.7.
8. Feldbæk, *Danske Handelskompagnier 1616-1843*, p.41-46, 1670-reglementet.
9. Erik Gøbel, 'Asiatisk Kompagnis sejlads på Indien 1732-1772', *Handels- og Søfartsmuseet på Kronborg, Årbog* (1987), p.22-86 (68-69).
10. Feldbæk, *Danske Handelskompagnier 1616-1843*, p.49-58, 1698-oktroj; 1699-reglement.

forty-five ships returned to Copenhagen with Asian goods to a total value
of 5,701,444 Rigsdaler (rd.). The value of the silver and goods sent to
Tranquebar was 2,926,258 rd. Seventy-eight per cent of the goods were
re-exported, and consequently Copenhagen had achieved status as a
northern European centre for Asian goods.[11] Not only had the
Copenhagen merchants made good profits in this trade. Also the Crown
gained a large – but unknown – amount of money on duties and taxes.

The Crown worked hard to re-establish an Asiatic company; partly
because it wanted to ensure the continued supply of Asian goods to
Copenhagen, and partly because it needed to maintain links to
Tranquebar. Feldbæk has repeatedly argued that the closure of the
East India Company and the establishing of the two interim Trade
Companies (in 1729 to India and in 1730 to China) in fact was a financial
transaction to get rid of the debts of the old Company. By doing this a
new sustainable company was created.[12] Both the Danish state and the
merchants of Copenhagen had a clear interest in ensuring the continued
supplies of Asian goods, because Copenhagen already was established as
a centre for Asian goods in Northern Europe. When the Company
needed restructuring to achieve this goal, both sides were ready to do
so. In all charters and conventions from the interim companies to the
new Asiatic Company, it was underlined that they were newly established
companies with no relation to the old East India Company and its debts.
At the same time various assets were purchased from the old Company.

Although the issue merits further investigation, it seems undeniable
that the new interim Company was in the pipeline, when the East India
Company was closed. In February 1730 the Crown issued a charter to an
interim China Company, and already a merger with the India Company
was proposed. On 20 April 1730 the investors decided to merge the two
interim companies. Thus, the basis of the Asiatic Company was created
two years before it was formally founded.[13]

The Asiatic Company 1732-1772

The Crown showed its clear interest in the company trade by installing
Crown Prince Christian as the pre-eminent director in the interim China
Company in the 1730. Almost at the same time as the first ship departed
for China, he was crowned Danish king on 30 November 1730. This is an
explicit sign of the Crown's close ties to the group of merchants who

11. Feldbæk, 'Den danske Asienhandel 1616-1807', p.108, and Johannes Brønsted, *Vore gamle
    tropekolonier*, vol. 1-8 (Copenhagen, 1966-1968), vol. 5, p.242-43.
12. Ole Feldbæk, *Storhandlens tid. Dansk Søfartshistorie 3, 1720-1814* (Copenhagen, 1997), p.49.
13. Feldbæk, *Danske Handelskompagnier 1616-1843*, p. 59-83, India Oktroj and Konvention
    1729; China Oktroj and Konvention 1730; India Oktroj and Konvention 1730-31.

were behind the temporary Asian companies. On the other hand, the Crown needed to indicate that it was an independent company, and that the Crown did not interfere in the internal affairs of the Company. This applies both in relation to the interim companies and to the Asiatic Company's charter in 1732. In the charters it was emphasised that it was for the shareholders alone to draw up and adopt the conventions just as changes of the conventions could be accomplished without royal inter-ference. Christian VI actually went so far that, in the charter of 1732, he promised that he and the royal family would refrain from using their voting rights as shareholders. A similar assurance was introduced in the West India and Guinea Company's charter of 1734.

The Crown gave the shareholders the right to decide who should be directors of the Company, but in the convention from 1732 it was determined that at least one of the directors should be of high rank. In the Asiatic Company the shareholders stipulated that the president would be a 'Höy Stands Persohn' – a man of high rank. This was important because it ensured close contact between the Company and the political leadership in Denmark. Finance Minister Christian Ludwig von Plessen was the first president of the Asiatic Company from 1732 to1743. He was then replaced by Foreign Minister Johan Sigismund Schulin. From 1750 to 1772 the leading minister, Adam Gottlob Moltke, was president of the Asiatic Company.[14] This arrangement was beneficial to both the Crown and the Company and it was a strong signal that they shared a common interest in promoting Asian trade. But gradually discontent grew among shareholders. Many shareholders criticised the aristocratic president and the close linkage between state and Company. These discontented shareholders were especially vocal when Moltke was president. This manifested itself at an annual general meeting when it was proposed that the Company should pay for an expensive equestrian statue of King Frederik V; Moltke was the main man behind the project. There was also growing discontent among the shareholders that the Company was responsible for the costly administration of Tranquebar and four commercial stations, which were established in the 1750s. It was something that could not only be directed to Moltke but to the Company's board of directors in general.[15] In 1772 the shareholders decided that it would no longer have a political president of the Company, but in this first charter-period from 1732 both state and Company had an advantage in maintaining this close contact. When the Company was re-established in 1732 it was very dependent on the Crown's political and financial support. The same was not the case in

14. Ole Feldbæk and Ole Justesen, *Kolonierne i Asien og Afrika* (Copenhagen, 1980), p.113.
15. Feldbæk, *Danske Handelskompagnier 1616-1843*, p.89-91.

1772. Over the forty years the Company developed to acquire a very strong financial position. It was increasingly controlled by large Copenhagen merchants with Frederick de Coninck and Niels Ryberg in the lead, who wanted to remove the links to the state. It is in this light we must look at the shareholders' decision in 1772 to remove the political president of the Company.

The Crown refrained from getting involved in the daily operations of the Company. One major reason for this was the difficulties associated with finding individuals who were interested in investing in the Company. In order to attract investors, it was necessary to assure them that they had power over the Company. This is illustrated by the fact that the Crown in 1732 guaranteed both domestic and foreign investors that they were free to invest money in the Asiatic Company. In relation to foreign investors, the Crown guaranteed the shareholders that they could sell their shares and get the money even though Denmark might be at war with the investor's home country. The Crown also offered the Asiatic Company an exemption from duties and taxes on goods being sent to Asia. The Company did not have to pay duties in Oresund on the returned goods, but it had to pay a one per cent tax on goods re-exported and a two and a half per cent tax on goods consumed in Denmark. It was not – as in the subsequent charter from 1772 – required that a portion of the manufactured goods to Asia should be produced in Denmark, that the ships be built in Denmark or that the Company recruit Danish nationals. Overall it shows that the Crown wanted to ensure that the new company would function and that they were careful not to impose too many responsibilities.[16]

Looking at the shareholder combination of the Asiatic Company in 1732 it is striking which groups invested in the Company. It had a total of 400 shares of 250 rd., equalling a total capital of 100,000 rd. In 1732 there were 144 named shareholders, and more than half of the shareholders were either nobles with close relations to the royal family or civil servants. The royal family owned seven per cent of the shares, while the nobles and the civil servants owned about two thirds of the Company shares. Christian Ludwig von Plessen owned 5.5% of the shares, Carl Adolph von Plessen 3.25%, Johan Henrik Gyldensteen 5% and Johan Henrik Desmercieres 10.5%. Christian Ludwig and Carl Adolph von Plessen were brothers and both members of Christian VI's government from 1730. Gyldensteen was the father of Desmercieres, both father and son were financial advisers of the Crown, and both were strongly involved in the establishment of the first bank in Denmark in 1736. So it is no exaggeration to say that men from the political elite in Denmark

16. Feldbæk, *Danske Handelskompagnier 1616-1843*, p.89-132, 1732-Oktroj and Konvention.

were the dominant investors in the Asiatic Company at its start. On the other hand, members of the merchant community only had 20-25% of the shares, while foreign investors were virtually absent. Thus, apparently the Crown in 1732 put pressure on the nobility and officials to make investments in Asiatic Company. It did not have the same opportunity to put pressure on merchants or foreigners, and it seems that they perceived the project as too risky. It is an area which deserves further investigation, the manner in which the Crown apparently was able to encourage nobles and officials to invest in the Company; whether they directly was forced or if it was by offering benefits. But it is noteworthy that not one of the first shareholders was a merchant who made major investments in the Company. Frederick Holmsted, a merchant and the mayor of Copenhagen in 1733, was the only exception to this because he owned more than four per cent of the Company shares in 1732.[17]

This picture changed strongly during in the following decades. Until the mid-1750s the number of foreign investors increased rapidly, as Dutch merchants especially bought shares in the Company. In 1755 there were approximately sixty-five foreign investors, and of these some forty-five were Dutch and ten French, while British investors were almost absent. In total, foreign investors owned some 20% of the shares in 1755. The nobility and the civil servants sold shares with good profits during the 1730s, but then some started buying again in the 1740s and 1750s and in 1755 these two groups still owned almost 50% of the shares. In the mid-1750s Danish merchants owned a very modest number of the Company shares – approximately 15% – which can be explained partly by the fact that there were only few wealthy merchants in Copenhagen in the middle of the eighteenth century.[18] Another explanation is that merchants generally were keener on investing money in their own businesses, while civil servants and the nobility could use Company shares to profit on the increasing Asiatic trade.

This picture stands in strong contrast to the corresponding Swedish company, the Swedish East Asia Company (SEAC). It was established almost at the same time as the Asiatic Company – in June 1731 – when the Swedish king issued a charter to Hindrich König & Company.[19] SEAC was to a large extent built on the recently closed Ostend Company, and many investors and other stakeholders of this Company attended

---

17. See Mogens Rostgaard Nissen, 'Asiatisk Kompagnis aktionærer 1732-1809', *Erhvervshistorisk Årbog* 51 (2002), p.164-93.

18. Nissen, 'Asiatisk Kompagnis aktionærer 1732-1809', p.164-77.

19. Leos Müller, 'Swedish East India Company and trade in tea, 1731-1813', paper presented in Kyoto, 28 October-4 November 2004, p.3, http://www.geocities.jp/akitashigeru/PDF/DiscussionPaper2004_11_01Muller.pdf, last accessed July 2013.

the SEAC.[20] Therefore foreign investors and other stakeholders played an important role in the Swedish Company from the beginning, which was not the case in the Asiatic Company.

During the first charter-period up to 1772 a very significant development took place in the Asiatic Company. After some initial difficulties in the 1730s trade progressed well.[21] It is calculated that ninety-eight shipments of Asian goods were sold at the Company's auctions in Copenhagen; of these fifty four were from China and forty four from India. The total value of the goods from China amounted to 31,233,155 rd. and the goods from India to 10,462,588 rd. This equals an average per ship of approximately 578,000 rd. of goods from China and around 237,000 rd. from India. Therefore, on average Chinese goods were sold annually for nearly 800,000 rd., and Indian goods for approximately 250,000 rd. The most important Chinese product was by far different types of tea – supplemented with porcelain and silk – while cotton was the main product from India, supplemented with saltpetre, pepper and other spices.[22]

Again this is a pronounced difference with SEAC, which almost exclusively traded with Chinese goods, and as Müller notes, the name 'Swedish Canton Company' would have been more appropriate.[23] SEAC did virtually no trade in other areas in Asia, it had no trade colonies and therefore it had a very small administration with corresponding very low administrative costs.[24]

On the other hand, the trade with China was very similar in the two companies, since tea was the overriding main product. In both companies more than 75% of the tea was re-exported to other European countries, primarily the Netherlands and the United Kingdom. Furthermore, the two companies sold approximately equal amounts of tea at the auctions in Copenhagen and Gothenburg respectively, just as the trade volumes changed almost simultaneously during the century.[25]

A quick calculation shows that there were annually, on average, 1.35 ships returning from China and 1.10 from India. Therefore the Company fulfilled the interests of the Crown and the merchants by ensuring that each year Asian goods were sold at auctions in Copenhagen. In all years after 1733 at least one ship returned from Asia, yet the above-mentioned

20. Leos Müller, 'The Swedish East India trade and international markets: re-exports of teas, 1731-1813', *Scandinavian economic history review* 53.3 (2003), p.28-44 (33-34).
21. Erik Gøbel, 'Asiatisk Kompagnis Kinafarter 1732-1772', *Handels- og Søfartsmuseet på Kronborg, Årbog* (1978), p.7-45 (35).
22. Feldbæk, 'Den danske Asienhandel 1616-1807', p.110-11.
23. Müller, 'Swedish East India Company and trade in tea', 1731-1813, p.3.
24. Müller 'The Swedish East India trade and international markets: re-exports of teas, 1731-1813', p.32-33.
25. Müller, 'Swedish East India Company and trade in tea', 1731-1813, p.5.

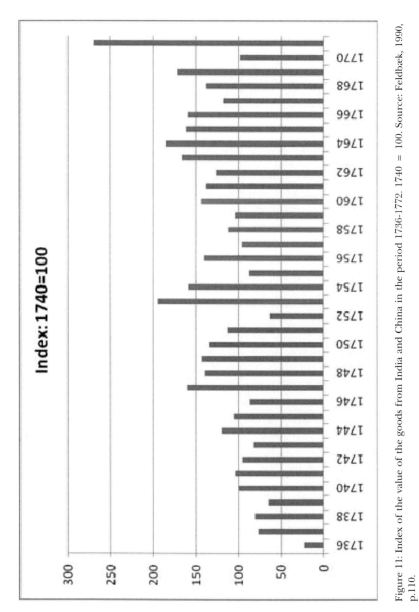

Figure 11: Index of the value of the goods from India and China in the period 1736-1772. 1740 = 100. Source: Feldbæk, 1990, p.110.

averages hide the fact that there were significant developments occur-
ring in the period. Until the late 1740s relatively more ships returned
from India than from China, while in the 1750s and 1760s markedly
more ships returned from China than from India. Thus the Chinese
trade was of much greater importance for the Company than the Indian
trade. Furthermore, the value of the sold goods in the 1760s was 50-100%
higher than it was in the 1740s.[26]

During the 1750s smaller trading colonies were built in Calicut and
Colachel on the Indian south-west coast (Malabar Coast) and in
Serampore/Frederiksnagore in Bengal close to Calcutta, and the Nicobar
archipelago in the Bay of Bengal was taken by conquest.[27] Together with
the administration of Tranquebar, this meant that the Asiatic Company
had considerable costs in India. In contrast, costs in China were relatively
small, because the Danish Company, like other European trade
companies, was forced to rent a commercial office in Canton, while
they were denied access to the rest of China. Although it was therefore
forced to do trade with certain Co-Hong merchants who had a monopoly
on the sale of Chinese goods to Europeans, the Company did not have to
create a costly organisation in China. In this way, trade with China had a
larger impact on the profits in the Asiatic Company than the trade with
India.

The Asiatic Company 1772-1807

The financial success of the Asiatic Company led to a growing dispute
concerning the Company's future. In March 1769 A. G. Moltke and the
board of directors submitted an application to the chancellery for an
extension of the charter for an additional twenty years on unchanged
terms. They prepared the ground for a continued monopoly on trade in
both India and China, but the chancellery and the state council was not
interested in simply giving the extension. The reason was that new
members of the college of commerce, such as A. P. Bernstorff and
Joachim Wasserschlebe, wanted to open up to the private merchants
trading in Asia. Therefore a commission, comprising two directors of the
Asiatic Company – who were also leading merchants in Copenhagen –
and two senior civil servants from the college of commerce, were
appointed. In January 1771, the Commission recommended a twenty
year extension of the Company's China-monopoly, while trade in India
and the rest of Asia should be opened up.[28]

26. Feldbæk, 'Den danske Asienhandel 1616-1807', p.110.
27. Feldbæk, *Danske Handelskompagnier 1616-1843*, p.27, p.89.
28. Aage Rasch and P. P. Sveistrup, *Asiatisk Kompagni i den florissante periode 1772-1792*
    (Copenhagen, 1948), p.16-17.

There was considerable disagreement about the terms of the new charter. The Company's directors wanted a twenty year extension on existing terms and conditions, but leading merchants and Company shareholders were opposed to this. The leading merchants had strong support in the government, where some of the members wanted to open up private trade in India. The later Foreign Minister, A. P. Bernstorff and the Finance Minister and leading merchant, Heinrich Carl Schimmelmann, supported the desire to open up the Indian trade, while A. G. Moltke requested an extension of the Company's Asia-monopoly. However, Moltke and the Company's directors soon recognised that it was impossible for them to get enough support for a continued monopoly all over Asia. Therefore, they suggested that the India trade should be opened exclusively for Copenhagen merchants, while merchants in other Danish cities – including Altona in Holstein – were prohibited from participating in this private trade in India. The background to this proposal was probably partly a desire to satisfy the Crown's interests in maintaining Copenhagen as a centre for trade in Asian goods, and partly an attempt to create discord among the merchants. The leading Copenhagen merchants Frederic de Coninck and Niels Ryberg supported the idea of opening private trade in India for Copenhagen merchants only. On the other side Finance Minister Schimmelmann was a strong opponent of a Copenhagen India-monopoly, because he had close connections to the merchant community in Altona. He therefore organised the sending of a letter from the college of commerce to the Company in March 1771 explaining that a partial authorisation for the Copenhagen merchants only was not acceptable.[29]

In his autobiography, Frédéric de Coninck has explained that the reason for the disagreement was that the Company had experienced a decline in the years up to the charter-extension. Spending was out of control and the Company had become too inflexible. So like other trading companies it could only survive because of its privileges. According to de Coninck, there was considerable political understanding of this opinion, especially among leading merchants but also among young politicians like Bernstorff and Schimmelmann. But in 1772 it was only possible to open up a part of the Asian trade and just because it was not expected that private merchants would take part in the risky China trade.[30]

King Christian VII had signed a new charter for the Company on 23 July 1772 after several years of discussions within the government, within the Company and between the government and the Company. Thus, the charter must be considered as a compromise between different political

29. Rasch and Sveistrup, *Asiatisk Kompagni*, p.14-22.
30. Rasch and Sveistrup, *Asiatisk Kompagni*, p.17-18.

and economic interests. The main difference compared with the previous charter was that the Company was only given a twenty-year
monopoly and only on the China trade. Trade in the rest of Asia was
opened to all citizens in Denmark. The Crown still demanded that Asian
goods were landed in Copenhagen, and the Company was still in charge
of the administration of the trade colonies in India. In exchange for
these administrative duties the Company received a fee from private
merchants, who traded in India. It was certainly not an optimal solution,
and both the directors of the Company and the merchants knew this
from the start. Furthermore, it created other problems, since the
Company could not prevent its directors and other employees from
participating in the private India trade. This was a common problem for
the European trade companies in India, especially for the British East
India Company. Feldbæk has demonstrated how the Danish Asiatic
Company from the 1760s transported vast amounts of 'black money'
for officials in the British administration in India to Europe.[31] Therefore
the board of directors of the Asiatic Company had extensive knowledge
of what might happen when the Asian trade was opened for its own
officials in India. In the 1772 charter it was also demanded that the
Company's ships should bring Danish manufactured goods to India and
China, and that ships normally had to be built in Denmark. In this way
the Crown wanted to ensure that it not only gained revenue from duties
and taxes, but also supported domestic manufacturing. At this time the
Company was so well established that there were no difficulties in
financing the expeditions. Both directors and shareholders knew that
the administration in India and the requirement concerning the domestic production would make a loss, but this was accepted because of the
prolonged China-monopoly.

An interesting paragraph in the charter dictated that no shareholder
could have more than three votes at the general meetings, including
proxy votes. The Crown had not interfered in the Company's internal
affairs for a long time, but now it decided to change the relationship
between big and small shareholders. Previously, a few leading
Copenhagen merchants accounted for a large part of the votes at general
meetings, which meant that it was almost impossible for smaller shareholders to wield any influence over the Company. According to Rasch &
Sveistrup it was the de facto prime minister, Johann Friedrich Struensee,
who recommended the voting restriction, just as he proposed to expand
the number of shares from 1200 to 4800, before he was removed from
power and executed in 1772.[32]

---

31. Ole Feldbæk, *India trade under the Danish flag 1772-1808* (Copenhagen, 1969), p.24-29.
32. Rasch and Sveistrup, *Asiatisk Kompagni*, p.19.

A few years later – in 1777 – an agreement was concluded deciding that the Danish state would take over the administration of the trade colonies in India. It was calculated that the Company had for ten years lost around 30,000 rd. annually in the administration of colonies, which was approximately one tenth of the value of the returned goods on one ship from India. Therefore, the Crown chose to follow the Company's wishes and took over the trading colonies because a calculation of the costs of administration showed that it would be offset by duty revenues. The compensation to the Company was 170,000 rd., but the important thing for the shareholders was to avoid the administration costs in India. As pointed out by Rasch & Sveistrup it was the 'enterprising young men' Ernst Schimmelmann and Christian Ditlev Reventlow, who were at the head of the College of Commerce that lay behind this decision.[33] At the same time as they were top civil servants they were also major investors in the Company; the Schimmelmann-family owed some 5% of the shares in the Asiatic Company, while Reventlow had approximately 1% of the shares.[34]

There is no source material left for the years 1756-1772 concerning investors in the Company but in 1773 foreign investors owned approximately one third of the shares. Dutch and French were by far the most prominent investors, owning 12-13% of the shares respectively. There might be several explanations behind this development. In the 1750s and 1760s Denmark managed to stay out of wars, and the Company made very good profits in that period. Thus, the Danish Asiatic Company offered high expected yields and a relatively low risk. In the following years, a large number of foreign investors sold their shares, and in 1784 only some 15% of the Company shares were owned by foreigners. This scenario was not obvious as the Company gained good profits due to the fact that Denmark did not participate in the American War of Independence (1776-1783), while most other European countries did, including France and the Netherlands. One explanation might be that French and Dutch merchants were forced to sell their Danish shares in an attempt to raise money for their domestic businesses which were suffering during the war.[35] On the other hand, one can argue that the Danish Asiatic Company offered Dutch and French merchants a good opportunity to gain on the trade with Asian goods in a period when the domestic trade suffered. But the fact was that from 1784 onwards foreign investors never owned more than 10-15% of the shares in Asiatic Company.

33. Rasch and Sveistrup, *Asiatisk Kompagni*, p.83-86.
34. Nissen, 'Asiatisk Kompagnis aktionærer 1732-1809', p.177-80.
35. Nissen, 'Asiatisk Kompagnis aktionærer 1732-1809', p.186-89.

At the beginning of the nineteenth century there were almost 1000 named shareholders. The shares were widely held by different social classes in Danish society. Obviously, the nobility, the merchants and the middle-classes were the most prominent shareowners, but a growing number of civil servants and employees in the Company also bought shares.[36]

The decades leading up to the turn of the century were characterised by wrangle and disagreement. One major reason for these disputes was the conflicting interests between small and big shareholders. Smaller shareholders continued to criticise the leading merchants, who were members of the board of directors. They were mainly accused of promoting their own interests. The disagreement broke out in earnest in 1783, when a major case of fraud in the Company was discovered. This happened almost at the same time as the economic depression following the end of the American War of Independence began. Together with its accountant and its treasurer, a director defrauded the Company for approximately 600,000 rd. The shareholders accused the board of directors of a lack of supervision. The matter was so important that Prime Minister Ove Hoegh-Guldberg tried to intervene and protect the directors against shareholder attacks. The reason for the government initiative was a desire to protect the Company's credibility and reputation, just as the government wanted to prevent possible bankruptcies among the private trading-houses in Copenhagen. The fraud case was settled in 1785 by reaching a settlement between the Company's shareholders and those involved. It was decided that the directors Ryberg, Fabritius and van Hemert each paid between 10,000 and 25,000 rd. to the Company, while a number of people affiliated the Company were forced to pay some compensation for their lack of control.[37]

During the period 1772 to 1792 new conventions were adopted; the first of these in 1778 in connection with the cession of the Indian trade colonies, and the second in 1787 after the completion of the fraud case. Neither of the two conventions resulted in major changes in relation to the decision-making authority in the Company, but the latter one especially was characterised by being very extensive. It introduced rules on just about everything, and a number of inspectors were employed to check that no officials defrauded the Company.

At the end of the 1780s negotiations regarding an extension of the charter started. At this late stage in the eighteenth century, all involved parties among merchants and the political leadership more or less agreed that the time had run out for the big trade companies. Neither

36. Nissen, 'Asiatisk Kompagnis aktionærer 1732-1809', p.180-85.
37. Rasch and Sveistrup, *Asiatisk Kompagni*, p.139-67.

in the government, nor in the Company's board of directors nor among the Copenhagen merchants was it a concern that private merchants would to take over the Chinese trade. It was expected that private merchants could cope with this trade in good years, but that they would fail in times characterised by recession. So although new liberal ideas had taken hold, the government did not want to risk the important Chinese trade. Therefore, in 1792 it decided to extend the Company's monopoly on trade in China for twenty years and this did not cause a strong opposition among the merchants. The depression following the end of the American War of Independence had convinced them that it was too soon to open up the Chinese trade. It was the last charter given to the Company, although it was extended several times. The Asiatic Company existed until 1843 and kept its China monopoly, but after the Danish participation in the Napoleonic wars from 1807 the Company's activities were very limited. This is much similar to the SEAC, which also almost stopped trade as a consequence of the Napoleonic wars. The French and Dutch Companies were already affected during the 1790s as a result of the revolutionary wars, from which both the Danish and the Swedish Companies profited.[38]

The Company's commercial peak was the period 1772-1807. In this period sixty-three Company ships and one hundred and twenty-one private ships returned to Copenhagen from India. The total value of goods sold by the Company was 35,272,229 rd. (approximately 560,000 rd. per ship) while the private ships sold Indian goods for 39,890,676 rd. (approximately 330.000 rd. per ship).[39] The Company gradually increased the return on sales of goods from India, while the private trade especially was flourishing in the mid-1780s and again in the mid-1790s. This indicates that the private merchants made use of the business cycles, whereas the Company's trade is better characterised by continuity with annual shipments of goods from India. In this way the Company and the private trade complemented each other.

It can be said that the relative importance of the Company's sales of Indian and Chinese goods changed during this period. Until the late 1780s the Chinese goods had a significantly greater impact on the Company's sales than those from India. This changed completely in the last part of the period when the Indian trade came to play a significantly stronger role than the Chinese trade. The main reason for this is that majority of the Danish imports from China during the period from 1730s to mid-1780s were re-exported to England. England had very high import tariffs on tea, which were circumvented by professional

38. Müller, 'Swedish East India Company and trade in tea, 1731-1813', p.5.
39. Feldbæk, 'Den danske Asienhandel 1616-1807', p.119.

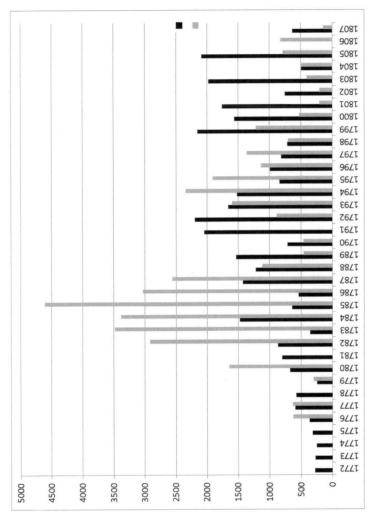

Figure 12: The value in 1000 Rigsdaler (rd.) of the goods from India in the period 1772-1807 shipped on Asiatic Company ships (black) and Danish merchant ships (grey). Source: Feldbæk, 1990, p.124.

smugglers, who bought the relatively cheap tea in Copenhagen and smuggled it to England. Since the English tariff on tea in 1784 was reduced sharply, a substantial part of the Danish-Chinese trade diminished. Consequently, the changing tariff policy in Britain had a much greater impact on the declining sales of Chinese goods in the latter part of the period than the end of the American War of Independence, the French Revolution or the Napoleonic wars.

In summary it can be noted that the debate on the pros and cons in relation to the monopolised trade companies in particular has significance in relation to the Danish Asiatic Company, whereas it is of less importance in relation to the SEAC. There is a general consensus among historians that the Chinese trade in the 1700s was so expensive and risky that few or no private merchants had the opportunity to cope with it. Therefore, the monopolised trade companies were well suited to develop this trade. In contrast, already at that time the issue concerning the monopolised trade in India and other areas of Asia was debated. Was the Company's trade monopoly a hindrance for the Asian trade at the end of the eighteenth century, or was it, on the contrary, to the benefit of economic development? It is very hard to say, and therefore it is still a topic for debate. It can be noted that the Crown and the government in Denmark followed a very pragmatic line. Though liberal views gained acceptance among leading politicians and the Copenhagen merchants in the latter part of the eighteenth century, the main focus remained on finding practical financial solutions. Thus, the Danish Asiatic Company – but also the SEAC – kept its privileges longer than might have been expected and longer than in other European countries.

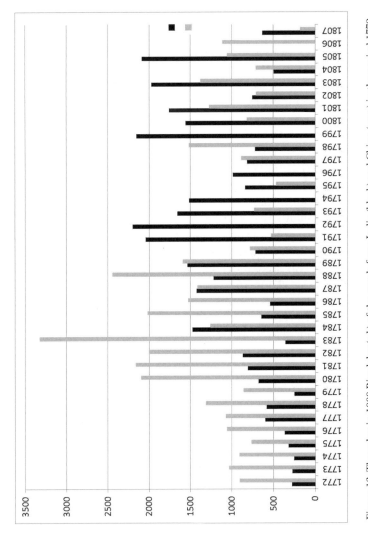

Figure 13: The value in 1000 Rigsdaler (rd.) of the goods from India (black) and China (grey) in the period 1772-1807 on the Asiatic Company-ships. Source: Feldbæk, 1990, p.124.

Whose pirate? Reflections on state power and predation on India's western littoral

LAKSHMI SUBRAMANIAN

Studies on buccaneer ethnography in the British context in the eighteenth century have revealed important insights on the close links between privateers and the making of empire, and on how representation of outlaws configured English colonisation, and impacted on the growth of English maritime power as well as on the language of imperialism. It is easy enough to see how the processes of nation-building and empire-making found it critical to define *legitimate subjects and citizens* and how in the process, a reclamation of the savage European pirate became possible, even desirable.[1] The same could not be said for the Indian pirate, encountered by the colonial power in the eighteenth century, whose ethnographic examination was initially framed within a predictable paradigm of lawlessness but which eventually turned out to be less than malleable. This chapter looks at the ways in which early colonial discourse in Western India developed a complex and multi-layered understanding of piracy and predation and how, in doing so, negotiated with tenuous and even ad hoc conceptions of maritime sovereignty on the one hand, and with personal predilections and orientations on the other.

Much of the ethnography on pirates and privateers of Kathiawar was spearheaded by early naval officers and Scottish administrators – notably Alexander Walker and James McMurdo, whose appreciation of the ground reality was as informed by immediate considerations of power and strategy as by their orientation to and appreciation of notions of traditional rights, clan honour and bravery. Just as figures like William Kidd (1654-1701) and Henry Avery were subject to multiple interpretations so were the 'Cooley rovers' of Kathiawad understood and described along different registers. Underlying the understanding of predation was the actuality of politics and market dynamics that added complex dimensions to the acts of maritime violence and contravention within the existing parameters of legitimacy and authority differently understood by different agents and actors. A second and related concern of the chapter is to consider the responses of coastal society to early

1. Anna Neill, 'Buccaneer ethnography: nature, culture and nation in the journals of William Dampier' *Eighteenth century studies* 33.2 *Colonial encounters* (2000) p.165-80.

colonial pressures and to consider the possibility of understanding early resistance through a maritime lens.

Piracy and its antecedents on the western Indian littoral

Piracy in India's western littoral in the latter half of the eighteenth century had its locus in the region designated in the colonial archive as the 'Northward' and which loosely comprised the territories north of Bombay comprising the coastal units of south Gujarat, Kathiawad and Cutch extending into Sind. It was in the second half of the eighteenth century that this sub-region emerged into greater prominence as a zone of piracy and multiple maritime claims, which happened to coincide with the growing advance of the English East India Company in Gujarat. The earlier decades of the same century had seen the fledgling Company settlement of Bombay articulate a policy against piracy in the southern stretch of the coast, known as the Konkan where a number of coastal chiefs and potentates of Maratha extraction had assumed rights to tax local trade, to enforce a system of passes and even – as in the case of Kanhoji Angria – to define rights of sovereignty over the high seas. The encounter in the Konkan was staged around the same time that the English East India Company and the British state began to revise its earlier position on the distinction between pirates and privateers. This persuaded the Bombay settlement in particular to take a harder stand against coastal claimants and competitors even while simultaneously embarking on a project of understanding agents of piracy and predation with greater rigour. Thus even though privateering especially in the waters of the Indian Ocean continued, the state began to be less tolerant of the lawless buccaneer in the Caribbean and Atlantic, reining him in and attempting to do the same with his Indian Ocean counterpart albeit with limited success.

The ferocity with which the category of the pirate was described and fixed was especially evident by the turn of the eighteenth century and found very quick application in the Indian Ocean. Pirates were described as worse than beasts of prey for the latter 'eat only to satisfy their hunger and are never found to prey upon creatures of the same species as themselves, whereas pirates prey upon all mankind, their own species and fellow creatures, without distinction of nations or religions'.[2] When it came to the treatment of coastal powers on the Konkan, notably Kanhoji Angria, the figure of the pirate assumed even more ominous connotations.[3] Described as a dreaded pirate, his political status –

---

2.   Neill, 'Buccaneer ethnography', p.167.
3.   Derek Elliott, 'Pirates, polities and companies: global politics on the Konkan littoral *c*.1690-1756', *Economic history working papers, LSE* 136.10 (2010).

especially in relation to the immediate local set-up – was not given sufficient recognition even though, in fact, he was the official commander of Suvranadrug fort from 1688. This position enabled him to articulate a set of specific maritime claims over the Konkan – a region that had already enjoyed a foretaste of maritime politics in the wake of the Portuguese offensive in the sixteenth century. The claims that the Portuguese had put forward amounted to monopoly control over trade and shipping and were enforced largely through the institution of the Cartaz-Cafila-Armada system, the implications of which were not lost on local powers and aspirants. Thus even as merchants suffered from higher trading costs owing to the protection system, coastal powers found the mechanisms useful to augment their claims over maritime trade and jurisdiction. Of these claimants, Kanhoji Angria was arguably the most enterprising and emerged by the first quarter of the eighteenth century as the strongest potentate in the Konkan able to challenge the English East India Company's claims of maritime hegemony. For the English Company in Bombay, hamstrung by lack of finances, the pretensions of the Angria were intolerable and the result was a sustained offensive against a power that they categorised as piratical. Kanhoji on his part functioned within the existing Maratha set-up of confederate chiefs with designated revenue claims and, like his Mughal counterpart, did not share the English notion of piracy. Rene Barendse in fact suggests that coastal navies began to be encouraged by land-based powers like the Marathas as part of Saranjam rights.[4] They allotted mercenaries to operate small naval forces with a concession for operating ships and authorising them to issue permits and to raise revenue. Such revenues first derived from taxing or ransacking fishing boats. According to Patricia Risso, Kanhoji saw himself as ruler of a coastal state and abided by personal agreements, and not by sovereign rights.[5]

The Company on the other hand saw Kanhoji as a serious competitor and, to neutralise his power, stepped up their naval strength in the form of an upgraded marine force. By the 1750s, when the Angria power was decidedly on the wane, the Company's reluctance to enter into any negotiation that gave coastal powers some leverage with local trade circuits was out in the open and it was made amply clear to all contenders that the Company authorities would not brook any competitor as far as the policing of high sea and coastal traffic were

---

4. Rene Barendse, *The Western Indian Ocean in the eighteenth century Arabian Seas 1700-1763* (Leiden, 2009), p.399-404.

5. Patricia Risso, 'Cultural perceptions of piracy: maritime violence in the Western Indian Ocean and Persian Gulf region during a long eighteenth century', *Journal of world history* 12.2 (2001), p.293-319. Also see M. N. Pearson, *The Indian Ocean* (London and New York, 2003).

concerned, and that the English pass was to be the single and sacrosanct insignia of legitimacy. The campaign against his later successor, Tulaji Angria, in 1756, followed by incursions against other coastal Maratha potentates like the Desais of Savantwadi in 1765, ensured the supremacy of the Bombay Marine as the arbiter of maritime politics, and any contravention of this was tantamount to aggression, maritime violence and predation. Interestingly by the end of the century, when the locus of piracy shifted to the Northward, the Maratha pirates became more acceptable agents and seen to be moderate in their manner and dealings in contrast to the northern pirates who were more enterprising, more ferocious and barbarous, fitting the character of the marauding pirate rather than the privateer.

Why and how did such a shift in ethnographic emphasis occur? Was there in the intervening period of more than half a century a context at work when anarchist marauding became rampant? Was there correspondingly a clearer conception of the underlying rationale behind the rhetoric against piracy framed within the paradigm of state formation and law? To what extent was this second wave of representation about piracy informed by personal conceptions and orientation by the men who undertook the study? Was there an attempt to domesticate the savage and make him part of a new regime of order? How did the subject respond? Was there in the response a clear sense of an alternative dispensation and moral economy? These are some of the questions that we shall turn to focusing attention on the long eighteenth century when substantive changes took place in the realm of political conceptions about empire, state and colony.

Between 1765 and 1800 a series of major changes occurred along the western Indian littoral. Politically, the region was not as yet completely subordinated to the authority of the English Company although in terms of naval control, the marine force of the Company seems to have held its own in enforcing English colours. Economically, the greater part of the eighteenth century was a period of political decentralisation with local potentates emerging as small-time actors and embarking on a programme of political expansion.[6] This was especially evident in the case of Kathiawar and Cutch where local Rajput and Muslim lineages aligned with merchants and opted for trade and commercial monopolies in order to enhance their resources. This not only resulted in the encouragement to trade and manufacture and urban growth but also in the deployment of coastal and maritime groups in extracting protection money from passenger shipping. What this meant in the long run was the

6. Lakshmi Subramanian, *Indigenous capital and imperial expansion: Bombay, Surat and the West Coast* (New Delhi, 1996).

crystallisation of coastal political units that became the basis for a more explicit conception of authority over the sea and shipping and that contested the supremacy of the English Company. Local merchants were not passive bystanders in this process; they found it profitable to dispose of goods seized from the Company-protected vessels and form a major interest group in developing a parallel circuit of trade and circulation. The period also saw the coming of age of Bombay, developing in the wake of a growing trade in cotton with China and coming under the pressure of its private merchants to safeguard the trade from any claims and attacks. The Company authorities in the city had to frame a strategy for developing an unambiguous policy of maritime control as well as for creating a community of consenting collaborators.

The emphasis on 'free and fair trade', and the protection of the 'fair' and 'benign' trader meant that the local privateer sanctioned by any merchant or ruler other than the English Company could no longer be tolerated. The distinction between privateer and pirate no longer had any currency; instead all forms of commercial piracy and privateering came under close scrutiny. At the same time, the financial consideration meant that colonial officials could not endorse a costly military campaign or even bypass the existing structures of authority and convention. It was this aspect of the situation that produced a complex taxonomy of piracy in the Northward, as officials encountered the paradoxes of privateering, random marauding, customary practices sanctioned by religious networks like temples and the working of black markets. Neither could they ignore the operation of a form of voluntary law (just as it operated in Europe) which included the right of every people to self-preservation together with attendant rights of self-government as well as the recognition of oceans as free spaces where the territorial rights of individual states extended no further than the power of protection reaches – that is to say within the command of gunshot from the shore. Establishing the distinction between legality and illegality was thus even more difficult in the Indian Ocean with its regimes of legal pluralism, and consequently the figure of the pirate, became even more complicated – barbaric, brave, savage and skilled, some working for small chiefs, others for wily merchants, some actually engaging in indiscriminate cruelty and violence against the crew, others doubling up as steersmen and expert navigators. The Northward also proved to be a difficult hunting ground. The limits of imperial authority in this region and the porousness of borders made for a geography that could not be easily contained or bounded. It also happened to attract the imagination of administrators whose ethnographic endeavours captured some of the complexities of coastal society.

Political ecology of the northward

The littoral region of the Northward consisted of Kathiawad and Cutch. Of the two units, Kathiawad was a well-watered region supporting a robust population and middle-sized urban centres like Jamnagar, Junagadh, Porbandar and Bhavnagar. What distinguished the political mosaic of Kathiawar as Howard Spodek has demonstrated was the multitude of feuding city-states, each of which was controlled by local warrior lineages (Rajput and Muslim) who negotiated with mainland powers when they demanded revenue and tribute claims from time to time.[7] By the latter decades of the eighteenth century, the Marathas had established themselves as major political claimants and arbiters, while the English settlement of Bombay kept a watchful eye on the province by insisting on the use of the Company pass as far as shipping was concerned. The pressures of the political situation and the workings of tribute-related politics persuaded local chieftains to develop partnerships with coastal groups and merchants in order to expand their sources of income. These included commercial monopolies, commission of licensed trade that the English East India Company saw as piracy. The rulers of Bhavnagar, Junagadh, Nawanagar and Jamnagar steadfastly put forward their claims on designated littoral spaces and worked closely with local merchants and navigators whose operations were like those of commissioned voyages. An account by the English Resident at Cambay in 1799 for instance, referred to the sanction given by the Raja of Junagadh to his dependants to conduct 'depredations', the principal directors being 'Syed Kharanjan and Khatoob'. Both brothers made use of the location at Novabunder, that was cut off at high water and remarkably well adapted for their purpose, inviting fortune-hunters to conduct the enterprise. The Syed brothers seem to have enjoyed the support of smaller rajas along the coast; notably Dwarka, Jagat, Gomti, Beyt, Positra and Aramra and would appear to have operated as small-time privateers but in tandem with marauders who were also occasionally supported by small time merchants operating grey markets.[8] The marauders themselves had no fixed base, wandering along the littoral and living presumably in small self-contained communities, but maintaining important links to political figures and merchants.

Two distinguishing features of the maritime profile of Kathiawad were its close contiguity with the bordering region of Cutch and the import-

---

7. Howard Spodek, 'Rulers, merchants and other groups in the city states of Saurashtra around 1800', *Comparative studies in society and history* 16.4 (1974), p.448-70.
8. Bombay, Surat Factory Diary no.697 of 1799, p.101. Letter from Mr Holford, the Cambay Resident to Bombay.

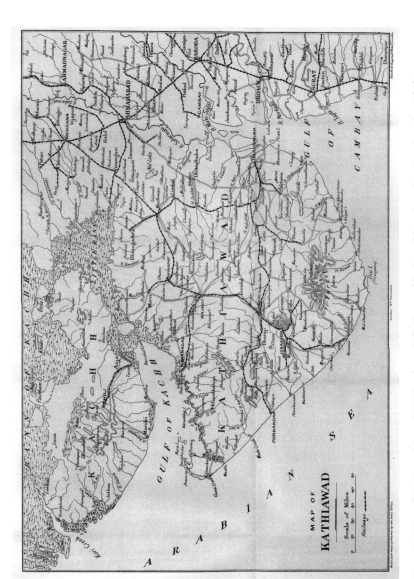

Figure 14: Map of Kathiawad from H. Wilberforce Bell, *History of Kathiawad from the earliest times* (London, 1916).

ance that the temple town of Dwarka assumed in the economy of predation. Not only did the temple with its minarets at Dwarka provide locational advantages by enabling groups to sight incoming vessels, but also the involvement of the temple committee in the proceeds and control of trade ensured a degree of religious sanction to the enterprise which the Company found difficult to bypass. As Seton the Cambay Resident mentioned,

> at these (Dwarka, Jagat and Beyt) posts are Dewals or Pagodas with very high minarets from whence they discern vessels at an almost incredible distance going to or coming from the Gulfs and having vessels always ready in conjunction with those of their phuttyas immediately when a vessel heaves in sight they put to sea after their prey, their boomrahs and dingeys during the season keep hovering at the mouth of the Gulfs and it seldom happens that but they must meet with success paying no respect to the colours of any power *except those who are the most formidable on their own coast.*[9]

The groups who seem to have actually commanded the operations are alternatively described as Cooleys, a subset of the Sanganians or Sankhadhar community,[10] and Waghers and who freely moved along the littoral. They were especially visible along the Cutchi littoral and along with the Jakus in Sind, freely offered their nautical skills to merchants and rulers alike.

As a region, Cutch was especially conducive to the support of hardy maritime peoples; isolated from the mainland, fringed by mangrove swamps and broken up by rocky cliffs, it was an archetypal maritime region where boats could remain hidden and prizes kept out of sight. In terms of agriculture, the region was arid although it was able to sustain a degree of coarse cotton cultivation. Its rulers fostered trade and manufacture with the result that by the eighteenth century Bhuj became well-known for its steel manufactures and cotton production, and linkages with Sind expanded. Mandvie emerged as a major port town with a semi-autonomous status under a governor enjoying substantive powers. The political set-up was also characterised by an alliance between the ruling class and merchant magnates who wielded considerable influence and were at the heart of the visible commercialisation of the province. In short, most of the chieftains in the Cutch-Kathiawar region were implicated in a complex structure of power and tribute sharing,

9. Surat Factory Diary no.697 of 1799, p.109.
10. Rene Barendse, *The Western Indian Ocean.* The Sankhdahars were coastal groups associated with the region of Okhamandal. Early travellers like Alexander Hamilton saw them as a criminal group residing in Bate whose people admitted of no trade but practised piracy. They seem to have been fearless and generally prepared themselves with intoxicants before embarking upon a skirmish. See Alexander Hamilton, *A New account of the East Indies* (London, 1930), vol. I, p.130.

operating the lower levels of the political system in the region, and subordinating themselves to the larger political authority that was assumed by the bigger chiefs like the Raja of Junagadh, the ruling Rajput house of Bhuj in Cutch and the governors in Mandvie. At the same time they maintained connections with local merchants and the temple circuits converging on Dwarka. Virtually all the coastal chiefs enlisted the services of seafaring groups or Wadellas as a convenient means of extending their revenue base and in the process integrating the subset of coastal seafaring activities within the larger political economy. These groups enforced their patrons' sphere of jurisdiction, attacked shipping and provided black markets with the goods that they seized. In such an arrangement, the pirates worked hand-in-glove with local chiefs and merchants and operated what seemed to be a localised economy of trade. Piracy was understandably a part-time occupation – many pirates were employed as steersmen and navigated ships for merchants when occasion demanded it.

The thrust to the Northward: touting the benefits of law and protection

The English East India Company directed its attention to the north-western littoral around the latter decades of the eighteenth century, by which time it had assumed a limited measure of political influence in western India in the form of a shared governorship in the city of Surat, of some territorial annexations in Gujarat and of the right to patrol and police the coast and high seas. In contrast to the politics of the Konkan, the Northward was viewed differently especially at a time when the discourse on piracy and privateering in the European context was assuming greater certitude and individual marauders stepped up their attacks in the Arabian Sea. Thus the imperative to step in and redefine the forms of privateering and piracy in more categorical terms became compelling, even as insurance costs went up and client merchants began to step up their demands for protection from the Company. Both coercion and negotiation emerged as necessary strategies and enjoyed particular attention from colonial administrators like Alexander Walker (Resident at Baroda from 1802 to 1810) whose ethnographic exercise showed sensitivity to the complexities of maritime and coastal politics and to local mercantile interests. The processes of law and protection worked together to create a more elaborate taxonomy of piracy. The new classification of predators and pirate states reflected older political considerations and more recent understanding of local merchant support that was contingent on the Company's efficacy in safeguarding property and security. What was foregrounded in the anti-piracy drive was the security to be advanced to merchants under the Company's protection and the application of force that alone could demonstrate the seriousness of the Company's intentions. It also demonstrated the maritime extension of the Company's growing territorial sphere of control in the larger region. As an interested party in the acquisition of political control in Kathiawar, the Company's compulsion to work with client rulers and merchants and thereby enforce their supremacy in territorial waters increased even though financial constraints precluded effective additions to the marine force.

The 1790s saw a steady escalation of attacks on local/coastal shipping and trade along the Sind/Cutch/Bombay axis as well as the trade between Bombay and the western Indian Ocean.[11] These attacks targeted local shippers as well as cotton boats that fed into Bombay's export trade with China. In both cases, merchants and their insurers pressed the Company authorities in Surat and Bombay for restitution of cargoes and vessels and alerted them to the necessity of eradicating the menace of predation. The circumstances were not especially propitious for the Company to take prompt and effective action – the fragility of their finances and the nature of claims they encountered meant that it was not easy to simply dismiss these attacks as barbaric and inevitable – and to pathologise the attacker as a born predator. Thus between 1795 and 1800 before the Company sent out its agents to make a more systematic survey of the region and its subjects, the emphasis was on securing the property of its client merchants by insisting on local coastal powers to restrain their subjects and to give undertakings about the sanctity of English colours and to make a more detailed survey of the nature of piracy in the region. What was repeatedly stressed in these initial years was the growing scale of attacks, the inadequacy of the Marine force and the importance of safeguarding coastal trade. As the Surat factors wrote to Jonathan Duncan in Bombay in 1799,

> the substance of intelligence recently received from Surat [...] is of a nature so alarming to the trade of this settlement that we deem it of great consequence. You must be informed of the great value of the commodities imported into Surat and Bombay from all the Northern ports during the period between this time and the middle of May and the beneficial consequences that ensue to the Company as well as to the merchants by the communication being kept as free as possible from the depredations of

11. Edinburgh, Walker of Bowland Papers Acc. no.M13674. See minute by the President of the Bombay Council dated 8 January 1808. This detailed the various attacks of the Collies from 1800. Also see Public Department Diary of the Bombay Government 14 December 1796, Petition from Govardhandas Bhucandas of Surat read by Kasidas Laldas. Also see petition from Framjee Pollojee read on 26 December 1796. More details of attacks are available in the Surat Factory Diaries.

various classes of pirates who infest the whole extent of the coasts from Cambay to this place. We shall now submit to your consideration the facts which have lately occurred to a fleet of boats from Broach in full, that you will see the necessity of speedily adopting some measures towards securing to the trade in question more efficient convoy.[12]

The same communication pointed out how the pirates were better equipped, how they were able to mount more guns on the ships they used and how they made use of local connections to secure provisions and to dispose of the goods they obtained. In fact, what emerged out of even the early proceedings was an acknowledgement of the multi-layered world of predation in the region, its links with markets and local circuits of trade and of its dynamics within a structure of tribute relations and distribution.

Thus there were pirate states whose subsistence came from the proceeds of predation, there were pirates who were forced into the profession to pay off old debts to merchants, there were independent seafarers who owed no allegiance to any specific power but all of whom belonged to an integrated maritime world that saw the Company's claims to maritime hegemony as tantamount to violence. As an obscure chief in the region of Okhamandal pointed out (in 1807), 'In these days all merchants have taken to the flag and protection of the Honourable Company and if I abstain from plundering them, where can I procure food and if I continue I fall under the displeasure of the Company'.[13] Nor was this an isolated expression of outrage; subsequent depositions indicated how the pressure of the Company's convoy and of local politics forced them to take up a course of predation. Between 1800 and 1818, the number of attacks on sea multiplied even though the nature of these attacks varied, especially after 1807 when piracy shifted to bases in Cutch and Sind whose rulers had pending issues against the English Company. What united these attacks was their integration to local markets where the confiscated goods found a ready sale. Who the pirates worked for was thus an important question that underlay the early efforts of the Company to write about them. Initially, the focus was on looking at the principal 'piratical states' of Dwarka, Aramra and Positra in Okhamandal, their claims over designated stretches, the moral-political economy of predation followed by a more critical view of Cutchi piracy – of the Jakhav pirates whose daring exploits fed into subsequent narratives of savage dare-devilry referred to by Kincaid in his account of the Waghers. It is also important to remember that Cutchi resistance through the agency of the Jakhav pirates and Fateh Muhammad, the

12. Surat Factory Diary no.697 of 1799, p.427.
13. Public Department Diary of the Bombay Government no.185 of 1807, p.6132.

principal officer at Bhuj, was also represented partly in terms of a larger anti-English offensive in which rulers like Tipu Sultan had participated.[14]

Between the latter half of the eighteenth century and the beginning of the nineteenth century, the Company authorities in Bombay were called upon by their client merchants to address the problems of random attacks on their shipping. The Mayor's Court was around this time required to sit in judgement over disputes relating to insurance claims over confiscated property and attacks by pirate powers. This set in motion a process of recording conventional insurance practices and also of insisting on the importance of securing merchant property against piratical attack and therefore of identifying pirates more critically. It also convinced the authorities of the usefulness of employing merchant collaborators to initiate the dialogue with piratical states and which lent its own inflections to the emerging discourse. Merchants had been in the habit of using multiple passes to protect their trade and it suited them to persuade the Company to take a harder line on those states that claimed the right to issue passes. In 1796, a Bombay merchant Kasinath Laldas petitioned the Bombay government for assistance against an attack by pirates of Gomti on his grandfather's vessel the Daria Daulat.[15] Successive representations complained of attacks by the Rajas of Dwarka, Gomti and Beyt and also of the Rajas of Porbanadar, Bhavnagar and Navangar who were in the practice of fitting out ships to raid local ships carrying English colours. In 1806, we have the mahajan of insurers claiming that his firm had sustained huge losses on account of piracy and how the situation called for effective and quick measures.[16] For the previous year, we have a letter from the Custom Master of Bombay informing the government about a merchant Pragjee Lacmidas whose vessel had been detained at Surat for carrying both the British pass as well as passes from other powers along the coast identified as 'piratical powers'. On interrogation, he replied quite categorically that he took this precaution because pirates paid no attention to the British pass and colours and that they seldom obtained redress even if the pirates were intercepted.[17] In

14. Walker of Bowland Papers MS 13914 (relative to Kutch), p.53-54.
15. Public Department Diary of the Bombay Government 14 December 1796, petition from Govardhandas Bhucandas of Surat read by Kasidas Laldas.
16. Commercial Department Diary no.45 of 1806, p.229, petition of Harjeevandas Jaitbhoy Mahajan of insurers of Surat dated 10 July 1806. The petition referred to attacks by the Nowanagar pirates. The term mahajan is used interchangeably to indicate either a senior merchant who commanded prestige and power or to an association of merchants representing a single profession or trade who represented the interests of the specific group before the local political authorities.
17. Commercial Department Diary no.45 of 1806, report from Custom Master read on 3 January 1806. The report was dated 19 December 1805.

fact between 1800 and 1808 when the Company stepped up its diplomatic and military offensive against the pirates and piratical states, the security of the merchants was presented as their most pressing concern. At the same time, there was a clear articulation of universal human rights under the framework of international law, even if this was rhetorical and completely ignored the actions of the Company and some of its allies. In 1808, the Bombay government in a communication to the Resident of Baroda Colonel Alexander Walker – who was critical of the Company's half-hearted military approach and sensitive to the ground level realities – mentioned that while they had shown restraint in their conduct towards piratical chiefs, the latter had not reciprocated and had interrupted the arrangements 'by their unprovoked and unjustifiable excess in contravention to the common rules of international observance among mankind in general'.[18]

The initial reluctance of the Company to embark on a direct and unilateral offensive against the predators was partly on account of its financial vulnerability and partly of its apprehension about interfering in a political system in which, they had as yet very little influence and which in spite of its deployment of piracy as a weapon of control and revenue was seen as enjoying legitimate authority. Thus the most important questions in which Company officials were interested was the identity of the pirate and whose patronage he enjoyed, for on that was predicated the nature of the military solution that could be applied. With a formal state, the claims of authority had to be more carefully worded – also there were possibilities of negotiation and alliances that could neutralise the more ambitious and independent piratical groups, many of whom had actually begun their careers as mercenaries working for different patrons. In 1797, some of the captured members of a pirate vessel stated in a deposition before the English Superintendent of Police that they were sepoys belonging to the raja of Dwarka and Gomtee, that they received about two rupees and had no share in the captured property. They also confessed that they entered this dangerous service because there was no other means of subsistence. What the confession revealed was how ruling chiefs in Kathiawad used maritime mercenaries as part of traditional practice and which the English Company could not so easily bypass. The legal position was not especially difficult to establish – theoretically, the Bombay Marine had the authority to police the seas, the Company's pass was meant to ensure merchants immunity from attacks and any contravention of this was seen as inimical to the Company's position on maritime affairs. In practice, the situation was

18. Walker of Bowland Papers Accession Number M13674, Bombay Government to Walker dated 4 February 1808.

a little different, as the Company was balancing its relations with the myriad rulers of Kathiawad whose policy towards trade and protection involved the use of mercenaries as well as of staking claims to maritime power. Understandably the Company could not strike out as unequivocally as it might have liked also because of its precarious finances. The result was a desultory military approach backed up by a discourse that was inconsistent but nonetheless grappled with the complexities of coastal politics on the western littoral, where religion, community, politics and coastal practice intersected to nurture a situation that could not be easily encapsulated in the rhetoric of fair trade and savagery. As Colonel Walker, Resident at Baroda, put it,

> in relinquishing piracy and any modification they conceived that they were relinquishing a right handed down to them from their ancestors, which was the gift of Krishna and secured to them by their religion and lawful source of livelihood. They exercised piracy as a trade and as a legal means of subsistence and this habit, which was favourable to their immediate interests and was supported by their prejudices would not probably yield to regulations.[19]

In fact Walker was quite in favour of military control which he believed was the solution – if this was not viable because of fiscal considerations, a more sensitive appreciation of the situation was warranted.

Pirate ethnography before Walker

Much of the early information on the Northward – on piratical states and their forces – came from either the English Resident in Cambay or from marine officers patrolling the coast. This gave decidedly military overtones to the representation and enumerated important details about organisation, technology and skills that the pirates possessed. In 1797, we come across a major report on the 'Piratical states of the northward' which included a detailed description of the petty states of Beyt, Aramra, Gomtee and Positra, all of which seem to have been led by small chiefs and whose territories were frequented by pirate vessels either managed by the chiefs or by others in the mainland, and for taking refuge if necessary. Topographically, these were small islands with access to creeks and heavily fortified. The report stressed how Beyt was the most powerful of the petty states and how its command of the passage to Aramra and Pisotra made its possession invaluable if piracy was to be checked. The report also pointed out how these 'pirate states' formed

19. Walker of Bowland papers MS no.13675, Letter from Walker to Bombay dated 2 December 1807. It is evident that Colonel Walker was wary of endorsing the conventional rhetoric on piracy. He was not reticent about interfering in Indian customs; he was for example at the forefront of the campaign against female infanticide. However, he chose to distance himself from the opinion of other commanding officers.

part of a complex and layered political structure that accommodated multiple shares ranging from those of temple trustees to larger officers in Cutch and Kathiawad. The use of coastal and seafaring groups was evidently integral to the politics of the region as we come across the claims and operations of the states such as Nawanagar and Bhavnagar. Reading against the grain, it could also be that the expanding presence of the English Company forced coastal groups to move along the coast and offer their services as a floating population of seamen who doubled up as navigators, fishermen and predators. Their fighting force was replenished by attacks on the Company's forces and partly by purchases of second-hand ships. It was the floating population and those who undertook the actual attacks who were described as Cooleys – a term that actually signified very little and was in all probability employed to indicate the lowest echelons of coastal labour switching occupations as and when the occasion demanded. Subsequently new appellations emerged – Sangarians and Waghers and Jakhav, all of whom were mobile Muslim groups with access to parallel markets subsisting on the fruits of predation. In 1798, the Surat Chief submitted a minute that gave an account of the forty-four boats the pirates had access to and how they generally worked for lesser chieftains who in turn were feudatories of bigger rulers like the Raja of Porbandar or the Nawab of Junagadh.[20] Of these states, the kingdom of Bhavnagar that entertained the most ambitious of maritime programmes moved rather rapidly into the Company's orbit taking a clear and public stand against piracy.

The emerging discourse on predation around this time was characterised by an attempt to relate the escalation of piracy to a narrative of misrule in Kathiawad and to a designated topos of piracy. In other words, the state of political insecurity and misrule in Kathiawad was seen to have encouraged adventurism that assumed a maritime dimension. This had produced a pirate corridor through the states of Beyt, Dwarka and Aramra whose rulers partook of revenues as much from piracy as from pilgrimage. Consequently the emphasis was not on the savage and dreaded pirate as on the politics of the small *piratical state* whose rulers had to be persuaded if not warned of the Company's intention. In 1797 for instance we come across a letter written by the English Chief at Surat to the Raja of Okhamandal asking him to release the boats that his forces had intercepted and how it was not 'proper to harbour pirates'.[21] What complicated the situation was the discovery that the rajas of Okhamandal were on many occasions joined by private merchants who were complicit in the attacks on Muscat and Bombay

---

20. Surat Factory Diary no.697 of 1799. See Consultation of 6 February p.75-76.
21. Public Department Diary of the Bombay Government no.124 of 1797. Consultation of 30 January 1797, p.164.

bound shipping and also that rulers like the Raja of Porbandar were traders with armed vessels but not pirates.[22] Clearly these actors could not be clubbed together and the gradations between pirates, chiefs and privateers could not be strictly enforced. The ethnography of piracy, therefore, in these years attempted a taxonomy that assigned the top place to the piratical states of Okhamandal followed by independent adventurers and even merchant sponsors and finally by the actual predators whose actions predictably were seen as ad hoc, random and almost unintelligible. The exercise was backed by spasmodic and desultory military action undertaken by commanding officers of the Marine against Beyt and Dwarka and demands made for restitution of property and compensation claims.

A minute by the President of the Bombay Council in 1808 written on the basis of older reports and surveys established the complex linkages between piratical states and groups with politics in Cutch and Kathiawar. It also recognised the consequences of conflict and political instability that had produced a dispersal of the coastal population who found their services to be in demand. Thus in 1803, when the Nawab of Junagadh expelled the Cooleys from his ports, they were received at Bate and Dwarka and quite openly flouted the so-called authority of the English pass saying that the latter could hardly hurt them. The minute also emphasised the random nature of predations and the complicity of ruling chiefs, and while there is little doubt that it was an attempt to justify the stand that the Company had taken, it did reveal the complex arrangements that rulers in Cutch and Kathiawad had entered into with certain groups, how shares and entitlements were formalised and also how states had come to rely on maritime control as part of their revenue base.[23] The moral legitimacy of this was of course questioned by the Company authorities and in doing so, there was a constant invocation of illegality and predation which was not necessarily shared by one and all.

Walker and the pirates of Kathiawad

With the appointment of Colonel Alexander Walker as Resident of Baroda who was entrusted with the charge of tackling the escalating problem of piracy, the ethnographic exercise assumed a different register. Unlike officials like C. W. Malet, whose representation of local society was naive and peevish,[24] Walker brought to his station an appreciation of

22. Walker of Bowland papers MS 13674. See Memorandum of Information given by Tucker Dewa Vakeel.
23. Walker of Bowland papers MS 13674. See minute dated 8 January 1808.
24. Joel Berlatsky, 'British imperial attitudes in the early modern era: the case of Charles Ware Malet in India', *Albion: a quarterly journal concerned with British studies* 14.2 (1982), p.139-52.

local traditions and practices as well as romantic notions of bravery and martial energy. Besides using the mediation of his trusted aide, Sundarji Shivjee, a merchant negotiator who enjoyed considerable influence and access along the littoral given his past commercial dealings in horses, he approached local bards for genealogical details and merchant- informants to piece together a history of maritime Kathiawar and Cutch. Thus notwithstanding his exhortations to the Supreme Government to pursue a policy of strong military intervention, his appraisal of the political ecology of maritime power was balanced. Acknowledging the impact of political conflict and dispossession, Walker chose to make a distinction not so much between piracy and privateering as between those states and chiefs who participated in actual attacks on sea and those who allowed individual predators or groups to fit out voyages from their ports. Nor did he subscribe to the idea of the unreasonable pirate – a position that kept him at constant loggerheads with the Company authorities over the question of indemnification and restitution. In his view, there was no real alternative to effective military action (even if expensive), but if this failed, there had to be a pragmatic resolution of the question by allowing the claimants to retain some of their entitlements. He thus made it a point to mention in his letters that Sadaram, the superintendent of Bate, had fitted out vessels at the commencement of a trading season but that they had instructions not to molest English property or the property of people trading under European protection. He also pointed out how pirates should be brought under Company protection, how they had no particular sense of being obliged to restore goods taken as they had no such demands made on them in the past and also because they could legitimately invoke the benefits of the customary pardon or *muluk sharista*. This observation indicated quite clearly how Walker was able to position the phenomenon of maritime violence in a larger context of politics and practice and not reinforce the conventional representations of piracy. However, this did not easily convince the Government of Bombay which insisted on restitution. It maintained that relinquishing claims were not

> founded on the general basis of right and equity, so much as that of political and temporary expediency, such as this government (feeling as they must for the sufferers) cannot acquiesce in the sufficient justice of it, or consequently authorise the renunciation of those well founded pretensions which may deem it on the contrary incumbent upon them to maintain as far as may prove compatible with the letter and spirit of the instructions from their superiors and to cause the same to be accordingly still intimated as already ordered to the chieftains.[25]

25. Walker of Bowland papers MS 13674. Bombay to Walker dated 4 February 1808.

The Bombay government insisted that the governments of the piratical states were in

> every view of reasonable construction equally answerable to other nations in both the instances adverted to, in which as far even as respects themselves, there exists only this immaterial degree of difference that their profits from the booty acquired by their own armed vessels is proportionately greater than the amount of their shares in that by private adventurers; there being none of any description in which the said governments do not more or less participate as well as temples, which are known to derive part of their support from the offerings made to them.[26]

Walker's response was telling. While fully acknowledging that the only way out was use of coercive tactics, he was candid in his rejection of the contradictions and inconsistencies of the Company's rhetoric against piracy as barbaric, illegal and immoral. Rather he made out a strong case for working within the confines of custom and usage and insisted that by compelling pirate chiefs to make good losses, they would be obliging them 'to continue their piracies'. He also made the point that many of the outstanding claims were obscure, ill-defined and/or the parties unknown or so vaguely specified that it would be 'impossible to fix on the actual thief'.[27] The circumstances of the pirates were in any case embarrassed and most of them were in debt and their revenues were precarious. The Resident was doubtful whether the rajas of Beyt or Dwarka had actually attacked Company protected shipping and furthermore acknowledged how they were trying to expel from their domain several piratical groups who in turn fled to Jackhav in Cutch and one that was identified as a the epicentre of piratical activity and recruitment. Thus for Walker not only were the profits of the pirates wildly exaggerated, it was important for the Company to initiate at least a dialogue that gave the states and chiefs an opportunity to enter into an agreement and even accept a British agent. Forcing chiefs to pay back was not an option and would, according to Walker, drive them to despair. In subsequent suggestions, he made the point that failing full military action, pirates would have to be allowed to issue passes or cowls to those merchants not subject to the Company. This had been a traditional practice to which they had been accustomed and to which merchants, both Arabs and Sindians further north, were likewise accustomed. In fact as late as 1817, Walker stuck to this point as he wrote that the granting of protection to pirates might also be a useful strategy for it would give some kind of compensation to them in lieu of their relinquishment of claims to the

---

26. Walker of Bowland papers MS 13674. Bombay to Walker dated 4 February 1808.
27. Walker of Bowland papers MS 13674. Walker to Bombay from camp at Kunderma Rana dated 29 November 1807.

property of wrecks and vessels stranded on their coasts which was a common practice of most nations.

Walker's ethnography thus acknowledged the complexities of the political context in which predation in late eighteenth-century Kathiawad had emerged. The Resident followed this up by deputing his confidante Sundarji Shivji to negotiate with the chiefs of Dwarka, Beyt and Aramra. Some of the key elements in the proposed agreement had to do with establishing the right of travel and trade at sea as on land, with refusing any protection to those who fitted out predatory expeditions from their ports, with the renunciation of all claims to shipwrecks and with the establishment of an agent in their territories. The agent was seen as a pivotal figure to deal with disputes – for as Walker pointed out, the rulers had a very 'confused and irregular notion of the right to property'.[28] In this he was echoing not so much the narrative of the barbarous pirate as he was of poverty and want that forced them to take to the act of predation which was part of an older cycle of activity and one which was supported by a thriving grey market. Thus as he put it, 'Among a people and in a country where robbery and plunder have so long been familiar, honesty and industry cannot immediately assume the legitimate ascendancy. Without the superintendence, the piracies that are now expelled but not suppressed would soon be excited by opportunity, want and property.' Further,

> goods got by piracy are immediately dissipated into various small shares, which even if they found a market at their full value are of little amount to each person who receives a part. It may be useful to remember that the small and confined income of the pirate have been the chief cause of their predatory mode of life and if their regular revenues are lessened their necessities might be expected to compel them to their former courses.[29]

In fact, Walker pointed to the fact that the Chiefs had made a legitimate demand from Sundarji 'for subsistence in consequence of their having renounced the means of support to which they have at times been used to resort and although this may appear *very unreasonable to a European, it is quite in conformity to their mode of thinking*' (italics mine). On an earlier occasion, he stated very categorically that the states in question exercised piracy 'as a trade and as a legal means of subsistence and this habit which was favourable to their immediate interests and was supported by their prejudices would not probably yield to regulations'.[30] For Walker then, piracy in Kathiawad was part of an older political economy, where chiefs relied on coastal communities to stake a claim to maritime resources and

28. Walker of Bowland papers MS 13675, Walker to Francis Warden dated 23 January 1808.
29. Walker of Bowland papers MS 13675, Walker to Francis Warden dated 23 January 1808.
30. Walker of Bowland papers MS 13675. Walker to Bombay dated 2 December 1807.

where there was an integrated network of pilgrimage, protection, trade and predation. Poverty and displacement in the wake of political conflict held the key to the way in coastal politics manifested and which was aggravated by the half-hearted attempts of the Bombay Marine to impose order and hegemony. The following years, however, saw Walker grapple with the escalation of piracy, this time directed from Cutch and ports in Sind that became epicentres of a different level and mode of predation. The focus of attention fell on the Jakhav pirates and who turned out to be an altogether different proposition and whose acts and self-representation gestured to a very different kind of politics. Of course even as Walker was issuing instructions to his confidant Sundarji in 1808, the close connections between Cutch politics and the piratical communities and chiefs in Okhamandal, the northern tip of the Kathiawadi peninsula, were evident to the Resident. Equally obvious was the fact that half a century of political contestation and of the Bombay Marine's political project had compelled mobile maritime groups to operate in a variety of ways ranging from mercenaries attacking ships at sea to fitting out voyages for their immediate patrons that included merchants to expert navigators and steersmen. Thus we find that the community of pirates was a mixed one and included what is referred to as Wadellas and Sangarians and even Moplas, as well as those bearing Indo-Portuguese names. The diplomatic and limited military pressure initiated under Walker in coastal Kathiawad pushed communities from Okamandal to Cutch and Sind where Mandvie, Kotiswar, Jakhav and Lakhpat emerged as important centres of piracy. To quote Walker again,

> The people of Kutch and particularly the ports under Fateh Muhammad have often betrayed piratical habits and of late have been more active in their depredations. The jumadar (Fatheh Muhammad) disclaims having afforded any countenance or authority for their practices and has promised to cause restitution to be made of the Nowree, which appears to have been seized by his orders. Fateh Muhammad has also generally condemned piracy and promised to exert his authority for rooting out the pirates and to extend his assistance to enable merchants to recover losses.[31]

The allusion to Fateh Muhammad was in fact to the contested political authority in the Cutch set up with the *de jure* rulers, the Jadeja Rajputs, subordinate to the authority of two influential officers namely Hansraj Shah the Diwan (in charge of Mandvie the port capital which had spearheaded an impressive maritime programme) and Fateh Muhammad (in charge of Bhuj the capital). Fateh Muhammad seems to have been especially active in mobilising the support and forces of the

31. Walker of Bowland papers MS 13675. Walker to Francis Warden dated 23 January 1808.

piratical communities and the states of Okhamandal in Kathiawar while Mandvie seems to have offered the best market for sales from piracy. The mission that Walker sent to negotiate with the states of Okhamandal balanced the interests of these rival contenders: it initially relied on the intercession of Mandvie on the assumption that Hansraj's interests as a merchant would persuade him to endorse the anti-piracy policy of the Company and to come forward as guarantor of the agreements being made with the states of Dwarka, Aramra and Positra. Hansraj on his part insisted that the recent depredations were being directed from Jakhav, which was under the jurisdiction of Cutch while Fateh Muhammad insisted as loudly that he never coveted plunder.[32]

What both these exhortations revealed was the steady escalation of maritime violence as a consequence of local politics and the intervention of the East India Company's marine force. Equally striking is the fact that by 1808, no longer were the Okha chiefs the subject of ethnographic attention but the independent and small predator crews who relied on community networks to scour the coast, to reject or accept the protection of political bosses and to engage in what might be seen as resisting all hierarchy and authority as an autonomous political subject. This representation, admittedly, was not part of the British story but more an element of the self-representation of pirates who were interrogated and came up with striking depositions. Here we shall refer to one such deposition to try and tease out the various strands that explain the nature of predation in this period and whether we can see in this a demonstration of subaltern action and whether this was at all reflected in later retrospective British histories of Indian piracy.

A deposition: the salty subaltern at work

On 25 May 1813, in the aftermath of successful Company attacks against the Jakhav pirates, Nakwa Kassow submitted a detailed deposition before the Company authorities at Porbandar. It was an eloquent statement of his ancestry, his activities and his politics, and identified clearly the dislocation that the Bombay Marine's politics had produced on the coast. As he said quite candidly,

> my family are originally natives of Bate, but have resided for about 20 years in Mandvee. My forefathers were all Pirates, and my father is the only exception in the family for seven generations – he navigated a boat belonging to a merchant in Mandvee until his death. I became a Pirate and joined Jecha nackwa many years ago, we used to carry most of our pirates to Verawal and the parts on that coasts at length the English came and interfered after which these places would not receive us.

32. Walker of Bowland Papers MS 13914 relative to Kutch, p.53-55 (57).

He also spoke of his service under Fateh Muhammad who authorised him to carry on his predation and for which he was paid 5 cories a day. He gave this up after 1812 as he felt 'Fateh Mohamad always took the plunder, and I got the blame'. He used whatever opportunity came his way to sign up with interested individuals to embark upon pirating cruises all along the littoral from Verawal down to the coast south of Bombay. He spoke of his acquaintance with other individuals – we hear of one Moosa Mapla in Bombay with vessels sailing right up to Mangrole and also came up with a brief inventory of the pirates in action and to the fact that almost all of them were to be found in places like Kotiswar and Jakhav where they had found protection after the Company action in Okhamandal.[33]

What does this deposition tell us? It is evident that, until his capture, Nackwa Kassau along with Jecha Kassow and his maritime gangs were active in raiding vessels either independently or working under the instructions of Fateh Muhammad and/or local merchants. Cotaseer and Jakhav part of Fateh Muhammad's jurisdiction had clearly emerged as major centres and markets – Lt. Blast in command of one of the expeditions in 1812 wrote, even while bitterly complaining of his rheumatic condition, how captured boats had been brought to Kotaseer by Jecha Nackwa and his gangs, and how their operations were quick and skilful and not always easy to intercept.[34] He also referred to the rapidity with which plundered goods were disposed of. We also have allusions to the debts that some of the pirates had incurred with local merchants forcing them therefore to take up this operation. Equally the deposition does indicate a degree of agency that the salty subaltern enjoyed as a consequence of his mobility, albeit forced – and that gave him access to a very different and constantly changing geography. Further, the irregularity of his reactions makes for a very different kind of political engagement that escapes easy representation. And yet it would not be far-fetched to suggest that, like other maritime actors, they were quite cognisant of the possibilities that transitional politics with its multiple levels and foci of jurisdiction afforded for their operations.

We come across cases of pirates and piratical crew working for other Europeans and the Imam of Muskat, and capitalising on what Benton might refer to as 'legal pluralism'.[35] Thus even if strategies were irregular,

33. Secret and Political Department Diary no.284 of 1813. See Deposition of Nakwa Kassow taken at Porebunder the 25 May 1813, p.18-23.
34. Political Department Diary of the Bombay Government no.283 A of 1812. See p.88 for letter from Lt. Blast dated 28 December 1811.
35. Lauren Benton, 'Legal spaces of empire: piracy and the origins of ocean regionalism', *Comparative studies in society and history* 47.4 (2005), p.700-24.

they were not irrational; there was an understanding of new claims being proffered by the Company even as there was a reinforcement of traditional claims to the seas and the privilege of issuing passes or cowls. Even with pirate chiefs such as Jecha Nackwa and Kassow Nackwa, there seems to have been at work an understanding of the possibilities and limits of resistance. The fact they could work both as private mercenaries for local chiefs, as well as operate as independent pirates, gave a very complex inflection to maritime violence, suggesting actors who could not be so easily contained in structures of hierarchy and authority. Jecha Nackwa for instance mentioned in his deposition the frequent attacks he made on Bombay shipping and how he was able to work with a network of crew and family members; how he chafed at the unfairness of both Fateh Muhammad as well as of the high-handed tactics of the Company. His deposition speaks of his travels to Sind, Cutch, Kathiawar and Bombay as it does of his employment as a private mercenary and his decision to break free as a pirate, a decision which frequently coincided with the mounting pressure of the Bombay Marine. 'I left Sind and came to Okhamandal', he declared,

> when the fort of Positra was destroyed by Colonel Walker about four seasons ago. I was at Aramra which I flew from and went to Lakhpat Bunder where I lived as a pirate under agreement to the jumadar Moor meah a part of the plunder for my part. I then possessed one boat and sent her on plundering, remaining myself at Lakhpat [...] My people then took a boat of Verawal Mangrole laden with sugar, suparee, sugar candy, dates and spices. She was brought to Lakhpat bunder and the cargo was sold at that place, 3000 cowries of it the jamadar paid to my creditors and 2000 cories he kept.[36]

He also mentioned subsequently how he was often asked by Fateh Muhammad to carry on his operations more stealthily lest he drew the attention of the Company to him. In fact, while the depositions carry details of the frequent raids organised by the pirates and the collusion of local chiefs in the enterprise, there is also a sense of autonomy that pirates like the Nackwas seem to have enjoyed; the decision they took in undertaking independent raids, and breaking free from either the local chiefs or of the Company's new legal regimes, does suggest a different political compulsion at work. Can this be seen as random marauding or as resistance born out of a pressing situation – indeed of a desperate attempt to break free from an increasingly restrictive legal regime? It is difficult to see the attacks as random marauding, for evidently the attacks were predicated on information and on the availability of a pirate crew that was mobilised along community and family lines, not to speak of the

36. Secret and Political Department Diary no. 284 of 1813, p.63. for the Deposition of Jech Nackwa.

extraneous support they enjoyed from local chiefs. There were elements of resistance – the displacement brought in by the Company's control over coastal Kathiawad was certainly the material context for the escalation of piracy which was seen as an integral part of the political arrangements that had evolved. For the Company officials, these pirates were not as easily accommodated as the chiefs of Okhamandal whose claims could be understood within a structure of authority and entitlement, however antagonistic it might have been to the Company agenda. Admittedly, by this time, the patience of the Company had been exhausted as expeditions were mounted against pirates more system-atically and Jakhav and Lakhpat were cleared of their predators. Even before this the expedition against the chiefs of Okhamandal, Positra especially signalled a new vigour in the Company's maritime policy.

How did the experience of confronting predation and the politics of piracy get written? This question has been central to the concerns of this chapter as it has attempted to tease out the multiple ways in which pirates were described and contained before they were overcome by force. I have argued that the exercise of ethnography was not straight-forward or even a continuation of a particular mode of representation that saw manifestations of coastal politics as illegal and predatory. There were different key moments in the articulation of a discourse on piracy, one that saw the coastal Maratha figure as a pirate whose operations had to be contained but who subsequently was seen as a more benign pirate than his northern Cooley/Sangarian counterpart. With the latter, the discourse on predation was intimately linked with narratives of mer-chant protection and fair trade and the question of sovereignty at sea was only an afterthought. The fact that the northern chiefs of Okhamandal defined themselves as pirates, and worked with communi-ties and crews of piratical extraction and their distinct location within a complex political system connecting the peninsula of Kathiawad with that of Cutch, meant that the English Company representatives had to elaborate a clearer taxonomy of piracy. The interest that Walker had in tracing the genealogies of pirate chiefs like those of Dwarka and other Wagher rulers suggests strongly that a parallel process of understanding the 'outlaw' co-existed with that of critiquing the marauder, a category which could not apply indiscriminately to one and all. Raja Mullu Manek of Dwarka was thus seen by the Resident to bear a favourable character and ready to enter into compensation agreements like any reasonable person. In such a narrative, it was the idea of fair trade and trader that prevailed. Walker emphasised repeatedly how the only means that appeared to him to have a chance of permanent success is to grant 'those people' the right to engage in commercial intercourse with foreign places 'from which they have been long interdicted or have practised only by collusion and stealth'.[37] The buccaneer seems to have been for Walker a thwarted merchant and privateer who was accustomed to a different moral and political economy and who could be contained either by complete military coercion or reformed by trade. Subsequently even as official narratives lost their enchantment with the potential of trade and preferred to attribute elements of savagery to the Jakhav pirates who with their counterparts in the Persian Gulf became embodiments of disorderly and marauding conduct, later retrospective histories continued to recuperate elements of autonomy in their actions. Alexander Kincaid was especially eloquent as he wrote of the Wagher outlaws of Okhamandal and teased out all the important elements in their story albeit in a romantic frame that appreciated all the motifs and symbols associated with them – bards and bravery, resistance and loot in conditions of strife and political dislocation[38].

37. Walker of Bowland papers MS Acc no.13917. Letter from Walker dated 21 May 1809.
38. Alexander Kincaid, *The Outlaws of Kathiawad* (Bombay, 1908), p.27. The following ballad is especially evocative: 'Amreli fears king Bava's might / And Dhari sounds the warning bell / E'en Waghir Manek flees at night / When you approach his citadel, / Where Gomti, fed by rains and tide. / Rolls past a hundred shrines its flood / You sacked and slaughtered far and wide / Till every wave foamed red with blood. / The sahib's helm, the sahib's sword / Had ne'er by child of Ind been ta'en / You, Bava, dared, bold jungle lord! / And ransomed back your wide domain.'

A comparative study of English and French views of pre-colonial Surat

FLORENCE D'SOUZA

As one of the buzzing hubs of trade and a regional political capital from pre-colonial times, Surat offers a rewarding subject for the comparative study of early European perceptions of India. From early Islamic times, around 750 AD, there was maritime indigenous Asian trade from Cambay and Surat to Mocha and Aden in the Red Sea, as also to Ormuz and Bandar Abbas (Gombroon) in the Persian Gulf, carrying Muslim pilgrims and trading goods such as textiles and pepper in exchange for precious metals and coffee.[1] In 1573, Emperor Akbar conquered Gujarat and shifted the focus of Western India trade from the traditional port of Cambay to Surat, as an outlet for Mughal merchandise from upper India (Burhanpur, Agra, Lahore). From 1600 to 1750, the pre-modern ports in Western India were at the mouths of rivers rather than along the coast, in order to avoid the dangers of coral reefs and to provide defence from pirates and hostile warships, forcing the larger sea vessels to accost at about 15 to 30 kilometres from the river estuary, and necessitating the transshipment of goods in shallow coastal boats.[2] Despite Surat's port being inland on the banks of the Swally-Tapti river, its harbour was on the coast at the outer mouth of the river, with a fortress (called Surat Castle) on the sea coast. Since Surat was able to provide cargoes, financial and shipping services, as well as loyal local merchants, from 1550 to 1750 it 'remained the unquestioned capital of emporia trading in the Western Indian Ocean'.[3] However, Surat's trading ships also plied to the Coromandel coast, to Indonesia and to China, even before the arrival of the Europeans in Asian maritime trade. After the British took control of Surat Castle in 1759, Surat's trade declined, giving way to Bombay (the British headquarters for the Bombay presidency) which became the foremost trading port of Western India, with its deep natural sea harbour.[4]

1. Kirti N. Chaudhuri, *Trade and civilisation in the Indian Ocean: an economic history from the rise of Islam to 1750* (Cambridge, 1985), p.80.
2. Chaudhuri, *Trade and civilisation*, p.116-18, 131, 161.
3. Chaudhuri, *Trade and civilisation*, p.102, 106, 118.
4. See Ashin Das Gupta, *Indian merchants and the decline of Surat, 1700-1750* (Wiesbaden, 1979).

Around 1520 the Portuguese, followed by the Dutch and the English around 1610 and finally the French in the 1660s, chose to establish trading factories in Surat soon after their arrival in India, despite having other factories: in Goa for the Portuguese, in Cochin and Pulicat for the Dutch, in Machilipatnam, Madras, Calcutta and then Bombay for the English and in Pondicherry and Chandernagore for the French. This was undoubtedly due to Surat's proximity to the Red Sea and the Persian Gulf, as also to Surat's exceptional facilities for traders (a safe port, banking facilities and loyal local merchants). K. N. Chaudhuri mentions the number of Dutch naval passes issued to ships in Gujarat in 1718-1719: Surat clearly dominated the region's maritime trade, with 23 ships belonging to Surat traders out of the total 32 ships registered by the Dutch authorities in Western India for that year.[5] To obtain an idea of the relative volume of Surat's maritime trade, Holden Furber supplies precise details: between 1720 and 1740, English country ships (owned by private English traders, as opposed to the official English East India Company's ships) expanded their trade, going from 17 ships a year to 28 ships a year and increasing the volume of the goods they transported annually from 3000 tons to 7000 tons. The Portuguese and the French, by contrast with the English, between 1720 and 1740, maintained a stable number of about 4 to 5 ships respectively per year, with a relatively unfluctuating volume of trade.[6] The Dutch, however, seem to have far exceeded even the English in the number of ships (32) and volume of trade goods they transported per year, over the same period. According to Furber, the Europeans (English, Dutch, French and Portuguese together) counted for about one third of Surat's total annual trade (worth an overall 87.5 lakhs of rupees per year, or approximately 875,000 pounds sterling), while the Muslim merchants and Hindu merchants represented respectively a similar third each of the trade transacted annually (28 lakhs of rupees transacted by the Muslim merchants of Surat and 28 lakhs of rupees transacted by the Hindu merchants of Surat).[7]

Of the three authors whose observations we shall examine in this essay, two were English and one was French. John Fryer (1650-1733) was a medical doctor who spent nine years travelling in Asia (principally in India and Persia). He was in Surat mainly in 1675-1676, in the wake of the Maratha leader Shivaji's attacks of the city in 1664 and 1670, and before the English shifted their administrative Western headquarters from Surat (where they had had a trading settlement from 1608 onwards) to Bombay in 1687. Fryer later returned to Surat, living there from 1679 until his final departure from India in 1681. Fryer's travel account, *A New*

5.   Chaudhuri, *Trade and civilisation*, p.157.
6.   Holden Furber, *Bombay presidency in the mid-eighteenth century* (Bombay, 1965), p.44-45.
7.   Furber, *Bombay presidency*, p.62-65.

account of East India and Persia in eight letters: being nine years' travel begun 1672 and finished 1681, was only published several years later in London in 1698, after the author had been elected a Fellow of the Royal Society in 1697. The epistolary form enables Fryer to use first and second person voices freely and to thus incorporate many personal judgements in his text. The other Englishman was an Anglican clergyman, John Ovington (1653-1731), barely three years younger than John Fryer, but who occupied the chaplaincy at the English factory in Surat from 1690 to 1693, some ten years after Fryer's departure. Ovington's travel account, *A Voyage to Suratt in the Year 1689*, was published in London in 1696. Ovington was in Surat after the 1687 transfer of the English administrative headquarters from Surat to Bombay. The third author whom we shall consider, Anquetil-Duperron (1731-1805), was a Paris-born scholar of Oriental languages and texts, who visited India some eighty years after Fryer and Ovington, from 1755 to 1761. He spent three years in Surat (1757-1760) searching for ways to translate into French the religious texts of the Ancient Parsis, the *Vendidad Sadé* and the *Zend Avesta*. The account of his experiences in India was included as a 'Discours préliminaire' to his French translation of the *Zend Avesta*, published in Paris in 1771.

Fryer, Ovington and Anquetil-Duperron visited Surat during its heyday as a centre of European trade in the western Indian Ocean. Before 1670, the Dutch, the English and the French were still consolidating their foothold in the trade of Western India; while after 1759, the English more or less eliminated the Dutch and the French from the trading scene in the region. Fryer, Ovington and Anquetil-Duperron each spent between two and three years in Surat, giving considerable weight to their observations on the city. Other European notices of Surat may be cited too. Sir Thomas Roe visited Surat between 1616 and 1619, but only briefly since the focus of his journey was the Mughal Emperor Jehangir whom Roe followed to Delhi and Lahore.[8] Roe was accompanied by the English clergyman Edward Terry, who also left an account of his travels in India, but this, like Roe's travel account, only refers to Surat in passing.[9] After 1760, there are the well-known accounts of their experiences in India by Anquetil-Duperron's brother, Anquetil de Briancourt, who was the French consul in Surat from 1774 to 1780,[10] and by the

8. Thomas Roe, *The Journal of Sir Thomas Roe, Knight, (1616-1619)*. Facsimile reprint from *The Calcutta weekly Englishman*, ed. Mr Talboys Wheeler (London, 1873), in *Travels in India in the 17th century: Thomas Roe and John Fryer* (New Delhi, 1993), p.1-130.
9. Edward Terry, *A Voyage to East India* (London, J. Martin & J. Allestrye,1655) first published in Samuel Purchas, *Purchas, his pilgrimes*, part 2, book 9, ch.6 (London, Henrie Fetherstone, 1625), reprinted in William Foster (ed.), *Early travels in India 1583-1619* (New Delhi, 1985), p.288-332.
10. Anquetil de Briancourt, 'Correspondence of M. Anquetil de Briancourt, French consul at Surat, 1774-1780', in Vinayak Gajanan Hatalkar (ed.), *French records relating to the history of the Marathas* (Bombay, 1978), vol.1.

Dutchman John Splinter Stavorinus, who visited Surat between 1774 and 1778.[11] Both Briancourt and Stavorinus, having stayed in Surat after the 1759 transfer of the regional English administrative headquarters to Bombay, mention the European trade in Surat being in a state of marked decline during the 1770s.

In studying Fryer, Ovington and Anquetil-Duperron's interactions with inhabitants and traders of Surat, I shall interrogate varying positions on both sides of the European/Indian divide beyond the reductive binary opposition between coloniser and colonised suggested by Edward Said's seminal work, *Orientalism* (1978). As Michael Dodson has pointed out in an examination of British orientalist philology in India between 1770 and 1880, colonial practices were inevitably double-sided, being grounded in and dependent upon Indian practices, while also displacing these for their own, colonial purposes.[12] This shifting instability of practices and discourses by both colonisers and colonised has been conceptualised by Homi Bhabha as a constant adaptation by all the historical actors in the colonial sphere to changing circumstances, with results that could not be fully controlled or foreseen by any of the participants concerned. Bhabha describes this process as an ambivalent 'negotiation' which allows agency without complete domination or hermetic sealing off on either side in exchanges between groups with cultural differences.[13]

I shall compare the observations on Surat between 1672 and 1761 of these three European visitors in two stages. In the first stage, I shall look at their comments on Surat's ethnic and religious diversity (friendly, hostile, curious?), and in the second, I shall compare their remarks on the trading practices used in Surat by the different trading communities there (beneficial, tedious, collaborative, conflicting, in need of reform?). I shall pay attention to textual evidence of the complexity of human exchanges in order to arrive at an overall estimate of the significance of Surat and its inhabitants in the eyes of these three Europeans over almost a century.

To begin with the ethnic and religious diversity of the inhabitants of Surat in the seventeenth and eighteenth centuries: Fryer, Ovington and Anquetil-Duperron all noted the complex administrative structure of the city, the simultaneous presence of several European powers for trading purposes (English, French and Dutch) together with the Portuguese stronghold at Daman nearby: 'As also passing by Balsore [Bulsar] (the first town of the Moors southward of Surat) and eight ships

11. John Splinter Stavorinus, *Voyages to the East Indies, translated from the original Dutch by Samuel Hull Wilcocke*, 3 vols (London, G. G. and J. Robinson, 1798).

12. Michael Dodson, *Orientalism, empire and national culture: India 1770-1880* (Basingstoke, 2007), p.1-17.

13. Homi Bhabha, 'Of mimicry and man: the ambivalence of colonial discourse', in *The Location of culture*, p.85-92.

riding at Surat River's mouth, we then came to Swally Marine, where were flying the several colours of the Three nations, English, French, and Dutch, on Flag-Staffs erected for the purpose, who here land and ship off all Goods, without molestation.'[14] Fryer points out that the customs dues on trade at Surat were collected by the *Shahbandar* or 'the Chief Customer, who has Chockies in all Inland Parts to receive Toll, and is responsible to none, only the Emperor',[15] and that the region of Gujarat was under the administration of a viceroy in Ahmadabad appointed directly by the Mughal Emperor in Delhi. At the Swally castle, on the coast to the north of Surat, the governor was an Ethiopian or Habshi with the title of *Sidi*, a hereditary post since the Sidis had wrested control of the Mughal Emperor's fleet at Surat through sea battles. Through Swally Castle, the Ethiopian Sidis controlled the sea traffic between Surat and the Persian Gulf and the Red Sea. Fryer observed separate armed forces and tensions between the Sidi governor of the Surat castle at Swally and the Muslim governor of the town of Surat.[16] Recent studies on Surat confirm this administrative structure with a hierarchy between Delhi, Ahmadabad and Surat, while within the town, authority is acknowledged to have been shared by the governor (titled *Mutasaddi* until 1732 and *Nawab* thereafter)[17] and the Ethiopian Sidi *Qiladar* or fortress commander of Swally castle who was also admiral of the Emperor's fleet. The English takeover in March 1759 of the Swally castle eliminated the Sidi *Qiladar* then in office and established a pro-English Nawab named Mia Achan in Surat to replace the weak Nawab Ali Nawaz Khan. Although this established the relative political supremacy of the English over Surat, Anquetil-Duperron observed that this did not change the ground conditions of administration; the only noticeable change being that the nominal Nawab of Surat was reduced to a mere external show of pomp in his *Darbar*, while the real political decisions in Surat were deployed by the English through their new political puppet, the Assistant Nawab or *Naib*, Fares Khan:

14. John Fryer, *Account of India*, facsimile reprint from *The Calcutta weekly Englishman*, ed. Mr Talboys Wheeler (London, 1873), in *Travels in India in the 17ᵗʰ century: Thomas Roe and John Fryer* (New Delhi, 1993), p.133-474 (265).
15. Fryer, *Account of India*, p.325-26.
16. Fryer, *Account of India*, p.289.
17. In 1732 a rebellion by the Surat merchants (representing all of Surat's trading communities) against a tax imposed on them from Ahmadabad obtained greater autonomy for the governor who was awarded the full-fledged status of *Nawab*. See Jorge Flores, 'The sea and the world of the Mutasaddi: a profile of port officials from Mughal Gujarat (*c.*1600-1650)', *Journal of the Royal Asiatic Society* 21.1 (2011), p.55-71 (esp. 57-59); and Lakshmi Subramanian, 'Capital and crowd in a declining Asian port city: the Anglo-Bania order and the Surat riots of 1795', *Modern Asian studies* 19.2 (1985), p.205-37 (210-11).

Ainsi finit l'expédition des Anglois à Surate [en mars 1759], bien conçue, mal concertée et encore plus mal exécutée. Ils y perdirent plus de deux cents Européens, quoiqu'ils eussent pour eux le nabab, qu'ils fussent maîtres de la rivière, que Bombaye fût presque à la porte, et ils ne durent leur succès qu'à l'imprudence d'un homme sans expérience (le Sidi) et au fracas, inusité dans ces contreés, que firent leurs bombes.

   Les choses dans la ville restèrent comme elles étoient avant la prise de la forteresse par les Anglois. Les Européens conservèrent leurs comptoirs, leurs privilèges, Miatchen garda le dorbar, mais Fares Khan, son second et l'homme des Anglois fut le vrai nabab, Vali Eullah [Bakshi] fut chargé des dehors de la ville.[18]

This continuation of the Mughal political regime in Surat after 1759 with the Surat Nawab's Darbar much in evidence is noted by Michelguglielmo Torri in his study of the social order in Surat between 1750 and 1800, where he insists that 'up to the last years of the century, in Surat the English ruled but the Mughals governed'.[19]

   Within the communities of Indians in Surat, the Anglican clergyman Ovington noted the co-existence of Hindus and Muslims:

To treat briefly of the Moors, who are allowed a precedence to all the rest, because of their Religion, which is the same with that of their Prince, and for this reason they are advanc'd to the most Eminent Stations of Honour and Trust; are appointed Governors of Provinces, and are intrusted with the Principal Military as well a Civil Employments. Very few of the Gentiles being called to any considerable Trust, or incourag'd any more, than just to follow their several Manual Occupations, or Merchandize [...]. And yet their peaceable submissive Deportment wins mightily upon the Moors, and takes off much of that scornful Antipathy which they [the Muslims] harbour against them [the Hindus].[20]

The degree of civic integration between the Hindus and Muslims of the province of Gujarat (during the riots in Ahmadabad in 1714)[21] as also of Surat (during the Surat riots of 1795)[22] has been the subject of reflection by various contemporary scholars. While Najaf Haider argues that in

18. Anquetil-Duperron, *Voyage en Inde, 1754-1762, relation de voyage en préliminaire à la traduction du Zend Avesta*, ed. Jean Deloche, Manonmani Filliozat and Pierre-Sylvain Filliozat (Paris, 1997), p.304, according to the initial pagination of the original 1771 edition.
19. Michelguglielmo Torri, 'Surat during the second half of the 18th century: what kind of social order? A rejoinder to Lakshmi Subramanian', *Modern Asian studies* 21.4 (1987), p.679-710 (698).
20. John Ovington, *A Voyage to Suratt in the year 1689*, ed. H. G. Rawlinson (New Delhi, 1994), p.140.
21. Najaf Haider, 'A "holi riot" of 1714: versions from Ahmedabad and Delhi', in *Living together separately: cultural India in history and politics*, ed. Mushirul Hasan and Asim Roy (Delhi, 2005), p.127-44.
22. Lakshmi Subramanian, 'Capital and crowd in a declining Asian port city'; see also Michelguglielmo Torri, 'Surat during the second half of the 18th century'.

Ahmedabad, during the 1714 Hindu-Muslim riots, the local Muslim administration played a neutral role in stopping the violence, as also in ensuring that justice was obtained from the imperial courts in Delhi by those who had suffered, he does not mention the presence of any Europeans in Ahmedabad at the time. Lakshmi Subramanian's hypothesis of an 'Anglo-Bania order' for trading purposes in Surat after 1759 – which more or less excluded the Muslim elite – is countered by Michelguglielmo Torri. Torri claims instead that the Muslim traders and Muslim governing elite co-existed side by side with the affluent traders of the Hindu, Jain, Armenian and Parsi communities in Surat between 1750 and 1800, as also with the English, Dutch and French representatives, with examples of ethnically mixed partnerships among the various Indians, among the various Europeans and between the Indians and the Europeans, despite occasional moments of dispute. Torri's position seems to be more or less corroborated by Ovington's remark quoted above, in which he points out a relative precedence of the elite Muslims in the public positions held in Surat in the 1690s, due to Surat's official administration being managed by Mughal authorities, with nevertheless a conciliatory attitude among Surat's Hindus which helped to defuse much of the tension that might have arisen from religious and ethnic differences. So we can see that not only were there no hermetically-bound ethnic groups, but that there was negotiation between all the parties and groups present in Surat during the period under study (1672-1761) with the aim of furthering their respective political, commercial and social interests.

Concerning the sports and leisure activities practised in Surat, Fryer and Ovington indicate ethnic differences between Muslims and Hindus, linking their respective preferences to the effects of climate and culture. Thus, Fryer notes that the Muslims enjoyed sports of speed, skill and 'bloody catastrophe' (horse riding, dart throwing, archery, hunting of various kinds and animal fights as a spectacle), while the 'Gentiles or Banyans' played at Chess or Tables, and also at pulling 'one another's Puckeries or Turbans off, being proverbially termed a Banyan Fight'.[23] Ovington, for his part, explains the liking of the 'Bannians' for relaxed indoor sports, such as chess, played in the shade, as also their universal esteem for animals of all kinds, as being due to 'the heat of the Country about Suratt', their 'Horror of Blood', and their belief in a 'Transmigration of Souls'. Ovington goes on to remark that the labouring classes of 'Pagans' resort to 'a pious Song' at different times of each day and during their various tasks, this being in Ovington's estimation just as 'apt to keep them active and awake at their Work, as it was to exercise the

23. Fryer, *Account of India*, p.310-11.

Devotion of their Thoughts'.[24] Anquetil-Duperron, in his turn, comments mainly on the leisure activities of the Muslim inhabitants of Surat: banquets, performances by dance artistes and public baths and massages (separate for men and for women), which he also attributes to Surat's hot climate.[25] Here, we can interpret the reactions of these three European observers to leisure activities that differed from what they were used to in Europe, as attempts to rationalise what they saw in the light of current European philosophical theories (such as Gassendi's and Locke's empirical sensualism, or Montesquieu's climate theory). Here again, their remarks can be understood as efforts to make sense of what was new to them, in relation to what they were already familiar with, rather than as a deliberate belittling of Indian practices in order to affirm European superiority.

Anquetil-Duperron presents some anecdotes that illustrate his personal negotiations with various parties in Surat. While trying to obtain access to ancient Persian manuscripts in 1759 from the Parsi Dasturs or priests in Surat who were reluctant to let their precious manuscripts out of sight, he enlisted the assistance of the Dutch representative, Taillefer, as also that of Taillefer's Indian agent or Dalal.[26] We learn that in 1759 Anquetil-Duperron attended the celebration in honour of the English chief, John Spencer (hosted by the recently installed Nawab of Surat, Mia Achan, at Surat's Salabatpura palace, where there were fireworks and a big crowd), and that the Frenchman rode in Spencer's own carriage on this occasion.[27] As an explanation for his proximity to Spencer, Anquetil-Duperron cites the Englishman's kindly temperament and the 'excellent relationship' he had forged with him, whereas he confesses that his relationship with Spencer's English successor in Surat, William Andrew Price, was much 'less cordial'.[28] In March 1761, when Anquetil-Duperron was trying to leave Surat to return to Europe for health reasons, the French in Surat were reduced to inactivity since the English had taken over Pondicherry just before in the course of the Seven Years War. His attempts to find a place on a Swedish ship, on a Dutch ship and on a Portuguese ship had failed (while resorting to Banians', Arabs' or Parsis' ships was out of the question since they were all under English control). So Anquetil-Duperron was reduced to pleading for a place on an English ship, which he obtained thanks to the kind intervention of his friend John Spencer (who had by then moved on to become a Councillor in the English Company's Council in Bombay in 1760). Thus ironically,

24. Ovington, *A Voyage to Suratt in the year 1689*, p.159, 164, 169, 173.
25. Anquetil-Duperron, *Voyage en Inde*, p.344, 355.
26. Anquetil-Duperron, *Voyage en Inde*, p.329-30.
27. Anquetil-Duperron, *Voyage en Inde*, p.341.
28. Anquetil-Duperron, *Voyage en Inde*, p.346.

despite English-French hostilities in 1761, Anquetil-Duperron returned to Europe on board an English ship.[29] Such details serve to illustrate that he could not afford to harbour an attitude of exclusiveness or superiority, but had constantly to make compromises with various parties in Surat.

Other remarks by Fryer, Ovington and Anquetil-Duperron that demonstrate processes of negotiation by the various parties in Surat, concern funeral rites. For example, between the walled gates of Surat and the island of Swally, along the banks of the river Tapti, there were the burial grounds of the Europeans, adjacent to the tombs of the Muslims, followed by the locality of Pulpara further away from the town, where the Banias and Hindus cremated their dead, and where the Parsis carried their dead to the Parsi tower of silence. Fryer comments on the 'handsome' and 'pargetted' [plastered and painted] tombs of the Dutch, the Armenians' tombs in a garden, the burial place of the Portuguese, the separate place where the French deposited their dead (this had only a single small tomb) and, among the English tombs, the impressive monument that marked the burial place of Sir George Oxenden, English president of Surat from 1669 to 1677.[30] Ovington notes a visible spirit of competition between the different groups of Europeans in Surat 'to outvie each other in magnificent structures and stately monuments' as repositories for their dead, with a particular mention of the tomb 'of a jovial Dutch Commander [unnamed], with three large Punch Bowls upon the top of it for the Entertainment and Mirth of his surviving friends'.[31] Anquetil-Duperron does not mention any European tombs, probably because there were not many French tombs in Surat. Among the Muslim tombs, Fryer describes 'a row of sepulchres of the Muttany or Bursta's Pilgrims [perhaps a reference to Bursa in Turkey] with the soles of their feet imprinted on the middle' with other round Muslim tombs 'by the side of a tank on an ascending mount'.[32] The locality of Pulpara inspires remarks from Fryer about many Brahmins in the River there 'doing their Devotions, which consists in Washing and Praying',[33] while Ovington dwells on the presence of ascetic 'faquirs' practising diverse forms of penance, amidst Pulpara's 'pleasant walks and Groves of Trees, near the gentle Stream of the River Tappy'.[34] Anquetil-Duperron mentions the pleasure garden at Pulpara constructed earlier in the seventeenth century by the Parsi merchant Rustum, and several ditches the size of a

29. Anquetil-Duperron, *Voyage en Inde*, p.430-36.
30. Fryer, *Account of India*, p.292-93.
31. Ovington, *A Voyage to Suratt in the year 1689*, p.235-36.
32. Fryer, *Account of India*, p.293.
33. Fryer, *Account of India*, p.294.
34. Ovington, *A Voyage to Suratt in the year 1689*, p.210.

human body along the river bank, in which a constant fire burnt for the cremation of Hindus.[35]

All three observers mention the tower of silence of the Parsis of Surat. Fryer's account mentions the birds of prey that dispose of the dead bodies 'and to that end, in the middle of this Enclosure is a Well for the filth to drain away', as well as on the role of the relatives who observe which body part the birds of prey lay hold of in order to make reports on the 'future bliss' or 'ill state' of the deceased person.[36] Ovington gives similar information on the circular structure 'made shelving towards the Centre, that the filth and moisture which are drain'd continually from the Carcasses, may by an easie passage descend into a Sink made in the middle to receive them', as also on the purifying ablutions carried out by the Company who attend the funeral rite in order 'to cleanse themselves from what defilements on these Melancholy occasions, they might have contracted...'.[37] Anquetil-Duperron's report of his trip to the Surat Tower of Silence closely resembles those of Fryer and Ovington though he also includes Parsi terms like '*Dakhmê*' for the tower of silence, '*Nesa Salars*' for the pall bearers and '*sag-did*' for the ritual of presenting a dog to sniff the dead body in order to make certain that the person is well and truly dead. Anquetil personally witnessed the deposition of a dead body on the day of his visit.[38]

Apparently then, all the different communities, Indian and European, present in Surat had been obliged at some stage of their development to negotiate the grant of a plot of land from the local Mughal authorities for the disposal of the dead bodies of members of their respective groups. That all our three European observers noticed these funeral grounds in Surat confirms the cohabitation within Surat of these different communities, Indian and European, for trading purposes, and the peaceful adjustment of their funeral rituals within the spaces allotted to them. Whether it was the functioning of the local administration in Surat, or particular leisure activities practised by different ethnic groups or personal arrangements made by individual visitors, or yet again the topographical distribution of the funeral grounds of the various communities present in Surat, the observations of Fryer, Ovington and Anquetil-Duperron on these various questions show that there were no hard and fast divisions or systematic oppositions between one group and another on ethnic, political, commercial or social grounds between 1672 and 1761. Continual give and take by all concerned seems instead to have characterised communal relations in the town.

---

35. Anquetil-Duperron, *Voyage en Inde*, p.361.
36. Fryer, *Account of India*, p.321.
37. Ovington, *A Voyage to Suratt in the year 1689*, p.220-21.
38. Anquetil-Duperron, *Voyage en Inde*, p.361.

This brings us to the second part of this essay. Here, I shall present particular aspects of the trading practices mentioned by the three selected European observers over the period between 1672 and 1761, with the aim of investigating whether there was any polarisation between the Europeans on the one hand and the different Indian trading partners they encountered on the other. First of all, they allude to the menace of pirates who threatened the smooth trading of any ships in the Indian Ocean, whatever their origin. Fryer presents the Arab pirates who plied especially in the Gulf of Persia as 'villainously inclined' and 'formidable' plunderers,[39] comparing their nuisance potential to that of 'the Moors of Algiers, Tunis and Tripoly' in 'the Narrow Seas of the Mediterranean'. This suggests an anti-Arab prejudice on the part of the English doctor. However in the clergyman Ovington's reports on acts of piracy in the Indian Ocean, three out of the four cases he mentions between 1689 and 1691, turn out to concern European aggressors who attacked either other European ships or Muslim ships, while Hindus do not feature in his depiction of piracy at all because they chose not to own ships, contenting themselves with buying and selling goods inland and at the ports.[40] Only in one case in 1690 recounted by Ovington are the attacking pirates Muslim Indian Sanganians, hailing from western Kathiawar, and Ovington indicates that even they were 'repulsed' and that they 'speedily withdrew' in the face of furious firing from the captain of the English ship under attack. Some ninety years later, Anquetil-Duperron reports a similar type of incident of piracy in what he calls 'the Fez Salem affair' at the end of November 1759, where again the aggressor-ship that captured a Muslim trading ship in Muscat was not Asian but was named 'le Condé' and directed by a French captain, while the victim ship belonged to the Muslim Chellabi trader of Surat named Abdul Kader who lost eight lakhs of rupees of goods on this occasion.[41] Among the cases of piracy in the Indian Ocean that appear in the written accounts of Fryer, Ovington and Anquetil-Duperron, a majority can be said to have emanated from European aggressor ships, outweighing by far the number of pirate attacks perpetrated by Asian or Indian pirates, belying the suggestion that non-European pirates were viewed by them as being more violent or corrupt than their European counterparts.

About the nature of Surat's maritime trade, Fryer is the most prolix, giving many details on the types of ships observable at the port of Surat, going from European 1000 tonners to Indian merchantmen that had thirty to forty pieces of cannon 'more for shew than service', smaller Indian frigates used more for river traffic than on the high seas, the

39. Fryer, *Account of India*, p.324-25.
40. Ovington, *A Voyage to Suratt in the year 1689*, p.64, 77, 99, 239.
41. Anquetil-Duperron, *Voyage en Inde*, p.346, 349.

Mughal Emperor's four great ships that carried mainly Muslim pilgrims to Mecca every year, with a passing mention also of 'the huge unshapen vessels called junks' belonging to the Muslim royal family of Bantam. Fryer adds precious information on the contents of Surat's exports (precious stones, indigo, cotton, cotton-yarn and silks) and Surat's imports (dates, Middle East drugs, horses, gold, silver and pearls), and on the seasonal variations in Surat's maritime traffic (European ships all year round, the arrival of ships from Basra in February and the appearance of ships from Jeddah and the Red Sea in August).[42] For his part, Ovington limits his description of Surat's sea trade to a rapid allusion to the warehouses and goods yards at the port of Swally where the larger European ships were permitted to accost, while the smaller Indian ships were directed 'either [...] to enter the river of Suratt, or to Anchor at the mouth of it', the residences and warehouses of the English, French and Dutch being situated between the Swally castle and the mouth of the river Tapti.[43] Anquetil-Duperron, intervening almost one century later, speaks of the 'immense riches' generated by Surat's trade and the 'considerable settlements' of the Portuguese, Dutch, French and English at Surat in the past tense, attributing Surat's present state of 'poverty' and 'weakness' to internal quarrels among Surat's Muslim governors and to mismanagement of their affairs by the chiefs of the European settlements.[44] These observations by Fryer, Ovington and Anquetil-Duperron enlighten us about the varied geographical and ethnic origins of the traders who participated in Surat's maritime trade, and draw our attention to the absence of discrimination by Surat's political and commercial authorities against customers and goods of any type. The decline in Surat's trade after 1750 turns out to be due mainly to personal greed and changing factionalisms (without evident religious or racial biases) for greater material gain among the Indian and European chiefs in power in this commercial hub.

A final point which enables us to consider whether trading was characterised by a spirit of cooperation and enterprise, or by manipulative domination on the part of the Europeans, is the portrayal of interactions between the Europeans traders and their Indian interlocutors. Already in 1672, Fryer is frank about the English being in a position of supreme advantage in Surat's trade, as compared to the other European powers, and he goes on to state that the Indian officials show respect for the English in the context of trade because of their naval strength and the English ability to impress:

---

42. Fryer, *Account of India*, p.288, 301, 302-303, 312, 314.
43. Ovington, *A Voyage to Suratt in the year 1689*, p.100.
44. Anquetil-Duperron, *Voyage en Inde*, p.264, 267, 270, 274.

So that we singly have the credit of the Port, and are of most advantage to the Inhabitants, and fill the Custom House with the substantialest Incomes. [...]

Amidst which it is time to return, to see what Grace we are in among this divided Multitude: our Usage by the Pharmaund (or Charter) granted successively from their Emperors, is kind enough, but the better, because our Naval Power curbs them; otherwise they being prone to be imperious, would subjugate us, as they do all others that are harness'd with the Apronstrings of trade. Supposing us then to bear the face of Ministers of State, as well as the sly visage of Mechanicks, they depose something of their Ferity [beastliness, savageness], and treat with us in a more favourable Stile; giving us the preference before others here resident and look on us with the same Aspect as they do on their great Ombrahs.[45]

Fryer explains the greater opulence of the English East India Company in Surat in comparison with the social standing of 'Vockeels or factors for money'd men up the Country' although the volumes of trade they dealt with were in fact similar to those transacted by the English Company, as resulting from concrete factors like independent fortification of the English warehouses, separate docks for English vessels and separate yards for the English Company's seamen, soldiers and ships' stores.[46] Ovington is quite explicit about the important impact of presents to Mughal officials by English factors, even necessitating close vigilance by the English presidents and higher echelons of the English administration in India to avoid complete monopoly of all English trade with India by the English factors. Such 'profitable blessing' ensured the English Company's trading interests by obtaining permission for the Company's servants to conduct 'private trade to all parts of the East'. Other factors included English 'Probity and Grandeur' which reputedly inspired respect for the English among the Indian population and the payment of comfortable compensation to Indian Brokers 'of the Bannian Cast' for the buying and disposing of the Company's Goods at the most advantageous 'Rates and Value'.[47] Such 'enlightened self-interest' advocated by Ovington might sound like pragmatism on the part of John Company.

Anquetil-Duperron in his turn provides a lively scene of public auction at the English factory in Surat in 1759:

L'adjudication se fit le matin dans la grande salle de la loge angloise. Les prix avoient été débattus et convenus auparavant entre le courtier et les marchands, et l'on sçait que ces marchés où il est souvent question de plusieurs millions, se font avec la plus grande tranquillité et la plus grande bonne-foi entre ces gens que nous traitons de barbares. [...] Nous entrâmes dans la salle de la loge angloise sur les dix heures du matin. Elle étoit remplie

---

45. Fryer, *Account of India*, p.275, 317.
46. Fryer, *Account of India*, p.317.
47. Ovington, *A Voyage to Suratt in the year 1689*, p.226, 227, 233.

de gens accroupis sur des nattes et qui d'eux-mêmes s'étoient placés selon
leur rang, c'est-à-dire selon leurs richesses. On y voyait des Indous, des
Parses, des Arméniens, des Maures, des Sidis (cafres), des Mogols et des
Arabes. [...] Lorsque nous eûmes pris séance, Jagrenat, courtier des Anglois,
fit la lecture du marché et présenta la liste des marchandises, on en apporta
même quelques montres pour la forme et chacun des adjudicataires redonna
sous le mouchoir sa parole à M. Spencer pour la partie qu'il achetoit. Les
présens furent ensuite distribués; ils consistoient en châles, pièces de
mousseline et paquets de bétel...[48]

Anquetil-Duperron appears sensitive here to the important role played
by the Indian broker Jagrenat on behalf of the English in ensuring the
successful unfolding of the public auction, through prior fixing of prices
with the Indian merchants present, in reading out the list of goods to be
purchased and by the distribution of gifts to the participants. The very
fact that Anquetil-Duperron chooses to portray the public auction at the
English factory, and not at the Dutch factory, or organised by Bania, Jain,
Parsi or Muslim traders, reflects that the English in 1759 were already the
foremost trading power in Surat.

Comparing the three European portrayals of Surat we have analysed:
Fryer's description appears concrete and rational; Ovington's approach
seems characterised by 'enlightened self-interest' on behalf of the
English, while Anquetil-Duperron's depiction is perhaps the most re-
alistic and complex, since it also accords an active role to Indian
complicity in the furtherance of English interests. Fryer's concluding
statement on Surat and her trade may serve too for this essay as a whole:

Were these difficulties [of security] removed, Surat, as if Nature had designed
her both by Sea and Land the Seat of Traffick, would have nothing to hinder
her from being the compleatest Mistress thereof in the whole World [...] The
commodiousness of the river serving to bring Goods in from Europe, Asia,
Africa and America; the long continued current from the Inland parts
through the vast wildernesses of huge woods and forest, wafts great rafts of
Timber for Shipping and Building; and Damar [Tar] for Pitch, the finest
sented Bitumen (if it be not a Gum or Rosin) I ever met with. [...] They have
not only Coir-Yarn made of the Cocoe for Cordage, but good Flax and
Hemp; and Iron from the mountains of the South. So that it may be
concluded, for the Benefit of an Harbour, for the disposition of the Natives,
for a convenient Supply (or more truly Abundance) of all things, for a due
imployment of them, but above all, the Commodities Exported, and the
Riches Imported, Surat cannot be fellowed in India.[49]

This comparative analysis of the observations on Surat by the English
medical doctor John Fryer (1698), by the Anglican chaplain John

48. Anquetil-Duperron, *Voyage en Inde*, p.341.
49. Fryer, *Account of India*, p.326-327.

Ovington (1696), and by the French orientalist scholar Anquetil-Duperron (1771) on the ethno-religious specificities of Surat's inhabitants and on the complexity of the trade practices there, helps us to understand two things in particular. First, that the political context was constantly changing with many unforeseen circumstances and crises which necessitated constant adaptation of the policies of all the parties concerned. And second, that the various European and Indian groups present were, in fact, on the same footing where trade was concerned, with each group trying to defend and further its own interests. While these interests resulted in a complex jostling of communities and persons, no pre-established teleological plan appears favouring the colonial ascendancy of Britain or any other European power. In fact, all the partners (European and Indian) involved in Surat between 1672 and 1761, seem to have practised ad hoc negotiations and to have improvised solutions to their problems, rather than resorting to any legalised fixities, institutionalised transactions or long-term arrangements.[50] In contrast with the very different picture of exclusive bilateral alliances – the 'Anglo-Bania order' – that emerges from Lakshmi Subramanian's notable reading of the later 1795 Surat riots, the accounts of Surat by Fryer, Ovington and Anquetil-Duperron between 1672 and 1761 would lead us to infer that medium-term trade profits and ambivalent, open-ended adjustments to a rapidly evolving setting were the determining factors behind the individual and collective actions of the Mughal administration, of the different European trading companies, and of the Indian trading groups in Surat during this period.

50. I am grateful to Professor Dirk H. A. Kolff of Leiden, author of *Naukar, Rajput and Sepoy: the ethno-history of the military labour market in Hindustan, 1450-1850* (Cambridge, 1990), for pointing out to me that 'Europe legalises, India negotiates'.

The Mughal decline and the emergence of new global connections in early modern India

SEEMA ALAVI

> *Iss ahad ko na jaanei aglaa saa ahad Mir*
> *Who daur abb nahin woh zamin aasman nahin*
> (This age is not like that which went before it.
> The times have changed the earth and sky has
> changed).[1]

This was the lament of the eighteenth-century Mughal poet Mir Taqi Mir (1722-1810) who had spent a lifetime in Delhi enjoying the patronage of the Mughal Empire and living on the largesse of the imperial court in Agra and Delhi. From the 1740s he saw the visible decline of the city: its degradation at the hands of Afghan and Persian invaders, the steadily rising political ambitions of the English East India Company, and the loosening of imperial control as revenue from its far-flung provinces became a trickle.

While Mir bemoaned the fading of Mughal Delhi, he was sceptical of the winds of change that saw power and patronage shift to the provinces. Indeed, the shrinkage of the old patrons had made provincial power centres the new havens of literary energy. In 1780 Mir, like many other Delhi littérateurs, very grudgingly shifted to the provincial town of Lucknow. However, his nostalgia of the imperial capital continued and produced the famous poetry of lament (*Sher-Ashob*). Mir introduces himself to the people of Lucknow in a patronising verse that reflects the cultural arrogance of the archetype Mughal court poet:

> *Kyaa bud baash puchi ho purab kei sakino*
> *Dilli jo ek shahar tha alam-i-intikhab*
> *Isko falak nei loot kei viraan kar diya*
> *Ham ko gharib jaan kei hans hans pukar kei*
> *Rahtei the muntkhab hee jahan rozgar kei*
> *Han reheni wale hain isee ujarre dayar kei*

> Why do you mock at me and ask yourselves
> Where do I come from, easterners?
> There was a city famed throughout the world

---

1. Khurshidul Islam and Ralph Russell, *Three Mughal poets: Mir, Sauda Mir Hasan* (Delhi, 1994), p.246.

Where dwelt the chosen spirits of the age
Delhi its name fairest among the fair.
Fate looted it and laid it desolate
And to that ravaged city I belong.[2]

Mir attributes the nasty fate of Mughal Delhi to the degeneration of the nobility and the corruption of office: *Hain jinhe kutch bhee rawaiyat-i-darbar sau farebandeh va maskari va gaddar* (Those having even a slight influence in court circles are cheats, tricksters and traitors, indulging in malpractices).[3]

And he is not alone in this assessment of imperial decay. His peer, the Delhi poet Sauda, echoes similar sentiments and is scathing in his critique of the incompetent new people who had emerged to control imperial politics: *Na rasm suleh kee samjhein na jang ka dastur; Jo in mein qaidah daan thei hue woh insei dur.* (The nobles do not know the art of making war nor peace while the wise among them have deserted them).[4]

The trope of decline referred to in the verses of Mir and Sauda contains several elements that were common to the Mughals and their contemporaries in the Ottoman and the Western Roman Empires: the degeneration and corruption of the body politic by luxury, sale of office or miscegenation. Some South Asianists have used this notion of decline literally and painted the eighteenth century as the dark ages.[5] Other revisionist studies have replaced the notion of 'decline' with ideas of 'decentralisation' and 'transformation'.[6] I shall focus on the critical role played by the myth of decline in the creation of wider conceptual spaces; such spaces, as will be shown, served as critical arenas for intellectual communities to connect in fresh ways to global influences.[7] This triggered a shift in the understanding of the self and the state: an atomised understanding that derived from a wider intellectual frame replaced one that framed perceptions in merely aristocratic literary and political genres. The de-centring of the state in the eighteenth-century narrative enables us to arrive at a more nuanced genealogy of the

2. Islam and Russell, *Three Mughal poets*, p.260.
3. Ishrat Haque, *Glimpses of Mughal society and culture* (New Delhi, 1992), p.66.
4. Haque, *Glimpses of Mughal society and culture*, p.67.
5. Irfan Habib, 'Eighteenth century in Indian economic history', *Proceedings of the Indian History Congress 56th session* (Calcutta, 1995), p.358-78.
6. Muzaffar Alam, 'Aspects of agrarian uprisings in North India in the early eighteenth century', in *Situating Indian history: for Sarvepalli Gopal*, ed. Sabyasachi Bhattacharya and Romilla Thapar (Delhi, 1986), p.146-70; Muzaffar Alam, 'Eastern India in the early eighteenth century "crisis": some evidence from Bihar', *Indian economic and social history review* 28.1 (1991), p.43-71. Chetan Singh, *Region and empire: Punjab in the seventeenth century* (Delhi, 1991).
7. For the idea of 'myth of decline' see Christopher A. Bayly and Seema Alavi, *Decline, decentralisation and diaspora*, forthcoming.

evolution of early modern political cultures as shaped, conceptualised and understood by individuals weathering the imperial crisis. This longer history of the court/state as conceptualised from 'below' invests discussions of the early colonial state with the kind of genealogical approach associated with the work of Norbert Elias.[8] It challenges the Foucauldian brand of nineteenth-century exceptionalism with its Eurocentric gaze; and allows us to move beyond the 'colonial' frame in understanding the political and cultural transitions that characterised eighteenth-century India.

  This chapter draws attention to the particular intellectual and imaginative histories of the three social groups that were impacted by the idea of decline. It elaborates, via their histories, the process by which the very illness and 'decline' of the imperial body led to the creation of a wider intellectual community occupying a newly envisioned conceptual space. One that was marked notably by, not merely the impact of western forms, but also the passage of knowledge within the global Indo-Islamic ecumene itself. The families of the Indo-Persian Mughal physicians, the communities of men of religion and the world of soldiering constitute three such social segments that raise an important set of considerations. Their stories reveal that the perceived dwindling of the Mughal court and its aristocratic culture became the trigger for wider social change.

Indo-Persian medical culture in transition

Mughal medical literature

The cloud of Arabic learning, with its trans-Empire appeal that straddled the Ottoman and Safavid literary circuits, always lingered over the heavily Persianised Mughal court. Muzaffar Alam argues that individual elite lives in Mughal India were entangled in larger processes that made Empire both territorially rooted and extra-territorially encased. An important case in point were the texts of political theorists like Nasir - ud Din Tusi, that borrowed heavily from Islam's Greco-Arabic legacy, and circulated freely in literary circles in Mughal India.[9] Mughal texts on governance, like Abul Fazl's Ain-i-Akbari, were impacted by such literature. The same was true for texts on medicine. Iranian *hakims* (physicians) such as Nur-ud-Din Shirazi and Muhammad Shah Arzani, who flocked into Mughal India in the seventeenth century, wrote encyclopaedic medical texts under the aegis of the court. Very much like Abul Fazl, they too borrowed from the Middle-Eastern or Arabic intellectual legacy of Islam (Avicenna, Aristotle and others). Stylistically

8. Norbert Elias, *The Civilizing process, vol.2: state formation and civilization* (Oxford, 1982).
9. Muzaffar Alam, *The Languages of political Islam in India c.1200-1800* (New Delhi, 2004), p.50-61. They were read by a small elite from the time of Humayun.

their texts, even though written in the court language, Persian, matched
the canonical stature of Avicenna's Arabic masterpiece the *Canon*. An
additional feature was their effort to combine Arabic knowledge with the
Ayurveda of Indic medical learning.

The late seventeenth-century genre of Indo-Muslim medical literature
in Persian underlined the idea of health as aristocratic virtue. This meant
that a good *hakim* was also a littérateur, a cultured man who had a
smattering of useful knowledge about the world. He wrote encyclopaedic
texts that displayed his wide range of knowledge and that laid out the
norms of proper conduct and deportment. He defined a healthy body as
a cultured body – one that had mastered the etiquettes and correspondence skills laid out in the literary genres of Persian texts.

According to C. A. Bayly, Rosalind O'Hanlon and M. Alam,[10] the
health of Mughal society was intimately connected to the health of the
Emperor who embodied social well-being. Persian medical texts
underscored the idea of health as individual aristocratic virtue and
proper social balancing by the Emperor that maintained political stability and societal harmony. They emphasised the salience of individual
comportment, proper conduct and correspondence as central to personal well-being that ensured the smooth running of society. The *Tibb-i-
Darashikohi* by Nur-ud-Din Shirazi, written in 1645-1646 and dedicated to
Shah Jahan's son Dara Shikoh (1615-1659), is an important case in
point.[11] The 1780s copy, prepared in Surat for a Parsi *hakim* called
Bizhan, is a huge encyclopaedic and ornate text in three volumes that
cover approximately 3000 pages. It follows the Islamic encyclopedic
tradition of Avicenna's *Canon*. And, like the *Canon*, it is said to have
borrowed extensively from a variety of healing traditions and pharma-
copoeias without always acknowledging them. It is unique because of its
ornate Persian style, its obeisance to the court, and the wide historical
canvas that it sketches for Unani. It offers a definitive history of Unani
spanning the pre-Islamic Greco-Arab world, the period of the caliphates,
and moves down to the pre-Mughal and Mughal medical tradition.
Shirazi delves into the philosophy of health even as he seeks to admin-
ister the body through the external agencies of proper conduct,
comportment and diet. For him, health is about individual well-being,
and an ideal state that can be achieved by a select few through proper
comportment.

10. C. A. Bayly, *Empire and information: intelligence gathering and social communication in India, 1780-
    1870* (Cambridge, 1996); Alam, *Languages of political Islam*; Rosalind O'Hanlon, 'Manliness
    and imperial service in Mughal North India', *Journal of the economic and social history of the
    Orient* 42.1 (1999), p.47-93.
11. Nur-ud-Din Shirazi, *Ilajat-I-Dara Shikohi*, p.857-59. MS supplément persan 342, 342A,
    342B, Bibliothèque Nationale, Paris.

The drift towards Arabic-style learning: Aurangzeb and Unani texts

The tradition of writing Shirazi-style medical encyclopaedias continued in the period of Aurangzeb, who is said to have weathered the worst political and economic crisis in the empire and overseen its demise. In this period of imperial crisis (1700), Muhammad Akbar Shah Arzani produced the *Tibb-i-Akbari* or Akbar's medicine. The *Tibb-i-Akbari* is the Persian translation of the Arabic text *Sharh al-Asbab wa al-Alamat* of Nafis bin Aiwaz Kirmani (d.1449). But in 1700 Arzani constructed and added his own commentary to it as well. The *Tibb-i-Akbari* tries to emulate the *Tibb-i-Darashikohi* both stylistically and in its content. It covers a wide canvas in its twenty-seven chapters, which deal with the history of Unani, symptomatic treatments of local and general diseases, and the properties of medicines and comportment regimens for individual good health.[12]

However, the second text of Arzani, *Mizan-i-Tibb*,[13] made evident the shift in medical learning. This is different from the average Mughal text. In its concise and user-friendly style it bends more towards providing useful medical knowledge as a guarantee of individual well-being. *Hakim* Arzani makes his intention to write a popular text of Unani clear on the opening page: 'My children and relatives were too busy to devote time to the study of the science of medicine. So I wrote this brief text to make simple the teaching of medicine. Even though it is a brief treatise it has many benefits. I named it *Mizan-i-Tibb*. I hope that God, the biggest hakim, should make it successful.'[14] The *Mizan-i-Tibb* claims to be a handbook of medicine for beginners. It is divided into three sections (*maqalahs*), each of which lays out medical wisdom rather than aristocratic virtue as the key to good health. Stylistically, it stands in sharp contrast to the voluminous and ornate Persian medical texts of the period. It is a short work of forty-eight folios, written in ordinary *nastaliq* style. The 1742 copy of the text seems to have been written by more than one scribe. Noteworthy is the effort of a third scribe, who makes corrections in the spellings and contents of the text and also offers supplementary clarifications and explanations in the margin. These marginal notes are in Persian. At times, the scribe translates the Persian into Hindi, using *Devnagari* to make it easy for the lay reader to recognise the medicines recommended. Thus, the Hindustani word *kewra* (a sweet fragrant edible potion for digestion) is inscribed in the margin to explain its Persian equivalent, listed in the text as *sharbat-i-kadar*.[15]

---

12. For copies of the *Tibb-I-Akbari* see Wellcome Institute Library, London: WMS. Per. 172, 374 folios, 1790, copied in Peshawar. Later versions are also available in the Wellcome collection.
13. Ad MS 17949, 48 folios, (British Library, London), 1742 copy.
14. MS 17949, folio 1, preface.
15. MS 17949, folio 1.

Written at the beginning of the eighteenth century the *Mizan*'s easy-to-read style and accessibility reflect the 'vernacularisation' of Persian and the loosening of the monopoly of scribes, families and court over the medical knowledge that it embodied.[16] It also reflects the turn to what Rosalind O'Hanlon calls the mushrooming of a more cosmopolitan intellectual 'connoisseurship' that now underpinned gentlemanly status.[17] With its emphasis on the useful knowledge of science and theology, it radiates the austerity associated with doctrinaire languages like Arabic.

Indeed the influence of Arabic religious literature was very much evident in the reading patterns and writing styles of late Mughal society. In this period Arabic texts like Jalal-ul-Din al Suyuti's *Tibb-i-nabawi* or the medicine of the Prophet[18] began to be included in their Persian translation in the medical compendiums of Mughal India. These defined comportment in the Arab tradition of the Prophet's life.

New medical learning in Arabic: Unani in early eighteenth-century India

In the early eighteenth century, as the Empire became 'ill', a cessation in the significance of physically embodied knowledge followed. As knowledge became disconnected from the person of the Emperor and all that he signified, it looked for a new authority framework. The turn to Arabic and the disembodied knowledge that it signified made scribes and families recreate their monopoly over medical knowledge by hooking it on to this doctrinaire language. The cloud of Arabic had loomed over medical knowledge from the days of Aurangzeb. But in the eighteenth century it was used to restore the prestige of older families and scribes who were worried about the spilling out of their medical knowledge by the increasing accessibility of Persian as exemplified by Arzani's easy to read text *Mizan-I-Tibb*.[19]

This by no means meant the disappearance of Persian. On the contrary its vernacularisation meant that the unalloyed Persian of high literary, religious and scientific texts was relegated more tightly than ever before to the realm of the exclusive urbane, elite aristocratic circuits of regional courts. In the early nineteenth century Alloy Sprenger, assistant to the British Resident at Lucknow, surveyed the 'Muhammadan libraries' of Lucknow aristocracy and notables. He reported that they

16. Alam, *Languages of political Islam*, p.317-49.
17. O'Hanlon, 'Manliness and imperial service in Mughal North India', p.50.
18. Charles Elgood, *A Medical history of Persia and the Eastern Caliphate from the earliest times until the year AD 1932* (Cambridge, 1951), p.63; also Charles Elgood, *Analecta medico-historica: Safavid surgery* (London, 1966), p.8.
19. For details see Seema Alavi, *Islam and healing: loss and recovery of an Indo-Muslim medical tradition, 1600-1900* (London, 2008), p.35-43.

had thousands of Persian manuscripts.[20] And a small collection of Arabic manuscripts. The same was the case in the southern kingdom of Mysore. Tipu Sultan too had a huge collection of Persian medical manuscripts and a smattering of Arabic ones in his library.[21]

However, beyond such courts and capital cities, literate elites looked for new means to legitimate their authority. The vernacularisation and popularisation of Persian weakened its efficacy as a tool through which local elite families could control medical knowledge. Thus, outside the capital cities of post-Mughal society, the dignity of medical science shifted from the Persian – in which it had rested since the time of the Mughals – to Arabic, which was now projected as the custodian of the Arabic sciences. As elite families leaned on Arabic, and the knowledge and prestige it embodied, the change was easy to discern. In the early eighteenth century the Arabic text on medicine, the *Sharh-i-Mujib*, rather than the Persian medical literature of the earlier century became the most popular text in the schools and libraries of North India. Now one could be a cultured gentleman without having read a single Persian text of medicine.

Arabic was the universal language of science in the non-European world. Thus the Indian shift to Arabic offered a wider ambit of literal and imaginary connections with the Islamic ecumene. At the end of the Mughal innings, when regional identities were being sharply articulated in local languages, it was the Muslims who established pan-regional links in science, medicine, astronomy and astrology in Arabic. The long arm of the politically-shrunk Mughal Empire, that leaned on Arabic to stretch into the non-European imperia, was a by-product of the widely circulated idea of decline.

The communities of religious learning

One remarkable manifestation of the myth of decline was the production of a new kind of reformist literature by men of religion attached to the seminaries of Sunni Islam in Delhi. As legatees of the Mughal Empire they met the new challenges posed by the sick Empire and its political successor the English East India Company by tapping both the indigenous resources as well as the networks laid out by the new English power. This enabled them to garner support and establish contacts beyond the territories of the still fledgling British India. Their efforts

20. A. Sprenger, assistant to Resident in Lucknow, to H. M. Elliott, Foreign Secretary to Govt. of India, 18 March 1849, Selections from the records of the Govt. of India, Foreign Dept, no. cccxxxiv, serial no. 82, report on Muhammadan libraries of Lucknow, 1896, p.18-19.
21. Charles. A. Stewart, *A Descriptive catalogue of the oriental library of the late Tipu Sultan of Mysore* (London, 1809).

were informed by the re-interpretation of the Arabic scriptures – the
Koran and the Hadith – that had global appeal. They invoked these texts
and popularised them via their commentaries and interpretations using
the vernacular Urdu language within India and Arabic outside its confines. Many still wrote in Persian. Indeed this reformist literature
produced in Urdu, Persian and Arabic reflected the multilingual
cosmopolitanism of the period. These were perhaps the last of the
multilingual authors before both British colonial drives as well as their
own drift towards Arabicist exclusivity in at least religious and scientific
knowledge would draw a curtain on people like them.

Many of these multilingual men were products of the Indo-Persianate
gentlemanly literate culture of Mughal India.[22] They traced their intellectual genealogies to the eighteenth-century Delhi Naqshbandi Sufi
Shah Waliullah. They re-interpreted his scripture-based eclectic tradition that was leader-centric and made it more individual-centric.[23] The
shift to the canon and the individual was a notable consequence of the
myth of decline. As the Mughal Empire and its successor states were
popularly perceived as moving into oblivion so did the Indo-Persianate
concept of the royal body and the court society as the embodiment of
knowledge of all kinds. In this period of transition both religious and
scientific knowledge spilled out of their bodily trappings. There was a
greater stress on the individual and his ability to create a doctrine that
ensured universal appeal and promised global connectivity.

This very distinct South Asian strand of Arabicist tradition became the
hallmark of the turn of the century Urdu and Arabic literature. The
reformists focused on the individual and his agency in interpreting
scripture. This added flexibility to the relatively prescriptive decorum
hitherto doled out at shrines, madrasas and religious gatherings by
leaders. Not surprisingly this Arabicist tradition of 'return to the scripture' and the salience of the individual opened a floodgate of intellectual
energy. South Asian intellectuals, warriors and traders interpreted scriptures in individuated ways as they came to terms with the reality of
British rule. It became an effective strategy to weave together diverse
people by offering them unprecedented agency. This individuation was
more than what is generally viewed as a mere self-purification exercise.[24]

---

22. For an elaboration of gentlemanly status see Seema Alavi, 'Medical culture in transition:
    Mughal gentleman physician and the native doctor in early colonial India', *Modern Asian
    studies* 42.5 (2008), p.853-97.
23. Francis Robinson, 'Religious change and the self in Muslim South Asia since 1800', in *Islam
    and Muslim history in South Asia*, ed. Francis Robinson (Delhi, 2000), p.105-21.
24. See Barbara Metcalf, *Islamic revival in British India: Deoband, 1860-1900* (Princeton, NJ,
    1982); Harlan Otto Pearson, *Islamic reform and revival in 19ᵗʰ century India: the Tariqah-I-
    Muhammadiyah* (New Delhi, 2008).

Rather, it was oriented more towards reaching out across the regional divide of India and forging connections with the world outside by using the new opportunities available at the turn of the century: newly laid English Company networks to access the trans-Asian labour market, print, imperial rivalries, trade and geo-politics.

Indeed, the regal, hyperbolic, eclectic Indo-Persianate world of the early eighteenth century was slowly giving way to the Arabicist orientation of the early nineteenth century characterised by its relatively sombre prescriptiveness and exclusivity within Hindustan, combined with a desire for a global hegemony via the universal appeal of the scriptures. Reformist texts both reflected this change and lent it momentum. They exemplified the Hindustani elites' interpretation of Arabic tradition. There was a greater leaning on the Sirhindi aspect of Arabicism that stresses exclusivity and less on the Ibn-i-Arabi style of accretion. Texts like the *Sirat-i-Mustaqim* continued to be penned in Persian. Arabic also continued to be the language of religious literature of this genre. But the bulk of the literature that circulated in India was in the local vernacular Urdu. However, even though written in Urdu, its tenor was Arabicist: individual-centric, austere, simple, prescriptive, exclusive and with a claim to universality.

One populist text of the period the *Nasihat-i-Muslamin* (Guide to Muslims), that was a product of the new turn to individuation, illustrates well this wider ambit of reformist Islam. The *Nasihat* authored by Karim Ali in 1823-1824 exemplified an ordinary individual's interpretation of the scripture. What emerged was a text that deleted conspicuously the devotional aspect of Sufi leadership that characterised reformist literature of the Indo-Persianate reformists like Shah Waliullah. Instead, in the *Nasihat* there was a ban on all forms of devotion and ritual centred on any single leader. *Tauhid* – belief in only one Allah – is the central pillar of the text.

The text lays out the new Arabicised orientation at its best. It divides the world between *ahmaq* (insane) and the sane. The former are those who deviate from the path of *tauhid*. They are to be brought to the right path (*sirat-I-mustaqim*). And of course the *ahmaq* is largely concentrated in the sub-continent where they have gone astray due to the Hindu cultural influence.

The small text, printed in sixty-nine pages, is divided into five sections. The first section provocatively titled '*Shirk kis ko kehtei hain*' (What is called *shirk*) defines the concept to mean the worship and dependence on many referents (*sajha*) of authority. Ali defines it against *tauhid* to refer to individual acts that adulate *pirs* and prophets for the fulfilment of one's own wishes (*apni hajjataun aur muradon kei wastei pir and paighambaron ki nazrein manei*). Thus the position of Allah is all-powerful and supreme, and for their problems mortals should approach no-one else except Him.[25] The second section in question-answer format ridicules those who commit *shirk*. Titled '*Shirk karnei walon kee himaqat ka bayan*' (Description of the foolishness of those who do *shirk*), it calls Muslims who turn to dead saints for help, *jahil* (ignorant/illiterate). Ali challenges the spiritual mentors of *jahils* to cite a single creation of theirs as compared to the entirety created by Allah. The deviants are seen as bereft of intelligence (*aql sei khaali*) and their actions are derogatorily called *himaaqat*-foolishness.

The third section lists prescriptive norms that are to be observed exclusively for Allah: *sijdah* (prostration), *rozah* (fasting), *zabah* (slaughter of animals), *nazar* and *mannat* (promising specific certitudes in lieu of one's prayer being granted). He compares this exclusive monopoly of Allah over certain forms of rituals to exclusive privileges that kings held in medieval times. Drawing on a regal allegory he argues that just as only the king could sit on the throne, Allah too has a singular and exclusive position of command and respect in the world. And, like the king, He too lays down certain ritualistic prescriptions to underline his singular and universal authority.[26]

The fourth section focuses narrowly on Hindu inspired customs that are listed as *shirk* and need to be avoided. This section called, '*Rusumat-i-shirk ka zikr*' (Discussion of customs that can be described as *shirk*) once again spells out Koranic injunctions in relevance to South Asian society. It lists some of the common customs observed in Hindustan that amount to *shirk*: finding auspicious dates for marriages from Brahmins, or ideal dates for travel etc.[27] In order to make the text easy to understand and popular he appended to it a few *nazms* (verse) as he felt that those would aid its popularity.

At about the same time the grandson of the Delhi Sufi Shah Waliullah wrote his masterpiece, the popular reader in Hindustani called *Taqwiyat-ul-Iman* (1826). Very much like the *Nasihat-i-Muslamin*, this book too, in a hundred and forty-one pages, is easy to read and interactive in tone and similarly uses the Koran and the Hadith to dismiss customs and rituals followed in Muslim society as *shirk*. Instead, it invites people to a belief in one God (*tauhid*) and explains what that means in great detail. *Tauhid* is the author's solution to end the ignorance of Muslim society in India (*mashere ko jihaliyat sei paak karnei ki nazar sei kitab likhee*).[28]

The book has an introduction that speaks to ordinary people who think that they are not knowledgeable enough (*itna ilm kahan*) to under-

25. Khurram Ali, *Nasihat-i-Muslamin* (Lucknow, 1823), p.15.
26. Ali, *Nasihat-i-Muslamin*, p.33-34.
27. Ali, *Nasihat-i-Muslamin*, p.40.
28. Maulana Shah Muhammad Ismael, *Taqwiyat-ul Iman* (Lucknow, n.d.), p.7.

stand the books of God – the Koran and the Hadith. Ismael Shahid strives
to make the scriptures user-friendly as a way of popularising his interpretation of the Arabic religious canon. He begins by disembodying
their knowledge locked in esoteric languages like Arabic, hence his own
text *Taqwiyat-ul-Iman* in simple easy to read vernacular Hindustani. He
also demystifies the canon reiterating that understanding the Koran does
not require any special scholarly skills. He dismisses the popular idea that
the holy books are difficult to understand by ordinary people and are
meant only for the scholars. He invokes the Koranic verses to state that
God has said that it is not difficult to understand the Koran, but hard to
follow it conscientiously (*iss ka samajhna muskil nahin balki inn par chalna
nafs parr mushkil hai*). Moreover, no special knowledge (*ilm*) is required for
understanding these books because they were written for the masses.

The English 'colonial' presence gave this individuation of religion a
new spin. It made it politically expedient that the doctrine be premised
on easy accessibility, simplicity of style and a kind of rationality that
enabled global connections. The individual with the agency to interpret
became the new connector who would enable this global reach. Indeed
the entanglement of men of religion in the post-Mughal political and
social moment – that was characterised by a tough contest over military,
trade, global diplomacy and the competition for politico-cultural supremacy between the Arabicist and the English colonial imperia – gave
new meanings and wider circulation to this individuated Arabicist view.

Individuated reformist energy became the impetus to form strategic
political alliances and further temporal ambitions. The reformists were a
ready reserve to be tapped by the best employer for state-building.
Within India the Tonk state relied on their labour completely. And on
the North-West frontier bordering Afghanistan, they played no small
role in the imperial rivalries between Russia, Persia and Afghanistan on
the one hand and the British Empire on the other. Many, like the
successors of the famous reformist Sheikh Ahmad Sirhindi, Murad al-
Bukhari, migrated to the Ottoman Arab territories: Damascus and the
Hijaz and set up Naqshbandiya seminaries in Mecca. Such men not only
exported the Indian brand of Arabic tradition abroad but also cashed in
on the Ottoman-British rivalries to their advantage.

Reformists doubled as traders and merchants as well. In a letter
addressed to an important wahabi leader Hussein Ali Khan of Azimabad
(Patna), the writer identified as Ikramullah, located in Sitana on the
North-West frontier, refers to his party of warriors as the *kafileh* (trade
caravans) and the Hindustani wahabis from Azimabad (Patna) as the
Toojar Mushruk (*tajir mashriq*) or merchants from the East. He directs them
to come with their *muiouzar* (implements). Significantly, the journey to
the North-West frontier region of Swat where the supposed fight for the

rule of Islam was to reach its culmination is referred as *toojaruth* or *tijarath,* that is, trading.[29] In 1852 P. Melvill, secretary to the Board of Administration, referred to them as 'traders', and hastened to clarify that 'for such they call themselves'.[30]

The new global connections via Muslim men of religion were clearly a spin-off effect of the myth of decline. They steered post-Mughal Muslim politics and society in new directions and pushed its frontier beyond Mughal India.

The culture of soldiering

The manifestation of decline in the military realm appeared in the form of the increasing reliance of Mughal provincial elites on European, particularly French and German, military entrepreneurs. This was most evident at the end of the eighteenth century when the English East India Company assumed political power in Bengal. As Mughal provinces inched towards regional autonomy, they perceived the shift of power from Mughal Delhi to the English Company headquarters at Calcutta. This urged them to garner greater resources and expand their military apparatus triggering a kind of 'military revolution'.[31] The change was not in the realm of technology alone. Rather, it was more social and cultural in its overtones. One, which leaned for sustenance on the earlier Mughal military tradition, but which also reached out, more than ever before, to the European mercenaries and free floaters to combat the English Company's military prowess.[32] As the European soldiers, particularly the French and Germans, came into the spotlight they enmeshed themselves in the politics and society of the subcontinent. They became the conduit for a particular kind of engagement with the European imperium, an engagement that was not framed in the sudden moment of late eighteenth-century European 'technological revolution' or 'modernisation' alone. Rather it was an engagement which reflected the intersection of the evolving South Asian and European political cultures that were driven by changes in comparable court societies with Eliasian long genealogies. Such long histories of the court and the state

29. Enclosure in L No. 86, Ikramullah, Sittana, to Husain Ali Khan of Azimabad, 26 July 1852, Political proceedings 15 Oct. 1852, Foreign and Political Dept., file no. 86, National Archives (NA), Delhi.
30. P. Melvill, Sec. to Bd of Admin., to Allen Esquire, Officiating Sec. to Govt. of India, Lahore, 23 Oct. 1852, Foreign Secret 1852, Consult. 26 Nov. nos. 63-69, file A, (NA) p.9.
31. This was different from the notion of a technological military revolution as given by Geoffrey Parker, *The Military revolution: military innovation and the rise of the West 1500-1800* (Cambridge, 1988).
32. Seema Alavi, *The Sepoys and the Company: tradition and transition in Northern India 1770-1830* (Delhi, 1995), p.11-55.

indicate that institutions like the military were not impersonal and bureaucratic in the Weberian way. Instead, they were shaped by individual conceptualisations of their worth and role in society.

The individual-driven political and military cultures connected eighteenth-century Europe and India in interesting ways. Individuals could cross cultures and relocate with ease as the courts both in India and Europe welcomed self-driven initiatives and expertise that suited their interests. For instance, the circulation of the myth of decline in late Mughal India benefited European, particularly French Protestant, jobber commanders immensely. The European jobber commanders, mainly Protestant, looked for new arenas of operation outside Europe as the going got tough for them in eighteenth-century Catholic France.[33] At the same time Indian regional polities, eager to reconfigure their military culture to combat the political aspirations of the English Company, looked towards them with hope. They offered European-style drill and discipline training and compatible combat technique.[34] The Indian courts, keen to streamline their armies to meet the more disciplined English armies, welcomed such experts with open arms. In 1775, an English military officer Col. Galliez reported the existence of around 200 Europeans in the Mughal province of Awadh alone. These included a large number of important French commanders like Monsieur John Baptiste Joseph Gentil, René Madec, Daniel du Jarday and Antonie-Louis Henri Polier.[35]

Needless to add, the French entrenchment in the political culture of the regional kingdoms was a source of immense concern for British Residents posted in North India. N. Middelton, British Resident at Awadh, continuously complained to the Governor General Warren Hastings about the local ruler Nawab Shuja-ud-daulah encouraging Frenchmen to settle in the area. He reported the double standards of the Nawab in following the British order to dismiss French military officers in his service like Monsieur Gentil and Madec.[36] Under persistent pressure from the English Company, Gentil was eventually dismissed from service by Shuja-ud-Daulah in 1774.[37] But this did not end the

33. The religious wars that rocked France in the sixteenth century led to the migrations of many Protestant families, like that of Polier's, to neighbouring Switzerland. Until the eighteenth century, Protestants lived in the shadow of these religious wars and looked for careers outside France. The opening up of political and commercial opportunities in the non-European world from the eighteenth century attracted them to India.

34. Alavi, *The Sepoys and the Company*, p.219-25; see Jean-Marie Lafont, *Maharaja Ranjit Singh: lord of the five rivers* (Delhi, 2002).

35. Muzaffar Alam and Seema Alavi, *A European view of the Mughal Orient* (Delhi, 2002), p.18-27.

36. BL, Ad MS 29135, N. Middelton to W. Hastings, 23 Sept. 1774; Ad MS 29134, N. Middelton to W. Hastings, 11 March 1774.

37. Persian Correspondence 1772-75, 1 June 1774, p.347-48. Enclosed with a parwana written to Monsieur Gentil.

problem. Given the military, engineering and surveying expertise that the Frenchmen lent to the Indian rulers they always remained an attractive pool of military labour in North India. And thus the recruitment of Frenchmen continued in the armies of the Persian regional satrap in India Najaf Khan, the successive rulers of the kingdom of Awadh, the Punjab and the Benares raj. Indeed the Frenchman Daniel du Jarday hogged the limelight, as he had become the confidant of Najaf Khan. He was given a handsome salary of 1000 Rs. and a land assignment (*jagir*). Middleton perceived the threat in du Jarday's access to the high portals of Indian powers. In a panicky note he wrote to Hastings: 'the object of Dejardu's nego[t]iations is said to be to effect an alliance between Nudif Cawn and the French nation and to engage his assistance in a war now meditating against the English in India.'[38]

The English Company also saw the benefits of French presence in the regional states. It was keen to resort to the French agents in the employment of regional rulers for news and intelligence reports. It was also not averse to employing them in its own administration for similar political ends. Frenchmen as good surveyors, architects, cartographers and topographical experts were equally attractive for the Company, which needed such expertise in the initial stages of its expansion in North India.[39] In 1791 Jonathan Duncan, the British Resident in Benares, transmitted to Edward Hay, secretary to the government, a map and journal reference which he needed and had extracted from a French resident at Mirzapur, Monsieur Devil Maubin.[40] He wanted to know if the Company desired him to get further information. And of course the most important and long-lasting French contact of the English Company was Claude Martin, the famous French soldier and surveyor who was in their service.[41]

The ambivalent relations that the English maintained with the Frenchmen showed the multi-vocal nature of early British rule in India. To a large extent this was a consequence of the myth of decline, a myth that intensified the garnering of military and political resources across the board. This consolidation of resources triggered by the perception of imperial collapse opened up, more than ever before, the space for the employment of the French émigrés. And this Indo-French conduit,

38. BL, Ad MS 29138, N. Middleton to W. Hastings, 25 March 1777.
39. For cartography see Ian J. Barrow, *Making history, drawing territory: British mapping in India, c.1756-1905* (Delhi, 2003). For French maps of Mughal India see Susan Gole, *Maps of Mughal India: drawn by Col. Jean Baptiste Joseph Gentil, agent for the French Government to the court of Shuja-ud-Daulah at Faizabad, 1770* (Delhi, 1988).
40. J. Duncan to E. Hay, 8 March 1791, Residents' Proceedings of Benares, Basta no. 31, Book no. 42, March 1791.
41. BL, Ad MS 29135, f.254. See Rosie L. Jones, *A Very ingenious man: Claude Martin in early colonial India,* (Delhi, 1991).

energised by individual initiatives, shaped the English East India Company rule in no small measure. The literature in Persian produced by one Protestant Franco-Swiss military officer, Polier, who served several masters – the Mughal Emperor Shah Alam, the ruling house of the erstwhile Mughal province of Awadh, the Persian freebooter in India, Najaf Khan, as well as the English Company – reveals how such individual bridgeheads worked.

Military engineer, commander, surveyor, architect and collector of oriental manuscripts, Polier was born of Protestant French parents. He was baptised in 1741 in Lausanne, Switzerland. His family had migrated there following the religious wars in France that saw huge Protestant migration to neighbouring parts of Europe. He arrived in India in 1757 to join his uncle who was employed with the English East India Company. He soon became a cadet and saw active service against the French under Lord Clive.[42] Transferred to Bengal in 1761 he struck a long-lasting friendship with British Governor General Warren Hastings. And on a posting to Awadh he developed good relations with the local ruler, Nawab Shuja-ud-Daulah. He served in his military, involved himself in private trade and amassed a fortune and considerable clout.

On account of his French origins and his friendships with Indian rulers, his relationship with the Company remained fractious. However Warren Hastings – realising his worth – remained his arch supporter. Indeed Hastings' dependence on this multi-faceted Frenchman also figured on the charge sheet that became public during his infamous impeachment proceedings.

Polier's literary compendium, the *Ijaz-i-Arsalani* (The Wonder of Arsalan) is a compilation of letters that he wrote in the 1770s and 1780s to a range of people – rajas, nobles and traders – while in the service of Nawab Shuja-ud-Daulah in Awadh and Najaf Khan in Delhi. These cover matters of private trade, politics, espionage, architecture and details of battles. The letters were put together under Polier's instruction by his Indian scribe (*munshi*) and are available in the Bibliothèque Nationale in Paris. Both the style and the content of the letters reveal that Polier had been completely sucked into the Mughal political and literary cultures. Indeed he enabled the Mughal legatees and legacy to occupy a wider conceptual space that was carved out by his own straddling of the Indian, the French and English Company culture.

His social categorisation and perceptions of Indian society stand in sharp contrast to the religion- and caste-based typologies of his British friends. Acculturated in the court culture of pre-Revolutionary France, and bereft of the political compulsions that framed the English Company

42. Alam and Alavi, *A European experience of the Mughal Orient*, p.1-9.

officials, Polier was comfortable with the Mughal way of engaging with society. And thus in continuance with the Mughal trend to identify people in terms of their relationship to court society, his notions of people and politics are based more on professional rather than religious signifiers. In contrast to British orientalists of his generation, like William Jones, who reinforced and often imagined caste and religious identities, his narrative skips such categorisation.[43] His appreciation of, as well as reprimands to people, are also couched in the elitist urbane, but caste- and community-neutral vocabulary that had gained currency under the Mughals.

His agents were drawn from different communities and were never referred to by their caste or ethnic identities. Diwan Manik Ram, Polier's trusted agent, is a Bengali. The text does not refer to his linguistic, caste, ethnic, regional or religious identities, whereas his professional title, Diwan, is always prefixed to his name so as to establish his identity in vocational terms. In a letter to Mir Suleiman he makes observations about local people in caste- and community-neutral terms. He writes, 'I have observed that people here are of a strange nature and are not trustworthy. When they observe someone's rising fortune they praise him keeping their hand on the head. But when someone is cursed with divine wrath the whole world puts its foot on his head'.[44] Again in contrast to the English Company view, his image of the Mughal Emperor is of a benevolent, humane and gracious figure. The tone of Polier's narrative on the Mughal Emperor Shah Alam is notably mild and avoids the derogatory style of contemporary British historians. The Emperor is projected as 'gracious', 'grave', 'reserved in public' and 'benevolent'.[45]

And yet despite this divergence between ideological and cultural positions regarding people and politics, the dependence of the Company on him was complete. Polier retained his rank of Major in the Company army and Hastings continued to support him. He continued to supply crucial intelligence information to the Company: about Najaf Khan and his alliances with the Jats, the developments in the Rohilla quarter during the 1774 Rohilla war, the activities of the raja of Benares and of course news from the important regional state of Awadh where he remained located in the service of Shuja-ud-Daulah for a considerable period.[46]

43. For William Jones see David Kopf, *British orientalism and the Bengal renaissance*; Surendra Nath Mukherjee, *Sir William Jones: a study in eighteenth-century British attitudes to India* (Cambridge, 1968, and London, 1987).
44. Translation of Ijaz, folio 35A, in Alam and Alavi, *A European view of the Mughal Orient*.
45. P. C. Gupta (ed.), *Shah Alam II and his court by A. H. Polier* (Calcutta, 1989), p.67. For the British contrast see Khalia Ahmad Nizami, *Supplement to Eliott and Dowson's History of India as told by its own historians* (Delhi, 1981), vol.2, p.1.
46. Alam and Alavi, *A European view of the Mughal Orient*, p.24-26.

Indeed, he remained the conduit between the Indo-Persianate world of the eighteenth century and the British and European imperia that loomed large on its horizon. He enabled the Mughal social categories and sociology of knowledge to occupy a space in the evolving English Company's archive of 'useful' knowledge. Thus he not only complicated the singular narrative of orientalist understanding of India but also ensured the relevance of Mughal knowledge in the making of Company power.[47] Straddling the local and the Western global frame he developed an ambivalent relationship with both. This contributed to the production of a hierarchy of knowledge about India, in which the European understanding contrasted with English orientalist underpinnings of colonial rule. And both came to be irretrievably entangled in the Indo-Persianate world that was enriched via this encounter. If Polier's intellectual and political inputs into Company administration fractured the myth of the reified and homogenous colonial power, it also reflected in no small measure the role that the myth of Mughal decline played in opening new and wider intellectual spaces in the eighteenth century: it softened the ground for indigenous initiatives to reach out to European jobber commanders to meet the threat of imperial decline. These larger conceptual arenas became the crucial intersections of the Mughal, regional, British and European strands that shaped eighteenth-century politics and society in India. Such multiple intersections stretched the Indian political and cultural experience beyond the Mughal and the Britain frames and brought them within the frame of European politics as well.

This chapter, then, contends that the role of ideas – including that of decline itself – must be brought back into the picture as active agents in historical change. Secondly, the chapter draws attention to the fact that the social and economic fragmentation of imperial polity in the eighteenth-century period of decline was accompanied by the emergence of new conceptual communities, which occupied the space of the former empires, or expanded far beyond them, capitalising on the ebb and tide of imperial legitimacy. Thereby, new empires of the mind came to populate the terrain of empires of the sword.

How does the trope of decline help us understand the larger movement of South Asian history in the centuries that followed? First, it dents the binaries of the coloniser and colonised as essentialised and reified social categories. While South Asian scholarship has effectively complicated the concept of the colonised Other, the 'colonial' Self still stands as a homogenous entity thanks to the influential post-modern scholarship with its Eurocentric gaze. In contrast, this chapter draws our attention to

47. Bayly, *Empire and information.*

other global imperia alongside the British colonial one that were shaping and being shaped as people worked their way through the myth of decline. The Islamic ecumene and its Arabicist strand, as well as the European French strand, were two such cases in point. Finally, the trope of decline and its critical role in bringing change brings to light the big challenge for South Asian scholarship to break out of the colonial frame and study Indian history at the intersection of global imperia. Norbert Elias underlined the significance of the genealogy of the state to understand its evolution as a regulatory body. He shifted the focus to the longer histories of change within individuals themselves that shaped the later more visible 'governmentality' that Foucault foregrounded. Similarly, this chapter has highlighted the long history of early modern Indian political cultures as conceptualised by individuals so as to de-centre the Eurocentric Foucauldian coupling of imperial knowledge and state power as the primary agents of change in the nineteenth century.

Summaries

A view from afar: India in Raynal's *Histoire des deux Indes*
Anthony Strugnell

Raynal's history of European trade and colonisation in the Orient and the New World was a best-seller throughout Europe and North America in the last decades of the eighteenth century. Raynal and the most significant contributor to his history, Diderot, neither of whom had any direct experience of the Indian subcontinent, nevertheless conveyed an authoritative account of the history, culture and contemporary situation there. They did so principally by drawing on published works, particularly British ones, while incorporating their own ideological and geopolitical perspectives. The resulting accounts, in their attempts to reconcile the principles of the French Enlightenment with French interests in the region, heavily compromised by the defeat in the Seven Years War, offer a necessarily distant, yet strongly articulated, vision of India which contrasts with the British one drawn from direct experience.

British orientalism, Indo-Persian historiography and the politics of global knowledge
Claire Gallien

This essay is a study of the narratives on Indian history translated by eighteenth-century British orientalists from Persian into English. Indeed, following British expansion in India in the second half of the eighteenth century, the directors of the East India Company started to commission works and translations that would help them set up a colonial administration. Thus, a new corpus of Persian narratives on the history and administration of India, collected and translated by British orientalists with the help of local scholars, was produced. This essay challenges Said's presentation of orientalism as a monolithic form of knowledge and highlights the dialogical and polyphonic nature of the corpus, resulting in the production of hybrid narratives. Additionally, it forces us to reconsider the concept of hybridity as defined by Bhabha in colonial contexts. Indeed, it reveals that orientalism could be based on local sources and rely on Eastern scholars while reinforcing, rather than disrupting, British authority and rule.

Globalising the Goths: 'The siren shores of Oriental literature' in John Richardson's *A Dictionary of Persian, Arabic, and English* (1777-1780)
Javed Majeed

This essay examines John Richardson's 'A Dissertation of the languages, literature, and manners of Eastern nations', prefixed to his *A Dictionary of Persian, Arabic, and English*. Richardson's opening out of these languages to each other forms the background to his reflections on the cultural and political origins of 'Englishness'. His revisionary global narrative of the 'Gothic' as a political category that underpins distinctively English freedoms and institutions locates 'Englishness' in a world historical context of overlapping and interconnected institutions and cultures. This narrative includes a transcultural conception of romance as a mode of writing which aims to broaden his readers' cultural horizons beyond the Hellenistic legacy of European civilisation. His arguments are placed against the backdrop of wider debates in Britain and India in the eighteenth century, and are related to his own complex subject position as a Scotsman whose class identity was fluid.

'Voyage of conception': John Keats and India
Deirdre Coleman

Towards the end of his life, 'straining at particles of light in the midst of a great darkness', John Keats went searching for an alternative belief system. Rejecting the gloom of Christianity's 'system of Salvation', he formulated his 'vale of Soul-making', a conception which invoked as part of its definition other world religions, including the 'Hindoos' and 'their Vishnu'. This essay argues that some of Keats's key aesthetic concepts – including 'negative capability' and its closely related paradox of 'diligent indolence' – were all touched by his understanding of Indian thought. Keats's circle also included two great champions of India, the literary critic William Hazlitt and the radical journalist Leigh Hunt, whose newspaper *The Examiner* carried notices and reviews of Keats's poetry alongside reports of Britain's 'Indian atrocities'.

'The country chosen of my heart': the comic cosmopolitanism of *The Orientalist, or, electioneering in Ireland, a tale, by myself*
Sonja Lawrenson

Published in 1820, *The Orientalist, or, Electioneering in Ireland, a tale, by myself* delineates the adventures of the 'orientalist', Stuart Jesswunt, as he endeavours to win both the hand of Lady Eleanor, daughter of Irish absentee landlord Lord Clanroy, and the parliamentary seat incorporating the Clanroys' Irish estate. This essay delineates how *The Orientalist* refracts contemporary anxieties regarding accelerated British imperial expansionism in the East through the particularised political prism of post-Union Ireland. Identifying *The Orientalist* as the work of a female novelist with a learned interest in 'Hindu' culture, it argues that the tale offers a parodic exposition of both Romantic nationalism and Romantic orientalism, whilst simultaneously disrupting the gender pre-scriptions of both. In so doing, it not only demonstrates why this long forgotten novel merits further scholarly attention, but uncovers the subtle insights into the intricacies of regional attitudes to imperial politics that its jocular irony affords.

Orientalism and 'textual attitude': Bernier's appropriation by Southey and Owenson
Daniel Sanjiv Roberts

François Bernier's *Histoire de la dernière Révolution des états du Grand Mogol* (1670) and *Suite des Mémoires [...] sur l'empire du Grand Mogol* (1671) were among the most influential European travel accounts of Mughal India throughout the eighteenth century, influencing numerous historical and literary representations of India. This study examines Bernier's influence on two English literary texts, Robert Southey's epic poem, *The Curse of Kehama* (1810), and Sydney Owenson's *The Missionary* (1811), in the light of what Edward Said described as a 'textual attitude' on the part of European authors, that is, their supposed reliance and interdependence on a corpus of textual material that defined the limits of European understanding of the orient. Both Southey's and Owenson's works were produced in the context of considerable metropolitan interest in India, which included a hotly contested pamphlet war regarding the issue of the East India Company's role in Indian governance. The study assesses the ways in which Bernier's text is appropriated by these writers in relation to their respective ideologies regarding native religious and cultural practices, and their responses to evangelical calls for the Christianisation of India.

Intellectual history as global history: Voltaire's *Fragments sur l'Inde* and the problem of enlightened commerce
Felicia Gottmann

Voltaire's *Fragments sur l'Inde* show that the Enlightenment could espouse a universalist vision that was truly global. The *Fragments* were published in 1773-1774 after Voltaire had engaged in a decades-long defence of commerce and luxury as the hallmarks of human civilisation. Yet without explanation, this text topples all of these arguments. India is the crucial factor in this. Even seen in the context of contemporary debates about Euro-Indian trade, of a renewed interest in Indian culture, and a nascent anti-colonialist discourse, Voltaire's stance was radical. He perceived India as Europe's equal. He found that luxury and commerce did not, in their interaction, lead to increased material comfort, humanity and civilisation as he had been wont to argue, but instead to its very opposite, namely oppression, slavery and exploitation in India. Thus in this work, he roundly rejected all of his previous pro-commerce discourse. The global and universalist nature of his vision of Enlightenment ultimately won over his European pro-commercial stance.

Fictions of commercial empire, 1774-1782
James Watt

This essay focuses primarily on three novels, the anonymous *Memoirs of a gentleman, who resided several years in the West Indies* (1774), Helenus Scott's *The Adventures of a rupee* (1782) and Robert Bage's *Mount Henneth* (1782), which it reads in the context of metropolitan debates about the gulf between the civilising possibilities of transnational commerce and the actual operations of the East India Company. It argues that these rhetorically unstable works at once rehearse anti-Company polemic and provide counter-narratives to the familiar story of corrupt nabobs. If they invoke the metaphor of circulation as a means of apprehending 'global connections', however, they are – unsurprisingly – unable to represent an India 'civilised' by commerce, and they generally eschew the sentimental tropes that other contemporary works mobilised in an attempt to negotiate spatial distance. As a result, it is suggested, the novels in question draw attention to the fictionality of their fictions of commercial empire, while rendering India – though also the scandal of empire – still more remote for their metropolitan readers.

The Spanish translation of Bernardin de Saint-Pierre's *La Chaumière indienne*: its fortunes and significance in a country divided by ideology, politics and war
Gabriel Sánchez Espinosa

The Spanish translation of Bernardin Saint-Pierre's *La Chaumière indienne* (1791), first published in Salamanca in 1803 by the printer-bookseller Tójar, who specialised in exotic, Rousseauian novellas, quickly caught the attention of both the Spanish reading public and the Spanish Inquisition. Could it be because it expressed the anxieties and inner doubts among the Spanish reform-minded minority about the feasibility of the

Enlightenment programme, as well as rejecting the orthodoxies of traditional Spanish Catholicism? It was soon reprinted in Valencia in 1811, amid the chaos of the Peninsular War, and was widely read both by patriot liberals and Spanish *afrancesados*. After the restoration of Ferdinand VII, it was repeatedly prohibited by secular and religious authorities, but all these prohibitions came to nothing against the tide of its continuous success with the reading public, as expressed by its multiple reprints up to the 1820s.

Displaying its wares: material culture, the East India Company and British encounters with India in the long eighteenth century
John McAleer

This essay considers how the East India Company, its history and the story of Britain's diverse encounters with eighteenth-century India can be understood through the production, collecting and display of objects and artefacts. Material culture formed a crucial part of the Company's mercantile, corporate and political identities. Cultural artefacts – variously collected, commented upon and displayed by the Company and its officials – had a significant impact on British understandings of India and Indians. And, through its collecting activities and the establishment of the India Museum, the Company also influenced the development of museum collections and played a role in shaping museum narratives. The study concludes by considering how changing historiographical trends have influenced the interpretation of this material culture in the recent past. In doing so, it suggests that the East India Company, its history and its material culture can act as a springboard for introducing both British encounters with India in the long eighteenth century and broader themes in the history of the British Empire.

The Danish Asiatic Company: colonial expansion and commercial interests
Mogens R. Nissen

This study focuses on the Danish Asiatic Company (Asiatisk Kompagni), which was the largest Danish trade company, and the company that existed, significantly, for the longest time. It was established in 1616 and closed down in 1843, but it is the period from the early 1730s to the 1790s that is the focal point in this study. It was during this period that the Company peaked financially, and it was in the latter half of the 1700s that the basis for private merchants' trade in India was formed. The focus is on the economic and political interests of the company. It is an examination of the political debates regarding the Company's privileges and responsibilities, including a growing debate concerning a continuation of the monopolised trade or a liberalised free trade for all Danish merchants.

Whose pirate? Reflections on state power and predation on India's western littoral
Lakshmi Subramanian

Studies on buccaneer ethnography in the eighteenth century have revealed insights into the links between privateers and the making of empire, and on how representation of outlaws configured British colonisation, impacted on maritime power and the language of imperialism. The processes of nation-building and empire-making found it critical to define legitimate subjects and citizens, making it possible – even desirable – to reclaim the savage European pirate. The same could not be said for the Indian pirate whose ethnographic examination was initially framed within a paradigm of lawlessness which proved less malleable. Much ethnography on pirates and privateers of Kathiawar was spearheaded by naval officers and administrators, whose appreciation was as informed by considerations of power and strategy as by notions of traditional rights, clan honour and bravery. Underlying the understanding of predation were the politics and market dynamics that added complex dimensions to the acts of maritime violence and contravention within the existing parameters of legitimacy and authority differently understood by different agents and actors. This essay evaluates moments in the articulation of an ethnology on piracy and its milieu.

A comparative study of English and French views of pre-colonial Surat
Florence D'Souza

Based on the observations of the trading centre of Surat by three significant European commentators – the English medical doctor John Fryer (1650-1733), the Anglican clergyman John Ovington (1653-1731) and the French orientalist scholar Anquetil-Duperron (1731-1805) – this study situates the views of these visitors in the context of the changing political and commercial scene in India between approximately 1670 and 1760. The comments of these observers highlight Surat's ethnic and religious diversity and the improvised trading practices used by the different trading communities (Indian and European) in Surat. The travel accounts studied furnish lively details on the role of Surat in the politics and trade of both Europeans and Indians in the region, prior to the full establishment of British colonial power in India. Constant adaptation to evolving circumstances by all groups concerned seems to have prevailed over any legalised stability or any long-term arrangements.

The Mughal decline and the emergence of new global connections in early modern India
Seema Alavi

This chapter offers a revisionist view of social change in eighteenth-century India. It connects the history of ideas with the narrative of the Mughal Empire's fragmentation so as shift the spotlight away from the state-centric view of social change. Instead, it focuses on the individual's perception of political transformation, which it foregrounds as an active agency in propelling the global reach of Indian society. Via the histories of men of religion, soldiering and medicine, it highlights how changes within such individual communities shaped the political culture and impacted upon the making of the more regulatory state apparatus of the nineteenth century.

List of contributors

Seema Alavi is Professor of History at the University of Delhi. She specialises in early modern and modern South Asia, with an interest in the transformation of the region's legacy from Indo-Persian to one heavily affected by British colonial rule. She has written on the military and medical cultures of the region from the early modern to modern times. Her most recent book is *Islam and healing: loss and recovery of an Indo-Muslim medical tradition,1600-1900* (2009). She edited *The Eighteenth century in India* (2002) and serves on the editorial board of several journals, including *Modern Asian studies*, and *Journal of the Royal Asiatic Society*.

Deirdre Coleman holds the Robert Wallace Chair of English at the University of Melbourne. Her research centres on eighteenth-century literature and cultural history, focusing in particular on racial ideology, colonialism, natural history and the anti-slavery movement. She has published in *ELH, Eighteenth-century life* and *Eighteenth-century studies*, and is the author of *Romantic colonization and British anti-slavery* (2005). In 2011 she published (with Hilary Fraser) a collection of essays, *Minds, bodies, machines, 1770-1930*.

Florence D'Souza is a Senior Lecturer in English at the University of Lille 3 (France). She is the author of *Quand la France découvrit l'Inde: les écrivains-voyageurs français en Inde, 1757-1818* (1995), and the editor of Book 4 of Raynal's *Histoire des deux Indes*, directed by Anthony Strugnell (2010). Her research focuses on European (in particular British) interactions with India.

Claire Gallien is a Lecturer in the English Department of the Université Paul-Valéry Montpellier III. Her first book, published in 2011, deals with the interactions between popular and erudite cultures of the East in eighteenth-century English literature, and is entitled *L'Orient anglais* (*SVEC* 2011:10). She is currently working on the construction of orientalist knowledge and is particularly interested in the question of cultural transfers, in the relationships between British orientalists and Eastern scholars and the role of these exchanges in the production of orientalist knowledge from the seventeenth century to the beginning of the nineteenth century.

Felicia Gottmann is a Research Fellow with the European Research Council funded project 'Europe's Asian centuries: trading Eurasia 1600-1830', directed by Maxine Berg at the University of Warwick, where her work focuses on the trade of the French East India Company. She received her D. Phil. from the University of Oxford for her thesis entitled 'The eighteenth-century luxury debate: the case of Voltaire' in 2010, and is currently writing a book on the impact of France's global textile trade in the long eighteenth century.

Sonja Lawrenson is a postdoctoral Research Fellow at Trinity College Dublin, funded by the Irish Research Council for the Humanities and Social Sciences. She is currently writing a book on Irish women's writing of the Romantic period.

Javed Majeed is Professor of English and Comparative Literature at King's College, London. His books are *Ungoverned imaginings: James Mill's 'The History of British India' and orientalism* (1992), *Autobiography, travel and postnational identity: Gandhi, Nehru, Iqbal* (2007), *Muhammad Iqbal: Islam, aesthetics and postcolonialism* (2009), and a critical edition of *Hali's Musaddas: the flow and ebb of Islam* (1997) with Christopher Shackle. He is currently writing a book on G. A. Grierson's *Linguistic survey of India*, which was carried out in the late nineteenth and early twentieth centuries.

John McAleer is a Lecturer in History at the University of Southampton. He was Curator of Imperial and Maritime History at the National Maritime Museum, Greenwich for six years. He is the author of *Representing Africa: landscape, exploration and empire in Southern Africa, 1780–1870* (2010) and, with H. V. Bowen and Robert J. Blyth, *Monsoon traders: the maritime world of the East India Company* (2011).

Mogens R. Nissen is Head of the Research Department and Archive for the Danish minority in Schleswig, Germany. His research interests are: Danish and European trade history from the eighteenth century to the present; Danish business history from the eighteenth century to the present; Danish and European agriculture in the nineteenth and twentieth centuries and Nazi economic policy in Denmark and other occupied countries. He is currently working on a research project concerning how Danish industries and companies have responded to the economic globalisation 1970-2010.

Daniel Sanjiv Roberts is a Reader in English at Queen's University Belfast. He is the author of *Revisionary gleam: De Quincey, Coleridge and the high Romantic argument* (2000) and editor of Robert Southey's *The Curse of*

Kehama (2004) as well as Thomas De Quincey's *Autobiographic sketches* (2003) for the definitive scholarly editions of these authors' works. He is working on an edition of Charles Johnstone's novel *The History of Arsaces, prince of Betlis* for the Early Irish Fiction Series.

Gabriel Sánchez Espinosa is a Reader in Spanish Studies at Queen's University Belfast. He has researched different aspects of the Spanish Enlightenment (autobiographies; transfer of ideas between Europe and Spain; printing history and book market). He is the author of *La Biblioteca de José Nicolás de Azara* (1997) and *Las Memorias del ilustrado aragonés José Nicolás de Azara* (2000), and has co-edited the volume *Peripheries of the Enlightenment* (2008).

Anthony Strugnell is an Emeritus Reader in French Enlightenment Studies at the University of Hull. He has published extensively on Diderot and Raynal, and is a former general editor of *SVEC*. He is the director of the new critical edition of Raynal's *Histoire des deux Indes*.

Lakshmi Subramanian is Professor of History in the Centre for Studies in Social Sciences, Calcutta. She has published widely on the economic history of western India and the Indian Ocean. Her research interests include history of music and cultural practices in modern India. She has been a recipient of numerous fellowships including, more recently, the Mellon fellowship in the University of Witwatersrand, Johannesburg and the Adam Smith fellowship in the University of Glasgow. Among her most recent publications: *Ports, towns and cities: a historical tour of the Indian littoral* (2008); *Veena Dhanammal: the making of a legend* (2009) and *A History of India 1707-1857* (2010).

James Watt is a Senior Lecturer in the Department of English and Related Literature at the University of York, where he convenes the 'Global eighteenth century' pathway of the MA in Eighteenth Century Studies. He is the author of *Contesting the Gothic: fiction, genre, and cultural conflict, 1764-1832* (1999).

Bibliography

Manuscript sources

Bombay, Maharashtra State Archives, Commercial Department Diary 1806.

Bombay, Maharashtra State Archives, Political Department Diary of the Bombay Government No. 283 A of 1812.

Bombay, Maharashtra State Archives, Public Department Diary of the Bombay Government 1796.

Bombay, Maharashtra State Archives, Public Department Diary of the Bombay Government 1797.

Bombay, Maharashtra State Archives, Public Department Diary of the Bombay Government 1807.

Bombay, Maharashtra State Archives, Secret and Political Department Diary 1813.

Bombay, Maharashtra State Archives, Surat Factory Diary 1799.

Delhi, National Archives of India (NAI), Foreign Secret 1852, Consult. 26 Nov. Nos. 63-69, file A.

Delhi, National Archives of India (NAI), Residents Proceedings of Benares, Basta No. 31, Book No. 42.

Edinburgh, National Library of Scotland, Walker of Bowland Papers Acc MS 13674.

Edinburgh, National Library of Scotland, Walker of Bowland Papers Acc MS 13675.

Edinburgh, National Library of Scotland, Walker of Bowland Papers Acc MS13914.

Edinburgh, National Library of

Scotland, Walker of Bowland Papers Acc MS 13917.

London, British Library, Ad MS 17949.

London, British Library, Hastings Papers, Ad MS 29134.

London, British Library, Hastings Papers, Ad MS 29135.

London, British Library, Hastings Papers, Ad MS 29138.

London, British Library, Oriental and India Office Collection (OIOC), IOR D/26.

London, British Library, Oriental and India Office Collection (OIOC), IOR D/29.

London, British Library, Oriental and India Office Collection (OIOC), IOR D/31.

London, British Library, Oriental and India Office Collection (OIOC), IOR E/1/54.

London, British Library, Oriental and India Office Collection (OIOC), IOR E/1/55.

London, British Library, Oriental and India Office Collection (OIOC), IOR E/1/60.

London, British Library, Oriental and India Office Collection (OIOC), IOR E/1/72.

London, Wellcome Institute Library, WMS. Per. 172.

Madrid, Archivo Histórico Nacional, Inquisición, leg.4501 (12).

Madrid, Archivo Histórico Nacional, Inquisición, leg.4461 (8).

Paris, Bibliothèque Nationale, Nur-ud-Din Shirazi, Ilajat-I-Dara Shikohi, p.857-9. Supplément Persan 342, 342A, 342B.

Primary sources

Ali, Khurram, *Nasihat-i-Muslamin* (Lucknow, 1823).

Álvarez de Cienfuegos, Nicasio, *Obras Poeticas* (Madrid, Imprenta Real, 1816).

Année littéraire (Paris, 1754-1790).

Anquetil-Duperron, Abraham Hyacinthe, *Voyage en Inde, 1754-1762, relation de voyage en préliminaire à la traduction du Zend Avesta* (first publication, Paris, 1771), ed. Jean Deloche, Manonmani Filliozat and Pierre-Sylvain Filliozat (Paris, 1997).

'Apuntes para formar la idea de la ciudad de Caalla, distante seis leguas de la Corte de Dradmi, reino de Naaspe, en los senos más recónditos de la India', in *Correo de Madrid* 409 (24 November 1790), p.52-54.

Asiatic researches, 20 vols (London, printed for J. Sewell; Vernor and Hood; J. Cuthell; J. Walker; R. Lea Lackington, Allen, and Co.; Otridge and Son; R. Faulder; and J. Scatcherd, 1799-1839).

Bage, Robert, *Mount Henneth*, 2 vols (New York, 1979).

Bernardin de Saint-Pierre, Jacques-Henri, *La Chaumière indienne par Jacques-Bernardin-Henri de Saint-Pierre* (Paris, Imprimerie de Monsieur chez P. Fr. Didot le jeune, 1791).

–, *La cabaña indiana y el café de Surate, Cuentos de Santiago Bernardino Henrique de Saint-Pierre* (Valencia, José Ferrer de Orga y Comp., 1811).

–, *La cabaña indiana y el café de Surate: Cuentos de Santiago Bernardino Henrique de Saint-Pierre* (Valencia, 1820).

–, *La cabaña indiana y el café de Surate. Cuentos de...* (Madrid, 1820).

–, *La Cabaña Indiana, y El Café de Surate, Cuentos de Santiago Bernardino Henrique de Saint-Pierre* (Burdeos, 1821).

–, *La Cabaña Indiana, y El Café de Surate* (Burdeos, 1822).

–, *La cabaña indiana y el café de Surate. Cuentos de Santiago Bernardino Henriago de Saint-Pierre* (Lyon, chez Cormon & Blanc, 1822).

–, *La Capanna Indiana...: tradotta dal Francese da Ant. Bruner, nativo di Roma* (Parigi, nella Stamperia di Honnert, 1796).

–, *Etudes de la nature* (Paris, P. F. Didot le jeune, 1790).

–, *The Indian cottage, or a search after truth: by M. Saint-Pierre* (London, printed for W. Lane, 1791).

–, *The Indian cottage: translated from the French of Monsieur de St. Pierre, author of Etudes de la Nature, Paul et Virginie, &c. &c.* (London, printed for John Bew, 1791).

–, *The Indian cottage: translated from the French of Monsieur de St. Pierre, Author of Etudes de la Nature, Paul et Virginie, &c. &c.* (Dublin, printed for J. Parker, J. Jones, W. Jones, R. White, J. Rice, R. McAllister, 1791).

–, *Die indianische Strohhütte aus dem Französischen des Herrn von Saint Pierre übersetzt und mit einigen Anmerkungen herausgegeben von Schröder* (Neuwied und Leipzig, Johann Ludwig Gehra, 1791).

–, *El inglés de la India, ó la cabaña indiana. Traducida del francés por D. M. L. G.* (Salamanca, Francisco de Tójar, 1803).

–, *Pablo y Virginia* (Madrid, por Pantaleón Aznar, 1798).

–, *Votos de un solitario y su continuacion, El café de Surate y La cabaña indiana*, 2 vols (Valencia, 1820).

Bernier, Francois, *Bernier's travels: comprehending a description of the Mogol Empire including the kingdom of Kashmir*, trans. John Steuart (Calcutta, 1826).

–, *A Continuation of the memoires of Monsieur Bernier*, 2 vols (London, Moses Pitt, 1672).

–, *The History of the late revolution of the empire of the Great Mogol*, 2 vols (London, Moses Pitt, Simon Miller, and John Starkey, 1671).

–, *Travels in the Mogul Empire*, trans. Irving Brock (London, 1826).

–, *Travels in the Mogul Empire*, ed. and trans. by Archibald Constable and revised by Vincent A. Smith (London, 1914).

–, *Travels in the Mogul Empire* (New Delhi, 1999).

–, *Voyages de François Bernier* (Amsterdam, Paul Marret, 1709).

The Bhagvat-Geeta, or Dialogues of Kreeshna and Arjoon; in eighteen lectures; with notes. Translated from the original, in the sanskreet, or ancient language of the Brahmans, trans. Charles Wilkins (London, C. Nourse, 1785).

Black, Joseph, ed., *The Broadview anthology of British literature, vol 4: the age of Romanticism*, 2nd edn (Peterborough, Ontario, 2010).

Blackwood's Edinburgh magazine 19 (January-June 1826).

Bolts, William, *Considerations on India affairs, particularly respecting the present state of Bengal and its dependencies*, 2nd edn (London, J. Almon, 1772-1775).

–, *Etat civil, politique et commerçant du Bengale, ou Histoire des conquêtes et de l'administration de la Compagnie angloise dans ce pays* (La Haye, Gosse fils, 1775).

Boswell, James, *Boswell in extremes 1776-1778*, ed. Charles McC. Weis and Frederick A. Pottle (London, 1971).

Burke, Edmund, *The Writings and speeches of Edmund Burke vol.5: India: Madras and Bengal 1774-1785*, ed. P. J. Marshall (Oxford, 1981), in *The Writings and speeches of Edmund Burke*, ed. Paul Langford, 9 vols (Oxford, 1981-).

–, *The Writings and speeches of Edmund Burke 6: India: the launching of the Hastings impeachment*, ed. P. J. Marshall (Oxford, 1991), in *The Writings and speeches of Edmund Burke*, ed. Paul Langford, 9 vols (Oxford, 1981-).

Calendar of Persian correspondence 1772-1775, being letters referring mainly to affairs in Bengal which passed between some of the Company servants and Indian rulers and notables, vol.4 (Calcutta, 1925).

Cambridge, Richard Owen, *An Account of the war in India, between the English and French* (London, T. Jefferys, 1761).

Carey, W. H., *The Good old days of Honorable John Company*, 2 vols (Calcutta, 1882-1887).

A Catalogue of Dyer's circulating library (Exeter, R. Trewman, 1783).

Catalogue of the London and Westminster circulating library (London, 1797).

Chardin, Jean, *Voyages en Perse et autres lieux de l'Orient* (Amsterdam, Delorme, 1711).

Chateaubriand, François-René de and Bernardin de Saint-Pierre, *Atala y René por Chateaubriand, Cabaña Indiana y el café de Surate por Bernardin de Saint-Pierre; bajo la dirección de José René Masson* (París, Masson e Hijo, 1822).

Clarke, Charles and Mary Cowden Clarke, *Recollections of writers* (London, 1878).

Clarke, Richard, *The Nabob, or, Asiatic plunderers: a satirical poem, in a dialogue between a friend and the author* (London, 1773).

Colebrooke, H. T., 'On the Sanskrit and Pracrit languages', *Edinburgh review* 9 (January 1807), p.289-93.

Coleccion de cuentos morales que contiene El Zimeo, novela americana; Las fabulas orientales y el Abenaki los da a luz traducidos del frances D. Francisco de Toxar (Salamanca, en la imprenta del editor, 1796).

Colección de historias, apólogos y cuentos orientales traducidos del frances por D. *** (Salamanca, par D. Francisco de Toxar, 1804).

Coleridge, Samuel Taylor, *Collected letters*, ed. E. L. Griggs, 6 vols (Oxford, 1956-1971).

Davidson, Alexander, 'Extract of a letter from Alexander Davidson', *Asiatic researches* 2 (1790), p.332.

Delisle de Sales, Jean-Baptiste-Claude, *Eponina. Traduccion libre del frances por don M.L.G.*, 2 vols (Madrid, 1821).

Desodoards, Antoine-Etienne-Nicolas Fantin, *Memorias de Typoo-Zaïb, Sultan del Masur ó Visicitudes de la India en el siglo XVIII... escritas por dicho Sultan; y traducidas al frances del idioma malabar; publicadas por... Desodoards; y vertidas al castellano por... Bernardo María de Calzada...*, 2 vols (Madrid, 1800).

Diario de Madrid (25 August 1806; 4 December 1811; 10 March 1813; 5 June 1819).

Diario de Mallorca (16 July 1811).

Diario de Palma (21 November 1813).

Dirom, Alexander, *A Narrative of the campaign in India* (London, W. Bulmer, 1793).

Dow, Alexander (trans.), *The History of Hindostan, from the earliest account of time to the death of Akbar: translated from the Persian of Mahummud Casim Ferishta... together with a dissertation concerning the religion and philosophy of the Brahmins, with an appendix concerning the religion and philosophy of the Brahmins, with an appendix containing the history of the Mogul Empire from its decline in the reign of Mahummud Shau to the present time; by A. Dow*, 2 vols (London, T. Becket and P. A. De Hondt, 1768).

–, *The History of Hindostan, from the death of Akbar, to the complete settlement of the empire under Aurungzebe* (London, T. Becket and P. A. de Hondt, 1772).

–, *Dissertation sur les mœurs, les usages, le langage, la religion et la philosophie des Hindous* (Paris, Pissot, 1769).

Du Pont de Nemours, Pierre Samuel, *Du Commerce et de la Compagnie des Indes*, 2nd edn (Paris and Amsterdam, 1769).

Du Pin, Louis Ellies, *The Universal library of historians; (viz.) the oriental, Greek, Latin, French, German, Spanish, Italian, English, and others: containing an account of their lives; the abridgment, chronology and geography of their histories...* (London, R. Bonwicke et al., 1709).

'The East India House', *Illustrated London news* (3 August 1861), p.125.

Earle's new catalogue (London, J. Nichols, 1799).

Francklin, William, *The History of the reign of Shah-Aulum, the present Emperor of Hindostaun: containing the transactions of the court of Delhi, and the neighbouring states, during a period of thirty-six years: interspersed with geographical and topographical observations on several of the principal cities of Hindostaun...* (London, Cooper and Graham, 1798).

The Freeman's journal (22 September 1820).

Fryer, John, *Account of India*, facsimile reprint from *The Calcutta weekly Englishman*, ed. Mr Talboys Wheeler (London, 1873), in *Travels in India in the 17th century: Thomas Roe and John Fryer* (New Delhi, 1993), p.133-474.

Gaceta de Madrid (8 July 1803; 30 January 1821).

Ghulam Husain Khan (trans. M. Raymond), *A Translation of the Sëir Mutaqharin; or, View of modern times, being an history of India, from the year 1118 to the year 1195, (this year answers to the Christian year 1781-1782) of the hidjrah, containing in general, the reigns of the seven last emperors of Hindostan; and in particular, an account of the English wars in Bengal, with a circumstantial detail of the rise and fall of the Families of Seradj-Ed-Döwlah, and Shudjah-Ed-Döwlah, the last sovereigns of Bengal and Owd: to which the author has added, a critical examination of the English government and policy in those countries, down to the year 1783. the whole written in Persian by Seid-Gholam-Hossein-Khan, an Indian nobleman of high rank, who wrote both as an actor and spectator* (Calcutta, James White, 1789-1790), 3 vols.

Gibbes, Phebe, *Hartly House, Calcutta*, ed. Michael J. Franklin (Oxford, 2007).

Gibbon, Edward, *The History of the decline and fall of the Roman Empire* (London, W. Strahan and T. Cadell, 1776).

Gilchrist, John, *A Dictionary, English and Hindoostanee, in which the words are marked with their distinguishing initials; as Hinduwee, Arabic, and Persian: whence the Hindoostanee, or what is vulgarly but improperly, called the Moor language, is evidently formed*, 2 vols (Calcutta, Stuart and Cooper, 1787-1790).

Gladwin, Francis, *Ayeen Akbery; or, The Institutes of the Emperor Akber, translated... by Francis Gladwin* (Calcutta, n.p., 1783-1786; London, 1800).

–, *Ayeen Akbery, or, The Institutes of the Emperor Akber*, ed. Michael J. Franklin (London, 2000).

–, *The History of Hindostan during the reigns of Jehangir, Shahjehan and Aurangzebe* (Calcutta, Stuart and Cooper, 1788).

'Grammars of the Sanscrita

language', *Quarterly review* (February 1809), p.53.

Greenblatt, Stephen, ed., *Norton anthology of English literature*, 8th edn (New York, 2006).

Grose, John Henry, *A Voyage to the East Indies*, 2 vols (London, S. Hooper, 1772).

Halhed, Nathaniel, *A Code of Gentoo laws or ordinations of the pundits* (London, 1776).

–, *Code des loix des Gentous ou Réglemens des Brames* (Paris, Stoupe, 1778).

Hamilton, Alexander, *A New account of the East Indies* (London, 1930).

–, 'Asiatic researches', *Edinburgh review* 15 (April 1808).

Hamilton Maxwell, William, *History of the Irish rebellion* (London, 1845).

Hastings, Warren, 'To Nathaniel Smith, Esquire. Banarism 4th October 1784', in *The Bhagvat-Geeta*, trans. Charles Wilkins (London, C. Nourse, 1785).

Hatalkar, Vinayak Gajanan (ed.), *French records relating to the history of the Marathas* (Bombay, 1978).

Hazlitt, William, *The Complete works*, ed. P. P. Howe, 21 vols (London, 1930-1934).

–, *The Plain speaker: the key essays*, ed. Duncan Wu with an introduction by Tom Paulin (Oxford, 1998).

Hickey, William, *Memoirs of William Hickey*, ed. Alfred Spencer, 4 vols (London, 1925).

Histoire universelle, depuis le commencement du monde, jusqu'à présent, traduite de l'Anglois d'une Société de gens de lettres (Amsterdam et Leipzig, Arkstée & Merkus, 1742-1802).

Holwell, John Zephanaiah, *Interesting historical events relative to the provinces of Bengal and the Empire of Hindostan* (London, T. Becket and P.A. De Hondt, 1766-1771).

–, *Evenemens historiques intéressans relatifs aux provinces de Bengale, et à l'empire de l'Indostan* (Amsterdam, Arkstée and Merkus, 1768).

Hume, David, 'Of luxury', in *Essays and treatises on several subjects*, 4 vols (London and Edinburgh, Millar and Kincaid, 1753-1756) IV, p.20-35, reprinted under its later title 'Of refinement in the arts' in David Hume, *Political essays*, ed. Knud Haakonssen (Cambridge, 1994), p.105-14.

Hunt, Leigh, 'Article and no article', *The Examiner* (27 September 1818), p.609.

–, 'India', *The Examiner* (20 September 1818), p.593-94.

–, 'Literary notices', *The Examiner* (11 October 1818), p.648-49.

–, 'Necessity of peace to our Indian possessions', *The Selected writings of Leigh Hunt: vol.1 periodical essays 1805-1814*, ed. Greg Kucich and Jeffrey N. Cox (London, 2003), p.46-48.

–, 'Review of James Mill, *The History of British India*', *The Examiner* (8 March 1818), p.156-58.

–, 'Superstition – its civil and political consequences', *The Examiner* (18 October 1818), p.657-63.

Islam, Khurshidul and Ralph Russell, *Three Mughal poets: Mir, Sauda, Mir Hasan* (Delhi, 1994).

Ismael, Maulana Shah Muhammad, *Taqwiyat-ul Iman* (Lucknow, n.d.).

Johnson, Francis, *A Dictionary, Persian, Arabic, and English; with a dissertation on the languages, literature, and manners of Eastern nations. By John Richardson. Revised and improved by Charles Wilkins; a new edition, considerably enlarged, by Francis Johnson* (London, 1829).

Jones, William, *The History of the life of Nader Shah, King of Persia: extracted from an Eastern manuscript, which was translated into French by*

order of His Majesty the king of Denmark* (London, J. Richardson, 1773).

–, *A Grammar of the Persian language* (London, W. and J. Richardson, 1771).

–, 'On the Hindu[']s', *Asiatick researches* 1 (1788), p.414-32.

–, *The Letters of Sir William Jones*, ed. Garland H. Cannon, 2 vols (Oxford, 1970).

–, *Poems consisting chiefly of translations from the Asiatick languages: to which are added two essays: I. On the poetry of the eastern nations; II. On the arts, commonly called imitative* (Oxford, Clarendon Press, 1772).

–, *Sous la protection des Universités d'Oxford et de Cambridge, et celle des Compagnies Angloises des Indes et de Turquie, prospectus de la réimpression par souscription d'un dictionnaire des langues Arabe, Persanne, et Turque, compilé et originairement publié à Vienne par Meninski en quarter volumes in folio: revû et corigé par Mr Jones* (Paris, 1771).

–, *Sir William Jones: selected poetical and prose works*, ed. Michael Franklin (Cardiff, 1995).

Journal encyclopédique (Liège, 1756-1793).

Jovellanos, Gaspar Melchor de, *Obras completas: diario 1*, ed. J.-M. Caso González (Oviedo, 1994), vol.6.

[Kauffman, C. H.], *The Dictionary of merchandize, and nomenclature in all languages: for the use of counting-houses: containing, the history, places of growth, culture, use, and marks of excellency, of such natural productions, as form articles of commerce, by a merchant* (London, 1803).

Keats, John, *Complete poems*, ed. Jack Stillinger (Cambridge, MA, 1982).

–, *Endymion: a poetic romance* (London, 1818).

–, *The Letters of John Keats, 1814-1821*, ed. Hyder Edward Rollins, 2 vols (Cambridge, 1958).

–, *John Keats: selected letters* ed. Robert Gittings, revised Jon Mee (Oxford, 2002).

Kincaid, Alexander, *The Outlaws of Kathiawad* (Bombay, 1908).

The Lady's monthly museum (July 1820).

Lemprière, John, *Bibliotheca classica; or, A Classical dictionary* (London, T. Cadell, 1792).

Lescallier, Daniel, *Le Trône enchanté: conte indien traduit du Persan* (New York, 1817).

Macaulay, Thomas Babington, *Prose and poetry*, ed. G. M. Young (Cambridge MA, 1970).

Mandeville, Bernard, *The Fable of the bees or Private vices, publick benefits*, ed. F. B. Kaye, 2 vols (Oxford, 1924).

Mandeville, John, *The Travels and voyages of Sir John Mandeville* (London, J. Osborne, n.d.).

Martín de Balmaseda, Fermín, *Decretos del Rey Don Fernando VII, año segundo de su restitución al trono de las Españas: se refieren todas las reales resoluciones generales que se han expedido por los diferentes ministerios y consejos en todo el año de 1815* (Madrid, 1819).

Maurice, Thomas. *The History of Hindostan; its arts, and its sciences, as connected with the history of the other great Empires of Asia, during the most ancient periods of the world: with numerous illustrative engravings, by the author of Indian antiquities*, 3 vols (London, printed by W. Bulmer and Co. for the author, 1795-1799).

Mavor, William, *Historical account of the most celebrated voyages, travels, and discoveries, from the time of Columbus to the present period*, 25 vols (London, Richard Phillips, 1796-1797; 1801).

–, *Universal history, ancient and modern; comprehending a general view of the transactions of every nation, kingdom, and empire in the world, from the earliest records of time*, 25 vols (London, 1802-1805).

McCrindle, John W. (ed.), *Ancient India as described by Megasthenês and Arrian* (New Delhi, 2000).

McGann, Jerome (ed.), *New Oxford book of Romantic period verse* (Oxford, 1993).

Melon, Jean François, *Essai politique sur le commerce* (n.p., n.p., 1734).

Memoirs of a gentleman, who resided several years in the East Indies (London, for J. Donaldson, 1774).

Memorial Literario ó Biblioteca Periódica de Ciencias y Artes 5 (January 1804).

Meninski, Franciscus a Mesgnien, *Lexicon Arabico-Persico-Turcicum, adjecta ad singulas voces et phrases significatione Latina, ad usitatiores, etiam Italica* (Vienna, 1780).

Mill, James, *The History of British India* (London, 1817).

The Modern part of an universal history, from the earliest account of time, compiled from original writers (London, S. Richardson, T. Osborne [*et al.*], 1759-1766).

The Monthly review, or Literary journal 63 (1780).

The Monthly review 92 (1820).

Morellet, André, *Mémoire sur la situation actuelle de la Compagnie des Indes* (Paris, 1769).

Moor, Edward, *The Hindu pantheon* (London, J. Johnson, 1810).

Moore, Thomas, *The Life and death of Lord Edward Fitzgerald* (London, 1831).

–, *The Poetical works* (London, 1841).

Lady Morgan, *Patriotic sketches of Ireland* (London, 1807).

–, *Book of the boudoir* (London, 1829).

A New catalogue of Bell's circulating library (London, 1774).

A New catalogue of Hookham's circulating library (London, 1785).

O'Connor, Arthur, *To the Free Electors of the County of Antrim* (Belfast, Miles's Boy, 1797).

O'Halloran, Sylvester, *An Introduction to the study of the antiquities of Ireland* (London, Murray, 1770).
–, *Ierne defended* (Dublin, Ewing, 1774).
–, *A General history of Ireland* (London, Hamilton, 1775).
Orme, Robert, *Histoire des guerres de l'Inde* (Paris, Panckoucke, 1765).
–, *A History of the military transactions of the British nation in Indostan* (London, J. Nourse, 1763-1778).
Ovington, John, *A Voyage to Suratt in the year 1689*, ed. H. G. Rawlinson (New Delhi, 1994).
Owenson, Sydney, *Woman, or, Ida of Athens* (London, 1809).
–, *The Missionary*, ed. Julia Wright (Peterborough, Ontario, 2002).
–, *The Wild Irish girl*, ed. Kathryn Kirpatrick (Oxford, 1999).

Paine, Thomas, 'Reflections on the life and death of Lord Clive', *Pennsylvania magazine* (March 1775).
Paterson, J. D., 'Of the origin of the Hindu religion', *Asiatic researches* 8 (1808), p.50-51.
Power, Thomas E. and John Stevenson, *A Selection of oriental melodies* (Dublin, *c.*1821).
El Procurador General de la Nación y del Rey (2 June 1813).
[Mrs Purcell], *The Orientalist, or electioneering in Ireland; a tale, by myself*, 2 vols (London, 1820).
Purchas, Samuel, *Purchas, his Pilgrimes* (London, Henrie Fetherstone, 1625).

'The Quarterly review – Mr Keats', *The Examiner* (11 October 1818), p.649.
The Quarterly review 1 (February 1809).
Quintana, Manuel José, *Poesías patrióticas* (Madrid, 1808).

Raleigh, Walter, *The Historie of the world* (London, R. White and T. Basset, 1677).
Raynal, Guillaume-Thomas, *Histoire philosophique et politique des établissemens & du commerce des Européens dans les deux Indes* (Amsterdam, 1770).
–, *Histoire philosophique et politique des établissemens & du commerce des Européens dans les deux Indes* (La Haye, Gosse fils, 1774).
–, *Histoire philosophique et politique des établissemens & du commerce des Européens dans les deux Indes*, 4 vols (Genève, Jean-Léonard Pellet, 1780).
–, *Histoire philosophique et politique des établissemens & du commerce des Européens dans les deux Indes*, ed. Anthony Strugnell *et al.*, 5 vols with atlas (Ferney-Voltaire, 2010-), vol.1 and atlas published to date.
Reybaz, Etienne Salomon, *Sermones de Mr ... precedidos de una carta sobre el arte de la predicacion; traducidos del Frances por D. Mariano Lucas Garrido*, 2 vols (Salamanca, en la Oficina de D. Francisco de Toxar, 1804).
Richardson, John, *A Dictionary of Persian, Arabic, and English. To which is prefixed a dissertation of the languages, literature, and manners of Eastern nations*, 2 vols (Oxford, Clarendon Press, 1777-1780).
–, *A Grammar of the Arabic language. In which the rules that are illustrated by authorities from the best writers; principally adapted for the service of the honourable East India Company* (London, 1801).
Roe, Thomas, *The Journal of Sir Thomas Roe, Knight (1616-1619)*. Facsimile reprint from *The Calcutta weekly Englishman*, ed. Mr Talboys Wheeler (London, 1873), in *Travels in India in the 17th century: Thomas Roe and John Fryer* (New Delhi, 1993), p.1-130.
Russell, Thomas, *A Letter to the people of Ireland, on the present situation of the country* (Belfast, 1796).
–, *Journals and memoirs of Thomas Russell, 1791-1795*, ed. C. J. Woods (Dublin, 1991).

Saint-Lambert, Jean François de, 'Luxe', *Encyclopédie, ou, Dictionnaire raisonné des sciences, des arts et des métiers, par une société de gens de lettres; mis en ordre & publié par M. Diderot... & quant à la partie mathematique, par M. d'Alembert*, 28 vols (Genève, Paris, Neufchastel, Chez Briasson, 1754-1772), vol.9, p.763-71.

Salvá y Mallén, Pedro, *Catálogo de la biblioteca de Salvá*, 2 vols (Valencia, 1872).

Scott, Helenus, *The Adventures of a rupee: wherein are interspersed various anecdotes Asiatic and European* (London, for J. Murray, 1782).

–, *The Adventures of a rupee: wherein are interspersed various anecdotes Asiatic and European, a new edition to which are prefixed, memoirs of the life of the author and to which there are annexed his remarks concerning the inhabitants of Africa*, 2nd edn (London, for J. Murray, 1782).

Scott, Jonathan, (trans.) *Ferishta's History of Dekkan, from the first Mahummedan conquests: with a continuation from other native writers of the events in that part of India to the reduction of its last monarchs by the Emperor Aulumgeer Aurungzebe; also, the reigns of his successors in the empire of Hindostan to the present day: and the history of Bengal, from the accession of Aliverdee Khan to the year 1780* (Shrewsbury, J. and W. Eddowes for John Stockdale, Piccadilly, London, 1794).

–, *A Translation of the memoirs of Eradut Khan, a nobleman of Hindostan containing interesting anecdotes of the Emperor Aulumgeer Aurungzebe, and of his successors Shaw Aulum and Jehaundar Shaw; in which are displayed the causes of the very precipitate decline of the Mogul Empire in India* (London, John Stockdale, 1786).

Scrafton, Luke, *Reflections on the government of Indostan* (London, W. Richardson and S. Clark, 1770).

Severn, Joseph, *Letters and memoirs*, ed. Grant F. Scott (Aldershot, 2005).

Smith, Adam, *Wealth of nations*, ed. Kathryn Sutherland (Oxford, 1993).

Southey, Robert, *The Curse of Kehama* (London, Longman, Hurst, Rees, Orme and Brown, 1810).

–, '*The Curse of Kehama*: by Robert Southey', *Quarterly review* 5 (1811), p.40-61.

–, *The Curse of Kehama*, ed. Daniel Sanjiv Roberts (London, 2003).

–, 'Periodical accounts relative to the Baptist Missionary Society', *Quarterly review* 1 (1811).

–, *Thalaba the destroyer*, ed. Tim Fulford (London, 2003).

Stavorinus, John Splinter, *Voyages to the East Indies, translated from the original Dutch by Samuel Hull Wilcocke*, 3 vols (London, G. G. and J. Robinson, 1798).

Stewart, Charles A., *A Descriptive catalogue of the oriental library of the late Tipu Sultan of Mysore* (London, 1809).

Strachan, G., 'Indian atrocities', *The Examiner* (27 September 1818), p.609.

Tavernier, Jean-Baptiste, *Six voyages de J. B. Tavernier* (Paris, G. Clouzier, 1679-1682).

Terry, Edward, *A Voyage to East India* (London, J. Martin & J.Allestrye, 1655).

'Teruna-Malli en la Costa de Malabar. Descripcion de una fiesta religiosa, sacada de una carta dirigida à Europa últimamente', in *Espíritu de los mejores diarios literarios que se publican en Europa* 118 (5 April 1788), p.13-14 and 119 (7 April 1788), p.19-20.

Thirty-two tales of the throne of Vikramaditya, trans. A. N. D. Haksar (New Delhi, 2006).

'Thomas Russell', *The Shamrock* 8 (October 1870), p.12.

Thomson, William, *Memoirs of the late war in Asia* (London, J. Murray, 1788).

Tójar, Francisco de, *La filósofa por amor*, ed. Joaquín Álvarez Barrientos (Cádiz, 1995).

Tooke, Andrew, *The Pantheon, representing the fabulous histories of the heathen gods, and most illustrious heroes; in a short, plain, and familiar method, by way of dialogue*, 13th edn (London, B. Law *et al.*, 1798).

Vallancey, Charles, *Vindication of the ancient history of Ireland* (Dublin, White, 1786).

–, *Ancient history of Ireland, proved from the Sanscrit books of the Brahmins of India* (Dublin, Graisberry & Campbell, 1797).

Vansittart, Henry, *The History of the first ten years of the reign of Alemgeer: written... by Mohammed Sakee* (Calcutta, Daniel Stuart, 1785).

Variedades de Ciencias, Literatura y Artes 19 (1804).

Vélez, Fray Rafael de, *Apología del Altar y del Trono ó Historia de las reformas hechas en España en tiempo de las llamadas Cortes, e impugnacion de algunas doctrinas publicadas en la Constitucion, diarios, y otros escritos contra la religion y el Estado* (Madrid, 1818).

–, *Apéndices á las Apologías del Altar y del Trono. Confrontacion de las citas que de la Apología del Trono hace el C. Vern... en sus Observaciones con la letra de aquella obra. Hacíala el autor de las Apologías* (Madrid, 1825).

Voltaire, *Corpus des notes marginales* ed. Natalia Elaguina *et al.* (Berlin and Oxford, 1979-).

–, *Correspondence and related documents*, ed. Theodore Besterman, *OCV*, vol.85-135.

–, *Dictionnaire philosophique*, ed. Christiane Mervaud, *OCV*, vols 35 and 36.

–, *Essai sur les mœurs et l'esprit des nations et sur les principaux faits de l'histoire, depuis Charlemagne jusqu'à Louis XIII*, ed. René Pomeau, 2 vols (Paris, 1963).

–, *Fragments sur l'Inde et sur le général Lalli*, ed. Cynthia Manley and John Renwick, *OCV*, vol.75B, p.55-262.

–, *Le Mondain*, ed. Haydn T. Mason, *OCV*, vol.16, p.295-313.

–, *Le Siècle de Louis XIV*, ed. Jacqueline Hellegouarc'h and Sylvain Menant (Paris, 2005).

–, *Lettres philosophiques*, ed. Frédéric Deloffre (Paris, 1986).

–, *Questions sur l'Encyclopédie A - Egalité*, ed. Nicholas Cronk and Christiane Mervaud, *OCV*, vol.38-40.

–, *Zadig ó El destino: historia oriental publicada en frances por Mr De Vadé; y traducida al español por D.**** (Salamanca, par D. Francisco de Toxar, 1804).

Wilkins, Charles, *A Catalogue of Sanscrita manuscripts* (London, 1798).

–, *A Dictionary, Persian, Arabic, and English; with a dissertation on the languages, literature, and manners of Eastern nations. By John Richardson. Revised and improved by Charles Wilkins; a new edition, with numerous additions and improvements*, 2 vols (London, 1806-1810).

–, 'Inscriptions on a pillar near Buddal translated from the Sanskrit', *Asiatic researches* 1 (1788), p.131-45.

Wordsworth, William, 'Essay, supplementary to the preface', *The Prose works*, ed. W. J. B. Owen and Jane Worthington Smyser, 3 vols (Oxford, 1974), vol.3, p.62-84.

–, 'Lines written a few miles above Tintern Abbey', *Lyrical ballads, with a few other poems* (London, J. &. Arch, 1798).

Secondary sources

Adas, Michael, *Machines as the measure of men: science, technology and ideologies of Western dominance* (Ithaca, NY, 1989).

Águeda, Mercedes, 'Goya y Bernardin de Saint-Pierre', *Cuadernos de Arte e Iconografía* IV.8 (1991), p.167-74.

Alam, Muzaffar, 'Aspects of agrarian uprisings in North India in the early eighteenth century', in *Situating Indian history: for Sarvepalli Gopal* ed. Sabyasachi Bhattacharya and Romilla Thapar (Delhi, 1986), p.146-70.

–, 'Eastern India in the early eighteenth century "crisis": some evidence from Bihar', *Indian economic and social history review* 28.1 (1991), p.43-71.

– and Seema Alavi, *A European view of the Mughal Orient* (Delhi, 2002).

– and Seema Alavi (ed. and trans.), *A European experience of the Mughal Orient: the I'jāz-i arsalānī (Persian letters 1773-1779) of Antoine-Louis Henri Polier* (New Delhi, 2007).

–, *The Languages of political Islam in India c.1200-1800* (New Delhi, 2004).

Alavi, Seema, *The Sepoys and the Company: tradition and transition in Northern India 1770-1830* (Delhi, 1995).

–, *Islam and healing: loss and recovery of an Indo-Muslim medical tradition, 1600-1900* (London, 2008).

–, 'Medical culture in transition: Mughal gentleman physician and the native doctor in early colonial India', *Modern Asian studies* 42.5 (2008), p.853-97.

Allen, Brian, 'The East India Company's settlement pictures: George Lambert and Samuel Scott', in *Under the Indian sun: British landscape artists*, ed. Pauline Rohatgi and Pheroza Godrej (Bombay, 1995), p.1-16.

Aravamudan, Srinivas, *Enlightenment Orientalism: resisting the rise of the novel* (Chicago, IL, 2012).

Archer, Mildred 'India and natural history: the role of the East India Company, 1785-1858', *History today* 9 (1959), p.736-43.

– and Ronald Lightbown, *India observed: India as viewed by British artists, 1760-1860* (London, 1982).

Asher, Catherine B. and Talbot, Cynthia. *India before Europe* (Cambridge, 2006).

Bakhtin, Mikhail, *The Dialogic imagination: four essays* (Austin, TX, 1981).

Ballantyne, Tony, *Orientalism and race: Aryanism in the British Empire* (Basingstoke, 2006).

Ballaster, Ros, *Fabulous Orients: fictions of the East in England, 1662-1785* (Oxford, 2005).

Barendse, Rene, *The Western Indian Ocean in the eighteenth century Arabian Seas 1700-1763* (Leiden, 2009).

Barron, W. J., 'Arthurian romance', in *A Companion to romance from classical to contemporary*, ed. Corinne Saunders (Oxford, 2004), p.65-84.

Barrow, Ian J., *Making history, drawing territory: British mapping in India, c.1756-1905* (Delhi, 2003).

Bartlett, Thomas, *The Fall and rise of the Irish nation: the Catholic question 1690-1830* (Dublin, 1992).

Bayly, C. A., *The Birth of the modern world 1780-1914: global connections and comparisons* (Oxford, 2003).

–, *The New Cambridge history of India: Indian society and the making of the British Empire* (Cambridge, 1988).

– (ed.), *The Raj: India and the British, 1600-1947* (London, 1990).

–, *Empire and information: intelligence gathering and social communication in India, 1780-1870* (Cambridge, 1996).

Belanger, Jacqueline, 'Some preliminary remarks on the production and reception of fiction relating to Ireland, 1800-1829', in *Cardiff Corvey: reading the Romantic text* 4 (2000): http://www.cardiff.ac.uk/encap/journals/corvey/articles/cc04_n02.html.

Bellamy, Liz, 'It-narrators and circulation: defining a subgenre', in *The Secret life of things: animals, objects, and it-narratives in eighteenth-century England*, ed. Mark Blackwell (Lewisburg, PA, 2007), p.117-46.

Benjamin, Walter, 'La tâche du traducteur', in *Œuvres I* (Paris, 2000).

Benton, Lauren, 'Legal spaces of empire: piracy and the origins of ocean regionalism', *Comparative studies in society and history* 47.4 (2005), p.700-24.

Berlatsky, Joel, 'British imperial attitudes in the early modern era: the case of Charles Ware Malet in India', *Albion: a quarterly journal concerned with British studies* 14.2 (1982), p.139-52.

Berry, Christopher J., *The Idea of luxury: a conceptual and historical investigation* (Cambridge, 1994).

Bhabha, Homi, *The Location of culture* (London, 1994).

Bowen, Huw, *The Business of empire: the East India Company and imperial Britain 1756-1833* (Cambridge, 2005).

–, '"The most illustrious and most flourishing commercial organisation that ever existed": The East India Company's seaborne empire, 1709-1833', in H. V. Bowen, John McAleer and Robert J. Blyth, *Monsoon traders: the maritime world of the East India Company* (London, 2011), p.91-125.

– (ed.), *Wales and the British overseas empire: interactions and influences, 1650-1830* (Manchester, 2012).

Brantlinger, Patrick, *Rule of darkness: British literature and imperialism, 1830-1914* (Ithaca, NY, and London, 1988).

British fiction, 1800-1829: a database of production, circulation and reception (Cardiff, 2004): http://www.british-fiction.cf.ac.uk.

Brønsted, Johannes, *Vore gamle tropekolonier*, vol. 1-8 (Copenhagen, 1966-1968).

Butler, Marilyn, *Peacock displayed: a satirist in his context* (London, 1979).

–, 'Orientalism', *The Penguin history of literature 4: the Romantic period*, ed. David B. Pirie (New York, 1994), p.395-447.

Campbell, Peter, 'At the British Library: review of *Trading places: the East India Company and Asia, 1600-1834* by Anthony Farrington', *London review of books* 24 (2002), p.31.

Campbell Ross, Ian, 'Prose in English, 1690 1800: from the Williamite wars to the Act of Union', in *The Cambridge history of Irish literature*, ed. Margaret Kelleher and Peter O'Leary (Cambridge, 2006), vol.2, p.232-81.

Certeau, Michel de, *L'Ecriture de l'histoire* (Paris, 1975).

Chaudhuri, Kirti N., *Trade and civilisation in the Indian Ocean: an economic history from the rise of Islam to 1750* (Cambridge, 1985).

Cheney, Paul, *Revolutionary commerce: globalization and the French monarchy* (Cambridge, MA, 2010).

Clark, Henry C., *Compass of society: commerce and absolutism in old-regime France* (Lanham, MD, and Plymouth, 2007).

–, 'Commerce, sociability, and the public sphere: Morellet vs Pluquet on luxury', *Eighteenth-century life* 22 (1998), p.83-103.

Coleman, Deirdre, 'The "dark tide

of time": Coleridge and William
Hodges' India', in *Coleridge,
Romanticism, and the Orient: cultural
negotiations* ed. D. Vallins, K. Oishi
and S. Perry (London, 2013), p.
39-54.

Colley, Linda, *Britons: forging the
nation, 1707-1837* (New Haven,
CT, 1992).

–, *Captives: Britain, empire and the
world 1600-1850* (London, 2002).

Connolly, Claire, *A Cultural history of
the Irish novel, 1790-1829*
(Cambridge 2011).

Cook, Malcolm, 'Bernardin de
Saint-Pierre, lecteur de Voltaire',
in *Voltaire et ses combats* ed. Ulla
Kölving and Christiane Mervaud
(Oxford, 1997) vol.2, p.1079-84.

Courtney, C. P., 'The abbé Raynal,
Robert Orme and the *Histoire
philosophique des deux Indes*', *Revue
de littérature comparée* 54 (1980),
p.356-59.

Coutu, Joan, *Persuasion and
propaganda: monuments and the
eighteenth-century British Empire*
(Montreal and Kingston, 2006).

Cullen, Fintan, 'Lord Edward
Fitzgerald: the creation of an icon',
History Ireland 6.4 (1998), p.17-20.

Dalrymple, William, *White Mughals:
love and betrayal in eighteenth-century
India* (London, 2002).

Deleury, Guy, *Les Indes florissantes:
anthologie des voyageurs français
(1750-1820)* (Paris, 1991).

De Almeida, Hermione, and George
H. Gilpin, *Indian renaissance: British
Romantic art and the prospect of India*
(Aldershot, 2005).

Demerson, Georges, *Don Juan
Meléndez Valdés y su tiempo* (Madrid,
1971), vol.1.

Desmond, Ray, *The India Museum,
1801-1879* (London, 1982).

Dew, Nicholas, *Orientalism in Louis
XIV's France* (Oxford, 2009).

Dirks, Nicholas B., *The Scandal of
empire: India and the creation of

imperial Britain* (Cambridge, MA,
2006).

Dodson, Michael, *Orientalism, empire
and national culture: India 1770-
1880*, (Basingstoke, 2007).

Douglas, Aileen, 'Britannia's rule
and the it-narrator', in *The Secret
life of things: animals, objects, and it-
narratives in eighteenth-century
England*, ed. Mark Blackwell
(Lewisburg, PA, 2007), p.147-61.

Dowling, John, 'Las *Noches lúgubres*
de Cadalso y la juventud
romántica del Ochocientos', in
*Coloquio internacional sobre José
Cadalso*, ed. Mario di Pinto *et al.*
(Abano Terme, 1985), p.105-24.

Drew, John, *India and the Romantic
imagination* (Delhi, 1987).

D'Souza, Florence, *Quand la France
découvrit l'Inde: les écrivains-voyageurs
en Inde, 1757-1818* (Paris, 1995).

Elgood, Charles, *A Medical history of
Persia and the Eastern Caliphate from
the earliest times until the year AD
1932* (Cambridge, 1951).

–, *Analecta medico-historica: Safavid
surgery* (London, 1966).

Elias, Norbert, *The Civilizing process,
vol.2: state formation and civilization*
(Oxford, 1982).

Elliott, Derek, 'Pirates, politics and
companies: global politics on the
Konkan littoral c.1690-1756',
Economic history working papers, LSE
136.10 (2010).

Escoto, Salvador P., 'Haidar Alí: un
intento frustrado de relación
comercial entre Mysore y Filipinas,
1773-1779', *Revista española del
Pacífico* 10 (1999), p.45-75.

Espagne, Michel and Michael
Werner (ed.), *Transferts: les relations
interculturelles dans l'espace franco-
allemand* (Paris, 1988).

–, *Les Transferts culturels franco-
allemands* (Paris, 1999).

Fabbri, Maurizio, 'Observaciones
sobre las dos redacciones del

Eusebio de Montengón', in *El siglo que llaman ilustrado. Homenaje a Francisco Aguilar Piñal* ed. Joaquín Álvarez Barrientos and José Checa Beltrán (Madrid, 1996), p.317-25.

Fairer, David, 'The *Fairie queene* and eighteenth-century Spenserianism', in *A Companion to romance from classical to contemporary*, ed. Corinne Saunders (Oxford, 2004), p.216-32.

Feldbæk, Ole, *India trade under the Danish flag 1772-1808* (Copenhagen, 1969).

–, *Danske Handelskompagnier 1616-1843: Oktrojer og interne Ledelsesregler* (Copenhagen, 1986).

–, 'Den danske Asienhandel 1616-1807. Værdi og volumen', *Historisk Tidsskrift* 15.5 (1990), p.104-52.

–, *Storhandlens tid. Dansk Søfartshistorie 3 – 1720-1814* (Copenhagen, 1997).

– and Ole Justesen, *Kolonierne i Asien og Afrika* (Copenhagen, 1980).

Festa, Lynn, *Sentimental figures of empire in eighteenth-century Britain and France* (Baltimore, MD, 2006).

Flores, Jorge, 'The sea and the world of the Mutasaddi: a profile of port officials from Mughal Gujarat (*c.*1600-1650)', *Journal of the Royal Asiatic Society* 21.1 (2011), p.55-71.

Foster, William (ed.), *Early travels in India 1583-1619* (New Delhi, 1985).

Foster, William, *The East India House: its history and associations* (London, 1924).

Franklin, Michael J., 'Accessing India: orientalism, anti-"Indianism" and the rhetoric of Jones and Burke', in *Romanticism and colonialism: writing and empire, 1780-1830*, ed. Tim Fulford and Peter Kitson (Cambridge, 1998), p.48-66.

– ed., *The European discovery of India: key Indological sources of Romanticism*, 6 vols (London, 2001).

–, 'Orientalist Jones': *Sir William Jones, poet, lawyer, and linguist, 1746-1794* (Oxford and New York, 2011).

–, 'Passion's empire: Sydney Owenson's Indian venture: Phoenicianism, orientalism, and binarism', *Studies in Romanticism* 45.2 (2006), p.181-97.

–, *Representing India: Indian culture and imperial control in eighteenth-century British orientalist discourse*, 9 vols (London and New York, 2000).

– (ed.), *Romantic representations of British India* (London and New York, 2006).

Fraser, Robert, *Victorian quest romance: Stevenson, Haggard, Kipling and Conan Doyle* (Plymouth, 1998).

–, *Rival empires of trade in the Orient, 1600-1800* (Oxford, 1976).

Fulford, Tim, 'Romanticism and colonialism: races, places, peoples, 1800-1830' in *Romanticism and colonialism: writing and empire, 1780-1830*, ed. T. Fulford and P. Kitson (Cambridge, 1998), p.35-47.

– and Peter J. Kitson, ed., *Romanticism and colonialism: writing and empire, 1780-1830* (Cambridge, 1998).

Furber, Holden, *Bombay presidency in the mid-eighteenth century* (Bombay, 1965).

Gallien, Claire, *L'Orient anglais: connaissances et fictions au XVIIIe siècle*, SVEC 2011:10.

Gifford, Paul and Tessa Hauswedell (eds), *Europe and its Others: essays on interperception and identity* (Oxford, 2010).

Gøbel, Erik, 'Asiatisk Kompagnis Kinafarter 1732-1772', *Handels- og Søfartsmuseet på Kronborg, Årbog* (1978), p.7-45.

–, 'Asiatisk Kompagnis sejlads på Indien 1732-1772', *Handels- og Søfartsmuseet på Kronborg, Årbog* (1987), p.22-86.

Gole, Susan, *Maps of Mughal India: drawn by Col. Jean Baptiste Joseph*

Gentil agent for the French government to the court of Shuja-ud-Daulah at Faizabad, 1770 (Delhi, 1988).

Goggi, Gianluigi, 'Autour du voyage de Diderot en Angleterre et en Hollande: la mise au point de la troisième édition de l'*Histoire des deux Indes*' in *Raynal, de la polémique à l'histoire*, ed. Gilles Bancarel et Gianluigi Goggi, *SVEC* 2000:12, p.371-425.

Gottmann, Felicia, 'Du Châtelet, Voltaire, and the transformation of Mandeville's Fable', *History of European ideas* 38.2 (2012), p.218-32.

Green, Martin, *Dreams of adventure, deeds of empire* (London, 1980).

Groseclose, Barbara, *British sculpture and the Company Raj: church monuments and public statuary in Madras, Calcutta, and Bombay to 1858* (Newark, NJ, 1995).

Gupta, Ashin Das, *Indian merchants and the decline of Surat, 1700-1750* (Wiesbaden, 1979).

Gupta, P. C., ed., *Shah Alam II and his court by A. H. Polier* (Calcutta, 1989).

Habib, Irfan, 'Eighteenth century in Indian economic history', in *Proceedings of the Indian History Congress 56th session* (Calcutta, 1995), p.358-78.

Haider, Najaf, 'A "holi riot" of 1714: versions from Ahmedabad and Delhi', in *Living together separately: cultural India in history and politics*, ed. Mushirul Hasan and Asim Roy (Delhi, 2005), p.127-44.

Haque, Ishrat, *Glimpses of Mughal society and culture* (New Delhi, 1992).

Hawley, D. S., 'L'Inde de Voltaire', *SVEC* 120 (1974).

Hirschman, Albert O., *The Passions and the interests: political arguments for capitalism before its triumph*, 20th anniversary edn (Princeton, NJ, 1997).

Hogle, Jerrold E., '"Gothic romance": its origins and cultural functions', in *A Companion to romance from classical to contemporary*, ed. Corinne Saunders (Oxford, 2004), p.216-32.

Hont, Istvan, 'The early Enlightenment debate on commerce and luxury', in *The Cambridge history of eighteenth-century political thought*, ed. Mark Goldie and Robert Wokler (Cambridge, 2006), p.379-418.

Impey, Oliver, 'Review of *The meeting of Asia and Europe*', *The Burlington magazine* 146 (2004), p.773-74.

Jack, Ian, *Keats and the mirror of art* (Oxford 1967).

Jackson, Anna and Amin Jaffer, 'Introduction: the meeting of Asia and Europe, 1500-1800', in *Encounters: the meeting of Asia and Europe, 1500-1800*, ed. Anna Jackson and Amin Jaffer (London, 2004), p.1-11.

Jasanoff, Maya, *Edge of empire: conquest and collecting in the East, 1750-1850* (London, 2005).

Jennings, Jeremy, 'The debate about luxury in eighteenth- and nineteenth-century French political thought', *The Journal of the history of ideas* 68 (2007), p.79-105.

Jones, Jonathan, 'Fugitive pieces', *The Guardian* (25 September 2003).

Jones, Rosie L., *A Very ingenious man: Claude Martin in early colonial India* (Delhi, 1991).

Joseph, Betty, *Reading the East India Company, 1720-1840: colonial currencies of gender* (Chicago, IL, 2004).

Keay, John, *The Honourable Company: a history of the English East India Company* (London, 1993).

Kee, Robert, *The Green flag: a history of Irish nationalism* (Harmondsworth, 2000).

Keirn, Tim and Norbert Schürer (ed.), *British encounters with India, 1750-1830: a sourcebook* (Basingstoke, 2011).

Kejariwal, O. P., *The Asiatic Society of Bengal and the discovery of India's past, 1784-1838* (Delhi, 1999).

Kenyon, John, *The History men: the historical profession in England since the Renaissance* (London, 1983).

King, Richard, *Orientalism and religion: post-colonial theory, India and the mystic East* (London, 1999).

Kirkpatrick, Kathryn, 'Introduction' in *The Wild Irish girl*, ed. Kathryn Kirkpatrick (Oxford, 1999), p.vii-xvii.

Kitson, Peter J., *Romantic literature, race, and colonial literature* (London, 2007).

Kliger, Samuel, *The Goths in England. A study in seventeenth and eighteenth century thought* (Cambridge, MA, 1952).

Kolff, Dirk H.A., *Naukar, Rajput and Sepoy: the ethno-history of the military labour market in Hindustan, 1450-1850* (Cambridge, 1990).

Kopf, David, *British orientalism and the Bengal renaissance: the dynamics of Indian modernisation 1773-1835* (Berkeley, CA, 1969).

Kozminski, Léon, *Voltaire financier* (Paris, 1929).

Lach, Donald F., *Asia in the making of Europe*, 3 vols (Chicago, IL, 1965-1993).

Lafarga, Francisco, 'Territorios de lo exótico en las letras españolas del siglo XVIII', *Anales de literatura Española* 10 (1994), p.173-92.

Lafont, Jean-Marie, *Maharaja Ranjit Singh: lord of the five rivers* (Delhi, 2002).

Lama, Miguel Ángel, 'Todo es exagerado y falso hasta cierto punto: nota a una lectura de las *Noches lúgubres* de Cadalso', *Dieciocho* 33.1 (2010), p.47-54.

Larson, Pier M., *Ocean of letters: language and creolization in an Indian Ocean diaspora* (Cambridge, 2009).

Leask, Nigel, *British Romantic writers and the East: anxieties of empire* (Cambridge, 1992).

–, 'Easts', in *Romanticism: an Oxford guide*, ed. Nicholas Roe (Oxford, 2005), p.137-48.

–, 'Kubla Khan and orientalism: the road to Xanadu revisited', *Romanticism* 4.1 (1998), p.1-22.

–, '"Travelling the other way": the travels of Mirza Abu Talib Khan (1810)', in *Romantic representations of British India*, ed. Michael J. Franklin (London, 2006), p.220-37.

Leerssen, Joep Theodoor, *Remembrance and Imagination: Patterns in the Historical and Literary Representation of Ireland in the Nineteenth Century* (Cork, 1996).

Lennon, Joseph, *Irish orientalism: a literary and intellectual history* (Syracuse, NY, 2004).

Little, Nigel, *Transoceanic radical, William Duane: national identity and empire, 1760-1835* (London, 2007).

Lock, F. P., *Edmund Burke: volume II, 1784-1797* (Oxford, 2009).

Logan, William, *Vain empires* (New York, 1998).

Low, Charles Rathebone, *History of the Indian Navy, 1613-1863*, 2 vols (London, 1877).

Lussier, Mark S., *Romantic dharma: the emergence of Buddhism into nineteenth-century Europe* (New York, 2011).

Lynch, Deidre Shauna, *The Economy of character: novels, market culture, and the business of inner meaning* (Chicago, IL, 1998).

Macaulay, Thomas Babington, 'A speech delivered in the House of Commons on the 10th of July, 1833', in *Archives of empire, volume 1: from the East India Company to the Suez Canal*, ed. Barbara Harlow and Mia Carter (London, 2003), p.54-58.

Mackenzie, John, *Orientalism: history,*

theory and the arts (Manchester, 1995).

Mackillop, Andrew, 'A union for empire? Scotland, the English East India Company and the British Union', *Scottish historical review* 87 (2008), p.116-34.

Majeed, Javed, *Ungoverned imaginings: James Mill's 'The History of British India' and orientalism* (Oxford, 1992).

Makdisi, Saree, 'Literature, national identity, and empire' in *The Cambridge companion to English literature, 1740-1830*, ed. Thomas Keymer and Jon Mee (Cambridge, 2004), p.61-79.

–, *Romantic imperialism: universal empire and the culture of modernity* (New York and Cambridge, 1998).

Mantena, Rama, *The Origins of modern historiography in India: Antiquarianism and philology 1780-1880* (New York, 2012).

Marsh, Kate, *India in the French imagination: peripheral voices, 1754-1815* (London, 2009).

Marshall, P. J., *The British discovery of Hinduism in the eighteenth century* (Cambridge, 1970).

–, 'British-Indian connections *c.*1780 to *c.*1830: the empire of the officials', in *Romantic representations of British India*, ed. Michael J. Franklin (London and New York, 2006), p.45-64.

– (ed.), *The Eighteenth century in Indian history: evolution or revolution* (New Delhi, 2003).

–, 'The great map of mankind', in *Pacific empires: essays in honour of Glyndwr Williams*, ed. Alan Frost and Jane Samson (Vancouver, 1999), p.237-50.

––, *The Impeachment of Warren Hastings* (Oxford, 1965).

–, 'John Richardson', *Dictionary of national biography* (Oxford, 2004), vol.46, p.818-19.

–, 'Taming the exotic: the British and India in the seventeenth and eighteenth centuries', in *Exoticism*

in the Enlightenment, ed. G. S. Rousseau and Roy Porter (Manchester, 1990), p.46-65.

McGetchin, Douglas T., *Indology, Indomania, and orientalism: ancient India's rebirth in modern Germany* (Cranbury, NJ, 2009).

Mehta, Binita, *Widows, pariahs, and bayadères: India as spectacle* (Lewisburg, PA, 2002).

Metcalf, Barbara, *Islamic revival in British India: Deoband, 1860-1900* (Princeton, NJ, 1982).

Meyssonnier, Simone, *La Balance et l'horloge: la genèse de la pensée libérale en France au XVIIIᵉ siècle* (Montreuil, 1989).

Motion, Andrew, *Keats* (London, 1997).

Mukherjee, Surendra Nath, *Sir William Jones: a study in eighteenth-century British attitudes to India* (Cambridge, 1968, and London, 1987).

Müller, Leos, 'The Swedish East India trade and international markets: re-exports of teas, 1731-1813', *Scandinavian economic history review* 53.3 (2003), p.28-44.

–, 'Swedish East India Company and trade in tea, 1731-1813', paper presented in Kyoto, 28 October-4 November 2004: http:// www.geocities.jp/akitashigeru/PDF/ DiscussionPaper2004_11_01 Muller.pdf.

Naushahi, Arif, 'ḠOLĀM-ḤOSAYN KHAN ṬABĀṬABĀ'Ī', in *Encyclopædia Iranica* http:// www.iranicaonline.org/articles/ golam-hosayn-khan-tabatabai.

Neill, Anna, 'Buccaneer ethnography: nature, culture and nation in the journals of William Dampier', *Eighteenth century studies* 33.2 (2000) p.165-80.

Nissen, Mogens Rostgaard, 'Asiatisk Kompagnis aktionærer 1732-1809', *Erhvervshistorisk Årbog* 51 (2002), p.164-93.

Nizami, Khaliq Ahmad, *Supplement to Eliott and Dowson's History of India as told by its own historians*, 2 vols (Delhi, 1981).

North, Michael, 'Production and reception of art through European company channels', in *Artistic and cultural exchanges between Europe and Asia, 1400-1900*, ed. Michael North (Farnham, 2010), p.89-107.

O'Brien, Karen, *Narratives of Enlightenment: cosmopolitan history from Voltaire to Gibbon* (Cambridge, 1997).

Okie, Laird, *Augustan historical writing: histories of England in the English Enlightenment* (Lanham, MD, 1991).

O'Hanlon, Rosalind, 'Manliness and imperial service in Mughal North India', *Journal of the economic and social history of the orient* 42.1 (1999), p.47-93.

O'Malley, Kate, *Ireland, India, and Empire: Indo-Irish radical connections, 1919-1964* (Manchester, 2008).

O'Quinn, Daniel, *Staging governance: theatrical imperialism in London, 1770-1800* (Baltimore, MD, 2005).

– (ed.), *The Travels of Mirzah Abu Taleb Khan: in Asia, Africa, and Europe, during the years 1799, 1800, 1801, 1802, and 1803* (Peterborough, 2009).

Paquette, Gabriel B., *Enlightenment, governance, and reform in Spain and its empire, 1759-1808* (Basingstoke, 2008).

Parker, Geoffrey, *The Military revolution: military innovation and the rise of the West 1500-1800* (Cambridge, 1988).

Parry, J. H., *Trade and dominion: the European overseas empires in the eighteenth century* (London, 1974).

Pearson, Harlan Otto, *Islamic reform and revival in 19th century India: the Tariqah-I-Muhammadiyah* (New Delhi, 2008).

Pearson, M. N., *The Indian Ocean* (London and New York, 2003).

Perrot, Philippe, *Le Luxe: une richesse entre faste et confort, XVIIIe-XIXe siècle* (Paris, 1995).

Pitts, Jennifer, *A Turn to empire: the rise of imperial liberalism in Britain and France* (Princeton, NJ, 2006).

Pomeau, René,'Introduction', in *Essai sur les mœurs et l'esprit des nations et sur les principaux faits de l'histoire, depuis Charlemagne jusqu'à Louis XIII*, ed. René Pomeau, 2 vols (Paris, 1963), vol.1, p.I-LXVI.

–, *Voltaire en son temps*, 2 vols (Paris and Oxford, 1995).

Pratt, J. C., 'The East India House', in *London pictorially illustrated*, Charles Knight (ed.), 6 vols (London, 1841-1844), vol.5, p.49-64.

Price, Fiona, '"Inconsistent rhapsodies": Samuel Richardson and the politics of romance', in *A Companion to romance from classical to contemporary*, ed. Corinne Saunders (Oxford, 2004), p.269-86.

Probyn, Clive, 'Paradise and cotton-mill: rereading eighteenth-century romance', in *A Companion to romance from classical to contemporary*, ed. Corinne Saunders (Oxford, 2004), p.251-68.

Puerto, Javier, 'El modelo ilustrado de expedición científica', in *Ilustración, ciencia y técnica en el siglo XVIII español*, ed. E. Martínez Ruiz and M. de Pazzis Pi Corrales (Valencia, 2008), p.129-51.

Qureshi, Sadiah, 'Tipu's Tiger and images of India, 1799-2010', in *Curating empire: Museums and the British imperial experience*, ed. Sarah Longair and John McAleer (Manchester, 2012), p.207-24.

Rahim, M. A., 'Historian Ghulam Husain Tabatabai', *Journal of the Asiatic Society of Pakistan* 8 (1963), p.117-129.

Rao, Velcheru Narayana, David Shulman, and Sanjay Subrahmanyam (eds), *Textures of time: writing history in South India, 1600-1800* (Delhi, 2001).

Rasch, Aage, and P. P. Sveistrup, *Asiatisk Kompagni i den florissante periode 1772-1792* (Copenhagen, 1948).

Rawlinson, H. G. 'Indian influence on the West', in *Modern India and the West: a study of the interaction of their civilizations*, ed. L. S. S. O'Malley (London, 1941), p.535-75.

Reig Salvá, Carola, *Vicente Salvá, un valenciano de prestigio internacional* (Valencia, 1972).

Rindom, Jan, 'Ostindisk Kompagni 1616-1650 – et spørgsmål om organisatorisk udvikling og interne magtkampe', *Handels- og Søfartsmuseet på Kronborg, Årbog* (2000), p.99-125.

Risso, Patricia, 'Cultural perceptions of piracy: maritime violence in the Western Indian Ocean and Persian Gulf region during a long eighteenth century', *Journal of world history* 12.2 (2001), p.293-319.

Roberts, Daniel Sanjiv, 'Newly recovered articles from *The Calcutta gazette* by Charles Johnstone', *Eighteenth-century Ireland* 26 (2011), p.140-69.

Robertson, Fiona, 'Romance and the Romantic novel: Sir Walter Scott', in *A Companion to romance from classical to contemporary*, ed. Corinne Saunders (Oxford, 2004), p.287-304.

Robertson, John, 'Preface', *Essai sur les mœurs et l'esprit des nations: II Avant-propos*, ch.1-37, *OCV*, vol.22, p.xxxvii-xliii.

–, *The Case for the Enlightenment: Scotland and Naples 1680-1760* (Cambridge, 2005).

Robins, Nick, *The Corporation that changed the world* (London, 2006).

Robinson, Francis, 'Religious change and the self in Muslim South Asia since 1800', in *Islam and Muslim History in South Asia*, ed. Francis Robinson (Delhi, 2000), p.105-21.

Rocher, Rosane, 'New data for the biography of the Orientalist Alexander Hamilton', *Journal of the American Oriental Society* 90.3 (1970), p.426-48.

Rohrbach, Emily and Emily Sun, 'Reading Keats, thinking politics', *Studies in Romanticism* 50.2 special issue (2011), p.229-38.

Rollins, Hyder Edward (ed.), *The Keats circle: letters and papers, and more letters and poems of the Keats circle*, 2 vols (Cambridge, MA, 1965).

Runte, Roseann, '*La Chaumière indienne*: a study in satire', *The French review* 53.4 (1980), p.557-65.

Said, Edward, *Orientalism* (London, 1995; first edition New York, 1978).

Sánchez Espinosa, Gabriel, 'Gaspar Melchor de Jovellanos: un paradigma de lectura ilustrada', in *El libro ilustrado: Jovellanos lector y educador*, ed. Nigel Glendinning and Gabriel Sánchez Espinosa (Madrid, 1994), p.33-59.

–, 'Un episodio en la recepción cultural dieciochesca de lo exótico: la llegada del elefante a Madrid en 1773', *Goya* 295-296 (2003), p.269-86.

Sapra, Rahul, *The Limits of orientalism: seventeenth-century representations of India* (Newark, NJ, 2011).

Sarrailh, Jean, 'Paul et Virginie en Espagne', in *Enquêtes romantiques* (Paris, 1933), p.3-39.

Schwab, Raymond, *The Oriental Renaissance: Europe's rediscovery of India and the East, 1680-1880* (1950), trans. Gene Patterson-Black and Victor Reinking (New York, 1984).

Sebold, Russell P., 'José Cadalso: sus

Noches lúgubres, su romanticismo', in *Historia de la Literatura Española: siglo XVIII* ed. Guillermo Carnero (Madrid, 1995), vol.2, p.726-43.

–, 'Novelitas de faltriquera', *ABC* (1 September 2000), p.58.

Shovlin, John, *The Political economy of virtue: luxury, patriotism, and the origins of the French Revolution* (Ithaca, NY, 2007).

Singh, Chetan, *Region and empire: Punjab in the seventeenth century* (Delhi, 1991).

Skrzypek, Marian, 'Le commerce instrument de la paix mondiale' in *Raynal, de la polémique à l'histoire*, ed. Gilles Bancarel and Gianluigi Goggi, *SVEC* 2000:12, p.243-54.

Smyth, Jim, *The Men of no property* (Houndmills, 1992).

Sonenscher, Michael, *Before the deluge: public debt, inequality and the intellectual origins of the French Revolution* (Princeton, NJ, 2007).

Spear, Percival, *The Nabobs: a study of the social life of the English in eighteenth-century India* (London, 1998).

Sperry, Stuart M., 'Keats's skepticism and Voltaire', *Keats-Shelley journal* 12 (1963), p.75-93.

Spodek, Howard, 'Rulers, merchants and other groups in the city states of Saurashtra around 1800', *Comparative studies in society and history* 16.4 (1974), p.448-70.

Stern, Philip J., 'History and historiography of the English East India Company: past, present, and future!', *History compass* 7.4 (2009), p.1146-80.

Storey, C. A., *Persian literature: a bio-bibliographical survey*, 5 vols (London, 1927-1997).

–, 'History of India, general', in *Persian Literature: a bio-bibliographical survey* (London, 1927-1997), vol.1, section 2, fasc.3, p.442-46. Available online via the PHI–Persian Literature in Translation website: http://

persian.packhum.org/persian/main. See also 'FEREŠTA,TĀRĪḴ-E' in the *Encyclopædia Iranica* online http://www.iranicaonline.org/articles/ferestatarik-.

Stronge, Susan, *Tipu's tigers* (London, 2009).

Strugnell, Anthony, 'A la recherche d'Eliza Draper' in *Raynal, de la polémique à l'histoire*, ed. Gilles Bancarel et Gianluigi Goggi, *SVEC* 2000:12, p.173-86.

–, 'Diderot's anti-colonialism: a problematic notion' in *New Essays on Diderot*, ed. James Fowler (Cambridge, 2011), p.74-85.

–, 'La réception de l'*Histoire des deux Indes* en Angleterre au dix-huitième siècle' in *Lectures de Raynal*, ed. Hans-Jürgen Lüsebrink and Manfred Tietz, *SVEC* 286 (1991), p.253-63.

–, 'Mixed Messages: orientalism and empire in the early British histories of India and their reception in France' in *Das Europa der Aufklärung und die außereuropäische koloniale Welt*, ed. Hans-Jürgen Lüsebrink (Göttingen, 2006), p.287-301.

Suleri, Sara, *The Rhetoric of English India* (Chicago, IL, 1993).

Subramanian, Lakshmi, 'Capital and crowd in a declining Asian port city: the Anglo-Bania order and the Surat riots of 1795', *Modern Asian studies* 19.2 (1985), p.205-37.

–, *Indigenous capital and imperial expansion: Bombay, Surat and the West Coast* (New Delhi, 1996).

Teltscher, Kate, *India inscribed: European and British writing on India 1600-1800* (Oxford, 1995).

Torri, Michelguglielmo, 'Surat during the second half of the 18th century: what kind of social order? A rejoinder to Lakshmi Subramaniam', *Modern Asian studies* 21.4 (1987), p.679-710.

Tracy, Robert, *The Unappeasable host: studies in Irish literature* (Dublin, 1998).

Tracy, Thomas, *Irishness and womanhood in nineteenth-century British writing* (Burlington, VT, 2009).

Trautmann, Thomas R., *Aryans and British India* (Berkeley, CA, 1997).

Trumpener, Katie, *Bardic nationalism: the Romantic novel and the British Empire* (Princeton, NJ, 1997).

Updike, Daniel B., *Printing types: their history, forms, and use*, 2 vols (Cambridge, MA, 1937).

Urzainqui, Inmaculada, 'Los redactores del *Memorial literario* (1784-1808)', *Estudios de Historia Social. Periodismo e Ilustración en España* 52-53 (1990), p.501-16.

Vauchelle-Haquet, Aline, *Les Ouvrages en langue espagnole publiés en France entre 1814 et 1833* (Aix-en-Provence, 1985).

Watt, James, '"The blessings of freedom": Britain, America, and "the east" in the fiction of Robert Bage', *Eighteenth-century fiction* 22.1 (2009), p.49-70.

Weiss, Judith, 'Insular beginnings: Anglo-Norman Romance', in *A Companion to Romance from classical to contemporary*, ed. Corinne Saunders (Oxford, 2004), p.26-44.

Whale, John, 'Indian jugglers: Hazlitt, Romantic orientalism and the difference of view', in *Romanticism and colonialism: writing and empire, 1780-1830*, ed Tim Fulford and Peter Kitson (Cambridge, 1998), p.206-20.

Wilson Foster, John, 'Introduction' in *The Cambridge companion to the Irish novel* (Cambridge, 2006), p.1-21.

Woolf, Daniel, 'From hystories to the historical: five transitions in thinking about the past, 1500-1700', in *The Uses of history in early modern England*, ed. Paulina Kewes (San Marino, CA, 2006), p.31-68.

Worden, Blair, 'Historians and Poets', in *The Uses of history in early modern England*, ed. Paulina Kewes (San Marino, CA, 2006), p.69-90.

Wright, Julia M., '"The nation Begins to Form": competing nationalisms in Morgan's *The O'Briens and The O'Flahertys*', *English literary history* 66.4 (1999), p.939-63.

–, 'National erotics and political theory in Morgan's *The O'Briens and the O'Flahertys*', *European Romantic review* 15.2 (2004), p.229-41.

–, *Ireland, India and nationalism in nineteenth-century literature* (Cambridge, 2007).

Yallop, Jacqueline, *Magpies, squirrels & thieves: how the Victorians collected the world* (London, 2011).

Yegenoglu, Meyda, *Colonial fantasies: towards a feminist reading of orientalism* (Cambridge, 1998).

Young, Robert, *The Idea of English ethnicity* (Oxford, 2008).

Index